UNTIL THE LAST TRUMPET SOUNDS

OTHER BOOKS BY GENE SMITH

American Gothic: The Story of America's Legendary Theatrical
Family—Junius, Edwin, and John Wilkes Booth

The Ends of Greatness

The Dark Summer: An Intimate History of the Events That Led to
World War II

Lee and Grant: A Dual Biography

High Crimes and Misdemeanors: The Impeachment and Trial of
Andrew Johnson

Maxmilian and Carlotta

The Shattered Dream: Herbert Hoover and the Great Depression

When the Cheering Stopped: The Last Years of Woodrow Wilson

UNTIL THE LAST TRUMPET SOUNDS

THE LIFE OF GENERAL OF THE ARMIES JOHN J. PERSHING

GENE SMITH

John Wiley & Sons, Inc.

New York • Chichester • Weinheim • Brisbane • Singapore • Toronto

This text is printed on acid-free paper.

Copyright © 1998 by Gene Smith

Published by John Wiley & Sons, Inc.

All rights reserved. Published simultaneously in Canada.

Library of Congress Cataloging-in-Publication Data

Smith, Gene.
    Until the last trumpet sounds: the life of General of the Armies
John J. Pershing/Gene Smith.
      p.   cm.
    Includes bibliographical references (p.   ).
    ISBN 0-471-24693-X (cloth : alk. paper)
    1. Pershing, John J. (John Joseph), 1860–1948.   2. Generals—
United States—Biography.   3. United States. Army—Biography.
I. Title.
E181.P57S64 1998
355′.0092—dc21
   [B]   97-33033
                                            CIP

Printed in the United States of America
10 9 8 7 6 5 4 3 2 1

CONTENTS

Prologue   vii

I   "You Are Not Going into the Army, Are You?"   1
II   Frankie   73
III   The Commander   137
IV   General of the Armies of the United States   215
V   Warren   247
VI   Dick   311

Source Notes   339
Bibliography   355
Index   359

PROLOGUE

IT WAS HARDLY A SURPRISE that the old man was finally dead, for he was rising eighty-eight—would have reached it in fewer than two months. When President Truman's train pulled into Washington's Union Station from Philadelphia, where he had just accepted the Democratic Party's nomination for another White House term, he was given the news. Then it was released to the public.

The papers ran obituaries prepared years earlier. There was a brief ceremony at the hospital chapel and then in the night the body was taken to lie in state under the Capitol dome. Before the hour set for public entry, President Truman walked in, coming, he said, in no other capacity than ex-captain of field artillery. After twenty-four hours of people filing by, middle-aged men sometimes coming to brief halt at attention with a salute, stance and motion of course not as sharp as once they had been, the funeral got under way. Some five hundred thousand people turned out to watch, nearly half of the District of Columbia's population, the Associated Press reported. Upper Sixteenth Street and Constitution Avenue were blocked off by police wearing black mourning patches beneath their badges.

To the beat of muffled drums and sound of dirges the mile-long procession moved at measured pace, the Army Ground Forces band of eighty-five pieces, the Third Mechanized Cavalry Reconnaissance's clanking half-tracks and jeeps and scout cars bristling with machine guns and radio antennae, a field artillery battalion of the 82d Airborne Division with thirty-seven vehicles and a dozen 105 mm howitzers, two squadrons of Air Force troops from Bolling Field, sailors of the Potomac River Naval Command, a company of marines, an engineer construction battalion, the Army Band of one hundred pieces, a battalion of the 504th Parachute Infantry Regiment, almost five hundred third classmen of the U.S. Military Academy, carrying M-1s, in summer whites with crossbelts and gleaming brass breastplates and officered by fifty-two first classmen, clergymen, and then the caisson drawn by six perfectly matched gray horses of the Ceremonial Company of the Third Infantry Regiment, three with soldiers aboard who held reins only in left white-gloved hand, the right kept at the side. The casket was of brown metal and covered with a flag. Behind came a jet black horse, saddle and trappings of black and with boots reversed in the stirrups and saber hanging, a soldier leading. There followed, held aloft by a flag-bearer, the dead man's personal banner, red and with silver stars, and then scores of marching generals, the out-of-the-army Dwight Eisenhower back in uniform for this and with Chief of Staff Omar Bradley by his side. Then came pallbearers on foot and honorary pallbearers in cars, and the family along with three thousand guests, the presidential widows Edith Wilson and Grace Coolidge, members of the cabinet and the U.S. Supreme Court with their wives, senators, representatives, admirals, foreign ambassadors with their military attachés in gilded dress uniform. A flight of Air Force P-80s screamed overhead, disappearing to make a turn and come back. Every American flag in Washington was at half-staff, and those at all army installations and every navy station and on every vessel.

The cortege went its slow way around the Lincoln Memorial and then on to the bridge over the Potomac. Rain started falling and Eisenhower asked Bradley if he thought they ought to get into cars. The answer was that he did not and so they went on, getting soaked along with everybody else. They had of course not known the dead man well, being only junior officers fresh from the Point during his great days of years before.

The head of the procession reached the entrance to the vast cemetery at Arlington. As the caisson went through the high and elaborate metal gates, artillery pieces began firing off a nineteen-gun salute. (The president had ordered that the customary twenty-one-gun salute due to himself upon entering a military installation be forgone upon this occasion.) The cortege made its way to the great marble amphitheater. Drum ruffle and bugle flourishes sounded and the casket was removed to a low bier. The rain swept off to be replaced by Washington's blazing summer sun glittering on the boxes lining the gallery around the amphitheater perimeter and the white stone benches on the terraced floor below, where sat the invited guests and great banked rows of flowers from the Old Employees of the American Battle Monuments Commission, the American Gold Star Mothers, hundreds of American Legion posts across the country, the Chinese Refugees from Mexico 1917, the Philippines Club, former president Hoover, the British ambassador on behalf of King George VI, Secretary of State George C. Marshall, Jr., and Frank P. Helm of Sausalito, California, who in the worst moment of the dead man's life held him in his arms for terrible hour after hour as he shivered and cried.

The services were stark, a few hymns, a few prayers. "Remember Thy servant John Joseph, O Lord," intoned Maj. Gen. Luther D. Miller, chief of chaplains, "according to the favor which Thou bearest unto Thy people, and grant that, increasing in knowledge and love of Thee, he may go from strength to strength, in the life of perfect service, in Thy heavenly kingdom." The casket was put back on the caisson and the horses drew it to the grave site. "The march of another soldier is ended," Chaplain Miller called out. "His battles are all fought and his victories all won and he lies down to rest awhile awaiting the bugle's call." The dead man had said something of the same nature years earlier, selecting his burial site: "When the last call sounds I want to stand up with my soldiers." The remark was unusual for him, for he rarely made reference to religious matters, and even more rarely employed poetic metaphors.

The family and the honorary pallbearers, many of the last with canes and hearing aids and in need of physical assistance, took seats under a canopy protecting them from the fierce sun. The coffin was placed for lowering into the grave, the old man within wearing four stars on each shoulder of antiquated uniform with Sam Browne belt and saber chain and on breast Distinguished Service Cross and Distinguished Service Medal, but none of the foreign decorations, France's Grand Cross of the Legion of Honor and Military Medal, Great Britain's Grand Cross of the Order of the Bath (which entitled him to be addressed as Sir John when on British soil, a practice he discouraged), Italy's Grand Cordon of the Military Order of Savoy and Grand Cross of the Order of St. Marizio e Lazzaro, Japan's Order of the Rising Sun, Montenegro's Oblitich Medal and Grand Cordon of the Order of Prince Danilio I, the Greek Order of the Saint Savior, the Serbian Order of the Star of Kara-Georges with Swords of the First Class, Romania's Order of Mihai Bravul, Poland's Polonia Restituta, the Grand Cross of Commander of the Order of the White Lion from Czechoslovakia, the others. All around the burial site, situated by itself on a rise distant from other graves, stood gum tree, oak, hickory, cedar, and sassafrass. It was four and a third miles to the Capitol where he had lain in state on the catafalque that once held Lincoln's body and later that of the Unknown Soldier who had served under him and whose last resting place was a short distance from his own.

Unseen artillery pieces with a second nineteen-gun salute, a firing party cracking out three volleys, "Taps" echoed by a bugler out of sight, removal of the flag from the coffin to be folded and handed to the next of kin; and the funeral was over. It was July of 1948. Flags rose to the tops of poles on Washington's buildings. They would remain down for another month at army posts from Berlin to Korea. The people went away from Arlington, the Army Band marching off in outdated and taken-from-storage gray uniforms the old man had ordered for the musician-soldiers' predecessors many years earlier during his active duty days. He had always been very involved with bands and indeed all musical activities, and one of the first things his future wife had noticed about him was how great he was on a ballroom floor—"Perfectly elegant dancer," she had written in her diary. Now perhaps, it was said, he was in Fiddlers' Green, the heavenly encampment reserved for cavalrymen only. In accordance with Arlington tradition for the burial of eminent persons, a sentry was posted and reliefs came and went for three days.

Then he was alone on his hill, solitary from other graves under a regulation government tombstone stating that he had entered service from

Missouri and had been general of the armies of the United States. That was a rank higher than those of Washington and Grant before him, and of all others afterward. It carried the right to wear six stars on each shoulder. A stamp shortly brought out showed him so adorned, although in life he had never chosen to put on so many. Twenty years went by.

Those who would in time become members of Yale University's Class of 1966 were little boys on that funeral day of 1948. Two decades later they were grad students, medical school, business school, Chinese studies, fellowship abroad. Many came on a spring day of 1968 to the Arlington hill where the tombstone was, its area bare of any other markers. By it, a few feet away, was a newly dug grave. The Yale men stood with Society people down from New York, with a classmate's twenty-two-year-old fiancée, his parents and relatives and army captain brother, and as on the previous occasion there was the crack of rifles, "Taps," the folding and handing-over of the flag, and the departure of mourners to go on with their lives.

The horses drawing the caisson that twenty years earlier carried the general of the armies went away, gear jangling and creaking. There was no riderless horse. This officer's rank did not warrant it. When the general of the armies of the United States made his remark about wishing to be with his soldiers when the last trumpet sounded he could not have had in mind the soldier whose last resting place was there by his side, for he had known him not as a soldier at all but only as little Dick, the little Dickie whose inscribed rank on the eventual tombstone would be that of the army's lowest commissioned rank, a second lieutenant lying by the highest-ranking officer of the country's history, brought back from Vietnam and the Tet Offensive and a Viet Cong hail of rockets and small-arms fire to be with Grandfather.

↠ I ↞

"YOU ARE NOT GOING INTO THE ARMY, ARE YOU?"

$\rightarrow$ 1 $\leftarrow$

HE STOOD, THE GENERAL STORE–POST OFFICE OWNER John Fletcher Pershing of Laclede, Linn County, Missouri, for the Union. As a young man he had taken rafts of lumber down the Mississippi to New Orleans, and what he saw on his trips turned him against slavery. Of Alsatian descent, his family had been in the New World since 1749, the first of their number an indentured servant. They contended against the Indians, one of their number dying at the hands of a British-paid band during the Revolution. John Fletcher Pershing's wife, the former Anne Elizabeth Thompson, late of Tennessee, but later of Montgomery County, Missouri, was from a pro-Confederate family. But like her husband she supported the Union.

All across their border state the most bitter kind of personalized conflict raged, the literal War of the Brothers, with neighbors ambushing and shooting and hanging one another from trees or barn rafters in the name of abolitionism or secession. Anne Elizabeth Pershing made an American flag her husband raised above their home. A group of their Confederate-sympathy neighbors came by and said they wanted that flag down. It would save everybody a good deal of trouble if he himself lowered it, they told the husband of its maker. If he did not, they would come by that night to do so themselves. John Fletcher Pershing replied that it would be better that they not come, but if they did they should carry with them a long pine box for each visitor, for he would shoot all who touched that flag. They did not come. When a trainload of Union troops came by to see for the first time since leaving St. Louis the emblem of the United States floating in the breeze, the soldiers erupted into cheers. Standing by, John Fletcher Pershing, he said later, was not ashamed to break into tears. Held in one arm as he waved with the other, he remembered, blue-eyed and very blond, so blond as to have hair almost white in color, was the first of his nine children, born September 13, 1860, the infant John Joseph Pershing.

Many of those who came into the world just then, the last days before the Civil War, took as their first memory their parents' reaction to the news of the assassination of Abraham Lincoln. Of that event John Joseph—usually "John" or "Johnny" to the town in which he grew up, sometimes "Jack" or "Jackie" to his family—retained but a vague impression. More clear was what happened when he was three months from his fourth birthday. His storekeeper-father was military provisioner, sutler, to the First and Eighteenth regiments of Missouri Volunteers, purveyor of such as wooden combs, spurs, pretzels, cigars, plug and smoking tobacco, epsom salts, smoked herring, salt, gingerbread, joke books, cookies, sardines, jackknives, pickles, toothbrushes, pipes, figs, raisins, liquor, quinine for gastric upset. His mother's people were engaged in fighting the troops buying the goods. (Nowhere did the term "Civil War" more apply than in the border states between North and South.) A band of irregulars who held themselves adherents to the beliefs of his mother's relatives rode into little Laclede on June 18, 1864, to conduct what was afterward alluded to as the Holtzclaw Raid.

It was around four in the afternoon. Men arrived, armed men, bushwhackers who were half Southern patriot and half bandit, yelling, jumping off their horses, and ordering all male citizens into a line in the public square. Then plundering began. The first objective was John Fletcher Pershing's store, for the raiders under Capt. Clifton Holtzclaw had not forgotten the manner in which he defended the American flag his wife had made. As the invaders burst in the front door, the storekeeper went out the back. At his home, men were demanding to know his where-abouts. His wife told them that he was not in the house; if they didn't be-lieve her, she said, let them make a search. They left.

Just as they went out, John Fletcher Pershing came in the rear door, carrying a loaded double-barreled shotgun. His home, five doors away from the store, faced the town square. Any question as to whether he was that type of sutler who was popularly said to be at the rear of all advances and in the front of all retreats was resolved when he prepared to fire on the invaders. But that would mean death, his wife cried—as indeed it meant death for two other men of the town, one who fired upon Holtz-claw's people, killing one before being killed himself, another who ran when told to halt. She flung her arms around her husband as—and all his life her elder son remembered it—she screamed at him and his little brother Jim to lie flat on the floor.

The demands of husband and father asserted themselves over desire and will to fight, and so the shotgun was lowered as in the square Captain Holtzclaw harangued his captives. If, he said, abolitionism and Unionism raised their heads again in Laclede, he would pay another visit, and one that would not be so lenient as this. As he spoke, his men took goods and cash wherever found, an estimated three thousand dollars or somewhat more. At Brookfield, five miles away, a detachment of Union troops was told of what was going on by two men who had slipped away, and soon a train appeared with soldiers. Holtzclaw and his raiders went away, and in the wake of their departure a company of Home Guards was formed in Laclede. John Fletcher Pershing was elected lieutenant, and later cap-tain. The Home Guards erected fortifications, mounds of dirt behind which they would fight. But Holtzclaw never came again. Perhaps it was because of the guards and perhaps because a post holding Union Army commissary stores was set up at Laclede, with Yankee soldiers there.

To Anne Elizabeth Pershing the bluecoats, including the officers, while representative of the cause of righteousness, were something other than exemplars in matters of morality and demeanor. To her son John they were seen through the eyes of a little small-town boy as, of course, heroes and demigods. "I recall distinctly going to the commissary and in all seriousness receiving from the sergeant a piece of hard bread and proudly carrying it home to Mother as my day's ration." She got hold of an army uniform and cut it down so that he could go about attired as a miniature soldier of the Union, getting the commissariat upon occasion to add bacon and coffee to the bread he bore home in approved march-past fashion. "I certainly saw a lot of soldiers as a child, and liked to be with them," he recalled.

The war ended, discharged soldiers from both sides straggling through Laclede on their way home. In later years he remembered them going along in either blue or gray. Some of them were slow to change the life they had lived of guns and killing, and for years there was turmoil in the area and great lawlessness, as seen in the exploits of Frank and Jesse James, and the Younger brothers' gang. Laclede was growing and in time would have hotels, restaurants, livery stables, clothing stores, dry goods places and millinery shops, a shoe shop, a hardware store, a tin shop, a harness shop, a lawyer, and a justice of the peace, with covered wagon prairie schooners passing through with set-tlers for the farther West. But "For some years it was what might be called a wild and wooly town. It was not uncommon during six or seven years following the war for rough characters to come into town on Sat-urdays, carouse at the two saloons, and then gallop through the streets yelling and firing their pistols in the traditional manner of the Wild West," he wrote in later years.

His father was doing very well, his general store expanding in such fashion that John heard him described as one of the richest men in Linn County. John Fletcher Pershing sold big agricultural implements, had a lumber yard, bought great swatches of land partially for speculation and partially to rent out for farming. The family lived in a fine house and had numerous servants, mostly ex-slaves a few years out of bondage. John was enrolled in a school where the tuition was a dollar and a half a month and the teacher was a young woman whose father was one of the two men killed in the Holtzclaw Raid. She was succeeded by the daughter of the town's Congregational minister, a kind, gentle, refined girl, he remem-bered, who often had her father come to open the school day with a prayer. In her class he made his debut in public speaking. "The verses assigned to me were from Mary and the Little Lamb." His mother dressed him in his best clothes, with a blue bow tie adding a special touch.

But when his name was called and he went to the front of the room to face the other students and an assemblage of parents come to hear the recitals, he was struck dumb: "The words would not come. They had left me. After a dreadful pause, Mother, who sat well up in front, came to the rescue." She whispered the opening lines. He got through the initial verse but was seized by forgetfulness for the second. Again she started him off. It went that way for his entire performance. In 1933, seventy years later, he still recalled those moments and wrote that ever after when he got up to speak to an assemblage he sometimes, oftentimes, thought of that first experience, the memory coming to him with full force.

At home in those days along the expanding frontier there were understood chores for children. He worked in the garden of the family's big new residence with a picket fence and high gables reminiscent of New England, the finest in Laclede. John graduated from plucking weeds and hoeing to planting and cultivating, each new assignment seeming one of an unfolding series of important events. There was waiting for the frost to be out of the soil so that beds could be made for early vegetables, preparation of the ground for seedlings transplanted from the glass-covered hothouses, and first showing of ripe strawberries about whose appearance he could "in triumph carry the word to the household." Beyond the garden with its fruit trees and past the stables for horses and cattle was a barn lot where he and other children could play the wildest games without protest from their elders that they risked destruction of shrubs or breakage of windows. There was a horse, Selim, who once threw his mother and made her thereafter gun-shy about riding so that she only got on, sidesaddle of course, anything else being unknown for a woman, when snowfall drifts were such that otherwise she would be entirely housebound. Selim was only being playful when he tossed Mother, John decided. Often he and two or three other children would jump up and on to careen about, playing circus.

Saturday in those days, Saturday night or sometimes on Sunday morning, a hot tub was an "absolute prerequisite," as was Sunday church attendance and an almost Puritan-like abstinence on that day from games.

Yet his parents, he felt, were a little more liberal than most. His mother took the lead in forming the first big Methodist church in town, his father making the largest individual subscription, and they encouraged their children in reading the Bible and Commentaries, and their home was the rendezvous of preachers and elders at the regular quarterly meeting, but they were for the place and day relaxed and open in their views. There were no children's books in the home, but *Pilgrim's Progress*, Shakespeare, Scott, Poe, Lord Byron, *Aesop's Fables*, *Robinson Crusoe*, and biographies of Daniel Boone and Davy Crockett. (Later he got hold of copies of Beadle's dime novels, to be read surreptitiously—"Often even in school when I was supposed to be studying. Several times I was so absorbed in the hairbreadth escapes of the heroes of those blood-curdling tales that I failed to notice the teacher prowling about the room and was caught with a novel hidden behind my history or geography."

On the edge of town were the breastworks thrown up in wartime days to defend against Captain Holtzclaw's threatened return to Laclede, and additional ones in the village square, where the men had been lined up as Anne Elizabeth Pershing implored her husband to put away his loaded shotgun, and there the children played on reminders of the days when the Boys in Blue and the civilian militias supporting them saved the Union. He remembered being carried about on his Confederate-supporting grandfather's shoulders when visiting the old gentleman's sawmill and home, whose occupants had uniformly served the rebels at every opportunity; but more dominant were the stories of how the Home Guards turned out to man the now-playtime barriers when rumors spread that secesh marauders were coming.

Once his father was named as grand marshal, of frock coat and red sash, for the annual Fourth of July parade to nearby Glovers Grove, where there would be speeches and a picnic. John was about nine. He was delegated to carry the American flag, recipient of great honor and responsibility. "I felt the burden of the nation resting upon my diminutive shoulders." The grove had a speakers' platform set among hickory trees, and plank seats for listeners, the Yankee veterans among them wearing little bronze buttons in lapels. Flocks of buggies and wagons and riders and marchers set off and despite the inspiring music of fife and drum it seemed to the flag-bearer that the distance to go under a hot sun seemed longer and longer. Once arrived, there were prayers and the songs of wartime, "John Brown's Body," "Marching through Georgia," the others. Throughout he held the flag aloft. Then there were speeches praising Washington, Lincoln, Grant, the war, the veterans. At long last he could lower his burden and make for a luncheon basket.

Camp meetings were also held at Glovers Grove, with ministers coming from far distances to speak to and pray with townspeople or country folk temporarily living in tents or, for some, including the Pershings, in rough shacks with rustic chairs and tables. Children were permitted to roam free during lectures and services reserved for adults, to imagine they saw in the woods animals of unexampled size and, at night, ghostlike apparitions such as the black servants used to talk about when gathered around the kitchen fire at home after dinner was over. John and his younger brother got their father to finance a refreshment stand. They built a hut of rough lumber and filled the shelves with candies and peanuts and other treats. They worked hard and managed to dispose of their entire stock but in the end barely came out even. "The conclusion in the family was that Jim and I ate the profits."

In the fall, when malaria was prevalent, children were given an occasional toddy from the demijohn always kept in the closet. In winter hot salt and vinegar were used as a gargle for colds, and throats were rubbed with tallow warmed by the log fire before going to bed with a red flannel around the neck. The spring tonic was sassafrass tea and a few doses of sulfur mixed with molasses. There were no shoes or socks for children in summer save for Sundays. In the winter boys wore heavy woolen stockings and copper-toed boots; the girls were in high shoes. Once, John remembered, he and Jim and some other boys raided old Mr. Hargreave's peach orchard and were eating and stuffing their pockets when the farmer himself stepped out of his cornfield nearby. They ran, but he identified them all. The next day they heard, or at least believed, that they were going to be arrested. A council was hastily called and John was delegated as emmissary to apologize to Mr. Hargreave and to promise not to repeat the offense. It was not the only sin of his youth; decades later a playmate of those days, Samuel Carothers, wrote to say investigation might clear up the mystery of exactly which Laclede boys mobbed a billy goat, and also explain why a certain man's turkeys were killed in self-defense when the selfsame boys were on a camping and hunting trip; additionally, Carothers thought, discussion could explode the old theory that green apples cause "tummy ache in the young and festive boy." There were taffy pulls and spelling bees and dips in the old swimming hole of the Locust Creek valley near where it was said the famous Princess Watta-Wa-Na refused to marry the conquering Musquakie king. And there was branding on the calves by teachers with switches—perhaps the use of the bundle of hedge cuttings always kept ready in a schoolroom corner was necessary, the mature John decided, and he doubted any boy got through the grades without a beating, but some of the teachers were overly severe. Fighting with his fellows was "an everyday pastime" in which, told by his father to stand up for himself, he was able to hold his own although sometimes he got more than he gave. He decided he would like to be a blacksmith of great powerful arms using two anvils to sandwich a charge of powder touched off by the red-hot end of an iron heated in the forge for explosions honoring the glorious Fourth. There were evening prayers each night before bedtime and a sister's joke on a visiting preacher who chewed tobacco and smoked and told good stories, Brother Sidebottom, called Old Side for short: she slipped out to the barn and pasted circus posters picked up somewhere all over Old Side's horse, the preacher laughing along with everyone else, although Mother "made a brave effort at being embarrassed." And he began to leave childhood behind.

In 1870 and 1871, he remembered, he read of the Franco-Prussian War in the *St. Louis Globe-Democrat* as "the wiseacres of Laclede used to gather in front of Father's store and Dick Mitchell's drugstore next door and while whittling in Missouri fashion hold forth on the strategy of the campaign—comparing the French and German generals to Grant and Lee." By then he had graduated to riding the lead horse of a team pulling a reaper over his father's fields of wheat, oats, or barley. The next promotion was to plow and harrow and sow, with cultivating and harvesting to follow. He broke horses, milked cows, used an old army rifle bored out and turned into a shotgun to go on the open prairie of foxtail, horseweed, and jimson and bring down quail, ducks, geese, wild turkeys, squirrels, and once, fooling with an old army revolver, loaded it, put on caps, and carefully turned the cylinder to have the hammer slip out of his grasp and produce a deafening explosion which sent a .45 bullet through the outside rail of the family's best mahogany bed. A sister screamed at the top of her voice and the mother raced up, thinking her daughter had been shot. "Thereafter I was forbidden to play with loaded revolvers."

All the Pershings were musical and some of his happiest memories were of gatherings around the piano, everybody singing together. He decided he would be an attorney, having with his father often gone to the county seat at Lenneus, six miles north, to see the family lawyer, Alexander Mullins, argue cases arising out of John Fletcher Pershing's numerous business ventures. Law's theoretical precision and exactitude appealed to him, and he pictured himself heading off to the University of Missouri at Columbia for undergraduate and then law school studies. But when he was thirteen his father told him all such ideas must be abandoned. For some time John had noticed that new family economies in spending were being imposed, had heard bits of disturbing conversation, seen from his parents' faces that something was seriously wrong. Now for the first time in his life Mr. Pershing spoke to him of business affairs. The father had disastrously overextended himself with purchases of two 160-acre farms, dozens of quarter sections of virgin land bought for speculation, and expensive farm implements obtained for sale at the store. All had been done on credit. Now he had no way of keeping current with obligations. As with millions of others rich and poor and in between, the Panic of 1873 had ruined him. "A rude awakening," John said years later of what his father told him.

The store went, the lands were foreclosed upon, John Fletcher Pershing left home to be a traveling salesman for a St. Joseph clothing firm, and Anne Elizabeth Pershing opened her house to boarders. One of the 160-acre farms, heavily mortgaged, was hung on to. It had to be depended upon, John was told, for food and revenue. He would run it, thirteen years old, with Jim, eleven, helping him. They must hire as few part-time assistants as possible. Every penny counted. Their attendance at school must be restricted to the couple of frozen-fields months when the corn was gathered and the wood for winter laid by.

For three years John and Jim worked the farm set in the Laclede out-lands. They departed the family residence turned hotel early each morn-ing with cold lunches to be eaten by the fields — the workhorses needed a midday rest and could not be utilized to take them home for a hot meal. He and Jim harrowed, planted, harvested. A plague of grasshoppers as-sailed them in 1875 and they also endured a severe drought in that year. The Panic dug in its claws and bit with cruel teeth and lasted and lasted, and when they got what they considered a prize crop of forty acres' worth of timothy bailed up, the price they got at St. Louis did not pay for the freight charges. By their efforts and their father's traveling-salesman in-come, such as it was, and the money their mother got from her boarders, the family ate well enough, although its members went about in patched clothing. (Mrs. Pershing was expert with a needle, as women were along the middle frontier.) In the end, the farm had to go. John, seventeen years old, got a job teaching in a school for black children. Years later a Laclede woman who kept a little hotel, Susan Hewitt, who was close to Mrs. Per-shing and to her son John, remembered how he used to come to her place and ask what the kitchen had that was good; told it was field apple pie, he would ask for a slice and then ask for another. Susan Hewitt re-membered also that when he went to be a teacher for the blacks certain of Laclede's boys jeered at the son of high estate now fallen and on his way to work: "Nigger!" He paid no attention.

He kept to his intention to one day be a lawyer. "Before I was twenty I had read all of Blackstone and all Kent's Commentaries." But there was no possibility that his father could help him with his education, for the Panic not only ruined but also ruined forever John Fletcher Pershing. His son obtained a single-year-only certification to teach in a white school, and in October of 1879 tried for appointment to one in Prairie Mound, some ten miles from Laclede. On his way to an interview with the school board, dressed in his best clothing, he went to pick up a promised letter of recommendation from a friend's father. "John," the man said, "that board down there don't take much to dress. A boy wearing kid gloves; you had better not wear them." He put the gloves in his pocket before the inter-view and got the job, one of the board members remarking another can-didate equally qualified had been turned down for wearing kid gloves.

The school had some forty-five students, ranging in age from six years up to twenty-one, two years older than the new teacher. His salary was forty dollars a month, a quarter of which went for room and board at the home of a school board member, an ex-lieutenant of the Union Army whose two adolescent daughters were members of the student body. He would teach the *First Reader* up to geometry and algebra and for the more advanced subjects would never be more than one jump ahead of his pupils. They early decided to try him out. He had to tell Tug Wilson, who was older than he, that he would stay after school for bullying a younger student. But when classes were dismissed the bully rose to leave with the others. The teacher came off his platform and stood almost in physical contact with him. "Wilson, I am here to run this school," he said, and told him to sit down or get a thrashing. Wilson sat. Not asking the school board to expel a student but dealing directly with a problem was the best way to handle things, the teacher decided. Once an outraged parent whose son had complained at home about something came on horseback, brandishing a gun. The teacher stood before his school, tried reasoning, got nowhere, and finally suggested that the man put away the gun and get off the horse so the matter could be settled with fists. The teacher won, then spent some time putting balm on his vanquished foe's wounds. He found teaching very valuable, and always felt he learned more than most of his pupils.

By the spring of 1880 he had saved enough money to enable him to attend for three months the state normal school at Kirksville,* eventual graduation from which would move him up substantially as an applicant for future teaching jobs in which he could earn enough to go to the University of Missouri and become a lawyer. At Kirksville his fellow students were like himself serious-minded, and he felt there was a studious atmosphere. The Latin professor wrote on the top of the blackboard an admonition regarding young men who chewed tobacco: "Those who expectorate on the floor must not expect to rate high in the class."

His grades were good but not exceptional and he never got a 10 nor a 9½ but did well in English grammar, written arithmetic, mental arithmetic,

---

*later Northeast Missouri State Teachers College

elementary physics, art of teaching, school management, penmanship, drawing, and methods of geography. He became a member of the Philomathian Literary Society and took part in its debates, did little at such sports as the college offered, and when the term was over went back to Prairie Mound feeling himself somewhat better qualified to practice his profession. At the end of the school year he returned to Kirksville to accumulate more credits toward his eventual advanced teaching degree, and repeated the alternately teacher-and-then-student process in 1881. His sister Elizabeth joined him in Kirksville for study, and one Saturday morning when he sat in her room reading the weekly from home he saw that two weeks in the future there was going to be a competitive examination for selection of a boy from their congressional district to attend the U.S. Military Academy.

His knowledge of West Point was hazy, but that Lee, Sherman, Jackson, Sheridan, and Grant graduated from there gave it to his mind "a romantic appeal." And it was free, a free education. He told Elizabeth he had a good mind to try for appointment. She said he ought to do so, and helped him review the subjects upon which candidates would be tested. He did not inform his parents of the matter but went to join seventeen other young men for the examination at Trenton, Missouri.

Most of the questions were written, but in geography and grammar the aspirants were tested orally in a spelling-beelike elimination contest. All the others were tripped up by questions on grammar until only he and one other boy were left. To them was propounded the sentence: *I love to study.* "Tell me the function of the infinitive 'to study," said the examiner to the other boy.

"It modifies the verb 'love.' "

The examiner turned to the second candidate. "The infinitive is the object of the verb." On that basis he was given the opportunity to travel to West Point and there be tested for appointment to the Academy. He decided he would attend a prep school just outside the Academy grounds where candidates boned up for the entrance exams. It would be opening very shortly. He would have to leave in a matter of days and for the first time in his twenty-one years cross the Missouri state line.

He returned to Kirksville for his things and to give the news, and was at once addressed as "General" by his fellows at the teachers college. A friend of his family called to him across a street, "John, I hear you passed with flying colors." "Yes, I did," John boomed back. The reaction at home was more restrained than that of those outside the house. "But John, you are not going into the army, are you?" his mother asked.

✈ 2 ✦

ONE DOZEN YOUNG MEN GATHERED for the four-month course at Colonel Huse's School in Highland Falls, just outside the gate of the U.S. Military Academy they hoped to attend. None of them, Avery Andrews remembered, was confident of passing the West Point entrance exam, and when after classes they walked up to the Academy and watched the evening parade, it was to Andrews "simply incredible" that they could get to wear that gray uniform and march with such perfect time and precision.

Pershing in early 1882 was physically strong, broad-shouldered, even-featured, well turned out, neat, serious, steady, interested in improving himself. In the pages of a Chicago clothing store advertising giveaway notebook, Mayer, Engle & Co. of Wabash Avenue, he penciled in the date of President Garfield's death a few months earlier, and that his successor, President Arthur, was a native of New York, along with reminders to himself to look up the definition of infinitives, passives, participles used as adjectives, the parsing of adjectives and relative pronouns and prepositions; also predicate nouns, their construction and parsing, and the use as conjunctions of modal adverbs. Also, Rel. Pro., Rel. Adj., Conj. Adverbs, the definitions of compound, complex, and simple sentences and mode, tense, person and number, gender and case, common, proper, collective, and abstract nouns, and that proper English usage was: "It could not have been *she*" and "I think I *shall* return home," along with "Giving money away liberally is far better than keeping everything to one's self." He noted that his great-grandfather was named Daniel and his grandfather Joseph, and put down parallels of latitude of various places, city populations, and the heights of mountains.

In addition to his itemization of random points, he gave attention to what he was being taught at Colonel Huse's for in common with his 11 fellows he passed the Academy exam along with 117 other applicants. Asked for a depiction of their parents' financial status, whether Indigent, Reduced, Moderate, or Affluent, almost all the new cadets, as with Cadet Pershing, indicated Moderate, although in his case perhaps Reduced might have been more appropriate. They went off to summer camp to live in tents, where before the warm weather passed, he later wrote, everything learned from Colonel Huse vanished from memory. It did not matter. West Point was little concerned with facts. Method and attitude and spirit mattered there. That and discipline.

It was such discipline so demanding and so brutal as had characterized the savage and cruel British Army, and the Prussian-automaton school of Frederick the Great. It had nothing in common with any other aspect or form of American life or experience; Cadet Pershing's classmate Cadet T. Bentley Mott decided in later years that to find its approximate parallels you had to travel to a Tibetan lamasery, or the Jesuit College in Rome. There were half a dozen daily inspections of a cadet's room and person and prescribed activities for every hour of every day; there was no smoking, and dismissal for anyone caught drinking a bottle of beer. Each class recitation inflexibly began with "I am required to solve the following . . ." All was cold, hard, ironlike. There was no leave for a cadet's first two years; during the entire four-year course one furlough was permitted. No money was allowed; a cadet could not possess it nor get it from home. (He was paid $540 a year and from that sum could charge necessary expenses.) Nothing could be done without reference to the book of regulations. When in 1882 the education of the Class of 1886 began, West Point's superintendent was the religiously inclined Oliver Otis Howard, the one-armed Christian Hero, so he was termed, of the Civil War. He was soon replaced by Wesley Merrit, who at twenty-seven had, along with George Armstrong Custer, commanded a cavalry division under Philip Sheridan. Removed from the scene of the Little Big Horn catastrophe, Custer now lay in West Point's cemetery. Wesley Merrit went on, remembered as the most severe disciplinarian of a West Point that had known many such.

One marched in a kind of goosestep and with little finger on trouser seam to classes, to meals, to field exercises, always in ranks and rigidly erect, chin in, head up, shoulders back, cadet officer file-closers barking as one went along. The "fourth-year classmen," equivalents of freshmen at a college but plebes at West Point, referred to themselves, when told to speak, in the third person: "Sir, Mr. Andrews begs to report," or "Sir, Mr. Mott is present as ordered," or "Sir, Mr. Pershing requests." In return they were ritually screamed at by upperclassmen as "Mr. Dumbjohn! Smack-head! Mr. Dumbwillie!" Men dropped out, went mad, killed themselves, broke down into weeping fits. Of the 129 plebes of 1882, 77 survived to graduate four years later.

When the summer camp introduction to their new life—"Beast Barracks"—ended, the plebes removed to the Academy proper, a place remindful of a medieval fortress of crenellated towers and sally ports and heavy great stone of commanding position above the Hudson and the Plain where booming drums and sounding trumpets and shrilling fifes sent the students on their stamping and pivoting way. The hazing of the plebes saw them yanked out of bed to be dragged along the company street, forced to sing, chew rags, go through calisthenics, roar aloud to extreme derision what their hometown papers had to say of their appointments to the Academy. One cadet managed never to reveal the brief notice in his local weekly: *John J. Pershing will take his leave of home and friends this week for West Point, where he will enter the U.S. military academy. John will make a good looking cadet with Uncle Sam's blue and we trust he will ever wear it with honor to himself and the old flag which floats above him. John here's our hand may success crown your efforts and long life be yours.*

The course of study included geometry, trigonometry, algebra, history, geography, ethics, English, drawing, philosophy, civil engineering, French, physics, geology, mineralogy, chemistry, all taught in recite-at-the-blackboard rote fashion, plus the military specialties of fencing, bayonetwork, musketry, gunnery, horsemanship with no rising at the trot, tactics at the company level, and, of course, endless marching and drill, inspections, parades, and guard mounts. All was unremittingly thorough, rigid, demanding, with academic standing rigorously calculated. Far, far more important was the extent to which a cadet was or was not alert, keen, smart, trim, erect, neat, straight-backed, willing—a soldier. A future officer. To produce such, cadets—and particularly plebes—were constantly chivvied at and harried after, given "skins" (demerits) for talking when standing in place, having clothing incorrectly put into a press, indifferently executing a command while horsed, misspelling a word when submitting a written explanation, having water about a washstand, laughing when in ranks, whistling loudly when going up a flight of stairs, wearing a torn blouse, wearing a cap on the side of the head, speaking in an unnecessarily loud tone of voice, improperly policing a tent or improperly fastening it down, failing to salute an officer, wearing muddy overshoes, being not conversant with the duties of a cannoneer at 3.2-inch gun drill, permitting and/or joining a conversation after "Taps," taking a rifle apart without permission, walking in an unmilitary fashion, swinging arms excessively while marching to church, swinging arms excessively while returning from dinner, not calling guards to attention for a passing officer, having an unauthorized sword in a tent, failing to correct a file of men for being out of step marching to dinner, approaching and addressing an officer without authority, executing the manual of arms in a careless and indifferent manner, wearing a sweater during barracks inspection, piling bedding sloppily, falling into ranks in improper fashion, drawing a bayonet at church formation, wearing dirty spurs, not sending all soiled clothing to the laundry, buttoning a blouse incorrectly, placing a broom in the wrong place at inspection, and for committing any other infraction of the rules, or of proper and understood conduct.

Cadet Pershing was academically somewhat above average although no class leader, foreign languages particularly not being his forte. Cadet Andrews felt it impossible for his classmate ever to show fear, but "his nearest approach thereto was his attitude towards his instructor in French." Cadet Charles Walcutt remembered how his roommate got deeper and deeper into troubles with French, which he attempted to remedy by missing meals to immerse himself in the textbooks, an expression of hopelessness and discouragement on his face. Sometimes he studied the language through Saturday nights.

While twenty of his classmates never got a single demerit during the four years, he got more than two hundred. Illicitly studying French after hours with a blanket hung over the window to hide his lamp, he and others heard an officer coming up the steps several steps at a time. The visiting Cadet Mott sprang across the hall into his room and Cadet Walcutt crawled under a bed. Pershing snatched at the blanket, doused the lamp, and leaped fully clothed under the covers. He did not confound the officer, and walked half a dozen punishment tours, marching up and down with a rifle. Primarily his demerits were for tardiness, for then and always he seemed entirely to lack a sense of the passage of time, almost, it was said, as a tone-deaf man lacks a sense of music and a color-blind one cannot know a rainbow.

But as an immaculate and snappy and severe and disciplined soldier of perfect military bearing, he was unsurpassable. He had the sharp-speaking, dominating, exacting qualities that made for a drillmaster, the command personality. The military ideal of complete precision married to the concept that if a job is worth doing it is worth doing well seized him. Even back at the state normal school in Kirksville he had been notable for stubbornly working through a study problem long after his roommate turned in. At West Point a perhaps inborn distaste for haziness, sloppiness, imprecision, haphazardness was summed up in a phrase that epitomized him then and afterward: "Let's get where we're going!" His fellows respected and appreciated him, and elected him class president. At the end of the plebe semesters the authorities appointed him senior cadet corporal of his year.

Recognition Day came, the end of the first year, with upperclassmen congratulating and shaking hands with and for the first time fraternizing with those they had deviled. Yearlings, as sophomores were called, the Class of 1886 went off to summer camp to haze and harry those coming in to replace them as entering cadets. In his own plebe year, Pershing recalled, "a burnt match left in the company street became a log" in the eyes of the supervising yearlings, "a scrap of paper was magnified into a trash pile"; now it was he himself coming into Cadet Charles Rhodes's tent to order that plebe instantly leave off washing his face for immediate picking up of a match and a piece of paper outside. Yet despite the severe and disciplinary manner, serious, conscientious, strict, one dealt with someone who lived up to his own precepts, remembered Cadet Andrews, for there was never any evidence of tyrant or despot in Pershing, no petty tin-soldier bullying. He was involved in getting to the matter at hand, doing the job. "His exercise of authority was then and has always been since," remembered Cadet Robert Lee Bullard, "of a nature peculiarly impersonal, dispassionate, hard, and firm. This quality did not in him, as in many, give offense; the man was too impersonal, too given over to pure business and duty. His manner carried to minds under him the suggestion, nay, the conviction, of unquestioned right to obedience. There was no shadow of a doubt about it."

At the end of two years at the Point, no contact with other schools, no organized sports as such, membership in a priesthood, the Class of 1886 was granted leave. Cadet Pershing, president of his class, senior officer of that class, went home to Laclede in Missouri. "Land o' mercy, Johnny, the Lord has been mighty good to you, boy, to bring you back here to your mother," said an old black woman who had known him as a child. He sat by a river where as a boy he had fished and swum with Charley Spurgeon, whose father told him not to wear kid gloves when applying for his teaching job, and Charles asked, "Well, John, how do you like it, anyway?"

"The training is a good thing," Pershing answered. "But as for following it as a profession—why, I don't suppose there'll be another gun fired in a hundred years. I'm going on and finish, though, just to get the education." After that, he told Charley, he'd serve the mandatory tour required of graduates, and then go to be a lawyer.

At the 1885 graduation ceremonies the cadet adjutant sang out the name of the man of the Class of 1886 who would hold the highest student position West Point knew, first captain of the Corps of Cadets. It was Pershing. "To stand first in studies," wrote Robert Lee Bullard, "to graduate at the head of the class, is as nothing to it." "Within five minutes," Pershing recalled, he had the chevrons of his new rank on his sleeve. "No other military promotion has ever come to me quite equal to that." Among his predecessors in the post was Robert E. Lee. Within a few weeks the entire Corps, for the first time in the years he had been at West Point, departed the Academy. Ferries took them across the Hudson to stand in long, straight lines as a slow-moving train came down the tracks, heading south.

Civil War veterans, graying now with their service twenty years in the past, stood by the railbed holding their old flags, with children in parents' arms. For down the tracks came the train bearing to its grave the body of Ulysses S. Grant. "Present arms!" called out the first captain and the lines behind him snapped to rifle salute. The soldier second only to Grant, Sherman, was often at the Academy, appearing tall and stately as he walked about, cadets making an effort to cross his path so they could salute and be saluted by the hero of the March to the Sea. Cheerful, jovial, offering humorous discussions of his own cadet days mixed with friendly advice, he was not the only icon to visit. Mark Twain came, learned that the first captain was from his state, came to his room, and kept everybody laughing as he told funny stories while frequently addressing Pershing as "fellow Missourian."

During the winter there were not many ladies from what Pershing called "the outside world" at the Academy, but in the warm months "there were droves of them." One went in summer white to hops— dances—to meet them and then walked about, often to Flirtation Walk, where tradition decreed that a girl could not refuse a cadet's request for a kiss. Pershing was far from being one of those cadets "who formed bachelor clubs and affected to dislike the sight of a skirt," he remembered. "He knew his way around Flirtation Walk," his later very close associate James G. Harbord was told by those who had known him at the Point. "He was a hop-goer, what cadets called a 'spoony' man," wrote Robert Lee Bullard. "He loved the society of women."

Graduation Day was coming. One hundred nights before that event, the Class of 1886 held the traditional down-the-stretch dinner for cadets in their position. Nine of their number were cited for unspeakable offenses. Among them was Pershing. The charge was: *Imposing on the feelings of the Corps by his tearful rendering of "Take Back the Heart That*

Thou Gavest." Perhaps his singing had declined since the days back in Laclede around the piano with his family.

Graduation came, June 11, 1886. In later years he remembered West
Point as making a philosophy class max, a maximum, the top grade, when
several visitors were present, including Civil War general William Rosecrans, pillow fights at Tatoo, marching with drawn saber while superin-
tending plebes policing up an area, light artillery drill, double-timing
around old Fort Clinton at morning squad drill. He remembered his first
guard tour. It was at night. Hazing upperclassmen attired as ghosts began
appearing from all directions. He challenged one: "Halt! Who comes
there?" The ghost stood still. "Halt! Who stands there?" The ghost produced a camp stool and sat down. "Halt! Who sits there?"

All his life he kept in mind what he had taken in from West Point
with its splendid, demanding uniforms, the cross belts and plumes and
glittering accouterments, the symbolisms and totems, the concept of
honor and, above all, duty. He loved his fellows of what they called "Old
'86," felt toward them almost as brothers. Now it was over and they
would, as the expression had it, doff cadet gray and don army blue. Gen.
Philip Sheridan came and spoke. President Cleveland's secretary of war
handed out diplomas. The first captain found a large and surprising
lump rising in his throat. He had not realized he was going to feel so
deeply sentimental. Hats sailed in the air and officers and professors
shook hands with the new graduates, something not done previously,
and they went down to the Hudson landing for the *Daniel Drew*, the
Corps they were leaving lined up on the river drive sending cheers across
the water, the *Mary Powell* coming upstream sounding its horn again
and again, other vessels offering whistled salutes. The graduates "howled
themselves hoarse" as they sailed south to New York City, Second Lieutenant Pershing remembered.

That night they gathered in a private room at Martinelli's Restaurant.
Everybody got drunk. "A sumptuous supper was served." Speeches were
made as "the spirit(s)" moved people to do so. Some dealt with Pershing's
showing as class president and first captain, with men predicting he
would rise to the highest military rank and be 1886's most outstanding
soldier. Second Lieutenant Wiley Bean declaimed that their classmate

would become president of the United States. More than fifty years on, Old '86's George Duncan asked Pershing if he recalled the drunken tributes and Pershing said, "I certainly remember all about it, and as a fact I never felt so embarrassed in my life." In response he himself offered "a few broken remarks."

The next day, "most of us feeling quite shaky," they wandered around the city in little groups. Pershing had spent a day there on his way to West Point four years earlier; now with others he left the Leland Hotel on Broadway to look at the *New York Tribune* building, the Equitable Life Insurance building, the great A. T. Stewart department store, the Fifth Avenue Hotel. They walked across the new Brooklyn Bridge, which since his previous visit had opened to be regarded as one of the world's wonders for its height and length and engineering magnificence, and he felt "awe and amazement that comes over one and gives him a timidity" but that probably, he decided, eventually would wear off if one saw the bridge often enough. They rode back uptown on the Sixth Avenue elevated railroad and visited the Eden Musée to see wax representations of Edison, Krupp, the French prince imperial dying at the hands of spear-wielding African natives, the German emperor, Lincoln, Victoria and the royal family, "all the noted musicians," Generals Grant, Hancock, and Butler, Robert Fulton, "Liebig of beef extract fame," Alexander "Clubber" Williams of the New York City police, "and many that I have forgotten." The Eden's Chamber of Horrors showed Indian barbarities, President Garfield's assassin, Guiteau, in his cell before execution, arctic suffering, hanging horse thieves, the Inquisition. There was an attached beer garden with solid mirrors for walls and so many plants that the place looked like an immense hothouse. Above was a gallery with stereoscopic views of interesting sights in various countries.

That night they all got together at Delmonico's to feast themselves again, and again to get drunk. One man fell asleep behind a curtain hanging and another scaled the heights of the gallery to wave a flag. They dispersed for summer furlough before reporting to their assigned units in September. The girls back in Laclede found extremely engaging a straight-backed almost-six-footer of some 180 pounds wearing glamorous, smart uniform.

In the fall Lieutenant Pershing went east to Washington to join classmates for a long train trip to their various posts in the West. From Chicago they headed outward over the tracks of the Atchison, Topeka, and Santa Fe. "A jollier crowd than ours never traveled. We told stories, sang class songs, cleaned out eating houses, fired at prairie dogs, hazed the peanut boy, and practically ran the train." Lieutenant Bean rang an old-fashioned doorbell to great hilarity until the sound aroused a fellow-passenger cowboy's ire. "The bell was retired."

Classmates dropped off at points along the line, and Pershing alighted into what he wrote was the "land of the burro, cactus, and tarantula." He got to Deming and then Silver City in the New Mexican blazing-sun deserts and harsh mountains so different from all he had known in the Missouri of his childhood and young manhood, and on the heights of West Point along the Hudson. He came to dusty parade ground, enlisted men's barracks, officers' quarters, flagpole, stables, commissary and quartermaster's storehouse, adjutant's office, Fort Bayard, and the Sixth Cavalry.

→ 3 ←

THE U.S. ARMY WAS IN THE MINDS of a vast proportion of the citizenry a little-considered and almost entirely out-of-sight insignificance. Anyone too young to have lived through the Civil War had likely never seen a soldier in uniform. As far as civilians were concerned, and they were very little concerned, the army was a faraway western police force shepherding Indians around.

There were fewer than twenty-five thousand usually semiliterate enlisted men, a large percentage Irish- or German-born, and some two thousand officers. Anyone above the rank of lieutenant was a Civil War veteran spinning out the long years since the days when the army was the Boys in Blue who saved the Union. One could be verging on forty years' service, have commanded a regiment at Gettysburg while holding temporary wartime rank, led charges at Lookout Mountain or seen Lee at Appomattox—and now be a gray-haired captain each morning inspecting horses' hooves.

Second Lieutenant Pershing's Fort Bayard was one of several posts manned by units of the Sixth Cavalry and outfits of other branches of the army, each a little community of some three hundred people living in a quadrangle around the parade ground. Another was Fort Stanton, and to establish communications between the two became the new officer's first military task: He was ordered to erect a chain of heliograph stations on

27

mountains twenty-five to thirty miles apart, immense mirrors reflecting the sun to send dot-dash messages. At once he loved the deserts and the work, which found him in the saddle through daylight hours and beyond. Back at the post there was reveille, and stable call after breakfast, drills, garrison courts, general courts, guard mounting, rifle and pistol and saber practice, jumping hurdles, dismounting to fight on foot, troop patrols with seeing to the "points," the flanks scouting to left and right in front of the column, trumpets sounding, bugles calling. The month after his arrival, in October 1886, his Troop L and another troop were ordered out to search the Mogollon Mountains for renegade Apaches led by Chief Mangus, who, following Geronimo's example, had left their reservations to raid where and how they might. The pack train was loaded before daylight, the new shavetail "amazed," he wrote, to find the soldiers, including the company first sergeant, intoxicated. His West Point conception of how regulars should take the field against a possibly deadly dangerous foe received a shock.

But once away the men turned earnest and were soberly efficient. The command went through the flourishing mining town of Silver City, nine miles from the post, some fifty from the Mexican border, and along the San Francisco River into mountain country. In the night, horses and mules stampeded and ran off. Perhaps coyotes frightened them, perhaps Indians did it. The cavalrymen were on foot in Indian country. They rounded up the animals and thereafter put on hobbles before loosing them to graze in the darkness. They learned that Chief Mangus, as with Geronimo, had turned himself in at a reservation.

That the men had been drunk starting out was not remarkable, for in addition to the post trader selling whiskey, around each of the 120 army posts dotting the vast areas west of the Mississippi were wretched little grog shops, "blind tigers," where the proprietor was never seen. One shoved money into a slot and was in return presented liquor on a revolving roundtable. In the army of those who had taken the queen's shilling, the enlisted men—"other ranks" in British parlance—were regarded, while of lesser value, as one step above the horses and mules; in America they were esteemed somewhat more highly, but not much. It was the duty of a company-level officer like Second Lieutenant Pershing to be banker,

counselor, teacher to and letter-writer for his men, but those men were
yet seen as beasts to be driven to their work, which was to protect the set-
tlers and the wagon trains and railroad lines and, when necessary, to be
put to building roads, repairing and constructing buildings, pursuing
horse thieves or deserters—both numerous—and cutting and storing ice.
It was quite different for those who supervised them, for such were to be
seen not only as officers but also as gentlemen. They paid formal calls in
full tog dress uniform upon their superiors of the garrison and those superiors' ladies, left visiting cards, listened to the musicale and applauded the
amateur theatrical, danced at the weekly hop to the strains of the post
band, drank of the punch, ate of the chafing-dish supper, tendered and
accepted invitations to formally elaborate dinners served on brought-
from-back-East china and eaten with heavy silverware.

Clouds of grasshoppers could obscure the sky, and clouds of dust;
summer was glaring light and brutal heat and dry creek out there in the
vast plains, in the prairie and desert—General Sherman liked to tell
about the soldier who died at Fort Yuma, Arizona, and went to hell, only
to come back for his blanket, for it was cold down there, the soldier complained; and for winter field duty one huddled shivering around dried
dung or mesquite fire as the wind howled. Pershing remembered an officer offering a warming drink and then dropping the bottle, which sadly
smashed, and an enlisted man coming up to ask, "Have I the captain's
permission to eat that snow?"

The mail came one hundred miles by buckboard from the nearest
railhead; but at the dinners one was in cavalry blue-and-gold comple-
menting the long gowns of the ladies of the regiment, and on the table
were red candlesticks and nuts or ferns in silver centerpiece and several
forks at the placings, and potted palms in the room corners. There were
costume parties with people turned out as skeletons, the Evil Eye, a har-
lequin, the devil; there were outdoor luncheon parties with hampers of
food.

His particular friends and housemates were Lieutenants Richard Paddock and Julius Penn, his Old '86 classmate, and as raw shavetails they
were, as the saying went, each so utterly a tenderfoot and green as to be in
danger of being eaten by a cow. The Three Green P's, a wit dubbed

them. Pershing and Penn went on a fishing expedition, Penn wrote home to Batavia, Ohio, and along with another companion got 240 trout; for Christmas they had roast chicken, mashed potatoes, French peas, rice and croquettes, jelly, floating island, and cake. "Our chinaman certainly knows how to get up a good dinner," Penn felt. To Penn at Fort Stanton from a field duty camp along Eagle Creek, Pershing wrote, "We are living like kings, we have milk, quail, wild turkey, a wagon load of vegetables, potatoes, carrots, turnips and onions—quails stuffed with them—plenty of grain and hay, good water, plenty of wood. The only thing lacking is—." (Decades later, General Penn, as then he was, former housemate of a man known for being a "spoony" cadet, took scissors or knife and clipped a few words from the letter before giving it to the Library of Congress.)

The workday ended early when in garrison, and from one in the afternoon until the late-day dress parade and Retreat of form and ceremony that saw the post turn out to wheel, pivot, slap weapons, stand rigid as the evening gun went off and "The Star-Spangled Banner" sounded and the colors were lowered and the troops passed in review, officers' time was almost entirely their own. They rode, drove, walked, drank, played billiards, played cards. Asked to sit in for someone called away for a moment from the poker table, Pershing protested he was ignorant of the game, was prevailed upon to play anyway, and won for the man a considerable sum. He took to playing frequently and got so involved as to see poker hands in his sleep. He decided to drop this amusement. It was typical that he not want endlessly to spend time over cards, for then and always he was of a studious nature, anxious to improve himself.

All around were the Indians who were the main reason for the army's very existence and its placings there in the little outposts so distant from what was called Back in the States. He saw one stalking a deer while wearing a white hunting shirt and a huge pair of antlers on his head, and felt he beheld a character out of some fable or legend of ancient times. He liked to talk with Indians and hear of their ways, wars, fights, customs, and see them dance as older chiefs recited stories of ancient victories and tom-toms sounded and shrill cries of "Hi-yi! Hi-yi!" rang out while in pantomime men followed the trail of an imaginary enemy, faces and bodies painted, wearing loincloths and moccasins and elaborate headdress of eagle feathers. They circled round and round a fire, and when a knife or arrow was stuck into a pot of boiled dog, a feast began. Indian spectators had a curious manner of expressing approval, he wrote home: They spat at dancers to show appreciation.

He was very good at dealing with Indians, and had an openness and honesty and earnest willingness to learn and know and understand not seen in soldiers and officers who felt what they considered savages to be a step above animals but a step below human, they with their painted faces and hair matted with mud, who could be shot or despoiled with no pangs of conscience. Once word arrived at Fort Wingate that two whites in a log cabin a few miles away were standing off some one hundred Indians. Pershing was dispatched with a dozen soldiers to rescue the men. He felt for Indians, but said to his noncom, "We are going to take those men away and if these bucks get hostile, remember we mean business." By parleying with the chiefs he got the job done, no shooting, no blood. Near Fort Wingate some cattle thieves killed a Zuni and tried to run off a herd to end up besieged along with guiltless cowboys by scores of warriors from the dead man's tribe. Pershing came with ten troopers and brought the trapped men away, managing through diplomacy rather than fighting to get the cowboys freed and the thieves to justice. Indians came to take him as being at a remove from most other whites, their estimation of whom had been long established. "Everywhere the naked, hungry, dirty, frightened little Indian children," wrote Lt. Britton Davis of the Third Cavalry, West Point 1881, "darting behind bush or into wikiup at the sight of you. Everywhere the sullen, stolid, hopeless, suspicious faces of the older Indians challenging you. You felt the challenge in your very marrow—that unspoken challenge to prove yourself anything else than one more liar and thief, differing but little from the procession of liars and thieves who preceded you."

Lieutenant Pershing was not seen as such, and once some Indians asked if he would for the sport of it wrestle their champion. Taught in West Point's great stone walls and rigid and uncompromising manner that it was an impossibility that a serving American officer should ever lie, he replied that the man was too dirty. They asked if he would race 110 yards

and he consented. Bets were laid, troopers putting their faith in the shavetail. Just short of the finish line Pershing's ankle buckled. He managed to
roll over, the winner by a hair. The Indians termed him Man-who-crawls-
to-win; he forbade his soldiers to collect on their bets, for Indians, he felt,
had given up enough and too much to the white man. There was much
that was fine in the Indian character, he felt, and that their "pathetic" situation was "mainly the result of government neglect and insincerity"
forming "the most cruel, unjust, blackest page of American history."

Yet they could be dangerous, as was the Apache who knocked Pershing out of his saddle with a blow to the head, prepared to tomahawk
and perhaps scalp him, and then decided it was better to grab his army revolver and run off. The incident in itself was trivial, but the possibility of
Indian uprisings on a large scale was not, and so it was the duty of the cavalry to practice to fight in force if necessary. All across three hundred
miles east to west and three hundred north to south, where Forts Apache
and Huachuca were in Arizona and Forts Stanton and Wingate in New
Mexico, mounted detachments played at Raiders And Pursuers, war-
game chases across creek and *cañon*, the Zuni Mountains and Agua Fria,
the San Andreas Pass, Pryor's Ranch, Cow Springs, Hermosa, Cuchillo
Negro, the Mescalero Agency, the White Sands and Bear Mountain and
the White Mountains, lead horses going along so that each man could
have two for getting across such places as the treeless plateau called the
Jornado del Muerte, the journey of death. Flying horse soldiers uncom-
mitted to slow infantry and not nailed down by the coattails to the artillery's heavy wagon trains, they ranged about seeking one another
through the scrubby mesquite and sage bush of the upland mesas and
along steep trails in the pine forests, around great volcanic cracks in the
earth, the prairies where not a tree or shrub could be found save for the
cottonwoods along the little streams, and past the watering-station towns
of saloon, dance hall, supply store, unpaved dusty street of one-storied
shop, gambling den, horse wagon and ox team, cowboy, prostitute,
hunter and miner, wooden hotel innocent of paint or wash and with
rooms defined by white muslin curtains showing the confines of a seg-
ment outfitted with shabby bedstead, chair, and small table with pitcher
and basin, the bar with villainous whiskey below. Raiders evading pur-

suers appropriated herds of cattle to drive over their trail and so destroy it. Lieutenant Pershing led a detachment 130 miles in forty hours, halting for seven hours one night and three hours the second night. Victory for raiders was marked when they were able to get within such range of their quarry that a sounding bugle could be heard. Pershing was great at the game and loved it, as he loved almost all in the West, antelope steaks for dinner, evening strolls along the creek past the graveyard headboards of those said to be awaiting the last reveille, the sixteen-mile ride to Gallup from Fort Wingate for dinner at the Harvey Eating House in the Santa Fe railroad station. But he regretted being sent to Wingate from Fort Stanton, writing Lieutenant Penn, who remained, "I have been there so long and had so much fun and know so many people, that I hated to leave. This post is a s.o.b. and no question, tumble down old quarters, the winters are severe, it is always bleak and the surrounding country is barren."

But there were compensations even there—the bracing outdoor life, friendships, hunting. Seeking deer, he once saw what he took to be a wild boar and fired, to learn it was a pig belonging to the Irish-born Mrs. Frank Lisnet, who with her husband ran a tavern. She was, of course, outraged. Years later, general's stars on his shoulders, he was back in New Mexico for an inspection tour. He saw the Irishwoman in the street. "How do you do, Mrs. Lisnet! Remember me?" "Sure, and that I do! Ye're the leftinant that was always killing me pigs!"

One trip came very close to giving him an unpleasant death. With the Sixth Cavalry's First Lieutenant John Stotsenberg, West Point 1881, he departed Fort Wingate for a tour of the Grand Canyon. It was a two-hundred-mile trip. They went with two packmules and a packer whose name, Stotsenberg later wrote, was significant: Minus. Their guide-interpreter was Sam, a Navajo. While to close friends Pershing was usually "John" while often being "Jackie" to his family, in the West he sometimes turned into Jackson. He and Jackson, Stotsenberg wrote, passed through Moqui pueblos and Navajo villages on their June 1887 trip. Having earlier visited Zuni encampments, he wrote, they did not mind the reek of the Indians nor the scent of the sheep manure burned for fuel. In native fashion Stotsenberg baked a loaf of bread in sand heated by coals, and they went along the Oraibi Mountain and across the Snake and Dog

Valley and up a high mesa. They stayed in a Mormon settlement and ate a meal composed exclusively of stewed gooseberries and soda biscuits, and with their hosts watched a traveling family circus of bar and trapeze and Punch-and-Judy ancient jokes. They went on, eating the sandy bread made with the flour they bore along and topped with bacon. The Navajo Sam's pony broke down and he went to find another one and did not return. Sam was famous for unreliability, Stotsenberg recorded.

Along the Little Colorado, Stotsenberg's pony kicked Jackson and then bit him on the arm. Jackson kicked back, in the ribs. They hunted a trail in the rocks, went through rough, flinty malpais, realized they were uncertain of where they were without Sam, and began running low on water. When they found some they filled not only their canteens but also their coffee pot, stuffing the lip and spout with grass so that none would be spilled. They wandered through canyons and high ridges in brutal sun, seeking a trail out, and Minus wondered aloud how long they could live.

They could not find a trail. Minus turned feverish for water, and after a night's sleep the two officers awoke to find him gone, along with the mules. They were alone in the heart of an unfrequented desert some twenty-five miles, they estimated, from a known water source. Their breakfast was biscuits soaked with whiskey—they could not afford to use what water they had. They pushed on, the sun merciless in the unclouded sky, the reflection off the stark rocks terrible. They slept under a little cedar tree and arose only with difficulty. Their lips and tongues swelled up and turned black. They panted with desire to put their heads under a bush away from the sun, did so, and fell asleep. He dreamed of rushing brooks and cool retreats, Stotsenberg remembered, and the awakening was terrible. Stotsenberg began to retch, and it seemed to him hardly worth the effort to get up. Pershing rubbed him down on face, neck, and chest with whiskey. It seemed to help. All they had left was a canteen cup's worth of water apiece, and Jackson offered his to his companion. It could not be accepted, of course, Stotsenberg wrote.

They agreed that if one could no longer go on, the survivor would. They divested themselves of things not absolutely essential to carry, Pershing throwing away his Winchester, a gift. Stotsenberg had earlier done the same with his army-issue carbine. Things looked a little grim, Stotsenberg observed. When they both smiled at the obviousness of the remark, the pain from lips and tongues was frightful. Staggering down a canyon, they saw a horseman. It was Sam. They sank into the shade of a rock. "Water" was the only word they could gasp out. Sam gave them some. They drank, and then Pershing made some coffee that was awful because he was afraid to let water boil, fearful he would "burn it," he said, precious beyond gold as it was.

Safe, they rested with Sam. Minus appeared, "A ghastly-looking sight, the man was absolutely crazy," Stotsenberg remembered. He had found a tiny seep of water after running off with the mules, and had been eating mud. His face and lips were covered with it. They went on to the cabin of a mountain man who made them welcome, and from a nearby bluff saw the Grand Canyon below. They dined on antelope with their host and headed back to Fort Wingate, a mule, Mollie, getting stuck in quicksand on the trip. Covered with mud, they dug and scratched trying to get Mollie out and finally Pershing suggested they tie her head to a pony's tail and so yank her loose. They stayed again with their Mormon friends and went on with no sustenance save some coffee beans in Stotsenberg's pocket and a little bacon. Pershing acted as chef and burned the first pan of bacon so that it was inedible; then he cooked two more pieces, which fell into the fire when he turned the pan. "I told Jackson that I did not care for supper anyway, and that he was the grossest man I ever saw." They met a squaw who had eggs and coffee and ground them corn flapjacks, and so at last well fed and safe, they got back to Fort Wingate. "We felt perfectly satisfied that we knew how not to go to the Grand Canyon," Stotsenberg decided.

There were those who felt the western posts of the army of the 1880s and 1890s were desolately narrow—one who did so was Pershing's classmate T. Bentley Mott, and it was fortunate indeed for him that he went to Paris as military attaché to spend decades in that capacity—but Lieutenant Pershing found stimulating both the work and the location. Homesickness and loneliness were the worst ills of those remote little garrisons flung down where one saw always the same people in the same setting of vast desert or prairie and lived by the same unchanging routine, and longed for differences in architecture, and for electric lights, hansoms, shop windows, late editions of the newspaper, new faces; and in time Pershing came to desire a transfer. But he took away wonderful memories, and half a century on used to go out on a horse around Tucson, where old as then he was he spent winters, and ride along and pretend to himself that he was back to being a second lieutenant of the Sixth Cavalry, young again and back there in the old days.

He was peripherally present for the final act of the long struggle between the red and white races, for the climax of what he called those "romantic yet tragic years." A medicine man of the Paiute in western Nevada, Wovoka, saw in a vision Christ, the white man's God, returning to earth to bring paradise to those the white man had pushed away. Death Song would be replaced by Ghost Dance which would bring back the Indian dead, relatives, friends, and with them the great vanished buffalo herds shot by the white man's guns for meat and hide. Tribal delegations journied to Wovoka to hear they must return to their people and have them dance the Ghost Dance so as to urge the Messiah on his way. Suddenly all across northern plains thousands of Indians were dancing, falling into trances, seeing their dead, saying they and the buffaloes were coming.

All summer and fall of 1890 the Ghost Dance spread, and in the eyes of the white settlers the Indians daily appeared more menacing and the dance seemed more and more a war dance. Back East the papers were filled with speculations about a volcanic outbreak. The most famous Indian of all, Sitting Bull, came to believe in the Ghost Dance. It was said he was about to break out from the reservation and lead his braves into the Dakota Bad Lands. If he took to the warpath, the papers said, anything could happen.

Orders to rush north came for the Sixth Cavalry, and the regiment departed New Mexico on the shortest notice. No travel rations were available and so the men hastily cooked up bread, and beef quickly spoiled. They left on November 23 and by rail made Rapid City, South Dakota, where winter clothing was issued, buffalo overcoats or blanket-lined canvas, fur-lined gloves, heavy felt boots, muskrat caps. It was decided to arrest Sitting Bull. There was a fracas and he was shot to death. That was on December 15. On the twenty-fourth the Sixth was ordered out to intercept Chief Big Foot of the Sioux, who was at large with a band of men, women, and children. Pershing spent Christmas alternately sitting by a fire and trying to sleep on a mountain peak as Big Foot turned himself and his people in at the Pine Ridge, South Dakota, reservation. On guard there was the Seventh Cavalry, Custer's old outfit. The troops attempted to disarm Big Foot's band, someone fired a shot, and there immediately followed along Wounded Knee Creek that massacre never forgotten. Hotchkiss quick-firing guns opened up, and the men of the Seventh indiscriminately shot everyone who moved, including women running away with babies in their arms. Shortly Pershing would be briefly assigned to the command of Troop B of Oglala Indian Scouts to patrol the Pine Ridge reservation, Thunder Bull his first sergeant and the men including Bear Nose, Running Shield, Red Feather, Big Charger, Black Fox, Broken Leg, Crow-on-Head, Eagle Chief, Has-White-Face-Horse, Yellow Bear, Ghost Bull, Iron Cloud, White Hawk, Wounded Horse, and Kills Alone. Undynamic in his reactions to the events at Wounded Knee and holding them simply one of the unfortunate incidents attendant to conflict, he purposefully drilled his Indian scouts in reconnaissance and the duties of a movement guard. But it was all second nature to them, and on their own they put out flankers and in perfect fashion covered main body advances. His concern for and even admiration for them aroused their loyalty, and when he took them to police up the scene of the massacre where here and there a relative of the dead could be seen walking about with what the Indians called "a bad heart," they without orders kept protectively close to their commander each time he left his tent.

Peace had come for all time between the red and white races on the American continent, although it was the peace of the grave for the Indians at Wounded Knee, and a mass grave at that, and to celebrate and perhaps also to show the Indians his power, the army's commanding general, Nelson A. Miles, ordered a great parade. Ten thousand Sioux were invited to attend. Great numbers of troops convened, and Pershing had a reunion with seven of his Old '86 classmates. He wore a cowboy hat with a silver band around it. "Three or four of the boys," he wrote Lt. Julius Penn, "got a little too full, one of whom I am which. I never went to a re-union yet that I did not wind up full as eighteen goats." Heavily wrapped in blankets, Indians watched as the troops marched through sand clouds of a shrieking prairie gale, great swinging columns of infantry, mules dragging the quick-firing cannon whose range was such that it was said to shoot today and kill tomorrow, three-inch rifled artillery pieces with carbine-holding soldiers on the caissons, the Sixth Cavalry with rifles slung to saddles, the black buffalo soldiers of the Ninth Cavalry, the bugle corps on white mounts, Hotchkiss gun batteries, hospital and supply trains and pack mules and finally with band playing "Garryowen" the Seventh Cavalry with blue capes flung back so that yellow cavalry lining was exposed. Chiefs were taken to Washington to be shown arsenals, guns great and small, mountains of ammunition, "as much to say, 'What General Miles has shown you at Pine Ridge is nothing to what we have in re-serve for you if you do not behave yourselves.' "

What had existed of Indian menace was gone, never to return, and with it the frontier, for 1890 is taken as the year when the strung-out settlements from the East reached the Pacific in sparse but unbroken line. A great historical epoch had passed so quickly and forever under his eyes, and Lieutenant Pershing departed the West to become professor of military science and tactics, and commandant of cadets at the University of Nebraska.

⇥ 4 ⇤

THE WRITER DOROTHY CANFIELD FISHER in maturity remembered the city of her youth as a shambling and energetic pioneer community that contained one "disciplined, really trained person." That such an admiring view was shared while though from a different vantage point from that of a twelve-year-old by a number of appraising young women, "one thousand of whom to my certain knowledge wished to change their name to Pershing," according to Lincoln, Nebraska, resident C. H. Morrill, was unremarkable. That it quickly came to be held by the highest officials of the University of Nebraska and hundreds of male students was less predictable.

For when Second Lieutenant Pershing arrived in Lincoln he came to a situation in which he was surrounded by people who had no comprehension of his aims and neither friendship nor concern for them. It was part of a state university's charter that a training battalion for students be maintained, but all across the country by long custom that maintenance was regarded in the lightest manner. The stipulated number of required military study hours was never observed, and assigned army officers philosophically accepted the impossibility of training collegiates. Nebraska students presented to the new professor of military science didn't want him at all, Dorothy saw, tall and careless and loose-jointed boys who had never stood straight in their lives and who but occasionally blacked the toes of their shoes and were against any fuss about neatness. There was never going to be another great conflict like the Civil War, it was universally held, and military training was out of favor with the faculty, who believed that if young fellows needed physical expression, the need was met by the growing enthusiasm for sports competition.

Midwestern states such as Nebraska had, it was true, produced outstanding soldiers in 1861–65, but of a type different from those of the East, who were officered by men elaborately adorned in elegant uniforms. Slouching Ulysses S. Grant was the exception to the rule, meeting Lee at Appomattox in muddy private's uniform with dingy lieutenant general's stars sewn on, and blouse incorrectly buttoned. He was in manner and style and sartorial presentation more akin to the men of the Army of the West who took Atlanta and marched to the sea under Sherman and put up with neither fripperies nor geegaws, and determinedly laughed at the pretentions of the Easterners. The college boys of the University of Nebraska in 1890 were the sons and nephews of Sherman's soldiers. What had they to do with a spit-and-polish, by-the-numbers West Pointer's views on their proper activities?

Pershing knew what they thought, knew the university. Two of his sisters had been students there before their parents removed to Chicago and clothing business employment for the father. (Visiting their brother in New Mexico, the sisters naturally got to know his friends, and in time Grace Pershing married Lieutenant Richard Paddock, one of the Three Green P's.) Nebraska's boys were great military material, the new professor of military science told the university's chancellor, James H. Canfield, Dorothy's father. "Watch me get it out!"

A certain number of students had to show up for drill, however reluctantly they came, and immediately Pershing impressed them as a powerful, resolute, mature, compelling personality, keen and resourceful. He appeared remarkably focused, able to call the roll once and be able ever after to connect name with man, seeming to require only a glance at a printed page to know its contents. Immaculate, stern, taking note of everything a cadet-student did, impossible to bamboozle, his aloofness and distant manner bred not antagonism among the young men but respect, and they began to find the precision of military drill an interesting means of individual training. Their commander's bearing and clear, clean-cut commands and masterful control "electrified" them, one remembered.

He demanded the best of them and got it, pouncing on an elbow raised half an inch too high, discussing a rusty rifle screw in rasping tone, making known in a voice heard in "the remotest classroom on the campus," Dorothy Canfield recalled, "that a tunic had a missing hook at the throat." He became very well known at the university and was always referred to as the lieut, pronounced "loot." The number of students volunteering to be cadets rose. When Pershing arrived, the battalion numbered 90. Soon it was up to 350. No other university department, Chancellor Canfield wrote, was making such rapid growth, "or has made a deeper impression on the people of the city and of the state."

"The boys all loved and tried to please" this inspiring figure, remembered Harry D. Estabrook of the university's board of regents. Some spent so much time polishing their equipment and practicing the manual of arms that the faculty complained studies were being neglected, professors suggesting that military drill be curtailed or abandoned. "I listened to the arguments of the learned faculty and cast my vote against them." The young men, Estabrook felt, were learning grace, discipline, poise, self-possession, elegant carriage. "I told the faculty that there was not a study in the curriculum that in my opinion meant half so much to these young fellows in after life as their military training under Pershing," Estabrook remembered. He was teaching obedience, promptness, sense of duty, temperance, cleanliness, deportment, "all that a useful and reliant citizen ought to be."

Chancellor Canfield agreed, saying certain professors might do well to take military training themselves. In company with his daughter, the chancellor found the lieut off-duty to be a charming man with a light touch and an irresistible, friendly smile. He lived off-campus and quickly picked up a circle of friends, including the struggling young lawyer Charles G. Dawes, who had come to Lincoln from Ohio to be shortly convinced, he later remembered, "that Horace Greeley's advice 'Go west, young man,' was not good short-range pecuniary counsel." The two regularly met for meals at Don Cameron's lunch counter, noted for inexpensive dining. Pershing was making a second lieutenant's $125 a month, not much, but at least it came regularly, Dawes told him. When the tails of his dress suit were worn bare he got a tailor to cut new ones out of an old pair of pants, which he replaced. The entire outlay was $6, an economy of which he was somewhat proud. (Dawes himself was in poor position to buy law books and so made a practice of borrowing them from Congressman William Jennings Bryan's Burr Block offices.) Both young men loved music — it was a passion with Dawes, and Pershing became known as one of the best dancers in Lincoln.

In November 1892, after six years in the service, Pershing was promoted to first lieutenant. He was thirty-two years old. With friends he celebrated in his rooms in the Hall-Lansing Block. After serious drinking they decided to organize the First Nebraska, Pershing to command, his troops consisting of the half-dozen young men eating the meal one of them prepared. With his pals he was easy and accommodating, jumping out of a window with Dawes to escape police raiding an illegal prizefight, quite different from the majestic figure he cut with his cadets, concealing "pretty well from your scholars," Dawes wrote him in later years, "some of your predominant characteristics which included a taste for the adventurous and skirting along the boundary lines of professorial decorum."

"There is no implication intended in the use of the word 'skirting.' "

The student battalion by then was a smartly functioning unit largely run by cadet officers the lieut appointed, and he complained to Chancellor Canfield that he really didn't have enough to do with his time. Then let him take over some classes in the university prep school, Canfield suggested, and he returned to the teaching he had left to go to West Point, his mathematics students including Dorothy Canfield, to whom he also gave fencing lessons, and another girl of even greater future literary eminence, Willa Cather. (He didn't know that he'd done a great deal for their future writing endeavors, Pershing said wryly in later years.) As a teacher he explained clearly how to step forward, where to go with your own two feet. If you needed crutches, Dorothy remembered, you got yourself transferred to another class and another instructor.

He taught in civilian clothes, usually pepper-and-salt business suits. Once his dual functions produced an unforgettable moment. The student battalion was drawn up in parade formation, the young men in blue uniforms with "U.N." on the collar, and on their caps a gold wreath surrounding "NUC," for Nebraska University cadet. All was in readiness for the lieut to appear on the ground. He did so, striding along erect and powerful, disciplined, each step precisely the same length of all the others. But as was instantly apparent, he had signally failed to utilize a mirror just before going to review the cadets, for incongruously on his head instead of a set-just-so military cap was—a derby. His appearance was a colossal absurdity. Anyone else, Dorothy Canfield Fisher wrote, would have been greeted with falling-down laughter, "any other man in the world."

All watched and waited in silence to see what would happen as he walked the length of the parade ground, turned on his heel, waited as the adjutant intoned, "Sir, the parade is formed," and saluted. Pershing returned the salute and at once realized he was wearing dramatically incorrect headgear. With neither hesitation nor delay the lieut turned and impassively marched off the field, left, right, left, right, in perfect rhythmic gait, to return wearing his officer's cap. Then in his trumpetlike clear and resounding voice—that voice calling "At-ten-shun!" was, Dorothy remembered, one of the most vividly recalled sensations of her childhood—he began the proceedings. "Did you ever in your life meet a man who would not have been laughed at in those circumstance? *I* have."

It seemed to her that the boys would have followed him off the roof of a house if he assured them they could do it, and they acceded to his suggestion that a selected number of them enter a nationwide drill team competition to be held in Omaha. Among the opposition would be Zouaves from Tennessee, a famous regiment from Boston, a crack corps from Baltimore, the Washington Fusiliers, the Texas Tigers. Pershing appointed as cadet captain of a forty-five-man elite team future governor George Sheldon of Nebraska, and for two months cadets worked before classes began in the morning and after they were over in the evening. Beside the thrill of victory and a gold cup, a $1,500 prize would be awarded the competition victors. The Nebraska group termed themselves the Pershing Rifles.

They departed for Omaha accompanied by a large cheering section, including Chancellor Canfield and Dorothy. The afternoon before the competition, the Pershing Rifles formed up for practice drill and performed marvelously. Omahans looking on applauded and they started college boylike to strut, jaunty and swaggering and certain they would walk off with the cup and money the following day. Back at their tent encampment, Pershing had at them. "Heavens, what an unpleasant voice the lieut could have when he wished to!" Dorothy remembered. He was ashamed of their vainglorious and self-congratulatory and popinjay attitude, he told the young men. They were a disgrace to the occasion, the university, themselves, and him. Plans for going out on the town that night were forsaken, and instead the Pershing Rifles spent hours brushing uniforms, polishing weapons and equipment, and blacking shoes—including the soles. They were in bed by nine. In the morning they again brushed and polished and fell into ranks in their sharply pressed trousers and blindingly white gloves. Pershing regarded them dourly. They marched off past him. His cap was low, eyes cold, arms folded on chest. When the last man went by he ordered a halt, lifted his chin, and in a voice remembered as silver-clear and ringing, called out in measured cadence: "Boys—I think—you're going—to win!"

They did. Everybody from the University of Nebraska rose from the grandstand, and waving hats and handkerchiefs made for the eight-foot-high fence surrounding the parade ground and got over it, even stout Chancellor Canfield "going like a feather," his daughter recalled. Everyone fell on the lieut with congratulations and almost carried the student-cadets away on their shoulders.

Pershing continued with his math teaching and in addition fulfilled his boyhood ambition, receiving his LL.B. from the university law school. "I say without the slightest reserve that he is the most energetic, active, industrious, competent, and successful officer I have ever known," wrote Chancellor Canfield. "We have the second-best cadet corps in the United States, the first being at West Point. Lieutenant Pershing has made the corps what it is today. He found a few men, the interest in the battalion weak, the discipline next to nothing, and the instincts of the faculty and president of the university against the corps. He has taught three hours a day in mathematics with just as much success as he has conducted his work as commandant. He is thorough in everything he undertakes, a gentleman by instinct and breeding, clean, straightforward, with an unusually bright mind; and peculiarly just and true in all his dealings. He is a man of broad outlook who sees things in their true relations and who desires to know and be more than he is."

The Omaha victory brought newspaper attention, and the inspector general's office of the army sent Maj. E. G. Fechet to study the Military Department of the University of Nebraska. "Too much credit cannot be given to its commandant," the major reported. "The high degree of efficiency is due entirely to the energy, ability, and tact to organize and command of Lieutenant Pershing. Previous to his arrival, but little, I understand, had been accomplished. Now it is just the reverse. I noticed especially the extreme soldierly bearing of nearly every individual cadet, and their eagerness to carry out drill in all particular points." Very few men missed training sessions, Major Fechet found, average attendance being 333, with but four absences. Arms and supplies were neatly kept, the bulletin board was comprehensive, as were the exercises in infantry disposition, artillery, field engineering, the delinquency book, record of drills, rosters, morning reports, sick books, target records. Once a month the cadet officers' lyceum met for lectures, with serving soldiers requested to speak, as Fechet himself did, on the Geronimo chases of 1885–86, in which he had participated.

The men, Major Fechet wrote, performed marching movements "with the utmost precision. They formed, presented, fixed bayonets, went to port arms, about face, parade rest, kneel and load and fire, rise and fire, column of fours to the left, column of platoons to the front, trail arms, double time in line of squads by the flank, fire, halt, fire, rise, rally by squads, deploy. All four of the companies showed a proficiency that I believe can be equaled by but a few military organizations. I doubt if there can be found a better drilled battalion outside of West Point. I know these are high words of praise, but I feel confident that any officer of experience, after seeing the battalion, would confirm my opinion."

At the close of the class year of 1895, the lieut's Nebraska tour ended. The cadets asked for a pair of his uniform pants and cut from them little strips for each man—campaign ribbons of a kind. But Pershing began to talk about leaving the army. What, after all, had he to look forward to? Retirement at the mandatory age of sixty-four as a cavalry major or, if he was lucky, a lieutenant colonel? He had his law degree, he could go into practice. But there was the disquieting example of his friend Charles G. Dawes before his eyes every day, a struggling young attorney of whom it could not be predicted that he would rise to be one of the richest and most prominent men in the country. It appeared to Pershing that staff rather than line position might bring quicker promotion, so he tried for a quartermaster office appointment, failed to get it, and in October 1895 was posted to the Tenth Cavalry at Fort Assiniboine, Montana.

It was a black regiment, officered by whites. Army doctrine decreed that in handling blacks strong treatment was needful; the circumstances were quite different from dealing with University of Nebraska college boys. Once when a soldier disobeyed an order, Pershing struck him in such fashion that he fell into a river. It was one of the two times in his career that he used physical force on a man. He did not approve of that sort of thing, he said; ideally it should not be necessary. But the corporals and sergeants and even the privates of the Tenth endorsed his action. He was behind his back Old Red for the color of his hair, and thereafter slackers were warned to keep to their work or Old Red would come along and knock them into a river. Racial matters did not appear of great interest or import to Lieutenant Pershing. It was efficiency that counted.

With his black boys in blue, so they were termed, he rounded up an 1896 band of Cree Indians who had fled Canada for Montana and the Dakotas, and got them over swollen rivers with a ferry of wagons lashed together with lariats and pulled with a lariat cable, dealt with death and childbirth among them, and measles, and headed them out of the lands of the Great White Father and into those of the Grandmother—Queen Victoria. An Indian who knew that the Canadians would hang him for murdering a priest committed suicide, the bullet he fired penetrating his body and passing directly between Pershing and another man. After 350 miles the nearly two hundred Crees and their five hundred horses were turned over to the Grandmother's authorities.

Out there in Montana, in Fort Assiniboine, he played in a post amateur theatrical presentation opposite the wife of his classmate Malvern Hill Barnum, who like the later commissioner of baseball Kenesaw Mountain Landis was named for a Civil War mountain of battle import. Five decades on, Pershing remembered. What fun it had been, he wrote Barnum, nick-named "P.T." for the circus impresario during West Point days and still so addressed when all were old, the two classmates and the long-ago young wife-actress. During his Montana time the commander of the army, Nelson A. Miles, came for an inspection trip. In younger days he was the Fortress Monroe, Virginia, prison warden of the Confederacy's Jefferson Davis; then he had gone on to leadership of the army and the great pass-by review of troops following the affair at Wounded Knee. He brought West his two hunting dogs, and Pershing organized a Christmas hunt. A party went by rail and then sleigh to Fort Buford and the Yellowstone to sleep in tents with snow banked around the outside walls. They bagged two dozen deer and great quantities of prairie chicken, and General Miles was impressed with the smart first lieutenant of the Tenth. He asked for Pershing's assignment as an acting aide-de-camp in Washington.

As such there were cavalry studies to be done, but primarily the work was of a social nature, accompanying Mrs. Miles and her daughter Cecilia in making prescribed calls, including to the White House for a meeting with the young Mrs. Cleveland, come there as a bride. Pershing's dancing capabilities were on full display. Early on he looked into the aides' room of the commanding general of the army, opening the screen door to admit his head, and saw sitting at a carved rosewood desk an old friend from the West, Lt. Guy Preston, who had also served with blacks. "What in hell are you doing here?" Preston whispered. The two chuckled together at being so close to the seat of army power, Preston remembered, "two cubs from nigger regiments being thus honored." They went about Washington together, and in old age Preston remembered Pershing lying in a filled bathtub to cool off from the capital's summer. Together they peered into the windows of the Arlington Hotel, where the annual Gridiron Dinner for the city's elite was under way, and Preston never forgot how his friend said that to be invited to attend was the proof that one had made his mark, worthy of consorting with senators, congressmen, cabinet members, the doyens of the press. Could he hope to be there one day? At the question Lieutenant Preston laughed.

The six months' temporary duty with General Miles concluded, and Lieutenant Pershing was assigned as assistant instructor in tactics at his

alma mater, the U.S. Military Academy. He would also act as assistant instructor in equitation and cavalry training, but being a tac officer was his
primary function. A former standout West Pointer, a brilliant performer
with the Nebraskans, it certainly could have been anticipated that he
would score a grand success in his new work, it appearing perfectly to suit
him, constituting as it did involvement with cadets' discipline, neatness,
attention to detail, smartness.

No tac riding herd on young men could expect to be loved, but Pershing seemed to go beyond accepted standards. Perhaps he expected too
much. Perhaps he expected all cadets to hold to the standards he had
held, and held, for himself. To his charges he seemed a heartless martinet, rigid, unforgiving, always ready to pounce on the slightest departure
from perfect performance, someone seeming ever ready—indeed anxious—to mark down demerits. The cadets detested him. In such fashion
that neither he nor anyone else could doubt the depths of their resentment, they made their feelings entirely clear. A West Point sign of extreme resentment, rarely invoked, was silencing. Pershing was silenced. It
was done in the most public and humiliating fashion. When he entered
the vast mess hall an instant noiselessness seized the corps of cadets. No
one moved a muscle as he went to his table. So palpable a display of ha-
tred could well destroy a career, for knowledge and mention of it could
be expected to follow an officer always. Its application did not affect Tactical Officer Pershing. He continued as he had begun, the embodiment
of what in any other situation would have been considered a petty fault-
finder. He went about with his notebook, unremittingly seeking cadet
flaws. They fought back as best they could, carefully balancing a filled
bucket of water on top of the door to Cadet Malin Craig's room when
what they considered their tormentor was expected. (A janitor came in,
and took the soaking in Pershing's place. In later years, chief of staff of the
U.S. Army Malin Craig averred that the thing was done without his
knowledge. He had known Pershing as a child whose father was a Fort
Bayard officer.)

In the end the cadets gained a more lasting revenge. Tac officers
were often given nicknames by their charges, the use of such being one
of the few methods by which young men could gain some feeling of

control and power. Those of Pershing's West Point days as a tac officer included Farmer John, the Keg, the Widow's Mite, Wooden Willy. Some of the titles displayed a rueful affection. Pershing's did not. For an officer of the Tenth Cavalry the cadets came up with what followed Pershing to a certain extent all his military career: *Nigger Jack*. He could not have been unhappy at leaving the Point, his opportunity to do so coming in dramatic fashion. For the United States was going to war against a foreign foe.

War. Against Spain. Newspaper headlines and boys flocking to recruiting stations and retrieval from storage of Civil War equipment, and military requisitions and order-placing. Pershing's acquaintance Asst. Sec. of the Navy Theodore Roosevelt went about drumming up volunteers for what would be called the First Volunteer Cavalry, the Rough Riders, men from the elite eastern colleges and society circles in which Teddy Roosevelt had found his existence, the sportsmen and clubmen joining hands with cowboys he came to know in his health-seeking days and years in the frontier West. He had met Pershing in January 1897, when both were guests in a Madison Square Garden box taken by Old '86's Avery Andrews for a military tournament. Roosevelt was a New York City police commissioner then. He was thirty-eight to Pershing's thirty-six. They talked about the West, Indians, the Plains, and the mountains, and they liked each other. Now Teddy, with not a moment of military experience, was preparing to go into battle and be addressed as "Colonel," while Lieutenant Pershing appeared trapped in West Point by a directive saying no officer on a stipulated tour of duty there could break away for field service.

He appealed to everyone he could think of, using all of his Nebraska connections and those of his home state, Missouri. He begged his chief in West Point's Department of Equitation, Capt. James Parker, the brother of a New Jersey congressman, to help him. He got James Canfield, gone from Nebraska to be president of Ohio State University, to write President McKinley. The National Guard, untrained volunteers—he would accept any post. The directive stood. He thought of resigning from the army to go serve with Teddy. But fortunately for Pershing, he had played a part in the life of former representative George D. Meiklejohn of Nebraska. They had known one another in Lincoln. At the expiration of Meiklejohn's congressional term, Pershing had told him he ought to apply for the job of assistant secretary of war. When Meiklejohn protested he knew nothing of military matters, Pershing explained the job was purely political, and talked up his friend's qualities to Gen. Nelson Miles. President McKinley appointed the Nebraskan to the post. Now Pershing wrote from West Point asking aid: "May I be relieved from here? George, I could no more keep out of the field than I could fly." During the absence from Washington of the secretary of war for a few days, Meiklejohn pulled it off. The Tenth Cavalry's black boys in blue had been marked for service against the Spanish in Cuba. Lieutenant Pershing joined them.

→ 5 ←

WITH REGIMENTAL BANDS ON DECK beating out ragtime, flocks of ships so numerous as to resemble after dark a lit-up moving city bore the U.S. Army toward Cuba. The men ate corned beef from cans, canned tomatoes, hard bread. Why they were going to Cuba, and what they would do when they got there were great questions. For three hundred years Spain had owned the island. Other possessions in the Americas had broken away, but Spain was determined to hold Cuba. A pronouncedly ragtag and decidedly unorganized group of native insurgents desired otherwise, and Americans endorsed their wish for freedom.

Spain also thought to hold the Philippine Islands. Suddenly that wish was very much in jeopardy. Urged on by the assistant secretary of the navy who would soon become Lieutenant Colonel Theodore Roosevelt of the First Volunteer Cavalry, the Rough Riders, Commodore George Dewey destroyed the Spanish fleet at Manila Bay. Like Sir Francis Drake of Elizabethan England, it was instantly said, he had dispersed the Spanish Armada. What this had to do with U.S. desire to aid the Cuban insurgents was unclear, and indeed most Americans were unaware of the Philippines' existence prior to the electrifying victory, President McKinley saying later that he had been unable to determine within two thousand miles where Manila was without consulting a map. Yet Dewey was now master of Philippine waters, and thousands of miles away the *Maine* lay at the bottom of Havana Harbor, blown up as a result of no one knew what; and Dewey's rivals and counterparts in the army saw themselves as his future equal if they conquered Cuba. The public of their country, hitherto innocent of a foreign policy, enthusiastically supported them.

It could not be thought, the soldiers felt, that the Spanish would put up much of a fight. Spain was a decayed entity, tired. That she had some 80,000 troops in Cuba—so what? The Americans were on the way, the greater number of the regular army's 28,183 officers and men gathered together from their little faraway Western posts and bolstered by rally-to-the-flag militias, National Guards, volunteers. Remember the *Maine*, to hell with Spain. Yet matters had not gone very smoothly as the young heroes of the Civil War now become the aging high-officer warriors of the Spanish War took in hand their forces. There was no plan of mobilization, no arrangements for assembling and transporting an overseas expedition. Nobody had had experience in handling large formations of troops since 1865, and staff work and purchase of hospital supplies, horses, mules, and foodstuffs would have to be quickly improvised. Politically motivated demands clouded everything, with governors and congressmen demanding preferred treatment for constituents.

The forces to liberate Cuba and rout the Spanish had gathered at southern staging points, Lieutenant Pershing and his black cavalrymen of the Tenth camping at Chickamauga National Park in Georgia, site of a renowned Civil War battle. Conditions were frightful, awful distribution of awful food, foul water, heat, and local storeowners forbidding entrance by blacks. They made for Lakeland, Florida, some twenty miles from Tampa, the port of embarkation for Cuba, where filled railroad cars with no bills of lading stood in endless lines to be opened up and gone through for indications of contents. Lackluster wooden houses stood in desertlike sands, the only area adornment Tampa's fantastic hotel of Oriental magnificence, minarets, towers, verandas with hundreds of rocking chairs upon which sat the army's officers to drink iced tea while preparing to execute the will of the American people and to respond to the demands of Joseph A. Pulitzer of the *New York World* and William Randolph Hearst of the *New York Journal* that Spain be punished for what she had done and what she was doing.

The fleet of improvised transports made Cuba. A beach was bombarded. There was no response, and so lighters began carrying men ashore. (Horses and mules were shoved out of cargo openings to swim themselves to land or, in some cases, to become disoriented, head out to sea, and never be seen again.) The heat was murderous, particularly to men outfitted in the blue uniforms suitable for Montana blizzards. Only the Rough Riders were in tropical khaki, with canvas leggings and broad-brimmed campaign hats dashingly turned up on one side. Their exclusive attire was of a piece with the haphazard prosecution of the war: John Jacob Astor at his own expense and initiative purchased quick-firing artillery pieces in Europe, and Astor's Battery, led by Capt. Peyton C. March, West Point 1888, immediately became the finest artillery unit in the U.S. Army.

The cavalry was commanded by Joseph Wheeler, late of the Confederate Army in which, as with the Union's Joseph Hooker of catastrophic performance against Lee at Chancellorsville, he was known as "Fighting Joe." He ordered an advance along a tortuous narrow trail by dismounted cavalry units—no horsed formation could get through the tangled Cuban jungle—including the Rough Riders and Pershing's Tenth. The squadrons worked their way forward and came upon Spanish breastworks. The Americans opened fire. Perhaps to their surprise in the wake of the unopposed landing, Spanish batteries replied. Cuban insurgents who had enthusiastically welcomed hoped-for liberators immediately decamped, not to be seen again for long hours into the future.

The skinny trail behind the on-foot cavalrymen jammed up as a militia outfit panicked, threw away its arms, and flung itself as one man on the ground. An American observation balloon appeared and hung in the air above the stalled troops. Spanish gunners correctly took it for an arrow pointing down to the target and poured out what Lieutenant Pershing called a "veritable hail of shot and shell." The balloon's officer shouted down, "The Spanish are firing at you!"

"Yes, we know it, you damned fool," men on the ground screamed back, "and you are drawing the fire. Come down! Come down!" Spanish snipers on heights above the trail or in trees rained down bullets, and the smokeless powder of the enemy artillery made their batteries difficult to locate. A young officer fresh from West Point was shot dead and lay on his back, his glazed stare directed at the trees overhead. Ants crawled over his eyeballs. The situation looked like it was turning into a disaster, but Pershing, remembered one officer, seemed as "cool as a bowl of cracked ice." The Tenth's regimental commander, Col. Theodore Baldwin, who had been all through the Civil War, felt he was looking at the coolest and bravest man under fire he had ever seen.

There was nothing to do but get forward or die in position, and so the jammed-together units went struggling through barbed wire hacked down with bayonets, thorned vegetation, high grasses, and thickets, with bullets from the Spaniards' Mauser rifles continually hitting home. Of the twenty-two officers of the Tenth Cavalry who moved up, eleven were hit. The Americans came on. Going back to order up reinforcements, Pershing halted to salute Fighting Joe Wheeler, who sat his horse in a shallow stream. A shell landed just between them, soaking them both. Pershing continued, delivered his orders, and rejoined his men; and Joe Wheeler was quoted back home as delivering the remark that made all America erupt in laughter, for when Spaniards retreated, the ex-rebel shouted, "We've got the damned Yankees on the run!"

There was a Spanish blockhouse on a rise pouring down fire, and the Americans made for it by little rushes, and then in a charge took it, the Spanish in their light blue and white uniforms running off as the Americans cheered, shook hands, jumped up and down. "We officers of the Tenth Cavalry could have taken our black heroes in our arms," Pershing remembered; but what the country remembered was the image of the accompanying Teddy Roosevelt taking San Juan Hill.

It was the single day of real fighting in what Secretary of State John Hay later termed The Splendid Little War. There followed negotiations, a naval engagement that saw the Spanish West Indies fleet dealt with as had Dewey with its Asiatic squadron at Manila, and a most unpleasant existence for American troops in Cuba. Torrential rains alternated with steaming heat, and the men had to deal with snakes underfoot or hanging on tree branches as they made do amid miasmal sodden vegetation while near-universally suffering from *el vomito*, yellow fever, malaria. Their provisioning was abominable—potted meats that had long since spoiled and showed so by a sickening discoloration, no tents, no decent water, no medical supplies, men living on hard bread, bacon, coffee, and little else. Three-quarters of the soldiers went sick, Pershing among them. (For a year afterward he suffered racking chills followed by raging fever on a clockworklike two-day schedule.) But he soldiered on, forcefully commandeering what supplies there were for his black troops. The rigidly by-the-book officer vanished, to be replaced by one who would take what he could as best he might. "You did some tall rustling," Colonel Baldwin said admiringly. He appropriated mules and wagons without requisition, clothing, blanket rolls, such extra food as was available. The Tenth suffered, as did all Americans in Cuba, but less than others.

The war ended. "Our regiment has done valiant service," Pershing wrote Assistant Secretary of War Meiklejohn. "No one can say that colored troops will not fight." By then the friend whose appointment he had pushed was practically supreme in the War Department, with Sec. Russell A. Alger made scapegoat for all the many inadequacies attendant to the army's dispatch to and maintenance in the tropics. "At my request the president has appointed you to the rank of major in the Volunteer Army," Meiklejohn telegraphed. It was a temporary rank, but as such Pershing went off on an inspection tour of western posts abandoned for the war. In Chicago his parents' doctor checking his malaria "pronounced my case alarming and said that I could not survive another chill. He gave me a heroic dose of quinine." That and a period of sick leave made the temporary major fit for service.

His next duty post was Washington, where under Meiklejohn he worked on problems and opportunities brought the army by the war. Cuba, Puerto Rico, the Philippines, and formerly Spanish-owned island coaling stations across the Pacific were now under U.S. Army rule, and a thousand questions arose concerning duties, taxes, tarrifs, customs, military and civil laws, responsibilities, administration, and church ownership of land. Pershing had a law degree, was industrious and thorough. He usefully dealt with the work. But out in the Philippines, thousands of miles away, a little war was going on, *insurrectos* declining the sovereignty of the Americans as they had the Spanish; and he was in Washington.

Meiklejohn wanted him there, and Charles Dawes, close now to President McKinley and on his way to the top of the country's financial and political life, told him to stay; but he said he didn't want to be behind a desk and got Meiklejohn to transfer him out there to the Philippines, to adventure, and to an entirely new world where he would stay almost uninterruptedly for going on fifteen years.

He sailed for the East via England, did the Tower of London and Westminster Abbey, strolled around Woolwich Arsenal. A guard mildly pointed out that it was against the rules for Great Britain's vast military stores to be inspected at leisure by casual visitors. Pershing identified himself as an American officer and on that basis was given a comprehensive tour. He went on to Paris, saw a Versailles street fair with the people in holiday attire on merry-go-rounds and at games of chance, spent time at the Louvre and Luxembourg galleries, made friends with art students who took him around the Academy Julien and the Beaux Arts and to their ateliers of the Latin Quarter whose parties and goings-on reminded him of the Bohemian-life George Du Maurier story of Trilby and Svengali published a few years earlier. "How did you stand the ordeal, General?" the sculptor Jo Davidson asked many years later, doing his bust. "I did my best to preserve throughout my military composure," Pershing replied.

He went south to Milan, Venice, Florence, visited art galleries, found Italian officers smart-looking, made Rome and Naples, and took ship to Alexandria and then on to Cairo and off to the Orient, Singalese tradesmen coming aboard at Colombo with pockets filled with jewelry guaranteed to be made of precious stones, children diving into harbor waters for pennies flung from the deck. He came to Manila. It was November 1899. The Walled City seemed to him to have almost the aspect of medieval days, with town criers and ringing church bells, night watchmen carrying staves, drums summoning the populace for the verbal publishing of ordinances, a sound like the buzzing of bees arising when people knelt en masse to pray, the moat and bronze cannons and ponderous masonry, the ancient walls remindful of the days of Spanish town battles fought by soldiers in armor. Through the groups of Filipino carriages and buffalo- or ox-drawn carts came the big American cavalry chargers. He was sent down to Mindanao, six hundred miles of enchanting journey that found his steamer going through island straits and past tropical flora, phosphorescent moonlit waters, native sailboats, strange birds and fish to be seen, royal palms and poincianas, the fire tree, and white coral sand beaches. He found the sky fascinating in line and color. The East of strange aromas, outlines of the distance quivering in the heat—the Orient and Asia and the tropics seized him, never to relax its grip. John Pershing was never bored in the Philippines.

Mindanao was the second-largest of the archipelago's one thousand islands, some three hundred miles long and three hundred miles across, ranking only behind Luzon. Aside from a string of coastal settlements it was almost entirely untouched by the twentieth century just coming in. Pershing arrived at the twenty-thousand-population Zamboanga of old Spanish buildings, monsoon breezes, and purplish distant hills on the first day of that century, January 1, 1900. The fortress there dated from 1636 and was the island's largest of its complement of forts and blockhouses, built by the Dons who had over the centuries scored easy victories over Mexico and Peru, the Maya and the Aztec, and the inhabitants of the northern islands of the Philippines. They had met their match and more in Mindanao. There they had broken their teeth, it was said, when they met the Moros of the blue seas and dark jungles. Of the same Malay ethnicity as other Filipinos, the Moro—Spanish for "Moor"—were fearsomely different. Conversion to Islam had come six centuries earlier, and from that religion its Filipino adherents had in unshakable and unreserved fashion taken the concept that to die was a warrior's highest aspiration. And they were warriors. Catholic Spain's cross shattered against Moro belief that to die for the Faith was glory, and Toledo steel against Moro *campilan* and *kris* and *barong*, weapons so sharply honed that a human hair dropped upon one fell to the ground in two pieces. Death to a Moro was nothing, his own or someone else's, and he went nowhere without his weapons wavy-edged and of double cutting surface with incised blood channels, they capable of severing body from shoulder to hip with one stroke, or decapitating with the precision of a surgeon's blade.

To the north, the insurrection of those opposing American rule was being suppressed by fifty thousand American troops, regulars and volunteers, the regs and vols, although not without losses, including that of Pershing's Grand Canyon tour companion John Stotsenberg, whose death in action leading a charge led to perpetuation of his name for designation of what was at one time the largest army post of the area, Fort Stotsenberg, P.I. There in the North the native was to the American soldiery enforcing what was termed pacification the Flip, the Gog, the Gu-gu, a slant-eyed and tree-climbing baboon whose children were pickaninny niggers. No such view was held of the Moro. "Civilize 'em with a Krag," soldiers defined their stated mission to uplift those Civil Gov. William Howard Taft would term Our Little Brown Brothers, the military tool to accomplish which was the Army's Krag-Jorgensen rifle. But a Krag was inadequate to stop a charging Moro gone *juramentado*. An Oath-Taker all of whose body hair was shaved, head, eyebrows, everything, and whose form was encased in tight white wrappings, he was in the most literal sense a holy terror, with edged weapons strapped to each hand with which he would ensure entrance into the next world by slaying as many Christians as he could. The number of houris greeting his heavenly entrance on a great white horse and his closeness to the Prophet in that world were determined by how many infidels he slew in his last moments. He could carry lead like a grizzly bear, soldiers found, like a buffalo. The army's .32 and .38 seemed almost to bounce off him. The .45 was created for him.

He seemed incomprehensible and lost to decency and humanity, the Moro, a believer in polygamy and slavery with filed teeth chewing betel nuts so that his saliva was blood red, a ferocious pirate terrifying Christian Filipinos with his terrible weapons so skillfully wielded. He had no government beyond shifting allegiances to tribal chieftains bearing feudal-like the most august of titles, maharaja, sultan, but who lived in bamboo shacks set a few feet above the ground littered with waste, and whose adherents could amount to no more than a few hundred souls. In that world murder was lightly regarded. Girls were sold at birth for later delivery. In Moroland it was held as faith that Americans had cloven feet.

Lieutenant Pershing studied the Moros. They and he were a long way from Laclede, Missouri. But of all the officers out there and down there in Mindanao, noted Robert Lee Bullard, who had been with First Captain of the Corps of Cadets Pershing at West Point, it was Pershing alone who actually found out things about these people, who worked to learn their language. "Pershing, you are the only man who knows anything about the Moros, I'm going to send you to Iligan," said the department commander, Brig. Gen. George W. Davis, in November 1901. The post was in north-central Mindanao, in the very heart of Moro country and near the great inland lake of Lanao, around which were clustered Moro strongholds. Sooner or later the area was going to have to be subjected to American suzerainty, but to achieve it with force would be a fearsome undertaking. "Do everything possible to get in touch and make friends of them," General Davis said.

Promoted captain after service of a decade and a half, Pershing arrived to conduct a Saturday morning inspection at Iligan. The post plaza, he saw, was overgrown with weeds, and the soldiers lounged about in careless disarray, their quarters badly in need of repair. He entered the mess shack of his new command, where the cook stood at attention. Pershing took down a frying pan that hung from a nail. He was wearing white gloves. He drew one finger across the pan's bottom. "He's gone and went and done it," an accompanying top sergeant said to himself. The glove looked, the sergeant thought, as if the new officer had found a piece of coal and was balancing it on his finger. "Never said a word but he swung back his arm and sent that pan sliding, banging along the floor toward Cookey."

The new commanding officer was reaching for the next pan as the cook gave a quick jump just as the first one came at him along the floor. "The same thing was repeated for the next pan and the next and the next—until Captain Pershing looked as though he had been cleaning a chimney with his gloves and the floor looked like a junk shop," the sergeant remembered. Not a word was spoken by anyone, and expressions did not change. The cook remained standing at attention, save for his leaps. Captain Pershing came to the mess shack's laid-out cutting utensils. "His eye fell on the big army meat cleaver, with a blade like a razor and heavier than the hoof of a stubborn horse." He took it from its nail and checked the edge as he threw a glance at the cook. As if propelled by a spring suddenly released, the man shot out the door.

"But the bark of a gun follows the bullet close. 'Come back here!' That voice went out the door, caught Cookey and dragged him back saluting with both hands. 'Yes, sir! Yes, sir! Yes, sir!' Pershing waited for him to get calm and then said: 'Not this time, but next Saturday . . .' and he looked from the cleaver to his dirty gloves and laid it gently on the table."

When Saturday came the pots and pans, the top sergeant remembered, gleamed like a double row of mirrors, and soldiers' boots were shiny, and chins were closely shaved and bunks neat. The men starting to look and act like soldiers, the captain turned his attention to the Moros. General Davis wanted them made into friends. Pershing sent out emissaries and letters to those everyone else considered inherently fierce and fanatical, wily savages, deadly barbarians, the literal Antichrist each one, lurking to do God knew what in the stiflingly humid and hellishly steamy jungles of decayed vegetation and menacing trails. On market day in Iligan some Moros from the surrounding countryside came in carrying chickens, eggs, rice, camotes, brasswear, baskets, varicolored cloths. The men wore wide pants with sashes into which were tucked fearsome cutting blades and brimless hats, Muslim fezzes. The women were in sarongs. By Pershing's orders all were made very welcome by every soldier of the two cavalry troops and three infantry companies of his command. He himself walked about greeting the people. "They liked to talk and wanted to speak with someone in authority," he remembered, "and in this they were given every encouragement."

A polite and respectful commanding officer in a newly enlarged marketplace asked about children, family relationships, the oxlike carabao plodding through canebrake or rice paddy with crude primitive carts, all sorts of things; and at length the most important leader to the north of Lake Lanao, Ahmai-Manibilang, came to meet Captain Pershing. They had exchanged several letters, each of the Moro chieftain's prefaced with the obligatory "Praised be God the Lord of Creation." Elderly, dignified, white-bearded, Ahmai-Manibilang arrived in great state, wearing a jacket of many colors and white trousers, a rakishly tilted turban cocked on his head, and riding a fine pony. A slave walked by each side of his mount, one bearing his master's gold-adorned kris, the other a highly polished brass box containing betel nuts, buya leaves, and a mixture of lime, all of which combined to make his chewing concoction. In the lead was a gun-bearing guard—Moros obtained firearms from Chinese traders—with another behind, followed by minor chiefs, relatives, and more slaves, all in choice finery. Ahmai-Manibilang stayed a night in Iligan to eat his own food, seemingly fearful that whatever Pershing offered might be prepared with forbidden lard.

The captain found his guest to be one of the most intelligent men he had ever met. Asked to describe his far-off country, he did so as best he could, not mentioning American distaste for slavery and plural wives. Invited to pay a return call, he went with an interpreter and native scouts, that was all, despite assurance of the residents of Iligan that he would never return unless attended by a heavy guard. (Americans were believed by the Moros to be the best fertilizer for an outstanding bamboo crop, he was told.) It was the first of many Moroland visits that he made entirely unarmed. Once his accompanying orderly, Frank Lanckton, stuck a pistol under his shirt. With the intense eye for detail that never left him, which in fact characterized him better than anything else, Pershing spotted a bulge. "Lanckton, a soldier's word is more important than his gun," he said, and the orderly had to put away his weapon.

He went to Ahmai-Manibilang to find the entire countryside turned out in welcome. His host's jungle home was a massive frame structure of hewn timbers, plank floors, and steep roof thatched with nipa, swamp-grown palm. Massed fighting men stood about. "I have never tasted more delicious chicken, seasoned as it was with native herbs, and the rice, steaming hot, was cooked to perfection, the grains still whole, as few Americans ever see rice cooked. None of the women of the house sat with us but the senior wife directed the serving in a quiet, dignified voice that was refined and pleasing." He noted then and thereafter: "I do not recall ever having seen a Moro wife or child abused in any way. No child, even by a concubine or slave, was regarded as illegitimate."

The next day, borne along waterways in a *vinta*, a canoe hewn out of a log and kept on even keel by bamboo outriggers, he visited *rancherias*, landholdings ruled by an elected or hereditary leader living with his vassals. He spoke with anyone who approached him. He returned to Iligan with a forty-man honorary escort, feeling Ahmai-Manibilang was now "a warm personal friend" certain to dissuade other *dattos* (chiefs) from opposition to the Americans replacing the Spaniards and possessing entirely different views. For the Americans of what those who were there came to call the Days of the Empire were involved, they said, not in suppression and still less in oppression of the islanders, but rather in construction of harbors, roads, warehouses, the encouragement of agriculture and handicrafts, with native labor employed at good wages. From his trip came endless expeditions into the interior of Mindanao: "On one of those visits, when I was spending the night and the time for retiring came, my host disappeared for a few minutes and came back with a most attractive member of his harem who, he advised me in the most matter-of-course manner imaginable, would accompany me. The announcement rather took me aback for a moment and my embarrassment was undoubtedly apparent, but I managed to express my thanks and declination without giving offense, the datto sending the woman away as nonchalantly as he had brought her in."

That night he declined. But there were other nights in those years in the Philippines. Protestant morality and American ways and old barriers melted away in the heat of the tropical sun. What was called the *querida* system was quite accepted. One went to a girl's father, asked what he wanted, gave half what was mentioned, and installed her in one's quarters. When one wearied of the *querida*, the sweetheart, one's houseman or boy said, "Time go home now, missy," so it was recorded, and a replacement moved in. John Pershing had been what West Point called a "spoony man," and the object it was said of a thousand women in Lincoln, Nebraska; and he was not at all behindhand in such matters in the Philippines. It was all quite familiar to those of the Days of the Empire, quite common; but one day it would come back to haunt him.

But that was neither here nor there to the Moros, to whom, as Pershing wrote, the offering of female company for the bed was but "an ordinary act of courtesy." His interest, his admiration, even, was what caught at a people hardly advanced beyond the dawn of civilization and now confronted with a representative of the twentieth century who almost alone among his fellows saw them as what Kipling called the White Man's Burden in its best and least ironic meaning. Nothing was too much trouble. He sat with the sultan of Bayan, squatting on his heels as was the fashion in that Moro world of bats with four-foot wingspreads, house snakes, monkeys, colossal reptiles, exquisite mangoes, brilliant vegetables of strange type, copra, gutta-percha, hemp, turbans covering knotted hair, brimless hats permitting one to touch forehead to ground, elaborately titled mandarins, paglimas, maharajas, hadjis, and a stenographer took down their ritualistically wordy conversation, which went on, as did all parleys, for hour after hour beneath a red parasol indicating Muslim authority. Everything was indirect, flowery. Patience was mandatory.

"I am very glad to meet the commanding officer on such a good day as this and to hear him express his friendship and that of the Americans for myself and my people," the sultan of Bayan said.

"This shaking of hands means that we will be friends forever. I hope this is the beginning of eternal peace," Pershing said.

"I hope my God will blow all bad feelings away. I would not have come but for the friendship I have for the commanding officer."

"I have a large tent in my camp where I meet all Moros and am going to send invitations to all Moros to come and visit me and discuss matters of interest. I will send a horse to you to take you up the hill as I wish to show everybody that you are a friend."

"I am too old to come to your camp. You have permission to use my name in bringing about peace."

"If you can possibly do so, come and visit us. I will wait patiently until you come as I would wait for my best friend."

He sat with Datto Gundar of Maciu, who asked, "If you have all different religions do you believe in God?"

"Yes, some of us are Catholics, some Protestants, and some of us believe in other religions but we do not fight because one differs from us."

"I have heard that many of the Americans are circumsized and as we are not, many of the Moros do not wish to live with them. Some say that soon the Americans will bring many hats here and make us wear them." The captain explained and explained again that it was not so.

Datto Acoti of Madalum: "I have heard that Russia and Spain are at war with the Americans and they are taking advantage of the war to make war upon us and to capture our men to fight for them."

"Who has said this?"

"Moros who go to Iligan have heard it."

"Who in Iligan has said this?"

"I do not know."

A Moro, the captain had decided, was like an unbroken horse. Harshness would not do. Gentling along was called for. He explained that Datto Acoti had been misinformed, repeated it, explained it again, and ended, "I want you to go home and tell all you have seen and heard and what I have said. If they do not believe you I extend an invitation for them to come and see for themselves. I hope they will not remain away in ignorance." He wrote out extensive vocabulary lists of the Moro language, studied translatings of old Spanish reports on the people. Pershing could be brutal when his view of duty commanded him so to be—"Damn it, let them die! They disobeyed my orders," he said when two soldiers contacted cholera after drinking from an off-limits spring; and the soldiers died—but when he reprimanded Moros it was in a reasonable and reasoning manner. "I am out of patience with the Moros who tell us they are friends and permit their people to steal from us," he told the sultan of Binidayan. "You have lived within two miles, have claimed to be our friend, and yet you allow your people to capture arms and cut the telegraph line."

"I am not responsible."

"You are responsible and it is your business to discipline your people. I have said all that I care to say. I want you to come in person next Wednesday and let me know what progress you have made." (A horribly tortured and fearfully mutilated malefactor, still alive, was delivered to the captain as a sign of the requested progress.) There would be no burning and no laying waste, no women-taking, Moro leaders were assured, but instead purchases of products, and work for those who wanted it; and the Moros came to have faith in John Pershing. For the first time in history they began to acknowledge allegiance to a governing power.

Pershing to the Moros became what no one before him and no one after ever was. "He is today the one great American to the Moro mind," wrote First Lieutenant George Bowman of the Fifteenth Cavalry to Assistant Secretary of War William Cary Sanger. "They regard him as a supernatural being. He always treats them fairly, never makes a promise which he cannot fulfill." Odd people seemed to wash up in Mindanao, déclassé Englishmen, peculiar Irishmen or Dutchmen, adventurers, remittance men—none came close to understanding the Moros as Pershing did. He was the last thing, Robert Lee Bullard wrote in his diary, from "some fool officer who ignorantly supposed that he could come and in an off-hand manner manage these savages."

To Pershing Moros were, and he meant it, "those we serve down here." They knew him for what he was and took him for what he did; and on February 10, 1903, he squatted on his heels with a great group of sultans and *panditas*—Muslim priests—and dattos and mandarins and maharajas. In their center was a Koran on a mat of fiber guarded by an aged pandita who wore gorgeous trousers of all colors and a robe of yellow silk. Each leader spoke. Each touched the Koran. So did John Joseph Pershing, U.S. Cavalry, late of Laclede, Missouri, and he was made a datto, and consecrated into priestly office and given priestly dignity. Such a thing had never been dreamed of before for a non-Moro. The men kissed him and he kissed them back. The betel-red saliva staining their beards did not affect him. They swore friendship together.

After that there was not a day that people did not come to him, leaders and followers alike, and he talked with them hour after hour and settled their grievances and sent them away happy. Women asked his blessings for their marriages. Men asked that he be honorary parent for their children. Girls and boys wrote to him as My Father.

That an American officer had been made a Moro datto was reported by Stateside newspaper articles in which Pershing became a god bowed down to by half-naked natives as he acted the part of a father and a prince, this "ideal administrator of consummate skill" and "brilliant record in our dominions beyond the seas, across the seas" bringing the "privileges and beneficences of Anglo-Saxon civilization."

The ceremony took place at Camp Vicars, along the southern shore of Lake Lanao, where he had been sent from Iligan. It was astonishing that he commanded there, for he was replacing a full colonel. The colonel, Pershing remembered, "was disposed to use force instead of diplomacy." That was why Pershing was there, a junior captain commanding the most remote, and one of the most important, posts of the army, two cavalry troops, three infantry companies, a field artillery battery, support units, an aggregation equal to a regiment.

He continued as he had begun in Iligan, purchasing Moro wood and hay, offering construction work, hiring Moro ponies and drivers to bring supplies up from Malabang along a brutally difficult trail through six-foot grasses and ending at the camp high on a mountain plateau overlooking the great lake. Sometimes it seemed necessary to him that he use some force while, as he put it, "waging peace," and so a column would depart Vicars, Captain Pershing always at its head. In the field he and his men lived on canned salmon, "goldfish" to the soldiers, and hardtack. Storms swept down as they huddled in their ponchos, and earthquakes shook the ground under their feet—Pershing remembered one that made the earth swell like the ocean as a soldier cried, "Steady, Lord, steady please, Lord," a request he himself endorsed—and rebellious Moros screamed from the darkness, soldiers gripping their Krags as they thought of murderously sharp Moro spears that could enter through the back of the head and emerge from the front with an eyeball on the point. The small-scale punitive expeditions punished bands who had jumped men for their guns or ambushed supply parties. Everything was done with such dispatch and restraint that Pershing was hailed as no less than a military genius by the *Manila American* while becoming mildly famous in the United States, the *New York Sun* saying, "No other officer has been more frequently or more favorably mentioned. Every few days we hear of his preaching the gospel of peace to some new datto out in the wilds of Mindanao. Interspersed with these accounts, others come to tell of his subjugation of some rebellious datto whose greatest need is just such a parental spanking as Pershing bestows upon him."

Unlike the Indians of the western plains, the Moros were not nomadic. After making a raid they retreated into cottas, forts with six-foot walls of earth stone faced or with sharpened bamboo stakes, and with a deep ditch in front. They had *lantecas,* small and crude cannons that fired lead, nails, stones, and seashells deadly at close range, and these they manned under war flags whipping in the hot equatorial winds as panditas chanted and tom-toms sounded. With mountain howitzers and rifles Pershing reduced such forts while leaving open avenues of escape for defenders to use if they chose. His dealings and displays of measured force made allies of most of the Lake Lanao rancheria chieftains, but not all. "Even though there are ten million of you, the more the better for we can then capture more rifles," wrote the sultan of Maciu. "This letter goes to you burned in six places to indicate that it means war," wrote the sultan of Bacleod. "You should not be here, for you are not like us. You eat pork. If you do not wish to leave this region, come and live in Bacleod under the sultan, who will practice circumsion upon you."

Pershing's reply was a letter sent to all Lake Lanao rancherias: "We have not interfered with the customs, habits, government nor religion of any Moro. We have demonstrated to the whole world that we are not here to make war nor dispossess the inhabitants of Lanao of anything that is theirs. Two or three dattos refuse our friendship simply because, as they say, they do not like the Americans. To those dattos I say that if they continue their opposition they must someday suffer the consequences of their stubborn ignorance."

Some of the letter's recipients were unimpressed. Their people slipped past outpost lines into Camp Vicars by night, cut the ropes holding up soldiers' tents, and slashed at the men struggling to get out. The bodies were done up in canvas and packed out slung across mules. (Men slain from ambush along the trail from Malabang and not immediately recovered were found decomposed from the terrific heat and humidity or eaten at by insects, reptiles, and the wild hogs who tore away the flesh. Or worse, as staked-out skeletons eaten to the bone by ants attracted to sweets laid on by the soldiers' captors.)

Pershing's patience was remarkable, his subordinates said. Lt. George Bowman remembered how two days out of Vicars a column came to a cotta whose walls were lined with Moros shouting defiance as they waved rifles, knives, spears. The fortress sultan sent word that if the Americans came close, the Moros would fight. Pershing sent back the information that he had come as a friend, that he would go away, but that he intended to come back again, and that in the meantime he would welcome a visit from the sultan to Vicars to talk things over. He marched the column away. How many American officers would let themselves be faced down by Asian natives, and how many British ones in India, Dutch in Borneo, French in Indochina? A lot of courage, Lieutenant Bowman thought, to walk away; and the sultan became a Pershing friend.

The powerful sultan of Bacleod remained unmoved. "Cease sending us letters," he wrote. "We do not desire your friendship." It came to Pershing and his superiors that failure to discipline the man was being seen as weakness all through the area. In April 1903 the captain moved against Bacleod with all the available troops in Mindanao, cavalry, infantry, artillery of Vickers-Maxims and mortar sections, a hospital corps, a pack train, native ponies laden with forage, medicinal supplies, ammunition, four hundred animals in all. It had taken quite some "military jugglery" to arrange for an officer of Pershing's rank to lead such an all-branches expedition of almost brigade size, remembered Robert Lee Bullard. It was done by the high command's assignment to temporary duty elsewhere of area officers senior to a junior captain, or by simply letting them sit idle at their posts. No other similar arrangements had ever been seen in the army's history.

He came to Lake Lanao's edge. For centuries the Spaniards had tried to subjugate the Moros there. As recently as 1891, hardly more than a decade past, they had by monstrous effort transported disassembled armored launches to the lake. Put together there, the gunboats had joined forces with four thousand soldiers to war upon Moro cottas. In the end the launches were scuttled in the lake and the soldiers went away. The impregnable fortresses, endemic fevers and diseases, natural obstacles of terrain—it was impossible to do anything with Lake Lanao, the Spanish decided.

The American column made ten miles over mountainous trails the first day, its leader as always looking to every detail, checking the animals, checking the men, permitting no delinquencies in bearing or tidiness to go ignored, his commands allowing no uncertainty and, even less, indifference. A letter was sent ahead to all rancherias: "We are coming exploring and we are coming peaceably. Do not try to oppose us." Camp was made near an old Spanish fort. In the night Moros from Bacleod came silently down the lake in vintas and fired on the soldiers, hitting two, one of whose arms had immediately to be amputated by surgeons. All night long the troops sent fusillades across the water to ward off additional attackers. In the morning it was found that horses' hooves had unearthed the bodies of people who appeared to have died of cholera and then been shallowly interred. The place reeked. The column went on for the fortress of the sultan of Bacleod. The previous day, going up and down slippery trails with the men hanging on to pack mules' tails to keep the animals from pitching forward when going down hill and to get a pull for themselves when going up, the Americans had visited Pershing's friend the sultan of Ganassi, his people seen in the fields waving cloths to drive away grasshoppers menacing the crops. Without doubt the sultan of Bacleod's scouts had reported the approach of so formidable a party, and it was possible its size would induce him to come to terms; but when the soldiers came to his cotta they saw war banners flying and heard Moros chanting threats and insults in chorus. The troops were at nine hundred yards' distance when snipers opened fire from the fort. It was on a high bluff overlooking the lake, with walls twelve feet high and fifteen feet thick. It had a moat thirty feet wide and almost forty feet deep.

Pershing opened with mortars and his Vickers-Maxims as the heliograph at Camp Vicars kept flashing requests for news until a violent storm blew up and made its use impossible. The *panandungan*, chief adviser to the sultan, periodically popped up on the fortress parapet, waving his sword. An infantry company was sent forward to within 350 yards of the fort, men sliding down hills slushy with rain, horses falling to roll with flailing hooves. The infantrymen concentrated on loopholes and shot down banner after banner flying from the roof while the Moros inside loosed off volleys from their primitive cannons. The rain came down. Upon occasion a lone juramentado came rushing out, a kris strapped to each arm. At once every American rifle was fired at him. Night came.

Through the route of escape to the lake upon which Pershing, as was his custom, did not fire, there fled women and children. But in the morning it was seen that the fort was still manned. Firing recommenced. When a truce flag rose on the parapet, all guns fell silent. The panandungan appeared and shouted down that he wished Pershing to walk up, alone. He was told to convey what he had to say through an interpreter, and did so. "If the Americans want to fight us, let them fight," the panandungan cried, "but tell them to fight like men. While American soldiers are besieging my fort I see them down by the waterside eating up all my coconuts. This is infamous, and is not war!" He hauled the war banner back up.

No one more looked and acted the soldier than John Pershing, cool, methodical, determined as he was, thought the author-explorer A. Henry Savage Landor, who had been permitted to accompany the expedition. He worked the fort over, personally posting guns and moving troops, twice parleying under truce flag in an effort to get the Moros to surrender. They said they would give up if allowed to keep their guns. He wouldn't have it. After a three-day siege the soldiers stormed the fort, going over the moat on a bridge of bamboo. They threw branches and shrubbery below so that men falling off would not have too hard a landing.

The bridge broke, but the soldiers converted it into a ladder and went up. Facing them above were Moros coming on, thought Lieutenant George C. Shaw, "like bees from a hive, in single file, swords in hand." The Americans fired storms of bullets and tossed in burning grass and wood. A Moro charged Lieutenant Shaw, who shot him at two-foot range. Another slashed down a kris that almost took off a sergeant's arm. The Moros fell one by one, and Pershing recalled his troops after setting fire to the cotta. Flames reached where the fort's gunpowder was, and there was a great explosion. When all was over, the bodies of some 120 Moros lay in a smoldering ruin. They had fought to the last man. Pershing's casualties amounted to nine wounded. That his losses were so slight, he said, made this the proudest day of his life. That many Moros had earlier escaped by his sufferance also made him proud: "We could have killed more but what's the use? As it is, it is better, although possibly not as brilliant"; but American papers headlined PERSHING CAPTURES BACLEOD; HUNDRED MOROS KILLED and FIERCE THREE DAYS' BATTLE AT BACLEOD along with details of gallant American assaults across the bamboo bridge and up the bamboo ladder, the scaling of ramparts in the face of desperate Moro resistance, bayonet against kris.

He went on his way, American flags sprouting on all the rancherias he approached. A couple of minor cottas stood firm against him; he reduced them without killing all defenders. Those who lived were released under an oath of allegiance, the binding quality of which was signified by a datto holding one end of a piece of *bejuco* as Pershing held the other while it was cut in half with a sword. Whole populations of villages walked behind as the column returned to Vicars in what amounted to a victory parade.

Within a few days Brigadier General Samuel S. Sumner, the new department commander, asked Pershing to go completely around the lake. No one had ever done that. He left Vicars on May 2, 1903, with five hundred men and more than four hundred animals. He preceded with two or three soldiers and a few Moro guides to pick out the way. For traversing an impassable bog he had his men cut brush and trees for footing with machetes and axes he had thought to bring along. When packmules bogged down, he had them off-loaded. Sometimes they had to be lifted out of mire by soldiers' hands and bent backs. His men did the work knowing that their leader wanted to spare them as much as he possibly could, and that they were appreciated.

Who were they, his soldiers out in what was called a howling wilderness of the vaguely known South Seas? It was said the army's enlisted-man personnel of nonofficer and nongentlemen rank had joined the colors for one of three reasons: Harvest season had given out, and they needed food and a place to sleep—the traditionally titled three hots and a flop; they were given a choice of jail or the army by a judge; had knocked up a girl and had to get out of town fast. It was not entirely so. Some were boys who couldn't think of anything else to do, or fellows with a taste for adventure and travel and desire to get away from Mississippi's pine forest or cotton field, Massachusetts' mills, with others foreign-born of imperfect English and few other prospects. That they were generally half literate and interested in roughhouse saloon liquor and whores, hard characters rarely getting mail from home—if indeed they had a home or anyone in it who cared to or had the ability to write a letter—that was hardly arguable. But while it was told of the duke of Wellington that he said of himself that he had never actually addressed, never said a word to an enlisted man, an other rank in British parlance, nothing less characteristic could be said of John Pershing. As he loved his men, so did he demand much of them. They gave it. His long, strung-out column completely circled Lake Lanao, and at home he was acclaimed as the soldier-diplomat showing the flag in velvet-glove-over-fist-of-steel, his gleaming battle-ax raised but not wantonly employed, a conquerer with better motives and finer accomplishments than, say, Cortez.

His malaria from Cuba acting up, he was ordered home, arriving in San Francisco on July 30, 1903. He was rising forty-three. At that age Grant had been the Lieutenant General Commanding the Armies of the United States. But military promotion was now strictly according to seniority. There were some 250 captains in front of Pershing, and each of them had to die, retire, or be promoted before he could be a major. The method of promotion did not have the approval of Theodore Roosevelt, made vice president as a result of the charge up San Juan Hill and president when McKinley was assassinated; and he said so in his annual message to Congress on December 7, 1903. Only the mediocre were content with the seniority system, Roosevelt told the assembled senators and representatives. It was ability that counted in life, he went on; but ability was shunned in the army. Brilliance, work, eagerness could not advance a man's career. A president could, it was true, make a promotion on his own—but only to the rank of a general officer. "When a man renders such service as Captain Pershing rendered last spring in the Moro campaign," Roosevelt declared, "it ought to be possible to reward him without jumping him to the grade of a brigadier general."

The legislators heard, pondered perhaps, but would take no action on the matter. When the president's speech was ended, listeners filed out, including the daughter of a particular western senator.

❧ II ❧

FRANKIE

→ 6 ←

MISS HELEN FRANCES WARREN of Cheyenne and Washington after graduation from Wellesley College with the Class of 1903 left the East for the Wyoming seat of her father's holdings. They were of such size, hundreds of thousands of acres extending east into Nebraska and south into Colorado, and with the animals grazing on them so numerous, that a colleague of Sen. Francis Emroy Warren once alluded to him on the Senate floor as "the greatest shepherd since Abraham." Senator Warren had been born in Massachusetts and during the Civil War served at the siege of Port Hudson in Louisiana with such distinction that he was awarded the Congressional Medal of Honor.

After the war he went west, winding up in Cheyenne, which when he arrived was part of Dakota Territory. He saw it as something other than a boom town that would fade away when the railroad construction crews moved on, and so he stayed to get active in the installation of sewer lines and the construction of permanent buildings. He was elected mayor. As the pioneer community grew he became accounted its first citizen. He built a hotel, bought lands for sheep raising, married a Massachusetts girl, was appointed territorial governor by President Arthur, was reappointed as such by President Harrison, was elected to the post when Wyoming became a state, and went to the U.S. Senate. By 1903 he had been in the Senate for thirteen years.

Senator and Mrs. Warren had two children. Their daughter, older than her brother by a few years, was originally called Little Helen to distinguish her from her mother, but by the time she was of high school age had dropped her first name in favor of Frances, or more generally Frankie or Frank. She was tall, filled with energy and go, jolly, outgoing, unspoiled despite her father's eminence and a financial status that made him known as the richest man in Wyoming. No one ever truthfully called Frankie Warren beautiful. But she had a good, kind face, was likable, and had the most delightful laugh.

Helen Warren died when her daughter was partway through college. That left Frankie to take up some of the duties of her father's Washington establishment as what a magazine termed a "maiden chatelaine" of careful respect shown senatorial wives to whom a single girl must display deference. She early on had social poise. "Though but a Miss in her 'teens," a paper reported when at a West Coast shipyard she christened the navy monitor *Wyoming*, she was "well known and liked by the people of the State. Charming, gracious, tactful and possessing fine buoyancy of disposition, Miss Warren is certain to be quite a leader in society and a powerful ally of her able father in his public life."

That summer right out of college, Frankie Warren happened across an unused diary for 1898, five years in the past. It had been given out by R. H. Hood, engineer and contractor, steel, timber, and masonry construction, Washington office at 7th and C streets, N.W. August 9 had been a Tuesday in 1898, but she wrote in Sunday for that date in 1903: "Felt an inspiration to begin keeping a diary, and found this among my mother's possessions which I was looking over today. Found Mother's and Father's love-letters to each other. Also some old diaries of Mother's. Did nothing but look over one clothes-basket full of things." Her twenty-third birthday was a week off. She had a wonderful time that summer and fall, playing golf, going to dances, making calls, writing and receiving letters, attending concerts, going to receptions, playing cards and reading novels—*The Senator's Secret, The Main Chance*. She had an enthusiastic nature, welcoming and never critical. The flowers and music at an affair were beautiful, Frankie told her diary, the fresh-caught trout and the fruit punch delicious, the Scotch whisky very fine. There was "beautiful furniture" and after a session of duck hunting a "gorgeous supper" was laid on, the moon rising just as the diners took their seats. Her fiancé, Bob, sent a "dear letter," a "darling" letter.

She went to meals that were "grand," had many tailors' fittings, often got in very late, and did not rise until 2:00 P.M. She read *The Heart of Hyacinth*, played cribbage and High Five and Razzle-Dazzle, had most often a "lovely time," "a delightful time," found people "perfectly charming." On November 30 her fiancé came to Cheyenne. "Had a very serious confab with Bob & broke my engagement to him," she wrote in her diary. That day she left for Washington, where her father would be taking up his senatorial duties of the new session. Once at the capital, where Senator Warren lived at the Willard, she visited the Library of Congress and, vacationtime novels dispensed with, told her diary she had taken out Ibsen's *Hedda Gabler* and Jacob Riis's *Children of the Tenements*. Daughter of a rich man and herself owning several income-bearing real estate properties in Cheyenne that brought a substantial income, she went to hairdressers, a millinery store, had hats sent home on approval. She dined at the Shoreham, went to the Tea Cup Inn for luncheon, made calls, received one from a lady who would be giving her a dinner, went to tea. On December 7 she was at the Capitol for lunch at the Senate restaurant and President Roosevelt's address remarking a particular army officer. Two days later: "Went to a hop at Ft. Myer with Papa and the Magruders at Lieut. Branch's invitation. *Perfectly lovely time*. Met Mr. Pershing, of Moro and Presidential message fame."

The next day, Thursday, she was At Home, receiving callers who included the wives of New Hampshire and North Carolina senators. On Friday she breakfasted with her father, read Balzac and the morning paper, received a woman friend calling to invite her to a box party, went to an auction house with Christmas presents in mind, and "had dinner with the Millards to see Capt. Pershing. It was *just great*. Have lost my heart." The following day, December 12: "Captain Pershing told Miss Millard* that I was a very 'jolly' girl and that he thought I could keep up with the procession. Oh, joy!"

The following Friday: "Went to dance at the Navy Yard. All the Navy and military there and all the swells of the city. Danced every dance but

---

*daughter of a Nebraska senator and Willard Hotel neighbor

one and have lost my heart to Capt. Pershing irretrievably. Perfectly elegant dancer."

"I've met the girl God made for me!" Pershing told an old Nebraska friend, Charles Magoon, future American civil governor of Cuba and the Canal Zone. Magoon had been asleep when Pershing arrived to deliver the news. But he was worried, the visitor said. He was twenty years older than she, what he termed an old man in love with a young girl. And she was accustomed to a certain manner of life, while he had nothing beyond his captain's salary. He went on and on until Magoon said, "Look, John, maybe you're in love and can live without sleep. But I'm *not!*"

They had known one another less than a week. "I see now it was love at first sight," Senator Warren said later. On December 23 she lunched at the Capitol with her father and Senator Clark, was introduced to Senator Hoar, talked with Senator Fairbanks, called on Secretary of War and Mrs. Root, and came home to find a floral offering obtained at the White House conservatory. "My dear Captain Pershing," she wrote, "I can't tell you the full measure of my joy at receiving your beautiful orchid. Just think of the combination—White House Conservatory! Orchid!! From Captain Pershing!!! (To be read crescendo.) Indeed, Captain Pershing, you have given me great pleasure both by the exquisiteness of your gift and by your thought of me. And now I am going to take this opportunity, if I may, of inviting you to be with us for a box party on the evening of December thirtieth. We are to see Irving, I think. Papa—whose opinion of you, by the way, I shall tell you later—is very anxious, as I am, to have you for that night. Hoping the best, I am most sincerely yours, Frances Warren."

Henry Irving played *The Merchant of Venice.* "Had a gorgeous time," she told her diary. "Supper afterwards. More gorgeous time." Pershing had accepted, of course. General George W. Davis, who sent him to Iligan because, as Davis said, he was the only man who knew anything about the Moros, once said to him, "Share your embraces with a good woman. An old bachelor doesn't make a good general. He needs to dandle something on his knee, first the wife and then the babies." But it was far more than the question of qualification for professional performance in the matter of John Pershing and Frankie Warren. In the years that were to come they wrote one another every day when they were apart, and sometimes twice a day, and not a one of those letters omitted mention of what each felt for the other:

Oh you darling, darling dear Boy. Darling, goodnight. I love you. Your Frankie. Darling Heart, It is ten o'clock and at this hour I take you in my arms my dearest one and kiss you. You are again with me and looking up into my eyes. I love you with all my heart. You are the dearest in all the world. I love you better than my life. Oh! how lonesome I am tonight my own darling. To be alone now seems so strange. I cannot see how I have lived all these years in this way. My best beloved, dearest darling. Jack.

On December 29, the night before the Henry Irving performance, the month in which they had met not yet out, they were together at a cotillion. Snow covered the sidewalks when the dancing was concluded. He saw her to her carriage. He, on a captain's salary, had none. She saw that he had no rubbers or galoshes. "Get in," she said. "I'll drop you off at your place."

A young woman to be seen leaving the dance in a closed carriage with a man not her husband? "I don't think it would be proper," Pershing said.

"All right. Walk ahead down to the corner. I'll pick you up there."

Some months passed. He was out to Oklahoma City, serving under Gen. Samuel Sumner, who sent him on the march around Lake Lanao. She went to Cheyenne. Her letters changed from "My dear Captain Pershing" to "My dear Captain Jack" and told of her disappointment that he could not come to Wyoming for a while. "But August isn't very far away now, and we must take these things as they come in the Army. (This is supposed to be diplomatic—to show what a philosophic Army woman I would make.)" His remained "My dear Miss Warren" and were signed "Your devoted friend" as he brought up to her the disparity between their financial situations. "I am trembling a little as I let this letter go from me," she wrote, and told him that she had had money and luxuries all her life, and in fact her annual income was $10,000, so that he was not rich meant nothing to her. August finally came, August of 1904, and he joined her in

Cheyenne to ride with her over her father's lands. They took to addressing one another as "Frankie" and "Jack." He was still worried about the financial question. She was not, writing: "Let me tell you right here, you dear old Jack Pershing, that you might just as well stand in the middle of a field and wave a red flag at a bull as to flaunt that word 'obstacle' at me. Here I am just urging and urging you to marry me. It seems that I have done nothing else since last February, and I am getting discouraged with you. I am going to bend all my efforts to fall in love with every attractive man I meet. Please may I kiss your nose?"

Still he hesitated. "You are incorrigible," she wrote. "Next time you get on the verge of taking my view of things, stay there till I come. One can get a fine ring for one dollar ($1.00), or if worst comes to worst, one can be procured along with a stick of candy for one cent—and I'll lend you that much." On Christmas Day in Washington he asked her father for her hand.

They decided on a June wedding, but two days after Christmas had to change their plans. Sec. of War William Howard Taft inquired about the captain's capability at bridge. The American minister to Japan wanted a military attaché expert at it. Pershing replied that his knowledge of the game was meager. There was another problem. He had heard that no married officer could be assigned to Tokyo.

"That's right," Taft said.

"Well, Mr. Secretary, I'm engaged to be married."

"You're not married now, are you? You have the appointment. Go ahead and get married. What you do after you have the appointment is your business." He asked the name of Pershing's intended. Told, he said, "You are a very lucky dog."

Tokyo and the Russo-Japanese War were waiting. There could be no June wedding. It would have to be done in a hurry. Newspapers announced their marriage would be on January 26. They would be leaving for the West Coast and a steamer immediately following. A few days before the ceremonies the prospective bridegroom called upon President Roosevelt to be told in what he thought was very surprisingly frank fashion of the president's concerns about the sudden rise of a Japan that but a half century before had been a medieval backwater of complete insignificance. Before their talk a White House aide came in and said, "Mr. President, John L. Sullivan and Jake Kilrain are here by appointment."

Nothing more typified the ebullient Teddy Roosevelt than his reaction and the ensuing conversation with the two retired prizefighters, John Pershing felt in later years. It was his most abiding memory of the man, more striking than when he heard the Rough Riders leader using unheard-of profanity during a Cuban crisis. The president sprang up, strode to the center of the room, buttoned his Prince Albert about him, stood in straight military fashion, and with a sweeping wave of his hand said to everybody present, "Ladies and gentlemen, we shall now receive John L. Sullivan and Jake Kilrain. How do you do, John, I am certainly glad to see you. How are you, Jake? It is certainly fine to see you fellows."

He would dearly love to see the two old competitors spar, Roosevelt declared. He patted Sullivan on the back in confidential manner. "There are several of them, John, who are not square fighters, but we know them, don't we, John? You and Jake were always on the square. John, I want to introduce you to one of our military fighters." Pershing came forward to offer and receive greetings. "The next time you come to town, John," the president told Sullivan, "I am going to have you here at the White House, you and Jake, and I want to have a little private exhibition, and I might put on the gloves myself and have a bout with you." The President roared with laughter, as did all his listeners. A few days later he arrived to be seated with the First Lady and his daughter, Alice, in the front row of Washington's Church of the Epiphany, all rising when he came in. The announcement of the January 26, 1905, wedding had brought to a forty-four-year-old bachelor no end of congratulatory messages mixed with expressions of some surprise from old West Point and army friends:

> I thought you would "get right" after a while. You'll find, old man, that it is a question of give and take, and selfishness must be put aside. I wish to present my sincere compliments to Miss Warren, and with them my congratulations, for I really believe you are a pretty good sort to tie to—you'll do.

> You have thrown quite a bombshell into camp. You have come to

the conclusion that most all of '86 arrived at long ago and are wise to desert those who are wandering around the world alone.

It is about time you got aboard the bandwagon where so many good men have been riding before you; if you had waited a little longer, your old joints would have been too stiff to make the climb.

I wish you would present my kindest regards to the bride, and say that I know she has most excellent judgment in bestowing her affections upon the gallant John Pershing.

From his sister Anna May, always addressed as "May" and to whom he was closest of all the family, whom people thought he looked like and with whom he had the most in common: "I was completely taken off my feet. What can I say to you? I can't think, my head doesn't work! I suppose the proper thing is to send you and Frances my very best hale and hearty congratulations. I'm sure you have done the best thing in the world by winning such a girl."

The wedding was, although so quickly arranged, the newspapers and society magazines said, the premier social event of that year's Washington winter season. The Senate convened an hour later than usual so that members could attend, Senator Stewart coming in evening attire under the apparent theory, speculated *Life*, that no matter what the hour such a wedding warranted one's best. The church was full to overflowing, the *Baltimore Sun* having it that "about 4,500 invitations were issued." Here was, said the magazine *Washington Mirror*, "a brilliant nuptial event." Miss Warren's portrait formed the magazine's cover. A full-page photograph of the groom was inside.

The decorations found the chancel with Easter lilies and palms with twined knots of trailing asparagus dotted with narcissus, mostly white with touches of yellow to represent the stripes down the breeches of officers of the cavalry branch of the service. Pershing was in epauletted and braided dress uniform, as were his ushers, officers of the army. Charles Magoon was best man. Anne Decker Orr of Pittsburgh, the maid of honor, Frankie's roommate at Wellesley, came down the aisle in white messaline with bands of pink panne velvet. Following her, on Senator Warren's arm, the bride was in white satin with elbow sleeves of lace and chiffon ruffles and a coronet of orange blossoms crowning her tulle veil. She carried roses, orchids, and ferns with streamers of long white tulle ribbon. The previous night she had in for dinner half a dozen Wellesley classmates, who now flocked into the church in elaborate gowns and hats while leaving their wraps in their carriages, an assemblage, the papers said, resembling a conglomeration of lovely flowers blossoming in Washington's January snows.

The wedding breakfast was at the Willard, two of its banquet halls secured for the purpose. The couple spent their wedding night in a Baltimore hotel suite reserved for them by friends of the groom, and then departed for the Pacific Coast. They stopped to see his family in Chicago, had a brief halt at Cheyenne, and boarded the outward-bound *Korea* on February 14. Among their fellow passengers were Gen. and Mrs. Arthur MacArthur, whom Pershing had known in the Philippines and whose son Douglas had, as with himself, been first captain of the corps of cadets at West Point. The general was being sent out as a military observer of the Russo-Japanese War.

Frances Warren Pershing proved to be a poor sailor and was violently ill. Her husband did not mind. "Love her more and more," he wrote. "She is the dearest girl in the world. And I the happiest man." They made Yokohoma on March 5 and that night went to Tokyo to stay at the Imperial. Japan's minister for war gave General MacArthur a dinner to which Pershing was invited. It was held in a very tense atmosphere, for off in Manchuria the climactic battle of the war was being fought, the massive affair at Mukden involving distances and troops on such scale as to make America's efforts in Cuba and the Philippines look like minor outpost skirmishes. The reports were that the Japanese were winning, and from the streets outside could be heard sounds of enthusiasm and shouts of "*Banzai!*" Bulletins came in and the Japanese officers all but lost control of their emotions, Pershing noted, and like the crowds, shouted, "*Banzai!*" "It is too frequently said by foreigners that the Japanese are inscrutable; they are human like the rest of us," he wrote.

American minister to Japan Lloyd Griscom found Frances Warren Pershing "jolly and friendly" and her husband an admirable man possessing the finest military carriage Griscom had ever seen. He also found that the new attaché had no interest in staying around Tokyo to play bridge. Without asking for instructions, Pershing invited himself to accompany MacArthur to the scene of the Manchurian fighting. They departed four days after arriving in Japan in a private railroad car put at their disposal by the Japanese government. "Said good-bye to Frances, saddest of all good-byes. She is the dearest in the world." She was on the station platform as the train pulled out, calling, "*Banzai*, Jack!"

→ 7 ←

THE GENERAL WESTERN VIEW of Japan before the Russo-Japanese War was such that when a citizen of that country entered the train compartment of the wife of the Belgian dean of the diplomatic corps in Tokyo, she cried out, "What! Are the natives allowed to ride first class?" So it came as a tremendous shock that they ran rings around the army and navy of Russia, seen as a Western, Christian country of first-rate military prowess.

The victorious army that Captain Pershing went to observe in Manchuria had very little ceremony about it, no pomp or show, no brass-buttoned ostentation and display and bravado. It was a scientific and businesslike force imbued with great energy and discipline. The men swung along in perfect step, their eyes fixed in an iron stare. They lived on next to nothing. Officers were dry-as-dust students of war, coldly colorless but tremendously effective, those of higher rank seeming to have foreseen any eventuality that might arise. They were very clever in masking troop movements, their medical service was exemplary, signals and field telephone marvelous, everything smoothly and correctly prepared. Hardly out of feudalism, the Japanese had mastered modern arms and strategy requiring technical understanding and national cooperation. They were operating far from home and over an extended sea and land line of supplies, but when their guns opened for the Battle of Liaoyang the effect was something the world had never previously seen. Accompanying foreign military observers had sat around campfires talking of what a great battle with modern armaments would be like, and here was one, with the Japanese loosing off a cannonade never before equaled. "This is great! This is great!" the American artillery officer Peyton C. March kept repeating.

That battle, and the even greater one at Mukden, were over when Pershing got to Korea on his way to Manchuria and the mopping-up operations. He and MacArthur debarked from a troop ship standing offshore in a flotilla of junks into which the soldiers were deposited in cargo nets, fifteen men at a time. The American officers were put ashore by a launch at the port of Dalny, created by the displaced Russians as the seacoast terminus of their railroad running down through Manchuria. It was filled with storehouses, barracks, and administration buildings whose construction had been one of the indications to the Japanese that the czar never intended to leave. That assumed intention, undoubtedly correct, had brought the war. The travelers were given passage in a supply train heading north and from its windows saw trainloads of Russian prisoners in open railway cars. They reached Liaoyang, where the first great battle had taken place, and found it a walled city with narrow, primitive streets in terrible repair and with reeking filth everywhere. At the headquarters of the Umezawa Brigade a celebration of the battle was in progress, and Pershing participated in doing honor to the dead as Buddhist priests offered addresses to departed spirits and burned incense. He joined in the burning ceremony when asked. He looked over a Japanese veterinary hospital for several hundred sick and wounded horses, the sight of which he found "harrowing," and went north toward Mukden seeing unburied Russian casualties of the fighting, fields strewn with articles of uniforms, rifles and equipment, shattered artillery pieces and broken-down transport sitting in bashed-in, ruined villages. There were no roads as the West knew them, only country paths with Japanese Army carts drawn by horses, ponies, bullocks, and coolies in white with topknots and chimney pot hats. Hogs scavenged in the muddy ditches or icy paddy fields. People wore wooden shoes with long pegs on the bottoms, so deep was the mud.

MacArthur went elsewhere, and Pershing, issued by the Japanese with a horse, a groom, servants, and a rickshaw, joined the little group of foreign military observers attached to the armies of Field Marshal Prince Iwao Oyama, who offered a feast of pâté de foie gras, chicken and mushrooms, eggs, bacon, and coffee. The attachés on the march rode behind the Japanese staff officers with Western newspaper correspondents following, the only people with round eyes—save for Russian prisoners—for many miles in all directions and, they termed themselves, "the albinos of the army" going on behind Japan's red-sunned flag. The representatives of America, Germany, France, Great Britain, Italy, and Austria sang together and told stories, with each offering a banquet to his colleagues on his country's national day—"But in using the word banquet I am stretching the word considerably, for we were living in primitive farm houses, mud-walled structures anything but clean; our respective chefs were only imitators of the art of Western cooking; and our supplies were by no means the best or most varied," Pershing remembered. The foreign officers were united by their irritation with the Japanese who in obvious determined fashion gave them picnics, dinners, and theatrical performances while denying them what they wished to know: what was actually going on. The Japanese made it all too clear they weren't giving anything away. "We are paying for this information with our blood," said Gen. Count Tamemoto Kuroki's chief of staff. The Imperial German Army's Capt. Max von Hoffman said with a snarl in return, "You are yellow—you are not civilized." Pershing was fond of what he called this "wild-eyed German" addressed as "Bloody Dutch," but was himself more subtle in indicating dissatisfaction. Knowing it would be intercepted and read, he sent a letter to the adjutant general in Washington saying that he was not being permitted to see anything of importance and might as well be elsewhere. The next day he was taken out with a Japanese horse regiment for a reconnaissance in force resulting in a skirmish with a Russian cavalry outpost.

Von Hoffman was not the only friend he made along the rising-cloud red dust trails going through twelve-foot-high millet fields or up and down the brutal mountains. The American war correspondent Frederick

Palmer felt Pershing was "the most pleasingly human and companionable" person met in Manchuria, a warm man who shared while stretching out "a welcome hand to accompany the smile which said: 'I like you. I want to do this for you.' " Palmer remembered how in an unforgiving rain Pershing came in a slicker to the correspondent's tent where he had been for hours gloomily listening to the water pour down, stuck in his head, and said, "Come on, I dare you. See me back to quarters. It's no farther for you to go than I have come to see you. You'll feel a lot better for it." He was right. After the walk Palmer felt better.

Pershing had his friends and was learning in spite of Japanese intransigence, but back in Tokyo was someone whose image was ever before his eyes. He wrote Frankie, "The kisses and caresses here and here and here and the dearest little dinners and breakfasts and coffee and toast and the delight I take in surprising you with flowers and oh! Frankie the fact is we should never be separated, it is too hard. Let's go back to Wyoming and go on a ranch and ride the range together, let's settle down in some place where our lives can be spent for each other."

But he knew that could never be, or could not be for many years; and knew also that she, understanding as she was and loving him as she did, knew it too. "I have been reading today of those brave old soldiers of our own Civil War," he wrote her, "and I really couldn't be anything but a soldier. Well: I must go to bed. Come to bed darling. Ah, and take me in your arms and hold me tight to you, press my cheek on your breast and kiss my hair. Sweetheart darling, dearest wife—I love you, love you, goodnight."

He was in Manchuria and Korea for six months, interrupted by a brief visit back to Tokyo and Frankie, during which time they worked to furnish a house they had taken. "I hope this blooming war will soon end," he told his irregularly kept diary when he returned to his duties. "I am just as forlorn as I can be. What lovely times she and I had together buying things. Only symbolical of a life, a whole life, of such happiness. I love her to madness." The war ended, Theodore Roosevelt convening representatives of the contending countries in Portsmouth, New Hampshire, and there mediating their differences in such fashion as earned him a Nobel Peace Prize. Pershing departed for Tokyo. "Frances," he had written her from Manchuria, "I wonder how long I am to grow in my love for you. Every day it seems greater and stronger. Oh! how dear are all those moments when you came to me with the sweet white wrapper and put your arms around me. Oh! My dear, you are my first thought every morning and my last every night."

Now they were together. They were received by the emperor with elaborate court ceremony in the palace whose grounds were cut off from Tokyo proper by a moat and earthen embankment like a Mississippi levee, and went through great halls with carved beams and ceiling lacquered in gold, green, and red, and with brilliantly painted screens. She wore a massive diamond-encrusted cross of her mother's she had previously never put on, and was in a gown of twelve-foot train. As according to protocol she backed off from His Imperial Highness after he greeted her, fearful that she might stumble into, and knock down, a paper wall. As a great honor they were invited to participate in a hunt of tame and pampered ducks in special marshland and lake where the weapons issued were large hand nets, like butterfly nets. Japanese ladies in kimonos and Western ones in elaborate gowns scampered about trying to catch the ducks, herded by attendants into narrow, funnel-shaped openings. "The customary dignity of social functions was entirely lacking," he noted. Secretary of War William Howard Taft came over for a visit with several senators and congressmen, including Frankie's father, plus Alice Roosevelt, and went with his group to the Philippines, Frankie accompanying them to ride over the trail from Malabang to her husband's former post at Camp Vicars on a horse he had left in the Philippines. "At Lake Lanao she got something of a shock when two Moro children, a boy and a girl, came up and announced that I was their father," he wrote long afterwards. (It transpired that the son of Datto Ahmai Tampogao and the daughter of the sultan of Ganassi had Captain Pershing as their honorary father.)

The military attaché's duties took him on visits to see the posts, bases, training camps, schools, and encampments all over the islands of the brilliantly victorious army of the late war, and often his wife accompanied him. He looked at stud farms breeding remounts for the Japanese cavalry—the results were not very good, as might have been expected of a country in which but fifty years earlier horses were almost unknown—attended the drills of infantry regiments, saw divisional headquarters, sent to Washington reports on fortifications, military police, the medical corps, observation balloons, engineering, espionage, target practice, the work of the judge advocate general, night attack practices, pensions, mail service, mapping, and machine gun utilization. He was indefatigable, dispatching uncountable requests to the appropriate Japanese Army authorities for information on the number of poles used by the field telephone service in the late campaign, the dimensions of the wire employed, the time required to train linemen. From ammunition supply staff officers he wanted to know the number of men and pack animals assigned different formations: "Is this train a separate unit attached to its particular regiment or battalion, or is it part of a brigade or higher unit?" He asked how many rounds were expended per man of the First Army in the battles of Liaoyang, Shaho, and Mukden, and requested personal interviews with officials to clear up other points.

He sent a letter of twenty-one questions to the chief of staff of the First Manchurian Army Corps and asked for a meeting with the unit's chief of artillery to discuss gun barrel wear and life, the highest velocities used, the weights of projectiles, the type of powder, the effect of weight of charges on the life of a gun, where wear first appeared, and whether the Japanese planned to change the rifling of their guns. He wanted a complete list of the articles needed to equip according to regulations a field hospital; a complete list of commissary supplies for issue or sale; the tools carried by a field engineering company and for a bridge company along with the dimensions of pontoon boats, transoms, baulks. He asked for photographs detailing the packing of an ordnance pony with small-arms ammunition, and one showing packing with artillery rounds. He listed twenty questions on the administration of military justice to be answered by the judge advocate of the Second Division, and followed up with eighteen more. His chances for getting anything close to what he desired were always minimal, he knew that. The Japanese didn't give out presents. "While the Military Attaché has been at all times courteously received by all Japanese officers," he wrote the secretary of the American legation in Tokyo, "yet it cannot be said that his attempts to obtain information even when such information was in no sense confidential have met with marked success. Written requests have often remained unacknowledged for several months at a time. Reference to such communications are usually met with a plea of pressure of business, lack of data, or the absence of some official who alone could give the data desired." He kept trying and was polite to all officers of the host country, sending out in August of 1906 letters to General Kumamoto at Nishijama, Colonel Abe at Sendai, General Yamada at Saghalien, General Watanabe and Colonel Yuhi at Hirosaki, Colonel Kuchiba at Sapporo, Gen. S. Yoshida and Col. H. Yoshida at Hokkaido, each man thanked for courtesies extended during his visits and begged to call upon him so he could return those courtesies. "Should you at any time be in Tokyo I shall regard it as a favor if you will do me the honor to call upon me and permit me to extend to you the hospitality of my home," he wrote. Had any or all of them come they would have joined as guests at the Pershings' soirees diplomats and military attachés from France, Belgium, Austria-Hungary, Great Britain, Germany, Brazil, Mexico, and other countries in addition to several members of the Japanese nobility. The captain and his lady had two homes that summer, actually, their main residence near the American legation in Tokyo, and a rented place on the seashore at Hayama, where they were able each morning to begin the day by looking up at Fujiyama's white heights. There were doors covered with translucent paper that slid into the walls, and beams so low he often bumped his head for neglecting to stoop. The bay was beautiful. "When the moon shone and light breezes rustled through the pines and caused the temple bells to tinkle, my wife and I felt that peace was as near about us as we should ever find it on this earth."

They were very happy in Japan with the travel and social life and with one another; and happy most of all because of something else. On what passed for their honeymoon, the trip over on the *Korea*, he wrote in his diary of how he and his new wife hung over the railing watching the twilight come and go and feeling they would go on forever together. "And oh! another sweet thought came over the waters, the voices of sweet children that are coming to have Frances for their mother and me for their father. So glad were they, and so glad we would someday be, when they came." They departed Hayama's shore to be in Tokyo for the birth on September 8, 1906, of their daughter Helen, named for Frankie's mother.

Twelve days later came news that Captain Pershing had been nominated by presidential fiat to be Brigadier General Pershing. In one sensational leap he went past 257 captains who were senior to him, 364 majors, 131 lieutenant colonels, and 110 colonels.

Such a move by a soldier recently become son-in-law of the chairman of the Senate's Military Affairs Committee threw the American officer corps into such uproar as may be imagined. "Selection by marriage." Favoritism. "Pull." Destruction of others' morale. PRESIDENT'S PET, read the headlines, reminding readers that it was Nigger Jack Pershing and his black Tenth Cavalry soldiers who had been with Teddy Roosevelt in Cuba and, some said, saved the Rough Riders from annihilation when the amateurs launched the charge that went to make Teddy a hero of great political future. Here was the payoff, with Senator Warren letting the president know that certain legislative matters might be facilitated if his daughter's husband was made a general. Something far worse immediately followed. For years, the papers said, it had been common knowledge in the Philippines that Pershing had with "gross immorality" lived in open fashion with a *querida*, that he had children by her. "The *Manila Times* publishes today," U.S. newspapers reported, "sensational charges regarding John J. Pershing, recently jumped over the heads of officers of superior rank and made a general." CHARGES AGAINST NEW BRIGADIER J. J. PERSHING. PHILIPPINE SCANDAL HITS PERSHING. SLUR ON PERSHING EXCITES WASHINGTON. CHARGE AGAINST PRESIDENT'S PET. The woman in question, it was said, was one Joaquina Bondoy Ignacio of Zamboanga. She with her sisters had run a shop frequented by army officers. She had come to an arrangement with Pershing. They lived in a cottage together. They had two children, one of whom died in a 1902 cholera epidemic. The other, Petronilla, four and a half years old, lived with her mother, who had married a man agreeing to be her husband as a result of monies offered by Pershing. NOW ACCUSED. HE IS FATHER OF CHILDREN OF FILIPINO WOMAN. WILL WAR DEPARTMENT BEGIN INQUIRY? The *Washington Herald* announced that Frances Pershing was thinking of asking for a divorce.

Whatever the truth of the paternity allegations—and Pershing's old friend Guy Preston, who had stood with him as he speculated about someday attending a Gridiron Dinner, in a letter suggesting that Pershing hunker down and let the thing blow over, remarked that "you know the course of our lives in the old days was such as to suggest the possibilities that the statements might have some foundation in truth"—Frankie did not dream of a divorce. "You will know that my love is the same whether it is true or not," she wrote her husband. "If they should be able to substantiate the charges, I would love you more than ever because your need of me would be greater. Oh, Husband, I love you until I am mad with love. Oh! I want you so! I want to take you on my breast and hold you—and love you, and love you, and love you." She wrote her father, "You stand by Jack, no matter what infamy may be said of him."

Pershing publicly denied everything, and the tone of newspaper articles changed to speculation that envious officers were behind the furor. SUDDEN RAISE CAUSES JEALOUSY. JEALOUSY BACK OF PERSHING SCANDAL. Frankie's father did as she suggested—or demanded. PERSHING'S LIFE CLEAN, SENATOR WARREN SAYS. The story of the alleged children followed him for years. It didn't matter. Frankie didn't care. Brigadier General and Mrs. Pershing and little Helen left Japan to take up a new assignment.

→ 8 ←

FOR SOMEONE WHO HAD BEEN a junior officer all his career, but was suddenly now a general, it was an awkward matter to take over the command of Fort William McKinley just outside Manila. The place was filled with men who yesterday ranked John Pershing. The officer he was replacing, Colonel Henry Kingsbury, had been a Sixth Cavalry captain fifteen years out of West Point when fresh from there the green-as-a-pea Second Lieutenant Pershing reported to New Mexico's Fort Bayard. The new general telephoned upon his Manila arrival.

"How are you, Colonel?" Pershing asked.

Kingsbury placed the voice. "I'm all right, General. How are you?"

"You don't like my coming here in command, perhaps?"

"Why, General, I don't see how that makes any difference. You are a general officer." That, of course, was the point.

"May I come over and see you?" The request was in contravention of the army custom that a subordinate officer calls upon his superior. Kingsbury might be envious of the jump upward, but at least Pershing was making a mollifying gesture. "I'd be highly honored if you did, sir." They had a long talk about old days in the Sixth.

With others who had ranked him, the majors, lieutenant colonels, and colonels of the post's two hundred officers, Pershing was for a time nervous and ill at ease. His situation was not made easier by being married to someone decades younger than subordinates' wives deferring to her as the commanding officer's lady who was also the daughter of the chairman of the Senate's Military Affairs Committee. Frankie Pershing dealt with her position in unself-conscious manner, cheerfully, warmly, the last person in the world to put on "side." She went to luncheons, played bridge, entertained, received, was at and gave receptions, went to and was hostess at teas and dances, and impressed everyone as an informal young mother impossible not to like.

Her husband had a brigade to work with. As he had in Missouri first-job days, and at the University of Nebraska, he functioned as a teacher. General Pershing's officers studied in detail the campaigns of the late Russo-Japanese War and went through map-reading exercises; the enlisted personnel were schooled in scouting duties and rifle and revolver firing and riding and swimming, and took classes in mulepacking, black-smithing, carpentry, clerical duties, and breadmaking. Officers and men were put to following trails, to reconnaissance, attack position preparation, construction of defensive emplacements, aid of the wounded, entrenching and the construction of fortifications, their leader very much an active presence. Once an engineering officer reported that he was unable to comply with the general's instructions to build a bridge across a stream for being unable to get a rope across. Pershing said: "I never ask the impossible. When you get an order you must find a way to execute it. Now come with me." He fastened a rope to his horse's saddle and swam the horse across.

McKinley was six miles up the Pasig from Manila, the Pearl of the Orient, with its Luneta of smart hotels and promenade for view of the quick sunset of the East, and Escolta for shopping. The delicious aroma of the ylang-ylang tree was like that of perfume. Manila was fascinating, exotic, foreign, filled with jasmine, begonias, Cadena de Amor vines, mimosas, four-o'-clocks, hibiscus. Under the portales people sold strange, spicy foods.

Fort McKinley was brand-new, built of Oregon pine on highlands overlooking the city and the bay. Nights after Retreat and the flag-lowering to trumpet and gun salute and turnout of troops, officers wore smart white high-collar tropical uniforms heavily starched and with gilt braid trappings of gold, while the ladies of the garrison were in filmy summer dance frocks or ball gowns. One dined off fine china and ate with good silver; and later, at the potted palm- and long-veranda Army and Navy Club, the band alternated between waltz and two-step. It was always warm, but the high elevation spared residents the greenhouselike steamy and humid heat of the lowlands, where natives monotonously pulled on *punkahs* so that officers at their desks might have a bit of breeze. The Pershings entertained on a grand scale. When William Howard Taft was guest of honor, the centerpiece of the table was in the shape of the White House Taft was soon to enter as president, made up of thousands of snow-white flowers and with an open door in it facing the visitor's seat. Just before the reception Pershing heard a loud cry from Taft's room, and went in to find the valet had forgotten to pack the white waistcoat worn with a tailcoat. Pershing scurried around to find one vast enough to fit the enormous guest of honor, and got it from the bulky Frank Helm, chief of the Island Transportation Department, which ran steamers to all points. (Large as Helm was, the waistcoat had to be split up the back and pinned to Taft's shirt.)

There were other guests. Pershing's former housemate in New Mexico, Richard Paddock, who married his sister Grace, had died while serving with the American forces helping put down China's Boxer Rebellion, and Grace also had died. Their son Richard, soon to enter West Point, was often with the general and his wife and little Helen. Frankie's Wellesley roommate and maid of honor, Anne Orr, came out for a long stay, eventually, like Frankie, to marry into the Army, although to a much younger man than Frankie's husband and one of lower grade, Lt. Walter O. Boswell. The general's sister May, very much like him in many ways, everyone said, came. She was a music teacher. She and her brother competed against one another in tennis and golf. Those were only two of the sports followed in McKinley. There was also polo, at which Pershing was quite capable; and there were literary clubs and theatrical organizations, and schools for the army children that very much interested Frankie, thinking ahead to when she would be the mother of a student or, as was soon apparent, students. (Writing from Washington, Senator Warren told his son-in-law that "everybody on the street" asked about Frankie, "and the inquiries also embrace yourself and her ladyship Helen. Mrs. Roosevelt inquired especially the other night at the vice president's, and I whispered in her ear, 'Frances has aspirations for March!' She was wonderfully pleased and seemed to appreciate the confidence.") In early 1908 Frankie went off to the army's high-country Camp John Hay, where the temperature rarely rose above 65°F, there to await her confinement. She took servants, a cook, a driver, and Helen and her nursemaid, who barely spoke English and addressed her charge in Chinese.

The train from Manila went only partway to the camp, and stopped at every little barrio. The rest of the trip was by mule wagon, relays changing every fifteen or twenty miles up steep mountain trails past native huts. Travelers spent the night in an inn of rustic logs and bamboo trimmings, with bamboo beds. The narrow road was a long series of horseshoe turns heading upward and finally leading to Camp John Hay, even newer than McKinley, with log cabins and tents and no running water or electricity, but with cool air sublimely invigorating. A doctor and nurse from the military hospital in Manila arrived to be in attendance, and nurse Gertrude Lustig found Frankie, as everyone did, sweet, natural, always with a smile Miss Lustig remembered as radiant: "It gave added charm to her pink and white complexion. Her hair was arranged in a coil on the top of her head. A few golden ringlets were playing about on her forehead."

"I'm so glad to have you both up here!" Frankie greeted the new arrivals. "Jack will be relieved, too. He is down in Manila just now. Isn't this a lovely country?" She waved her hand toward the mountains. "We are just camping up here," she remarked, and indeed the house was primitive and unpretentious, still unfinished but with a wide veranda on all four sides and view of canyon and open country. There were kerosene oil lamps, and candles in brass holders. Blankets were needed at night. Little flaxen-haired Helen, just able to toddle and prattle a few words, had her mother's winning smile.

It was difficult to find ready-made clothes for infants in the Philippines, so the nurse and expectant mother set to work with Chinese materials and laces, and sewed each night. "I have never been called very domestic, but really I do enjoy sewing here with you. It is a novel experience for me," Frankie told the nurse, and threw back her head and gave a hearty and infectious laugh. "She had a sweet, well-modulated speaking voice—and a very melodious singing voice as well. She sat on the big porch those moonlit nights. Her voice rang out in strains of song, into that clear stillness. It sounded like a bell pealing over the mountains," Miss Lustig remembered.

They made a bassinet lined with silk, with fine lace and ribbon trimmings, and a pretty utility basket to match. "Won't Jack be pleased when he sees how domestic I'm getting to be!" the general's lady said. Her husband came up from Manila, and late on the night of March 25, 1908, ran off to get the doctor, who was staying in a tent. Anne Orr Pershing, named for Frankie's dear friend, was born in the early hours of the twenty-sixth. "One of the first things we noticed was that she was the very image of her father," Nurse Lustig noted. "Even to the dimples. A pretty dimple in each cheek, and one in the chin. It pleased the general immensely to have visitors remark that baby Anne looked like him! Those kind gray eyes would light up." The infant's mother agreed with what people said. "Yes, she resembles you a lot," she told her husband. Anne lay in her new bassinet out on the veranda for most of the day—The Fresh Air Baby, they called her. Nights after the sudden coming of darkness—there was no twilight in the Philippines—the family sat by an open graystone fireplace with great logs blazing. The decorations were richly colored woven hemp-cloth hangings crafted by head-hunting Igarottes, and there was wicker and bamboo furniture. "Frances." Pershing said, "you are beautiful in that fluffy pink robe. You are even more beautiful than you were when I asked you to marry me. I love to stand here and look at you."

Helen seemed to adore her little sister, and it appeared to nurse Lustig that the little girl's eyes just danced with delight when she was permitted to fondle Anne. The infant must have seemed a pretty doll to her, the nurse thought. Often General Pershing stood by the bassinet and looked down with a smile. From the Igarotte huts nearby came the sound of fiesta music at night.

When she was up and about, Frankie went marketing for her Chinese cook, riding in a covered army wagon pulled by a brace of mules. She visited native farms and markets, bought tiny strawberries, mangoes, chickens that had run free. Sometimes the general's coachman took the family for an evening drive up winding mountain roads. Years later the Pershings met Miss Lustig again. "Anne, do you remember me?" the nurse asked. "Daddy said you knew me when I was so big," Anne said, holding her hands about ten inches apart. "I remember your white dress," the little girl averred.

The family of four returned to McKinley, and its head to his work, at which as ever he was a stern taskmaster thinking of nothing but efficiency while remaining, said *The Army and Navy Journal*, "cordial, kindly" — when things went right. But his health was not good. Even up in cool Camp John Hay, running a temperature, he had taken to his bed. Asked by Frankie to see what she could do, nurse Lustig offered an alcohol rub. He said it made him feel better. But the years of service in the tropics, added to the lasting malarial symptoms from Cuba, were telling on him. It seemed also, he thought, that manifestations of heart trouble were making themselves known, disturbing palpitations. The end of his McKinley tour of duty approaching, he and Frankie decided to go back to America for a change of air. That was always the recommended solution for men run down by prolonged stays along the equator.

They decided to go via Asian Russia and the Atlantic rather than across the Pacific. It would be a diversion. They would be on a long and presumably interesting journey through many countries. They would be together. "Frank, you may think I am a baby or a booby, but I don't care what you think. I simply cannot live without you," Pershing had written her while they were briefly separated when in the early stages of her pregnancy with Anne she went with Helen to Japan to be in a cool place of less rusticity than Camp John Hay. "Frank, I am not going to stay in the service away from you," he wrote. "Damn the service. Damn everything and everybody that takes from me or ever has taken from me one minute of your time or one thought of your mind. Oh, Frances, I need you every moment. I cannot live without you. And I shall not try. It is only half a life. It's so incomplete, so aimless."

A good-bye party at Fort McKinley sent them on their way, more than four hundred people appearing, and on August 1, 1908, they and the children sailed for Japan. They stopped for sightseeing at Hong Kong, made Nagasaki, went to Kobe, went to Kyoto, went to the port of Tsuruga where he arranged transport across the Sea of Japan to Vladivostok and a train heading west out of Siberia. Russia as they found it was high-booted czarist soldiery, bearded *mujiks* in tight-collared smocks, long-robed priests and the drivers of droskeys pulled by high-yoked ponies. Everywhere were towering spires and domes.

They negotiated with porters to load the luggage that would follow in one or more droskeys the one occupied by the family and Japanese maid. The luggage, its size and weight appearing untoward to the droskey proprietors, consisted of containers large and small, suitcases, baskets, one of which, filled with books, was "heavy as lead," a carpetbag, a roll of rugs, souvenir ikons and tea urns, all the accumulations of long residence abroad. Even more trunks had been sent on directly to Paris. Discussions about transport fees mixed with appeals for drivers' great care poured out of General Pershing in English, Spanish, West Point French, Japanese, and Moro. Frankie had taken German at Wellesley, so her contribution was in that language. The listeners understood nothing. Yet they indicated complete disagreement with whatever they were being told. "Everywhere the heathen rage," Frankie recorded, "porters gesticulate wildly, point to our baggage, wave their arms in despair & pour out torrents of Russian. But Jack, with a fierce mien, pours out an even more voluble torrent. His voice gradually drowns them out, & they retire sadly and leave him victorious on the field of battle." A caravan made for the depot.

There remained the matter of making good for the tickets. He had to find a bank willing to cash a draft on the Riggs Bank of Washington. A droskey took him to one suggested by the ticket agent, his vehicle rocking over hilly streets like a ship in a storm. The bank was closed. He found another, got the equivalent of U.S. $600 in rubles, rushed back to the station, paid up, got everybody settled in their seats, and found that after paying for everything—tickets, excess baggage, the droskeys, tips—he was left with three rubles—$1.50 in American money. He faced a trip with his family of thousands of miles in a train often not exceeding twenty miles an hour before they reached their first real stop, Moscow; and food purchased in brief halts from station vendors or in the dining car was not being given away. Frankie sat rigid. "Jack, what shall we do?" He had no answer. The train started, and they were on their way.

The children were hungry, and their nurse demanded that they be fed while their mother's eyes filled with tears. Pershing took a box of first-rate Manila cigars and went into the train's corridor. He saw a Danish naval officer met on the ship coming over from Japan and went into the man's compartment. "Anything was pardonable to save those we love," he wrote later, and to the Dane offered a cigar and his matchlessly unhappy story. His listener found the situation hilarious—a general of the U.S. Army begging, if not in the street, then on the train. A loan was arranged.

Sometimes for an entire day they saw nothing of civilization but an occasional village of a few scattered houses, sometimes for hundreds of miles the only break in the silver birch and fir forest was the line over which they traveled. They saw a prison train with barred doors and windows taking the czar's enemies into exile; looked at the guards on the bridges; crossed the Tunguska, Yenisie, Ob, Irtisk, Ishim, and Volga rivers, and rubbed shoulders at half-hour stops with Koreans, Chinese, and Machus, Mongols, including lama priests in red or yellow robes, Buriat horsemen, Turkomans, Muslims with veiled wives, cossacks with curved scimitars, Gypsies in fantastic garments of many colors, people whose type they could only guess at. They saw blue-eyed Slavs with curly, flaxlike hair, Mongols with jet-black hair, men with full shocks and others with shaven skulls, and women in trousers and men in gowns. They were never bored, there was always something of majestic beauty to see out of the window, the vast plateau, the plains of pastel coloring, the somber forest with black, mysterious depths, the mountain ranges with dark storm clouds massing. They were some ten days on the train, living on the Danish officer's advances.

They stopped in Moscow, where in addition to banks there was the Hotel Metropole, from which each day for a week and a half they departed with a guide to visit, among other places, the Kremlin of clusters of enormous domes and bells and eight hundred artillery pieces captured from Napoleon just short of a century before. He went to the Château Petrovsky, where Napoleon lived when his forces occupied Moscow, saw Sparrow Hill where the emperor had his first view of the city. What an inspiring sight for a conqueror to behold, Pershing thought. They saw penitents carrying golden banners said to weigh five hundred pounds that even when the flag-bearer was assisted by friends forced collapses to the ground; saw the church where czars were crowned with gold and silver, it seemed to the visitors, by the ton; saw sabers of Oriental pattern with highly jeweled hilts, saw robes of emperor and empress in massive churches, thick-walled. They went to bazaars, toured Moscow's outlying precincts of unthinkable squalor and misery.

At the palace where Napoleon resided, little Helen caused some commotion when, spotting what she thought was a butterfly resting on an embroidered screen, she ran through furniture purchased by Catherine the Great to capture it. She was halted in her chase, for the butterfly was a jeweled masterpiece. More appropriate playthings were offered on her second birthday, September 8, 1908. "Gave her a toy wagon in the morning," her father wrote, "and some colored pencils, a doll from the guide, and a pipe to blow soap bubbles. In the afternoon Frances went with the guide to an arcade and bought her a red dress, a hood, some leggins, and a coat. We all came home at 5 o'clock and arranged candles on Helen's birthday cake, had some tea, put her moo-cow and the horsey on the table and brought Anne in to witness the ceremony. Helen cut the cake (with papa's assistance) and Mama gave her a few bites. She was very much pleased with the day, and went to bed happy." Five days later, on his forty-eighth birthday, Frankie and the girls gave him a ruby set in gold from the time of Ivan the Terrible.

They went on to St. Petersburg encumbered with even more luggage, including a samovar Frankie had to have, saw the Winter Palace and the changing of the guard there, the Hermitage, a monastery of silver sepulcher and icon and altar in front of which, Frankie wrote, a Western ranch girl yet despite Wellesley, "one of the monks swang a censer of incense." They had planned to duplicate their ten-day Moscow stop in St. Petersburg, but when they learned on the third day there that two servants of their Hôtel d'Europe had just died of cholera, they gathered their two little girls and made for Warsaw. The *première classe* tickets the general purchased guaranteed a washroom, but when the conductor showed them a compartment lacking such, Frankie pushed into one so equipped and plumped down, proclaiming in not entirely grammatical German that she was going to stay there. Pershing put in his bit in English—"Jack got into the game," she wrote. The train personnel capitulated.

Warsaw in Russian Poland and the Bristol Hotel followed, and a ride through the ghetto, the "Israelite Quarter" to the general looking at the skullcaps and long robes of "this enduring stock" of "oppressed race" whose children, even, "seemed to be of Old Testament lineage." He went to watch cossack mounted drill. "Excellent, but no better than our own cavalry." They visited the former palace of the kings of Poland, stopped at a tavern offering wines of what were said to be vintages three centuries old. ("One cannot believe all one's guides declaim," Pershing noted.)

In Berlin, at the German War Office, he called on the brother of an officer with whom he had served as fellow observer in Manchuria during the Russo-Japanese War, and was shown how the brother's artillery regiment was ready for the reception of its reserves should there be a war. Everything was ready to the proverbial last button. Germany had the finest military machine that had ever existed, the visitor decided. They went to parks and palaces and museums by day and at night theaters and operas, seeing *Tannhäuser*, with Geraldine Ferrar as Elizabeth. They held hands as they listened. Frankie thought *Salome*, music by Richard Strauss, theme by Oscar Wilde, "a horrible thing, but very thrilling in places." They were two weeks in Germany, and he saw a cavalry demonstration and an inspection of the Empress Augusta's Guards Regiment.

When in Brussels he did not let pass the opportunity to visit nearby Waterloo, and there came into his mind a poem memorized long decades before when he was a boy back in Missouri. *There was a sound of revelry by night/And Belgium's capital had gathered then/Her Beauty and her Chivalry.* In Paris they found great crowds looking at bulletins posted up before newspaper offices, and saw them buying special editions of those papers. Austria-Hungary had annexed Bosnia and Herzegovina in the wake of North African tensions between Germany and France, and the threat of a general European war was in the air. The situation was tense enough for Gen. J. Franklin Bell, the army chief of staff, to cable that Pershing was to hold himself in readiness for duty as a military observer. Waiting on developments, the family went to Tours for a course of study aimed at polishing up his always shaky West Point French. He and Frankie studied it together. In the end there was no war and they went to England to take ship for America and Washington.

The general's health was still a matter of concern—to Frankie's father he looked terrible, drawn, pale, thin—but he found himself appointed a member of the Inaugural Ball Committee for the incoming president replacing Teddy Roosevelt, William Howard Taft. His assignment, he felt, was not lacking in comical content, for it included supervision of a group of men selected as the most physically appealing representatives of their respective native hearths. There were two from each state. Oddly enough, he remembered, none of America's handsomest was anything but a good Republican. At the last moment it was found that no stipulated or prominent place at the inaugural ball had been designated for "the group of Apollos" and that "these stars, who expected to form a galaxy of satellites around the new President, were about to go into eclipse.

"They made an appeal to me to save them from this humiliation." He grouped them about a fountain past which Taft and his party soon paraded, where their wondrous looks were "especially conspicuous." His own appearance suggested medical intervention, and the army's surgeon general recommended extended leave. It was also suggested that he give up tobacco. He had smoked since he was a boy and was accustomed to a dozen cigars a day. "All right, I'll stop," he said. Asked if he could do so just like that, he said, "I guess so." He never smoked very much again for the rest of his life.

Abstinence from tobacco would not alone restore his health. He went off to a Watkins Glen, New York, sanitarium for three months, followed by a one-month stay at the Army and Navy Hospital in Hot Springs, Arkansas. His 1886 West Point classmate Maj. George Deshon, who had gone to be a doctor, took charge of him there. After a series of procedures, Deshon—always "Shonny" to those of Old '86—said, "John, we have subjected you to every known test, and in my opinion and in that of my associates there isn't a damn thing the matter with you. Tomorrow morning two saddle horses will be ready at seven o'clock and we shall take a ride."

Deshon led the way, at a walk. The next day the pace was increased. Soon, Pershing remembered, he found himself "galloping over the hills as I had when a lieutenant." All was well, he wrote a friend—two hours on a horse each day, lots of sleep, a good diet, forty minutes of calisthenic exercises followed by a salt rub, a daily hour nap; and soon he was ready and fit for duty. Back on her family's Cheyenne holdings, equipped with governess, housekeeper, handyman, nurse, and chauffeur for a big new automobile, Frankie waited to give birth for the third time. Her husband joined her to welcome a son born in June 1909 and named for the senator—Francis Warren Pershing, twelve pounds. Father and mother and the two girls and one boy lingered in Wyoming for a couple of months to be a part of Cheyenne's fabled Frontier Days of August, living on one of the Warren ranches with complete staff plus horses and rigs, traps, landaus, gigs, and the car driven by the chauffeur—for Pershing never learned to drive. He went back to Hot Springs for a final checkup by Shonny, who pronounced him "entirely fit for duty in the Philippines"; and so he returned to where he had served so long and done so much, this time as military commander of the Department of Mindanao and civil governor of Moro Province.

→ 9 ←

A MAGNIFICENT HOME CAME with his new positions, with rooms so numerous that it almost could be called a palace. Off the Strait of Basilan came cooling breezes to reach the broad second-floor veranda filled with palms and plants and profusely hung with orchids. The dining room could seat sixty people.

They hardly ever closed their doors and windows save for typhoons, and there was hardly a morning when they did not cross the twenty paces over pure white coral sand beaches for a dip off the pier in the turquoise waters. "The children took to the water like ducklings, but in this I was like an old hen. I was never at ease when out of my depth and often fluttered about the shore in dismay when my wife would swim half a mile straight out into the sea." Afternoons around four the Pershings usually went riding. The children were taught horsemanship as soon as they could sit a pony, the boy Warren—he was never called by his first name, Francis—before he was three. They used little Java Thoroughbreds, not ponies but perfectly proportioned small horses, sorrel and roan, whose young riders always wanted to gallop as fast as their mounts could carry them. In the stables were big carriage horses, and mules for the Doherty wagon similar to a stagecoach and called an "ambulance" by the army. The specially matched mules were groomed to a glitter by Bill Johnson, the family coachman, one of the enlisted men assigned to duty with the commanding general. A second longtime participant in the family's life was the orderly Frank Lanckton, corporal now, court-martialed private then, sergeant on occasion. The two functioned amid an assemblage of Days of the Empire native and nonnative houseboys—the cook Ah Chong and his assistants, cleaners, watchmen, *amahs* (nursemaids) guards, groundskeepers, several officer aides.

Once Johnson, drunk, driving the family to an affair, kept falling asleep on the box. The horses sped up when he slackened the reins. He wakened to a canter, pulled them in, dozed off again. The military commander of the Department of Mindanao and civil governor of Moro Province realized the situation, climbed forward onto the box, heaved Johnson off, and himself drove to a destination, where upon arrival all who saw him at his work were convulsed with laughter. The orderly Lanckton accompanied his general to assignment as American representative at the funeral of the Japanese emperor, Sec. of State Philander C. Knox sailing from America to be delegation leader. President Taft had specifically requested that Frankie accompany her husband on his mission, and she brought the children to ride in rickshaws also carrying the cook Ah Chong, a nurse, and two maids. They were, Lanckton noted, a novelty to Japanese viewers in the streets, particularly three brightly blond children. Each of the party was alone in what seemed to the orderly a caravan of a dozen conveyances, the general in civilian clothes, the children with their attendants, himself, Lanckton, in uniform, attracting the most attention. People tipped their hats and bowed. Lanckton returned the courtesies, constantly saluting and inclining his head and taking off his hat. An American voice from the sidewalk shouted, addressing Lanckton as "General Pershing," a request for information as to how he liked Japan. Lanckton offered a salute in return. "That's the way, General!" the American called. "How do you like Yokohama?"

"Fine!" yelled Lanckton. Behind him the rickshaws shook with laughter. Pershing and the other American representatives joined the brother of the German emperor, Britain's Prince Arthur of Connaught, and Spain's Prince Alfonso as the mikado's midnight funeral began, the dead ruler in a catafalque drawn by white oxen, a chamberlain carrying his shoes behind. To signal the departure of Emperor Mutsuhito's body from

Tokyo to its burial place, a great boom of artillery sounded over the city; and at that boom Gen. Count Maresuke Nogi, who in the late war had captured Port Arthur and turned the Russian right wing at Mukden, routing therewith the Russian commander Kuropatkin, plunged a blade into his stomach at his modest mat-floored and paper-windowed home. His wife did likewise. They had lost their elder son at Port Arthur on the heights of Nan-Shan, and their younger in an assault against the Russians at 203 Meter Hill. General Nogi had been quiet, mild, stoic, reserved, offering sometimes a smile and a little jest. As a military attaché Pershing had noted his stately appearance. He had served his dead emperor from boyhood and now had no interest in living on. "The dignity of this man's modest existence and terrific death could not but hold one in awe," Pershing wrote. He represented Secretary of State Knox at the funeral.

They returned to the great house at Zamboanga. Their third daughter was born, her name arrived at by her sisters Helen and Anne. One wanted "Mary," the other "Margaret." She became Mary Margaret. The general's classmate George Duncan wrote that this could likely be the last baby of '86, and that a cup ought to be awarded to her father. He was quite alone just then in Zambo, he wrote his fellow officer Joseph Dickman, for Frankie and their son and three daughters were off in the mountains in the cool air, "and I am very lonesome without them." That was an abiding theme, for as it was not considered wise that children should steadily be in the heat of the low-lying tropics, Frankie periodically took them off to the highlands, or Japan, and even to the United States. "It is hardly worthwhile for me to say that the house seems very deserted," the general wrote his sister Mary Elizabeth Butler, "and I shall be very lonesome while they are gone." "I wish that I had gone with them, as this is about as lonesome a place without one's family as can be imagined," he wrote his friend William Tracy Page. "I wish to the Lord that I had gone with them." His devotion to Frankie and their children was known to all; when she sent word to her father that she was coming home for some fresh air, the senator responded to her cable, "I was both glad and sorry to get it — glad, because of the prospect of seeing you and the children, but sorry because I knew how lonely you'd leave Jack." The letters between husband and wife remained as they had been: "To the sweetest, dearest woman in all the world. I am mighty lonesome for you. Last night, I simply gave way and couldn't keep back the tears. My Heavens, I simply worship you." "My own darling, darling Heart—my great lover—oh, Jack, I just go mad for love of you—I adore you, I love you from the top of your dear curly head to the very end of your toes!"

He maintained two offices, one for attendance to military matters, the other for his work as civil governor of the half-million inhabitants of the island, thirty-eight thousand square miles, the size of a midwestern American state. He dealt with unpredictable Moros and the impenetrably primitive tribes of the deepest interior of Mindanao who were routinely referred to as the Wild People, the Wild Men, the Pagans, and to suppress occasional incidences of violence, murderous gangs in remote hills, organized stealing of cattle or *carabaos*, ordered out columns of Kragmen, so the soldiers were called, carrying along with their rifles bacon they fried and beans they boiled to eat along with grease-fried hardtack. (At base they dined on corned beef hash, Canned Mystery to them, roast beef in tins called Embalmed Horse, beef stew termed Slum, and cornmeal dubbed Chicken Feed.) One carried in a pocket a few pinches of coffee to be dropped into boiling water. When a coconut fell on a galvanized iron roof everyone jumped for fear that it was a shot. All troops wore sidearms in case a juramentado suddenly appeared. Officers were regarded by soldiers in the British Army tradition followed by the Americans as beings from a different world, Society people, noblemen almost. But General Pershing could hold up an entire troop movement until an unrusted canteen could be found for a man.

He did not romanticize his forces but knew them and could never be taken in by soldiers' tricks. When Johnson and Lanckton got going in the bootlegging business, bringing liquor into camp in such quantities that one party got out of hand with tables broken and dishes shattered, their general called them in and said, "I think you two have got all the shoes you need. I don't want you to buy any more." They never learned how he knew it was they who brought in the alcohol, and that they transported bottles in shoe boxes. Once in some complicated manner Lanckton managed to let loose horses who entered the general's house with predictable messy results. When Pershing found out, Lanckton stuck close to little

Warren, correctly feeling the general would not humiliate him in the boy's presence. All he received was a glare. Lanckton taught Warren to ride, using a hobbyhorse until the child was steady enough on his feet to try a pony. Little spurs were on his moccasins, put there by Lanckton. When the pony did not respond readily, Warren yelled, "Bad boy!" That became the pony's name. By age five he was riding cross-country with his father. Visiting Hong Kong with the family, Johnson and Lanckton went on a spree and were late for the boat going back to Zamboanga. When they hurried up, Pershing had the captain raise the gangplank and shouted at his men, "Stay in China!" They had the last laugh. They got another boat and beat the Pershings back and were waiting on the pier to meet them. The general rubbed his eyes and said that as he couldn't get rid of them he'd have to make the best of it.

In his civil capacity the governor was very active in letting contracts for the construction of bridges, ports, warehouses, markets, wagon roads, railroads, and industrial enterprises; he worked to encourage the growing of tobacco, rubber, sugar, coffee, rice, corn, cotton, kapok, sisal, hemp, and the teaching of American ideals to those who were his wards to be uplifted. The Anti-Tuberculosis Society was a particular interest, and he was active in setting up more than three dozen medical stations staffed by members of the army's Medical Corps. People who could pay did so. Others were not charged. He had a children's dispensary, and printed a widely distributed pamphlet on children's health, written in Spanish, Moro, and English. Smallpox vaccination was introduced. Under the governor's sponsorship shops were set up for the sale of native products, silver, brass and copper utensils, ornaments, edged weapons, and cloths. The troops bought them in profusion for souvenirs, as did all visitors to Mindanao. A school for girls was opened. Each incoming student got a bath and a new white dress. At Pershing's orders telephone lines, bridges, wharves, and municipal buildings came into being. The people responded to what he did and what he wanted to do. Hundreds of Moros volunteered to work on projects without pay.

The officers of the army serving as his district governors were told to use force only as a last resort—really he was a pacifist and not a warrior, Robert Lee Bullard felt—and were forbidden to use troops to intimidate laborers, as was desired by *los illustrados.* Many of the officers became, as with Pershing, keen to develop Mindanao, to ship out products and make money for the natives. The model farm at the penitentiary with imported stallions to improve the island's horses, the building of sidewalks, the voyages on vintas up rivers he had ordered dredged and through the cleared mouths of those rivers, the erection of electric plants, trips through Parange Ward, Lati, Tin Can Camp, Langkusan, San Ramon, Bun Bun and Twai-Tawi and Siasi districts, there to deal with Iman Pasaim and Maharaja Agga, and the Headman of Looc and Datu Mandi—he felt exuberantly useful, fulfilled, of service in exotic lands of romanticism of duty. The stern military carriage never relaxed nor the eye immediately catching a soldier's unbuttoned tunic, but he remained approachable—not only, for example, as when in June 1911 he joined nine classmates of Old '86 for a twenty-fifth graduation anniversary dinner at Manila's Army and Navy Club. He ranked them all in the wake of his startling elevation from captain to brigadier general, but it would have been utterly out of character that he patronize such as Malvern Hill Barnum, still dear old "P.T." for the circus man. The menu printed in embossed silver began with caviar and oyster cocktails and martinis, and ended with biscuit glacé, assorted cakes, Camembert, café, dry Monople, and Scotch. His openness showed when on an upcountry tour with Governor General of the Philippines Cameron Forbes their group found at a marketplace a crew of Moros saying they wished to play a game of baseball with the visitors. (That the sport and the new popularity of boxing were replacing the Spaniards' fighting of bulls was accounted a triumph of Anglo-Saxon civilization.) The challenge was accepted with Pershing and Forbes playing infield positions while aides and secretaries filled out the team. They beat natives who only yesterday went about half naked with spear and shield and blowgun and who, it was true, might well do so tomorrow.

His children grew, the older ones, Helen and Anne, attending a little kindergarten in the home of an officer's wife. The teacher, Bonnie Bloedel, the wife of Capt. Robert Bloedel, thought of the sisters' mother and father almost as if they were a boy and girl in love. She used to see them walking along the street hand in hand, happy and full of fun. Mrs. Bloedel picked up other charges each morning in a wagon, but Helen and Anne were delivered by the general. He lifted them out of his Doherty and sent them in with good-bye kisses. "Tell Helen that Terrell is taking very great care of the pony," he wrote Frankie when she was away with the children for a trip back to Cheyenne, "and that the little pony can trot as fast as any big horse. His mane is trimmed up nicely and his tail looks as well as Helen's hair does after Mary has fixed her up for luncheon. Say to Anne that Papa has her little rocking horse fixed up and the wagons and other toys are all in good repair, so that when she comes home she can go right to play with them." Frankie herself he informed that it was a good thing that just then he was entertaining many guests — "This occupies my time and thought and keeps me from being too lonesome." But "I cannot tell you how I long for you to assume a few of the burdens of housekeeping. It is rapidly driving me to an early grave. The house is beginning to look shabby, and I don't seem to be able to do anything about it. The sooner you come back the better." That things were run down seems improbable, but when she was away he was never happy, although able to make weak jokes about it: "People take pity on my widowerhood. Mrs. Bond made the remark to me the other evening at the hop that I never came to hops when you were here. I told her that you and I had so many differences that we spent most of our time quarreling about them, and for that reason had no time to go to hops."

Perhaps they did not go often to dances, but they regularly played tennis and golf and baseball and polo at the Zamboanga Country Club, of which he was the first president. Its athletic and recreation fields were second to none in the Philippines, the clubhouse transformed from a jail abandoned when the new model farm-prison was set up. So passed five years in Zamboanga in their home with special orchid house and maidenhair ferns and Cadena de Amor he loved to tend himself, with high arches and great fountain and, on the post, shaded drives bordered by tropical plants and great palms, fire trees, and a canal lined with wild almond, talisay, the foliage of which at night offered shelter for exotic huge bats, flying foxes with two-foot-long wings coming to feed on the almonds. Japanese lanterns glowed from officers' porches, soft light touching rustling leaves. On the beach were Moro fishing craft of sharp prow and outrigger and sails of vivid color, and the surf rolling up from the

Sulu Sea. To others it seemed that he was wasting away there in a place no one in America cared about anymore—"Don't sizzle your time away in the Philippines any longer," wrote his doctor-classmate Deshon; "Leave, Jack, and come home with Frances and the babies," wrote his friend John A. Ryan, teaching languages at West Point. "Come back to the white man's country. Don't forget you want another star soon, stars don't fall in the Philippine Islands, they may start to fall, but when they reach the earth it is upon the shoulders of some brigadier nearer to Washington than Mindanao." But he had things he yet wanted to do out there. In February 1911, after extensive preparation, he opened the week-long Moro Province Fair, the greatest such event ever held in the Philippines. There were delegations from forty peoples, primitives who lived high in Davao's trees, Samal fishermen, Yakans from Basilan, Subano tribesmen down from their hills, the sultan of Sulu leading his people in pants resembling ballet tights, residents of the Cotabato Valley marching in all but naked, the princess of Maguindanaw borne in a purple palanquin surrounded by dancing girls.

The Tirurais came laden with jingling bracelets and ankles, the Bilanos in coats gorgeously decorated with shell sequins, the Manobos with spears fifteen feet long, Dibabawans with roosterlike headresses, Mansakas of ruffled trousers, Tagacaolos, Atas, Guagngas, Calagans, Mandayans, Sangils, all different one from the other with their beaded jackets and bells and brass and silver ornaments of brilliant Oriental splendor, seeming in the eyes of the fair's organizer representative of all the dramatic color of the non-Western world, wild-men savages from the beginnings of civilization. The fair had parades and the display of industrial products housed in temporary bamboo and nipa structures enclosing a plaza blocks across with a temporarily installed electric light plant which when darkness came was put into function to flabbergast with brilliant illumination thunderstruck people declaring that of a sudden night was turned into day. Groups were taken to board and tour American warships standing in Zamboanga Harbor, the cruisers New York, New Orleans, and Albany. Regulars and Jackies bands played, and those of the Philippine Scouts and the Constabulary. The displays of moving automobiles left viewers stunned.

Pershing had planned and saw performed dances, sports contests, exhibits, displays of horsemanship, a water parade with high diving, fireworks, races, hemp stripping competitions, floral processions with decorated carriages and floats, horse and cattle shows, races by foot, bicycle, goatcart, the tug-of-war, and saw, it seemed to him, that tribes' eyes were opened to the fact that other tribes were not as bad as had been imagined from millennia past. Peoples cheered their representatives' showing against other peoples. It seemed to him there was a palpable lowering of suspicion among the disparate elements of the varied population he ruled, and goodwill from one to the other, even kindliness. The American mission to uplift, teach, lead—here at the Moro Province Fair was its most vivid demonstration. He rode in an open car to the cheers of twenty thousand spectators with Panglima Diki-Diki of Sulu, "the smallest among Uncle Sam's uncivilized wards," he termed him, he the leader of a midget race who himself was thirty-one inches in height and twenty-five pounds in weight, and smoked a cigar literally as long as his arm. Hundreds of men warred against in his days of circling Lake Lanao threw their turbans in the air and cheered when they passed the review grandstand. Pershing could scarcely hold back tears.

He had one final duty to perform. For years there had been discussions about disarming the fierce Moros. Murder for profit or revenge or real or imagined slights was a common occurrence in Mindanao. Also running amuck, going juramentado. But to attempt to take weapons from this warrior race was always thought to risk bringing ungovernable outbreaks of violence. Pershing believed otherwise. As civil governor he issued an order forbidding the carrying of guns or cutting weapons. As military commander it was his duty to make that order stick.

Some people did what he demanded, accepting generous government compensation for what they turned in. A less compliant group of Moros responded by attacking an American outpost, flinging themselves regardless of pain on the barbed wire of the perimeter. Pershing led a punitive expedition against them in person. "I would give anything to end this business without much fighting," he wrote Frankie, up in Camp John Hay's coolness with the children. "But the Taglibi seem vicious. They have shown their teeth and snapped at us. You can't talk a fellow around to much of anything if he is shooting at you all the time." Five columns of troops scattered the rebellious tribesmen. A letter of appeal to their chiefs followed: "I am sorry to know that you and your people refuse to do what the government has ordered. I am sorry the soldiers had to kill Moros. All Moros are the same to me as my children and no father wants to kill his own children.

"Now, I am writing you that you may know that I want my children to come in and stop fighting. We do not want any more killing. Too many Moros and their women may be killed. Your people are better off not to have guns as we can then have peace. The government will pay for all guns. If you leading men do not stop fighting, you will be responsible for the lives of your women and children. You have no right to lead all these people to follow you into a fight. Give up the guns and save your own lives and the lives of your people."

They did not listen, but made to hole up with their families in a cotta atop Bud Dajo, a high peak. They had done that in years past, and Pershing's precedessor General Leonard Wood had brought in artillery and taken Bud Dajo with slaughter not only of warriors but also of women and children. Pershing would not have such a thing on his conscience for the fame of Napoleon, he told Frankie. But he would have to go in. "I am very sorry these Moros are such fools. I shall lose as few men and kill as few Moros as possible." He threw a thousand soldiers around Bud Dajo and so squeezed it off that, as he wrote Frankie, "a cat could not sneak out." There was a surrender. He took Bud Dajo without killing more than a dozen Moros. Three Americans were wounded.

One last campaign to bring disarmament remained. Thousands of Moros—ten thousand according to estimate—moved into great fortified cottas atop the extinct volcano Bud Bagsak. From there they mounted expeditions to kill those who had surrendered their weapons, and to take their cattle and possessions. They must be annihilated with artillery, it was said. That was what was called for. Pershing hesitated. "I am not prepared to rush in and attack while they are surrounded by women and children."

But their war gongs beat and their war drums sounded; and even as he begged them to leave off, it came to him that they took restraint for weakness. He ordered the withdrawal of all troops from the area. From Bud

Bagsak emerged women and children, and some of the men, returning to their fields to plant and cultivate. It was what he had hoped for. Several hundred men remained in the mountain fortress. That also had been his hope. There on Bud Bagsak were, he felt, the dregs of Mindanao, inveterate outlaws lost to reason. He had always said Moros were like untrained horses: if you attempted to ride them at once you got bucked off. If you approached gently you could get good results. But sometimes a situation demanded harsh curbing, a bit, a whip. He went back to Zamboanga and let it be known that he was off on a recreational leave with his family. Then sailing with lights out and accompanied only by one aide, Lt. James L. Collins, he made for Bud Bagsak, collecting troops as he went along, swiftly, secretly. There was no warning to soldiers that he was docking; officers in dress whites paying social calls found him suddenly materializing with orders that they immediately muster troops and come along.

With some twelve hundred men he made a rush at the mountain stronghold. It was June 11, 1913. His guns opened with shrapnel on outlying cottas. Moros fired back, screaming. On his hands and knees he went through shrubs and tangled vines with Lieutenant Collins to conduct a reconnaissance, getting so close to Moro forts that the sound of conversations inside could be heard. He ordered an assault. Philippine Scouts, infantry, dismounted cavalry went forward. Moros poured out to meet them, spears and barongs flying. His line broke. He went to the place of its rupture, general side by side with junior officer and sergeant, and steadied his troops and by encouragement and example got them moving forward. The Moros were fifteen yards away. He pushed them back. What he had done, soldiers said, merited the Congressional Medal of Honor. He did not agree. He met a need and was where he should have been, he said.

His men slashed through bamboo entanglements, through flying pointed weapons. His guns roared. The Moros atop Bud Bagsak died to the last man. Their passing was magnificent, he thought. Not a man had surrendered. His Bud Bagsak foemen lived up to the deepest traditions of a great warrior race. John Pershing never forgot, always admired.

They had perished in a poor cause, he felt, but at least it all went for something. The issue of disarmament in Mindanao was decided. Peace reigned, and the rule of law. Now it was time for him to leave the Philippines and the East. He was run down and thin. And he and Frankie wanted the four children to have an American education and to know their country. A great Zamboanga farewell was offered; the town plaza was filled. The Pershings went up to Manila and the Army transport *Sherman* departing in December 1913. They watched the harbor drop down the horizon, and also Corregidor and Bataan, and put to sea. Father and mother and children were on deck most of the day, the last-named on their feet all the time save for meals or when their mother or governess read aloud or told them a story. "I romped and played with them," their father wrote, "getting as much fun out of it as they did." On Christmas Day there was a tree, gala dinner of turkey with plum pudding for dessert, and presents for the children purchased back in the Philippines. At Honolulu Helen and Anne and Warren and Mary Margaret thrilled to swimmers coming out to meet the *Sherman* and then diving for coins; "ashore they each had to have a lei, one of the garlands of fresh flowers hung about the necks of visitors."

They made San Francisco, Senator Warren journeying out to the West Coast to meet them. He came clambering up a Jacob's ladder from an army tug to the deck for embraces by his daughter and son-in-law and four grandchildren. "Help!" he cried, a child in each arm, one on his back, and one pulled along behind. A couple of years earlier he had married after a decade of being a widower, to Miss Clara Morgan, a vivacious woman hardly older than Frankie. All the family adored her. Along with the senator were ships' news reporters and photographers to do stories about the return to America of a man defined by the *San Francisco Examiner* as the officer who had had so "rapid and remarkable rise in rank and fame," with Bagsak described as "the famous battle against the Moros marking the zenith of his fighting career." The children were grouped together for photographs appearing in the next day's paper, the "four globetrotting youngsters" born in Japan, Camp John Hay, Cheyenne, and Zamboanga, each with the lightest blond hair, that of Anne and Warren appearing to be almost white.

Their father's next assignment was to command the Eighth Brigade at the Presidio, the ancient post hard by where the *Sherman* made port in

San Francisco. A choice of quarters there was available to an officer of the general's rank, and before meeting the ship Senator Warren had looked the possibilities over. One suggested itself to him, big—not as big, of course, as the almost-palace in Zambo—with a spacious yard facing out on the post's parade ground. Its only possible flaw, the senator thought, was that wind might blow up dust as it swept across open space. But they took the house in preference to an even larger one because Frankie felt the children needed a nice big play area. General and Mrs. Pershing got active in the extensive preparations for the coming Panama-Pacific International Exposition of 1915, a great world's fair. Planning delegations from all American states and many foreign countries were coming to San Francisco, and it was interesting to meet and be with them, and the Presidio's and the city's social life was exhilarating if exhausting. They found the climate toniclike after the oppressive Philippines heat, went to the theater and to concerts in the city almost entirely rebuilt after the earthquake of nearly ten years earlier. The municipal parks and surrounding mountains they found enchanting. Riding horses and children's ponies had been left behind in Zamboanga, but they had a motorcar and someone to drive it, and there were fine roads leading to the Yosemite Valley and elsewhere.

In April of 1914, three months after their arrival, Frankie was involved in a Sutter Street accident. She made light of it in her cheery manner—the laughing lady, her husband's brother Jim always called her. She was being driven home from a shopping trip in a horse-drawn little coupe, she wrote her father, Senator Warren, when she saw a runaway automobile bearing down. "There was a crash and the carriage rose in the air. I did not know anything more until I felt myself merrily sliding down the street; even then it was like a dream, my only sensation that I was sliding on my arm and hat and vaguely wondering what I was doing it for. The horses ran away. I was either inside the carriage or else in falling out I became caught and was dragged along." After half a block the horses slammed the overturned carriage into a telegraph pole. Frankie was flung clear to lie half on the sidewalk and half in the street. "Why my head was not fractured or my neck broken in the process remains a mystery.

"Though I have Heinz's 57 varieties of cuts and bruises, I escaped without any broken bones or internal injuries. People have been perfectly lovely. My room looks like a flower store—the loveliest roses you ever saw. I have about eight or ten dozen American beauty roses; four or five dozen red roses (Jaquemont); pink roses, yellow roses, Easter lilies, white roses, hyacinths, and pansies. I have also had books, notes, telegrams, and Jack says he has done nothing for two days but answer the telephone. There is nothing like being alive and attending your own funeral. I am afraid I shall acquire a habit of being run into or away with. The advantages seem to outweigh the discomforts.

"Thanks so much for the telegrams from you and Clara, and lots of love to you both.

"Your affectionate rubber ball."

During her stay at Letterman Army Hospital the general took the children and their governess to the combined Buffalo Bill Wild West Show and Floto's Circus. He had known William F. Cody, Buffalo Bill, out on the frontier a quarter century previous, and was sent complimentary tickets by his old friend. Other old acquaintances were among Bill's performers: Sioux scouts once commanded by Lieutenant Pershing in the wake of the bloody Pine Ridge affair at Wounded Knee Creek in South Dakota now had become bareback stunt riders for staged cowboy-Indian battles. "It reminded me of old times to see those Redskins on the mock warpath again, and the children sat in wonder at this and other thrilling performances. The kiddies were in ecstasy," Pershing wrote.

"To them, who had spent most of their lives in the Philippines, everything in America was new, strange, and wonderful. In the menageries the animals they liked best were the bears. This was probably because they remembered hearing from their nursery books the story of the three bears. On leaving the big tent at the end of the performance we passed again through the zoo, the elder children under the guidance of the governess and the youngest in my arms. As we passed the bears' cage the baby waved her hand and said, as if speaking to an old friend, 'Good-bye, Mr. Bear.'"

Discharged from the hospital, Frankie declared herself, as she put it, fit for duty. It was well that she was so, for her husband's presence was required elsewhere. In the wake of the unexpected fall from power of Mexico's iron-fisted ruler of more than a quarter of a century, the neighbor to the south had fallen into anarchy of the most violent nature. Generalissimo, caudillo, assassin, insurgents, outlaws, irregulars, private armies, and armed bands, each espousing the cause of freedom and the People sprang from the ground as Porfirio Diaz entrained for Vera Cruz and a ship to exile in Paris; and across from Mexico's Ciudad Juarez America's El Paso blocked its windows with mattresses to protect against bullets and artillery shells flying across the border. Mindless executions, rape, robbery, the sacking of trains and despoiling of towns, completely lawless chaos, seized Mexico. Unrest, tension, the possibility of American intervention—and the Eighth Brigade was ordered to Fort Bliss.

There its commander drilled its elements and sent them patrolling along the miles of barbed-wire border through the sand and cactus and rattlesnake-infested little railroad tank towns. It was impossible to know how long Pershing would be there on the border, conducting what President Wilson termed watchful waiting, so Frankie took the children and went off to Cheyenne and her father's domains. Helen and Anne enrolled in school there. Whenever he had the chance Pershing was with his family, spending time at the ranches and going East with his wife to attend the June graduation at West Point of his nephew Richard Paddock and to visit her alma mater, Wellesley. From Fort Bliss he stayed in constant touch with her and the children, and they with him.

I bought Warren a corduroy suit in regulation Norfolk jacket pattern. He was so delighted that he told the conductor on the car all about it. You should see your children. They all look so blooming. Mary Margaret is a perfect little fascinator with cheeks like a red apple. Anne wrote you a darling letter. She dictated her thoughts,and Helen was her secretary. Both did a pretty good job, I thought.

Grandpa Warren and Grandma Clara came home yesterday are you glad. I am Anne and I have a new dress. They are very pretty. Are you having a nice time. We are having a nice time are you. Your loving daughter Helen.

Well, Helen and Anne have finished bathing the others and un-
dressed themselves, so I want to go up and read to them. Am also going to bowl a while later. I love you, dearest, dearest. Never has time
dragged so interminably as since I decided—or we decided—not to
go to Texas. What do you think of the Mexican situation?

What he thought was what everyone thought: that it was unpredictable. So also was the leader of the most powerful group in the areas
adjoining American territory, Francisco (Pancho) Villa. In equal parts
Robin Hood, patriot leader, murderous assassin, he favored the Elite
Confectionery in El Paso for its splendid ice cream and often went over
the wooden International Bridge spanning the Rio Grande for a visit
there. Once he came to call upon the leader of the Eighth Brigade, arriving, Pershing noticed, with revolvers bulging from pants pockets. Villa
had charm and appeal, but it was nothing for him to sit in a courtyard and
offer prisoners a chance to get over a wall, freedom their destiny if they
succeeded and death their potion if he could put a bullet in their backs.
He did not often miss. Usually found with ammunition-filled bandoliers
crisscrossing his chest, he often had a large fountain pen stuck in his
handkerchief pocket. That he could use it to form intelligible words was
doubtful. He was always accompanied by an aide no less feared than Pancho himself. When the two men walked in for their call upon Pershing
the aide neglected to doff what Americans always called a "sombrero,"
the ubiquitous tall-capped head covering of Mexico, and Pancho said
with a hiss, "Take off your hat, you brute, you animal." They posed for
pictures, the Eighth Brigade commander grinning. Each afternoon at
four-thirty Pershing went for tea at the Hotel Sheldon, headquarters for
newspaper correspondents waiting for something to happen and regarded
as the hub of the border universe. Everyone found him cheery and socia-
ble, different from the usual run of high officers who, Pershing's West
Point contemporary Robert Lee Bullard noted, appeared automatically to
demand with cold look that one give an account of oneself. But he was
not happy. If a day passed when he did not receive a letter, Frankie could
be certain she would receive a telegram asking assurance that everything
was all right. PLEASE ANSWER IMMEDIATELY.

She often went bowling, she reported, rolling about 120 or so. The children each night put on circus performances. Sometimes they varied the production. Each would then stand on a chair and deliver a speech. They were really quite remarkable, she thought. She told him of one of Anne's:

Ladies and gentlemen, my speech has begun. Now about Longfellow—here he is (Holding up rock.) You know, you know, he lived in this little house. (Here she points to a doll's cardboard house on a chair.) Now you know, you know, when he was one year old, he was in the oneth grade at school. Then there was Washington. He lived about fifty years ago.

Dear Papa, I am sending Virginia a easter basket are you going to send any easter eggs. I am going to give people easter eggs are you. We dyed some eggs to give to Virginia and Dorothy. We will have a nice time on easter will you. We will. I do not know anything else to say. Your loving daughter Helen.

Dear Papa, I love you. Baby, Warren and Helen are having a nice time. This is all I can say. From Anne. To Papa. The end.

The first day of April 1915 came—he had been able to get away to spend Christmas in Cheyenne—and they were, the older girls wrote him, April fooling everyone. Their drawings went out to be with him there on the border, those of Anne showing full-figured women with long dresses and in hats with feathers. There were math papers from school: $2 \times 8 = 16$, $4 \times 8 = 32$, 12 divided by $3 = 4$. He wrote back to Dear Old Anne to ask about the ponies they were riding, Scamp and Rascal, and how they liked the snow so alien to the life they had known back in Zamboanga. He was hoping to come and pull them along in a sled, he said.

June 1914 had come and gone, that month in which in remote Sarajevo in Bosnia the heir to the Austro-Hungarian throne died from a bullet put into him by a tuberculosis-doomed adherent of Greater Serbia. With Archduke Francis Ferdinand died his wife. Nothing could less concern the Americans. If report of the incident made a paper, it would be found in the back pages among the want ads, personals, and rooms for rent. In Cheyenne the following June, Helen Pershing received a certificate stating she had successfully completed her studies in the third grade at the Churchill School. Anne Orr Pershing was awarded a similar certificate saying she had completed the course of study for the first grade. Their father went to gather them along with their mother and the smaller children and bring them back to the big house on the post across the drill field at the Presidio in San Francisco. Things were reasonably quiet across the Rio Grande, or at least less wild than was customary, and so he was able to stay for a while, supervising the varnishing of the floors. But neither parent had bargained for the lengthy enforced separation, fourteen months in all since they had come from the Philippines. "I'm tired of living alone," he told a friend when he went back to duty on the border. "I'm having my quarters fixed so that my wife and children can join me."

Yet before going off to be with him at Fort Bliss there were things Frankie wanted to take care of. It would be great for the children to see and remember the Panama-Pacific International Exposition, a stone's throw from their house, and she volunteered to be at the Fair's Montessori School booth—that method of education greatly attracted her. And she was active in working for a forthcoming conference on women's suffrage to be held in the area. Finally, Wellesley's West Coast alumnae were planning a San Francisco get-together she didn't want to miss. After the reunion—the Off-Campus Rally, it was termed—she would make for El Paso and Fort Bliss and the border, where the family could be together. Meanwhile they were as always in touch by letter:

Just finished a very successful bowling party and aftermath at our house. Everyone on the post turned out. I'm certainly glad to be bowling again. Did rotten as far as playing is concerned. Haven't played so poorly since I can't remember. Very poor balls all night. Made 60 or 68 I think. I must go to bed. No letter from you today, darling. I love you so much—I am getting weary of being away from you. What about this Mexican situation. I suppose it will warm up so you can't get away. If only you were here! I'm getting so sick of being away from you. Oh, I love you, dear one!

August arrived. The Wellesley affair would be on the twenty-fifth, and on the twenty-eighth she and the children would make for El Paso. Meanwhile she worked to get the Collegiate Alumnae Association to pass a resolution in favor of women having the vote. (She had sent word to the Equal Franchise League of El Paso that she wanted to join when she got to Texas.) A friend paying an afternoon call asked how the general was, and she replied with a laugh, "I had a letter from Jack in which he said: 'Suffragettes I suppose only write once a month to their husbands.' " She was in a rose-colored gown with lace and had on what the friend, Laura McClernand, considered a very becoming hat, which she said her husband had given her. After admiring an opal worn by the visitor, she went to get and show an opal pendant of her own. She came downstairs with it and some scissors and cut flowers for Laura McClernand to take away.

His claim that she wrote once a month could not be less accurate, of course. On August 15 she told him that Anne reported that a girl said her father was richer than Anne's father:

I said to her, "The next time anyone says that, you tell them that your father is the finest man in the world." I explained to her that it was a matter of no consequence whether we were rich or not—we all had enough to wear and to eat and if we didn't, we could all go to work and earn.

That night she was at the Greek Theater in Berkeley. She wrote, "Oh, Jack, it was wonderful. I did so want you here. The night, the light on the stage like moonlight, the wonderful music." The Wellesley affair was held ten days later, August 25, in the Massachusetts Building on the Exposition grounds. All the women were given hats to wear, an ancient one of shepherd's curves dating from the 1880s assigned a recent young graduate, gray-haired alumnae handed those of the most youthful and modern vintage. Frankie was given a mortarboard she perched at an angle on her light hair. She sat with old friends from college days, including Anne Orr Boswell, her roommate and later maid of honor married to one of Frankie's husband's aides. A number of graduates had been asked to speak, Frankie being one of them, and she seemed in the eyes of Caroline Hazard, Wellesley's president in Frankie's student days, gay and bright while also somewhat preoccupied, thinking of her coming remarks. When she arose she was witty and amusing.

"Miss Hart," she said, indicating a longtime faculty member in attendance, "thinks, no doubt, I have forgotten all about unity and coherence, but whether or not we can practice all that we have learned, we have not forgotten it; somewhere in our minds and hearts and natures the lessons of college are stored and daily bear their fruitage. To the fine women who must have thought at times, in teaching me, they were casting their seed on rocky soil, I want to acknowledge my debt." She talked about collegiate hijinks, of how, up to mischief, she was crawling through a transom over a door when her trailing and dangling leg was firmly grasped by an official demanding to know what she was trying to do. "I called back to Miss Pendleton, from the other side of the transom where my head was, that I wanted to get into that room to take a tutoring lesson in mathematics." Then she turned serious, saying the good times were a background against which a deepening inner life went on as Wellesley "quickened the desire to know."

What inspired students and might afterward be explored in depth was a part of the school's offerings, Frankie went on, that and an ability to lay hold of knowledge, to get at what graduates needed and desired, and also a latent power to meet new situations.

"It has helped me in every kind of crisis, great or small, from the time they brought me and laid in my arms my first baby, to the time I backed out of an audience with the emperor of Japan in a train twelve yards long." Her voice had, thought Professor Sophie Hart, rich, sweet notes, and it came to the teacher that her former pupil had a gift for public speaking. (In fact Frankie had been on the debating team back in college days.) She had, Miss Hart felt, utter unconsciousness of self along with her ready and fitting words, their happy variety. The professor had earlier noted Frankie's excitement regarding women's suffrage, the enthusiasm for that cause. A woman of genuineness, glad-hearted, Miss Hart thought, with a merry nature and an appealing simplicity.

I have just come from the Wellesley rally and a toast which I had to make to the eighty-some alumnae present; and slept with Anne while she fought a case of acute indigestion; have had a day of it and a night of it last night—and so I'm just going to say goodnight. Anne and Polly said they thought my toast next to the best there. I thought I did rottenly myself. I'll send it to you tomorrow to let you judge. Anyway, I was one of the first there in number of children—one woman having five and two of us four. Goodnight, dear heart. Your Frankie.

The next day, the twenty-sixth, she talked with Frank Helm, the physically imposing friend who back in the Philippines gave his waistcoat to Secretary of War Taft when it was discovered such item of that gigantic individual's things had been forgotten by a valet packing his bags. Frank and Laurie Helm were good friends, back in the Philippines. Childless, they had shared two Christmases with the Pershings and the Pershing children. Helm had found that a tree closely resembling that familiar to American families for holiday use grew on the island of Palawan; decorated with cotton balls doing duty for snow and surrounded by toys, it offered a tropical substitute for the real thing. Blowing a tin horn, the general marched around it with his little ones. Now the Helms were in San Francisco living at the Colonial Hotel on Bush Street while he held down a Stateside position. They wanted to take the children for a return visit to the Wild West show-circus attended with the general during Frankie's stay in the hospital following her carriage accident, and it was agreed they should do so on the following day.

That night, August 26, Frankie had house guests. Anne Orr Boswell, for whom little Anne Pershing was named, came with her two boys, James, six, and Philip, three, to play with Frankie's children. It was Anne who along with Polly Storm Walthall, another classmate, offered the complimentary appraisal of Frankie's Off-Campus Rally speech mentioned in her letter to her husband along the border. Another guest was a Mrs. Margaretta Gray Church, who had approached Frankie at the Exposition's Montessori booth. She had known Frankie's mother years back in Cheyenne, Mrs. Church said. Now she was out to San Francisco seeking to get her daughter out of a mental institution, where the daughter had been committed by a beastly husband. It was obvious that Mrs. Church was in financially difficult circumstances, and hearing her speak of her mother, Frankie asked her to the Presidio house to stay there and be tided over while they discussed ways and means to help the daughter. That night Anne Orr Boswell went out to dine with Major and Mrs. Henry H. Whitney, old friends of hers and the Pershings from the Philippines. Frankie and Mrs. Church dined at home. At about ten-thirty the Whitneys brought Anne back to the house. The children were, of course, in bed. Frankie and Anne and Mrs. Church sat around the dining room's grate coal fire opening on the floor whose varnishing the general had supervised. It was very foggy outside. They chatted for a time. Midnight approached. They retired to their beds upstairs. Mrs. Church had mentioned that she knew some Pittsburgh friends of Anne's, who was from that city, and seeing the woman's financial situation Anne asked herself if it were not possible that she help out an old acquaintance of Frankie's mother. Frankie stopped into her room for a moment, and they talked about Mrs. Church briefly. It was late. Frankie went to the two rooms her daughters occupied. She would be sleeping there, for little Anne, Anne Orr Boswell's namesake, was still not completely recovered from the indigestion Frankie mentioned in her letter of the previous day to her husband. A few hours later the telephone rang in the general's Fort Bliss headquarters.

→ 10 ←

THE CALLER WAS NORMAN WALKER, Associated Press correspondent in El Paso. He had been looking at the teletype in the *Herald* office. Believing that news of a story coming over it would have reached General Pershing, he phoned and thought he recognized the voice of his social acquaintance James L. Collins, the general's aide.

"Lieutenant Collins, I have some more news on the Presidio fire."

"What fire?"

It came to Walker that he was not talking to Collins.

"What fire?" the voice on the phone repeated. Walker recognized whose it was. He stumblingly said he would read the dispatch that had come over the teletype. He did so.

"Oh, God!" Pershing cried. "My God! What's that? Read that again!"

Walker did so. "My God! My God!" Pershing cried. "Can it be true?" Walker tried to offer his sympathies. But nothing came back over the line. There was a long silence. The correspondent thought to hang up. Then Pershing said, "Wait a minute. Who is this? Who am I speaking to?"

Walker identified himself.

"Thank you, Walker. It was very considerate of you to phone."

* * *

After Frankie left her room, Anne Orr Boswell fell asleep, briefly to wake up a couple of hours later—it must have been about two in the morning, she thought. There was light coming from the crack beneath her closed door, she saw. Frankie, across the hall with her children, must have turned on a lamp. Anne dozed off, woke. The light seemed more intense. She opened the door. A great gust of smoke and terrible flashes of flame came at her. She began screaming, "Frank! Frank!" at the door on the other side of the hall. It would be impossible to cross over to it. The foot of the stairs leading down to the first floor, she saw, resembled a furnace—a great roaring mass of flame. Screaming, she slammed her door shut. There was a porch roof outside the window of the room where her two boys and maid were. She got them up and through the window and stood with them as flames shot up through the roof of the house, cinders pouring down on their heads. Below, the signal gun going off brought running soldiers, and members of a businessmen's training group encamped on the Presidio grounds.

In another room Mrs. Church half awoke to hear the crackling of fire and to say to herself that Mrs. Pershing had very efficient staff getting up early to have the house warm when the family arose. She heard noises and decided the children must be having a roughhouse. She got up, opened the door to her room, saw densest smoke and flames, got dressed, gathered her things, entered the bathroom, and from there went out of the window and into the arms of a soldier below. From the porch roof Anne Orr Boswell threw her little boys down at outstretched hands. Her maid jumped off the roof. Then she herself leaped, to land in a flowerbed, where she lay prostrate in her nightgown. Mrs. Church came up and said she would take pneumonia if not moved somewhere else. Fire shot up through the house. Coals from the dining room grate had fallen out onto the floors whose varnishing General Pershing had supervised, ignited the varnish, and brought flames and smoke and destruction.

It was about four-thirty in the morning. Fire hoses laid on streams of water, clouds of smoke and steam rising to mix with fog and enshroud the area in a darkness that made people think the rescued children they saw were the Pershing children. "Thank God there's nobody left in there," one bystander said. Then it was realized that little James and Philip Boswell were in fact not the Pershing children. There was a rush to get into the house. Men went in to grope through smoke and to be driven back by overwhelming heat and fire. They tried again, forced their way in. They came out bearing burdens in their arms. Frankie had just turned thirty-five years of age. Helen was eight. Anne was seven. Mary Margaret was three.

Someone asked about the son, Warren. Pvt. Fred Newscome took a lantern and went through great smoke. His lantern made as to flicker out for lack of oxygen, so he went down on his stomach and squirmed blindly along floors before coming upon an unconscious but still breathing form in a separate bedroom. Newscome made for air and handed over Warren for swift delivery to Letterman Army Hospital. Frankie and Helen and Anne and Mary Margaret did not have a mark on their bodies—asphyxiation had taken them. Even their hair was not scorched.

On a train headed west from El Paso with Lieutenant Collins, General Pershing screamed and cried. The train came to Bakersfield, California. Frank Helm was at the station. Collins led him to the general's stateroom. "I can understand the loss of one member of the family, but not nearly all!" Pershing gasped. He put his arms around Helm's neck and held him so, constantly weeping, as the train made for Oakland. He did not change his position as they went on. It seemed to Helm that his old friend was in such state as to make him believe that if Warren had died along with the others he would have lost his mind. He told Collins to wire ahead for a doctor to be at Oakland with a sedative.

They got across the bay to San Francisco with the medical officer and to the undertaker's establishment of Clark and Booth, on Geary Street. They went where the four caskets were, and the general asked to be left alone. Standing behind heavy drapes, Collins and Helm and Maj. Edson Lewis, the doctor, looked on as the general got down on his knees before the first casket. He stayed so for some ten minutes, then went on to the next and stayed before it in the same fashion, and the next, and the next. After nearly an hour he arose and said he wanted to go to the Presidio. Helm tried to say that perhaps he ought to have a rest first, but left off his remonstrances when he saw the general would not be satisfied until he saw the house. They looked at the burned hulk. That Warren's bedroom door and the bathroom one separating him from his sisters' rooms had been closed had saved his life. Even so, the smoke that took away theirs left the walls of his room blackened to the ceiling.

They went to the hospital and the general talked with Anne Orr Boswell, who was unable to stop crying. Warren was there under the care of Major Whitney's wife, other friends, and the medical staff. The door to his room was opened and the father went in. After a time the two came out and in an auto made for the Stewart Hotel, where the general and his six-year-old would be staying. Warren sat on his father's knee. Passing the Exposition grounds, Pershing managed to ask the boy if he had been there. "Oh, yes," Warren said. "Mama takes us often." Pershing began shaking so violently that Frank Helm reached over and took the child on his lap.

Senator and Mrs. Warren and his son Fred and Fred's wife arrived, and it was decided that interment would be in the family plot in Cheyenne. They would leave on the Overland Limited after brief services in the Clark and Booth funeral parlor chapel the next day. That was the day Frankie had planned to take the children and entrain for El Paso and Fort Bliss. Quoting from a prayer attributed to British prime minister William Gladstone, her husband wrote in a notebook: *Tell her, O gracious Lord, if it may be, how much I love her and miss her and long to see her again, and if there be ways in which she may come, vouchsafe her to me as a guide and a guard, and grant me a sense of her nearness.*

After Episcopal services at the Geary Street undertaking establishment, some one hundred people present inside and others gathered in the street, he walked to a car in dark civilian clothes, his head down and never looking up. He was arm in arm with his brother-in-law Fred's wife, Bessie, who pressed a handkerchief to her mouth. Three of the four coffins were so pitifully small.

They made Cheyenne, and the dead were interred. Warren would not, of course, remain six years of age forever. Decades later, handsome, charming, likable, very rich by virtue of his Wall Street activities and by his marriage to a great heiress, Warren came into his summertime place at Narragansett Pier in Rhode Island. He was in golfing attire, cleated shoes. Warren was a fine golfer. He saw the older of his two sons. Warren picked up the nearest thing available to his hand, an open leather sandal used for going to the beach. With it he began to beat the child. He beat him and beat him. The boy was John for the general, Jack as the general had been, not much older than Warren had been when his mother and sisters died. Even as he cried and ducked and pleaded, he was aware that there was behind this savage beating, the worst he ever endured, something coldly and terribly restrained and disciplined. He had, little Jack in Rhode Island, been playing with matches.

General Pershing had been in the little constricted familylike U.S. Army for, including his West Point time, more than thirty years; and from all over the world, from its members and their women, and from others, there poured forth more than a thousand attempts to say what was in people's minds.

> Our beloved friend: All day my thoughts have been with you and the remembrance of those we loved, together in that little happy span of days in Japan. How peopled is my garden with their shadows, Helen and sweet baby Margaret and Anne! I think of Frances with the grateful consciousness that we came to understand and love each other in those happy days. My dear friend—if I have hurt you with this expression of my heart and thoughts, in this forgive me. It seems as if I have been choking with the grief of it. I have wanted to cry it out to you.

> Words fail . . . Appalling loss . . . May God help you to bear it. . . . This awful tragedy . . . How we wish we could comfort you. . . . I pray that Divine Love may find a way to make this trial a little easier for you to bear. . . . God give you strength in your hour of need. . . . I can scarcely put pen to paper. I wish, my dear friend, I could comfort you. Warren is your solution.

People wrote of Frankie coming with a rose to the Fort McKinley hospital to greet a friend's newborn; of how dear and kind she had been to a sick and miserable army wife alone on a journey to the Philippines. They wished they could do or say more to alleviate the suffering of this sorely

wrung heart. That he must accept this decree of Providence with the for-
titude of a soldier. He heard from the Japanese ambassador, former presi-
dent Roosevelt, playmates of the girls signing themselves Your Little
Friend, the governor of Texas, the Speaker of the House of Representatives, people in the American consular service in Bombay, in the Canal
Zone, on Corregidor Island, former University of Nebraska cadets,
Philippine Scouts, Senator Henry Cabot Lodge, from Fort Meade, South
Dakota, the Depot Quartermaster's Office in Boston, the Sixth Infantry in
Macon, Georgia, and former president Caroline Hazard of Wellesley re-
membering Frankie's speech at the Off-Campus Rally: "And in thirty-six
hours that radiant spirit was gone, gone with her three little daughters!"

> The Service mourns with you. . . . Oh! dear friend, she was so young,
> so fair, so gentle and kindly, and the sweet innocent children. To be
> snatched away so suddenly. I am numb with misery. I feel that never
> again in this life can I be "Auntie Horne" to anyone. . . . Our Savior
> said: "What I do thou knowest not now, but thou shalt know here-
> after." Job in the presence of the great mystery could only say,
> "Though he slay me, yet will I trust in him." . . . What can I say to a
> man so bereft as yourself? So fearfully alone! What can anyone say?
> Those pleasant days at home; and now the blackness of this night!

He must go through storm and darkness now, the wreck of home and
hopes, people wrote, Mrs. Arthur MacArthur, Sec. of the Treasury
William Gibbs McAdoo and his wife who was President Wilson's daughter, classmates from the state normal school at Kirksville and the days of
his young manhood, and from Cheyenne, "Dear General Pershing and
little Warren, In behalf of the boys and girls in the Churchill school who
knew and loved Helen and Anne—" with the signatures of three teachers.

> Great God! Words fail me to express my feelings. A lump in the
> throat, a numbness in the head. I can only say, May you have strength
> for the boy's sake. . . . Dear old John, we can think of nothing else.

Great bereavement; overwhelming affliction; and from a young student teacher at Mary Margaret's school a description of how on the first
day of the session the little girl wore a lavender dress and so to the young

student teacher became Wisteria. Mary Margaret fitted pegs in holes, traced geometrical forms, talked with the other children, carefully washed her hands when told to do so. And then of a morning, "My little Wisteria did not come."

> Thank God you have your dear boy left. May he be your joy and blessing. . . . Tragic calamity . . . Our bright, cheery Frank . . . Inexpressible sorrow . . . Tell little Warren, Peggy sends her love. . . . Dear John, every friend you have sorrows with you. That makes many mourners. . . . The why of such we cannot understand. Sufficient it is to have faith that it will be all right—sometime—somewhere.

He went back to Fort Bliss in El Paso with his son, his spinster sister May coming along. Pershing was about to turn fifty-five. The marriage had lasted ten years. Endlessly he blamed himself for applying the flammable varnish; it seemed for a time all he talked about. But the matter was not discussed in front of his son. The fire was never mentioned. Warren Pershing in all his life never heard a word from his father on what had happened in the Presidio in the early morning hours of August 27, 1915, not then, not in adolescence, not in maturity as the father of the general's two grandsons. Warren in those Fort Bliss days was surrounded by his father's people he had known and grown up among back in the Philippines, Lieutenant Collins, Lt. Richard Paddock his cousin, Johnson the coachman, Lanckton the orderly. But everything on the border was temporary, including the large number of troops accumulated there for the unrest just across the line in Ciudad Juarez and all the way south. He needed a permanent home. It was decided such would be offered by Aunt May and Aunt Elizabeth Butler, who lived together in the Lincoln, Nebraska, house left to Aunt Bess by her late husband. Warren went off to begin his new life.

His father, always a hard worker, became even more so as he drilled his Eighth Brigade. Withdrawn, more coldly businesslike than in the past, he jumped on mistakes, a schoolmaster in uniform. He was fearsomely lonely. Nothing connected him to the family life he had loved save letters from Nebraska. *Dear Papa, I hope you are having a nice time. I was promoted to second grade to-day. We have hard words. In our book. I take a music lesson every day. I send you all my love and kisses. Warren Pershing.* The boy's seventh birthday approached. "Last year his dear mother had a party for him and his sisters were there," the general wrote Frankie's father. "This year his aunties will have a party for him but it will be vastly different." Aunt May was asked to give him a bicycle in his father's name. She wrote of how the boy hung a stocking outside his door when going to bed, and got up early and came running down to his aunts to show what he had found in the stocking. At his place at the table he found new handkerchiefs, neckties, clothes, cuff buttons, and things Anne Orr Boswell had sent. There was also a letter from Warren's father. It said a bicycle would soon be delivered. "O, he just jumped up and danced when he found that he was to have a wheel," Aunt May wrote her brother on the border. "I never saw a child so delighted. Well, the bicycle was sent out about noon. It is a Ray-Cycle and is considered first class in every way. It cost $22.50. He is not able to ride it alone yet but is learning. Of course, I have to restrict him and he is very good about minding." A party began at three. There was a cake with his name in pink icing across the top, and ice cream and candy for his guests, new friends made in his new life. "Warren served every child himself before he sat down and played the host to perfection. They all had a beautiful time and I think Warren was the happiest boy I ever saw." Already mother and sisters were fading into vague memory. Warren sent a sample of the invitations he had typed himself and an accompanying letter with numbered lines:

1. *Dear Papa*
2. *To-day is my Birth*
3. *day. Aunt May got*
4. *a new wheel for me. I*
5. *thank you very much.*
6. *I had a nice Party*
7. *with 25 children.*
   A kiss. Papa I love you.
      Warren Pershing.

By then, mid-1916, the general's letters back were on stationery marked Headquarters Punitive Expedition, U.S. Army, In the Field, Mexico.

⇥ III ⇤

THE COMMANDER

→ 11 ←

In March 1916 the former mayor of Cleveland was appointed as new secretary of war. President Wilson's choice was esteemed an odd one, for so ardent a pacifist was Newton D. Baker that it was said he once declined the leadership of Ohio's Boy Scouts on the basis that he would have nothing to do with so militaristic a body. He was jockey-sized, an eyeglass-wearing and mild-mannered soul who when first seen with the weather-beaten horsemen comprising the army's officer corps was often taken for an attending clerk or stenographer. Baker was given little time to get acquainted with his new duties, for on the day he accepted his post the United States was thrown into a crisis involving his area of responsibility, the military. Pancho Villa had taken it into his head to go rampaging into American territory and into the tiny hamlet of Columbus, New Mexico, there to shoot up the town, set fires, and send a great "¡Viva!" into the desert air. Two months earlier he had yanked more than a dozen Americans off a Chihuahua train, stripped them naked, shot them dead, and run off with all they had.

Why the Columbus raid? The reason was never fully explained. It was Pancho Villa's way. The marauders galloped off, bodies left in the sandy streets of the little settlement set in the flat and dusty and bleached, unshadowed land of shimmeringly hot and dry winds, sage-bush and rattlesnakes. It was the last straw for the Americans. For years *pronunciamentos* of *presidente* and *caudillo* were followed by constant fighting, confiscations, irregular armies battling each other, bullet-pocked walls, expropriation of American property in Mexico—and now this. President Wilson dreaded getting involved in Mexico's problems. But the Columbus matter could not be let go. A long-standing treaty permitting troops of both Mexico and the United States to enter one another's territories in pursuit of "barbarians"—Indians—would be utilized: America would pursue the band or bands that had so disturbed its peace. "I suppose," Secretary of War Baker said to a group of officers whose acquaintance he had made only hours before, "if we are going to send an expedition, the first thing to be decided is who is to command it." He himself had no suggestions, hardly knowing the names of any officers save the ones just introduced to him. One of them was Assistant Chief of Staff Tasker H. Bliss, who spoke of the Eighth Brigade leader. Pershing would be a logical choice, Bliss told Baker. Baker said, "If there is no difference of opinion on that subject, we will consider it settled." Orders went out from Washington. Above all things, Pershing must not get involved in a real war with Mexico. Across the Atlantic, Europe was in flames, with the great Battle of Verdun just under way. America could not get bogged down south of its border. Pershing must walk on eggs.

He gathered cavalry, infantry, and field artillery to be formed into two parallel columns seeking Pancho Villa. Trains filled with troops, hustlers, adventurers, prostitutes, some traveling on flatcars, poured into a Columbus that previously was innocent even of electricity but that now suddenly possessed newspapers, hotels, saloons, gambling halls, bordellos, keno parlors, acres of tents on rocky areas amid prickly pear cactus and thorny mesquite by the railroad tracks running through what passed for the center of town. The Old West gathered for its final moment in the sun, old-time trappers and prospectors hiring out to the army as guides through uncharted Chihuahua, Apaches who knew the area, gunfighters looking to sign on, muleteers and college boys and taxi drivers, assorted hands who wanted to exchange a seat on a cow pony for one behind a steering wheel on one of thirty trucks swiftly purchased. An officer of field artillery was put in charge of the trucks. He had never driven anything in his life. He got hold of an automobile, took three lessons, learned more or less how to move the machine from one point to another. He likened gas, oil, and water to oats, hay, and water, held "stables" every evening with "feed" for his trucks. The First Areo Squadron, Aviation Section, Signal Corps, arrived, canvas-and-wood-covered Curtis JN-2's, Jennies, their pilots equipped with yokes to rest on their shoulders for use in banking a plane into a turn. The pilots carried pistols. There were no other armaments.

Pershing's traveling headquarters would consist of two clerks, an orderly, a cook, a couple of officer-aides, and a few trailing journalists from the Sheldon Hotel bar in El Paso. One officer not detailed to accompany the group camped outside of Pershing's Fort Bliss quarters and never permitted him to pass without begging for assignment. "Everyone wants to go," Pershing said. "Why should I favor you?"

"Because I want to go more than anyone else," replied Lt. George S. Patton, Jr. One morning Patton's phone rang and Pershing asked when he could report for duty. Patton replied that his things were already packed. "I'll be goddamned," Pershing said. He had been reminded of himself as a lieutenant when, told he must stay at his West Point assignment while others went off to the invasion of Cuba, he desperately pulled strings to join them. And he was fond of Patton. Even more so was he of Patton's sister Anne, always addressed as "Nita." They had gotten to know one another at Fort Bliss when she made a protracted visit from California to her brother and her brother's wife. She was twenty-nine. Previously something of a wallflower, and all her life in the shadow of Georgie, as her brother was called, Nita Patton suddenly blossomed at Fort Bliss. "Beaus galore," she wrote her mother. Of General Pershing: "He is awfully good-looking."

A week after the Villa raid, the two columns moved, Pershing leading on horseback. It was March 15, 1916. All Columbus turned out to cheer. All spit and polish, Pershing offered salutes. His health had sadly declined in the wake of Frankie's death, and he had thought of resigning his commission, but the sudden call to duty invigorated him. He was certainly presented with a challenge. Trapping Villa in the limitless deserts or in the mountains of the Sierra Madre was as likely a prospect, he said privately, as locating a rat in a cornfield or a needle in a haystack.

The Mexicans met on his way, he knew, would be as anxious for him to capture Pancho as had been the denizens of Sherwood Forest that the sheriff of Nottingham do the same for Robin Hood. Villa was unpredictable and really not normal in his casual manner of taking life and taking women—but at least he was Mexican, and few countrymen of his preferred the gringos. And everyone knew that the last time the Yankees came to Mexico, in 1846, the result was that Mexican territories were taken to make up four American states.

Pershing headed south through great plumes of dust raised by the hooves of the horses from ground that had not seen a drop of rain in months, equipment thumping and thudding and squeaking, sabers and pistols and pennons and the horse-drawn artillery pieces, the trucks and a few touring sedans groaning in the rear, laden as they were with forage for the horses and rations and ammunition for the men, great slabs of bacon strapped side by side with drums of gasoline, tins of hardtack, bedding, rifles, and bags of water for the steaming radiators. Men wore goggles and tied bandanas over their mouths. The heat during the day could rise to 110° or 115°F; it was freezing at night.

He pushed his men 140 miles in the first thirty-six hours. Villa was somewhere to the south. Perhaps the Americans could get behind him. Vague desert trails ran out, and the men negotiated by compass or by the purple mountains in the distance. Pershing did not sleep under cover, but lay on the ground in a bedroll. Wearing a four-dented campaign hat, he bathed naked when he could in half-dried trickling streams or water holes, the region's intensely alkaline water making lathering up difficult and sometimes blistering the skin. No one ever saw him anything but clean-shaven and usually wearing a tie. He split his leading elements to fan out seeking Pancho, men going up into mountain fastnesses while leading their horses for hours and pack trains following, the trails inaccessible to wheeled transport. Even on the flat, trucks came to rocky points where wheels hopelessly spun and soldiers massed together to shove. Rattlesnakes seeking warmth came to your sleeping bag in hopes of making you, it was said, a snake-warmer. Lieutenant Patton killed two one morning with a pistol as people asked why he hadn't used a saber—he had been named Master of the Sword at Fort Riley and detailed to teach his specialty there. (Georgie replied that an officer should be proficient in all arms, and additionally sabers were for use when mounted.)

Overhead the Jennys took pictures while taking rifle fire from the ground, the shooters Mexicans who might be allied with Villa, or an independent band, or freelancers, or very likely identified with what was called the de facto government. The Americans came across men in varied uniforms, some in the blue with red piping of Porfirio Diaz's old *federales*, some in the now-tattered white of his *rurales*, others with nothing but belts filled with cartridges and bandoliers slung across their chests to identify them as military adherents of one group or another adding their bit to Mexico's chaos. Those who definitely followed Pancho Villa wore hair-woven hatbands with a little silver buckle. Every Mexican save for those actually firing at the gringos was by Pershing's orders to be treated with patience and restraint. Under no conditions must the Punitive Expedition incite such feelings as might bring on a general uprising of the people.

General Pershing had spent years negotiating with Moros, and now his diplomatic skills were needed for dealing with Mexicans. Once as he sat with a tiny group detached from other elements of his spread-out command, a couple of dozen men, a band of some two hundred armed Mexicans appeared. They circled the little camp. Pershing rubbed his chin. The situation wasn't very good, the reporter Frank Elser of the *New York Times* unnecessarily told himself. The Mexicans' leader, General Luis Herrera, who had fought with, and then against, Pancho Villa, came up. A Pershing orderly ceremoniously took charge of Herrera's horse; Pershing's cook swept an area clean of litter and offered empty gas tins for the two generals to sit on. Herrera had fine white teeth and spoke in a low voice, Elser noted. He wanted to know how many Americans there were in Mexico, how far south they thought to go, and how long they would be staying. Pershing in turn asked how many Mexican troops were hunting Villa, and where they were. Herrera bowed with Latin courtesy and took his departure. The next time Americans ran into his men, there was shooting.

The cavalry of the Punitive Expedition performed some of the most extraordinary marching feats in the world's history of mounted operations as it sped into Mexico. Soon the army's line of communication and supply back to Columbus was longer than that of Sherman on his Georgia–South Carolina March to the Sea, five hundred miles past wrecked railroad stations shot up during the years of irregular warfare, and blown bridges, through little one-street towns where the troops negotiated purchases of frijoles, tortillas, goat brains, soft drinks, half-candied bananas in thin wood boxes, *huevos rancheros*, cactus candy, cinnamon-flavored chocolate, cane sugar, enchiladas and tamales sold from trays women carried on their heads or displayed on little three-legged tables in rutted roads before adobe houses by tinkling fountains. The fact that the Americans paid with good money was astonishing to vendors often forced to accept cheap-paper bills printed by bands carrying their printing presses along with them. Pershing looked wonderful, reporters thought, the inspiring picture of how a cavalryman looks and acts. He got along on little sleep, often rising before his men to sit with maps and papers or to censor the dispatches reporters got the Jenny pilots to fly out to a telegraph station. He munched soda crackers, went back to smoking after a decade of doing without. He was easy with the newspapermen, one of them remembering how he asked the general where Villa was, anyway. "Your guess is as good as mine," Pershing answered, taking a swig of tequila.

Once in the little ranch settlement of San Geronimo, nearly three hundred miles from Columbus and seventy-five hundred feet up in the sierras, cold murderous, snow falling, his little group stretched a bull hide between two poles and built a fire in its lee. There they crouched, grimy, pestered by the blowing sand. There were thirty of them, hired scouts and guides whose directions were always questionable in the light of what Pancho would do if he ever got hold of them, reporters, a handful of soldiers. There was no tent for the general commanding, no table, no folding chair. Dinner was hardtack fried in bacon grease—some fish taken from a stream had proved not to be trout, as hoped, but suckers. Dusk approached. Pershing was sitting on an empty box. A rickety wagon came into sight carrying four peons with musical instruments and a woman with children. The musicians got out, a fiddler, a guitar player, a cornetist, and a man with a huge bass viola. No one said anything. The men began to play and sing, very sweet and very sad Mexican love songs. Then they played rollicking dance tunes, and couldn't resist "La Cucaracha," the unofficial anthem of Villa's people. The listeners all applauded and yelled, "¡Más!" With a battered sombrero American silver was collected and for an encore the players offered "Adeleta," singing it in the high, wailing, falsetto Mexican manner. Pershing got up and moved away to stand by himself. The Mexicans stood shuffling, fearful, the Americans saw, that the *jefe* was somehow offended. Reassuring looks were offered and they strummed their instruments, awaiting a suggestion. "Play 'La Paloma,'" someone said, and they began and then halted suddenly, for Capt. James Collins had raised a hand commanding them to stop. "That was a favorite tune of Mrs. Pershing," he told the other Americans in a low tone.

Everyone looked at the general, standing apart. He came closer. "I liked that," he said. "Why did they stop? Tell them to play 'La Paloma,' please, for me." They did and then went on their way, the Americans standing by the fire and watching as they vanished into the darkness of the valley.

Villa was dead, assassinated, cremated, he was dying, he was gone, he was going, Pershing was assured. In fact he lived on, and the Americans never got him. But the Punitive Expedition had been sent south, its orders read, to break up the band or bands that had plagued the border, Villa's name not mentioned for fear that if he ran away to the ends of the earth the U.S. Army would have to pursue him there. At least what was required had been accomplished. The days of the Villistas firing in the air from moving trains as they sat dangling their legs out of boxcar sides, their goats and chickens tethered on the tops, shouts for Villa aides rising—"¡*Viva la brigada Francisco Portillo!*" or "¡*Viva la brigada José Ortiz!*"—were over. Many of his people had in the day's shifting-loyalty manner of Mexico gone over to Pancho's enemies, or were dead. The important Villista colonel Julio Cárdenas was dead, for Georgie Patton killed him with a pistol at a shoot-out in a walled hacienda along with another man. A third was killed by Patton's soldiers. The bodies were strapped onto the fenders of a Dodge touring car like deer bagged during a hunting expedition and brought back to camp. After that Pershing referred to Georgie as The Bandit.

But it was evident that Villa was beyond reach and that to continue aggressively to seek him might end the complicated family fights of the Mexicans and unite them all in violent opposition to the Punitive Expedition and so involve the United States in an all-out war. Frank Elser handed Pershing a dispatch to the *New York Times* for the commander's censorship: "General Pershing from a military standpoint for the time being has come to the end of his line," it began.

"Is that your deduction?" Pershing asked. The reporter nodded. "All right, send it." He knew Elser was right. The Americans settled down in isolated way station outposts and in the main camp at Colonia Dublán, some two hundred miles south of Columbus. The summer of 1916 came and went. In September Brigadier General Pershing was given a second star. His West Point classmate T. Bentley Mott sent congratulations from his military attaché post in Paris, and in reply the new major general referred in sad, oblique fashion to what had happened back at the Presidio: "All the promotion in the world would make no difference now." In California at her parents' home Nita Patton did not see it that way: "Dear Major General Pershing: Do you feel horribly dignified now, or can you still smile occasionally?"

November came and with it the presidential election back home to the north. Warren was very interested in the Wilson-Hughes contest, Aunt May wrote her brother in Colonia Dublán, and had set up a box so that all the household could cast ballots, and then found out where the real polling places were and went about and observed what went on and came back to tell all about it. Christmas was coming, and the general asked May to do his shopping, mostly candy to be sent to the children of friends, and boxes of fruit candy for their wives. She was to get a tree for Warren and in the boy's name send presents to Frankie's father and stepmother, and the children of Frankie's brother Fred and Fred's wife, Bessie. Would she please send cards in the general's name to some one hundred people on a list from the preceding year? He had left it with her. And please append his name to any presents she gave their mutual relatives? For himself, he was busy with preparations for a Christmas celebration with his soldiers.

By his orders a great tree was constructed out of small firs. It towered sixty-five feet in the air and had hundreds of lights which flicked on after fireworks shot up into the sky. In the glare of massed truck headlights the American flag was seen to be floating from the top of the tree. A soldiers' chorus of four hundred that had practiced for weeks burst into "Joy to the World." For each of the ten thousand men in Mexico there was a gift. NONE IS OVERLOOKED IN DISTRIBUTION OF PRESENTS, headlined the *Washington Post*. Christmas dinner was a feast, with the men singing "The Battle Hymn of the Republic" and "America." Pershing's army by then, after nine months in Mexico, had worked out methods for improving truck performance and the use of tractors for pulling guns, trained drivers and wireless operators, created air photography experts, and was completely drilled in unit exercises that its commander devised and whose results he rigorously studied. It was a brilliant little army so strongly disciplined in health matters that its incidence of disease was as nothing to what afflicted the troops of the Civil and Spanish Wars.

Pershing knew by name every scout, knew after a lightning storm how many horses were hit, the limit a wagon could be expected to carry; accepted that regulars were tough, hard-bitten, rootless save for the service, and required prostitutes, whose housing he arranged. He was approachable, made up his mind quickly, gave completely clear orders. He could be reasoned with by his subordinate officers. For reporters he always had questions about what was going on and was himself able to tell them what was fact and what was only the nosebag gossip of the picket line, or latrine rumor. When papers arrived from the States he scanned them quickly and kept up with what was happening in the outside world and in the European war. In later years, when Pancho Villa turned into a folk hero, Mexican legend had it that Pershing ran away dressed in woman's clothing; in actuality the commander and his columns crossed over the international border barbed-wire fence at Columbus on February 5, 1917, bands playing "When Johnny Comes Marching Home," Chinese who had served the troops as launderers and cooks coming along for fear of what Mexicans might do to them if they stayed. The Punitive Expedition passed into history. Columbus lapsed into the somnolent place it had always been save for its brief moment of excitement. Pancho Villa was shot to death from ambush six years later.

Pershing's next assignment was commander of the Southern Department, with headquarters at Fort Sam Houston. First he went off on leave to the California estate of Georgie Patton's people. "Nita may rank us yet," Georgie told his wife, Beatrice, an heiress whose money joined to his made him known as the richest officer in the army, the owner of strings of polo ponies and a yacht. Nita made Georgie very nervous as he saw his commanding officer paying court to a sister always in his shadow. (Her first memory was of portraying the horse who dragged the body of Hector around the walls of Troy, a dead sparrow representing Hector with Georgie, of course, being Achilles.) Georgie fidgeted nervously when she was with Pershing, Nita reported to their mother, "so afraid I will say the wrong thing." Her mother was all for the romance, while her father was less enthusiastic, feeling the general was socially beneath a young woman springing from Virginia aristocracy the menfolk of whose immediate family, himself and Georgie, he regarded as the nearest American equivalent to noblemen. Georgie's wife, Beatrice, less nose-in-the-air, accustomed herself to the idea that she would become Pershing's sister-in-law, and had her little daughters send him cards and letters in Mexico which, Georgie saw, reminded him of his own daughters and filled his eyes with tears. Beatrice boldly asked him what he felt for Georgie's sister and he said he was "crazy about Nita." Perhaps he meant it at the moment he said it. Beatrice asked, "Do you think it would be a good thing for Nita if she married you?"

"Yes. I do." When he left California for Fort Sam Houston it was with a definite understanding that they would wed. A month later, President Wilson asked Congress for a declaration of war on Germany, and Senator Warren telegraphed: WIRE ME TODAY WHETHER AND HOW MUCH YOU SPEAK, READ AND WRITE FRENCH. Pershing telegraphed back that he had studied it at West Point—he did not discuss the progress he made with it there—and had much refreshed his knowledge of the language when he and Frankie worked on it in Tours in 1908 during their return from the Orient via Europe. He then spoke it quite fluently and could read and write it well, and could easily reacquire his then-proficiency in it, he told the senator, an estimation of the past and projection of the future he later defined as "comparatively accurate." There followed orders to report to the chief of staff, Maj. Gen. Hugh L. Scott, at the War Department. He wrote May in Lincoln:

I am ordered to Washington for consultation. No one knows what it means. May, do you remember Miss Patton? She is here for a few days. Well, May dear, she is the finest and best woman. I had thought I could never love, but she has made a place all her own.

I am telling you all this, May, you and Sister, *very confidentially.* So please do not mention it to a single soul in the world. I have been so wholly broken-hearted and bereft. It will make a home for little Warren.

He went with Capt. James L. Collins through New Orleans to Washington, where General Scott told him he would command a scraped-together division showing the flag in Europe. He went in to meet the secretary of war and was taken aback to find him so very youthful-looking and "diminuitive." Two days later Baker said the plans had been changed. Instead of taking a division of thousands of men to Europe, Pershing would leave almost immediately with a tiny staff. It would be the nucleus for a future great army. He would command that army. He would command it with minimum interference from Washington. Baker would give him but two orders. The first was to go. The second would be to come home. Now the first was issued.

With a group of fewer than two hundred men—officers, enlisted personnel, civilian clerks, and interpreters—and three newspaper reporters, the commander in chief of the American Expeditionary Forces took a train to New York and the Astor Hotel in Times Square, the city's traditional place for officers, where reduced-rate accommodations were offered. The Patton family had come East to see off Nita's intended and Georgie, who would command the headquarters company of motorcyclists, drivers, signalmen, guards, and mechanics, forty-six men. It seemed likely to the aide Captain Collins, going along in the same capacity in which he had served the general in the Philippines, at Fort Bliss, and in Mexico, that an engagement announcement might be made before the sailing. There was none. In civilian clothing with a straw hat, Pershing went with Collins to the Governor's Island headquarters of Maj. Gen. J. Franklin Bell, commander of the army's Eastern Department. Former head of all Philippine Islands troops, former army chief of staff, he had in years past done everything for the new commander in chief of the American Expeditionary Forces. As soon as the appointment had been announced, Bell wrote asking for European service under his former subordinate. Now face to face, he repeated his plea. In Pershing's eyes Bell was an officer and gentleman the superior of whom the U.S. Army never produced. But Bell was old, and, Pershing saw, not well. He was noncommittal about offering an answer to Bell's request. The little group of men who once ashore would constitute hardly more than a landing party assembled for transport on the government tug *Thomas Patten* from the White Star pier down the harbor to Gravesend Bay and the SS *Baltic*. The wife of the army chief of staff was present to see off a group that included her son, David Scott. He would never return. Her husband, like Bell, had desperately wanted service abroad. But General Scott, like Bell, was old. His first assignment out of West Point had seen him serving with the Seventh Cavalry and occupying the drawing room of the quarters just vacated by the grieving Mrs. George A. Custer, she departing Fort Abraham Lincoln to live out almost sixty years expressing reverence for her husband. Scott was of that era, Libby Custer's contemporary of those days of the Old Army whose passing had been marked, although not universally comprehended, in the doings of the Punitive Expedition of trucks, field telephones, and airplanes. Scott had hoped for a moment that Baker would choose him to lead the Americans in Europe. Told it would be Pershing, he manfully said that the secretary could not have made a better choice.

The day was raw and cold and with a driving rain, May 28, 1917. Hardly more than three months earlier, Pershing had been drilling his men in the sands of Colonia Dublán. Now, thought his chief of staff, Major of Cavalry James G. Harbord, he led his tiny group on a trip no less romantic than that undertaken by Jason and the Argonauts, who sought the Golden Fleece. *Thomas Patten* made *Baltic,* and the party went on board. They slipped out headed for Nantucket in rainy darkness, paper covering each porthole for fear a German submarine would see a light, and with smoking on deck strictly forbidden. The general had a spacious stateroom to himself, with Harbord in the adjoining one. All night long the ship's whistle blew for engulfing fog, a blast sounding every three minutes. At nine in the morning they made the lighthouse on Nantucket Shoals. Classes in French were held at ten in the morning and four in the afternoon, and there was a good deal of talk about submarines. (The crew advised the wearing of warm clothing if *Baltic* went down, and the taking along of a flask of brandy.) They would soon be picking up an escort of U.S. Navy destroyers, but wore civilian clothing as they entered the danger zone, for if *Baltic* was sunk it could be expected that a sub commander would fire upon uniformed lifeboat occupants. *Rowan* and *Tucker* came into sight to take up station on either side of *Baltic,* and the weather turned fine. Each day the general worked with his staff on the formation and training and equipping of what he felt would eventually become a million-man force he must create virtually from scratch. He wrote for dispatch upon arrival in England, "Your papa is going to miss his little boy very much and it may be a very long time again before I see you."

Late springtime's green shores of Wales appeared, and the American destroyers fell away as *Baltic* went up St. George's Channel to Liverpool and dropped anchor in the Mersey and in the morning docked. Lt. Gen. Sir William Pitcairn Campbell, K.C.B., came up the gangplank, his selection as first welcomer to the Americans revelatory of what was always true, that the British knew long historical memory; for Sir William's ancestor Major Pitcairn had on April 19, 1775, faced another group of Americans, at Lexington, and cried, "Disperse, ye rebels!"

With the Liverpool lord mayor and lady mayoress and others Sir William invited the travelers to debark, preceding them down the gangplank to be on shore where formally he turned about and offered greetings. The Third Battalion of the Royal Welsh Fusiliers was drawn up as a guard of honor. In front was the unit mascot, a white goat with a silver plate hanging between its horns. The regiment had charged at Bunker Hill. Among the rigidly at-attention left-shoulder-arms soldiers there could have been very few of Great Britain's well set-up prewar Tommy Atkins, for those were dead in the retreat from Mons in 1914 or decaying in the mud along the path of 1916's Somme offensive, the Old Contemptibles, so a remark of Kaiser Wilhelm had dubbed them. Pershing went down the line of the new men replacing those of before-the-war gone to glory for king and country, gloved, sword at his side, perfectly turned out by the vigilant Corporal Lanckton, to both British and American eyes the model soldier, perfect posture, groomed, attentive, trim, smart, showing no touches of military gaudiness, the British reporters felt. On his breast was a single row of ribbons for Indian, Cuban, and Philippine campaigns. A band played "The Star-Spangled Banner" followed by "God Save the King."

A royal train stood ready. At London's Euston Station dignitaries waited, American ambassador and British field marshal. There followed audiences with the king, dinner with Lloyd George, Balfour, Lords Derby, Curzon and French, Admiral Jellicoe, Chief of the Imperial General Staff Robertson, Churchill, Smuts, all the civil and military greats of the home islands and the empire. Officers of the American party were lodged at the Savoy; the enlisted personnel commanded by Captain Patton were in the Tower of London chamber where Sir Walter Raleigh spent his last night.

Services in Westminster Abbey where reposed the flags of regiments gone to the war, left there in accordance with ancient custom for safekeeping; attendance at the Hippodrome's musical extravagance *Zig Zag* where before "God Save the King" the orchestra played "The Star-Spangled Banner"; King George telling America's general it had always been his dream to see the two great English-speaking peoples, the Anglo-Saxon race, as he called it, uniting in a battle to save civilization; talks, receptions, conferences, a visit to Savile Row for fittings for new uniforms, a call upon Parliament, a march-past by British troops; and then departure from Charing Cross for Folkestone and a channel boat for France and the war.

→ 12 ←

On June 13, 1917, at about ten in the morning, the American reporter
Floyd Gibbons took note of a little boy in a red stocking cap that to Gibbons's eyes seemed not unlike the Liberty caps worn by the stormers of
the Bastille in 1789. The boy was standing in shallow water at the Port of
Boulogne and yelling, "*Vive l'Amérique!*" From a ship coming in, Maj.
Gen. John J. Pershing tendered a salute to the first person welcoming him
to France. On shore were officials, officers, long lines of *poilus* standing
rigid at the Present. There was a brief tour of the city and then the train to
Paris. For a long time the French had made no occasion of the arrival in
their capital of visiting dignitaries; they came with no public notice. It
would be different for the Americans who now were here, so Paris said,
and Marseilles and Lyons and Nice, to save France from the Boche who
killed Son and Father and bled France white in a thousand tragedies
along the Western Front.

So the train was timed to arrive at the Gare du Nord at six-thirty in the
evening when the office workers and factory people would be in the
streets heading home and able to see that succor for suffering France in
horizon blue had come in American khaki. The train halted before a red
carpet. Waiting were marshal of France and United States ambassador
and a great mass of people who broke into such cheers that, the reporter
Gibbons thought, the sooty girders of the station quivered. The band of

the Garde Républicaine burst into "The Star-Spangled Banner" and followed with "La Marseillaise." Pershing rode in an open car with Minister of War Paul Painlevé. Station gates were battered down as people poured out, and when he saw the sea of humanity in the streets Pershing became stunned and shocked. Perhaps nothing similar had ever occurred in Paris, certainly not in the life of anyone living. Flowers bought by shopgirls from their meager earnings, or by war workers, or soldiers' wives, simply poured from windows. Little American flags waved everywhere in people's hands. Windows blossomed with them. Children screamed from the trees they had climbed; and on the sidewalks their elders wept. ALL PARIS OUT TO SEE PERSHING, the papers headlined. AMERICAN GENERAL AND HIS STAFF PELTED WITH FLOWERS. Trapped by the rampaging crowds, a line of ambulances carrying wounded poilus from a hospital train came to a halt. Here was symbolism, reflected the American Embassy's Clementine Phelps, looking at the pale and broken French soldiery and then at the upright American general: the war as it had been and would be.

The line of automobiles crept through great masses, motors overheating at the slow pace, to the Place de la Concorde and the Hôtel Crillon. A magnificent suite was waiting, filled with banks of flowers. Crowds surged outside calling for the deliverer of France. Pershing stepped onto the suite's balcony to bow and smile, women below thinking him very handsome with his silver-gray hair and bronzed complexion and straight posture, carrying himself so well and looking younger than his fifty-six years. Massed on the balcony, with the Tuileries Garden in view and the long stretch of the Champs-Élysées and the gold dome of Les Invalides, were Allied flags on staffs. A breeze caught the French standard. He caught it and touched it to his lips.

The next day he was taken to the Invalides past saluting old men who had gone to the Crimea before he was born, one of whose hands he took to say it was a great honor to greet an old soldier of glorious service. He was taken into the vast rotunda hung with battle flags and then down to the crypt. Marshal Joffre, who in 1914 saved France along the Marne, was along. With Pershing he went to where a bluish light streamed down on a red porphyry sarcophagus and tinged it purple. A massive door was unlocked, and Joffre and the American and his staff silently went down a flight of marble stairs to where on an altar surmounted by a cabinet of glass and gold lay the golden chain Napoleon Bonaparte wore when crowned emperor. By it was a *chapeau* worn at the Battle of Eylau, and the sword of Austerlitz. Joffre saluted. The others followed suit. An aged general took out a golden key and slowly unlocked the cabinet and took the sword, and faced about and holding it before him walked to Pershing with slow steps. John McA. Palmer of Pershing's staff never knew a tenser moment in his life: "What a magnificent gesture! Here was France presenting her most sacred military symbol to the new American general. What would he do with it? Would he take it in his hands?" All kinds of thoughts flashed through Palmer's mind; the possibilities for the wrong move seemed all too prevalent. Everyone seemed in suspense save for Pershing, who stood at attention and then with no hesitation, not moving his hands from his sides, bent forward and kissed the sword hilt and then straightened up, at attention once more. "Magnificent!" exclaimed a French officer behind Palmer. The American military aviation pioneer Billy Mitchell thought that Pershing had shown that, untried, he did not feel worthy to take Napoleon's sword in his hands. The gesture was unforgettable, Mitchell thought.

There followed state dinners on Sèvres porcelain in rooms with Gobelin tapestries on the walls, attendance at the Opéra Comique to wild acclaim, a visit to the Chamber of Deputies where the members rose to their feet and cheered for moments on end, demonstrations of French airplanes, conferences on shipping and food, a pilgrimage to the Picpus Cemetery where he laid a wreath and where Col. Charles F. Stanton, Quartermaster Corps paymaster for the American Expeditionary Forces, something of an orator, Pershing knew, uttered the phrase always associated with the head of the AEF, although a thousand times he explained that he never said it: *Lafayette, we are here!*

Within a few days a couple of battalions of the newly thrown-together U.S. First Infantry Division arrived in France. Pershing by then had departed the Crillon—if he'd had to pay for the palatial temporary quarters, he remarked to Billy Mitchell, he'd be ten years meeting the bill— for the 73 rue de Varenne residence offered by Ogden Mills, heir of the

Comstock Lode's Darius Ogden Mills. Its rococo interior foamed with flamboyant bows of carved ribbons, gold brocade, great paintings, tapestry hangings, marble steps, and flowered rugs. Its garden, large enough to gallop a horse, put Major Harbord in mind of a dream of Paradise. (When Pershing's old friend of University of Nebraska days risen from struggling lawyer to rich banker and newly minted AEF officer came for dinner, the two sat at a marble table large enough for sixty and Charlie Dawes, as irrepressible, spirited, cheery, lively as he had been in their young manhoods, said, "John, when I contrast these barren surroundings with the luxuriousness of our early life in Lincoln, Nebraska, it does seem that a good man has no real chance in the world." "Don't it beat hell," Pershing replied.)

He was well housed, he had made a good impression, he was well liked by all who met him in France, and the children referred to him by a pleasing joke on his name, Père Sing, Father Monkey; the British commander Field Marshal Sir Douglas Haig wrote his wife of him, "Quiet, gentlemanly bearing—so unusual for an American," and the enlistment stations back home were jammed with men signing up; but what role was he to play in the Great War? In his first days abroad the Allies had seemed to expect that he would immediately be followed by massed legions. They appeared unable to comprehend that there existed a great continental power that, unlike the French, the Germans, the Russians, the Austro-Hungarians, had no great standing army and no ready-to-go reservists of the type for whose reception into depots Pershing had so admired when he was in Germany with Frankie and the children nine years earlier. When they got that clear in their minds they came up with a future use for the Americans that to their thinking was entirely logical. Germany had knocked Russia out of the fighting just as the Americans declared war. Very soon German divisions from the Eastern Front would be hurrying to the Western one. It could be expected there would be a German push across the ground contested in France and Belgium for three terrible trench-warfare years at what cost was well known. Now there was a new entrant into the Great War. The new entrant's officer corps had never handled large numbers of troops, it had no logistical backup, its air fleet consisted of fifty planes of which five were considered battleworthy under European conditions, it had no trench helmets, few rifles, no heavy field artillery, and its entire stock of accumulated ammunition would not suffice for the requirements of one day's firing for one regiment under Western Front conditions. The United States, Great Britain and France felt, should be regarded as a giant recruiting ground for the deplenished legions of His Majesty's forces and for the descendants of La Grande Armeé. Gathered into platoons, or companies of fifty or one hundred fifty men commanded by American lieutenants and captains, let them be inserted into British or French regiments for utilization as seemed best to commanders of long Western Front experience. There need be no intensive training for these soldiers, for the only way to learn to fight in this war, Paris and London believed, was to learn by doing. The only Americans needed in Europe, General Pershing was informed, were infantrymen and machine gunners. Let the Americans not bother themselves about majors and lieutenant colonels, and still less colonels or generals. The Allies would provide them. The Allies would also do the strategic and tactical thinking.

Nothing conceivable could appeal less to Pershing at the head of his corporal's guard. "The United States will put its troops on the battlefront when it shall have formed an army worthy of the American people," he announced a month after his arrival in Europe. Brave words, surely. But how much better, the British and French said, that he operate within the framework of established organizations. To wait for the Americans to produce their own equipped and formed army could invite disaster and a lost war. Pershing, they said, was a conductor with a baton but no orchestra, a symbol. His army was not even a skeleton army. He would be at building up regiment, division, corps, while the Germans perhaps marched through Paris and drove the British into the sea. Pershing was living in a dream, Marshals Ferdinand Foch and Sir Douglas Haig decided. Tragic delusions had seized him. He *must* feed his men into other countries' armies. King George came over to France to tell him that. But he could not agree. "I should have liked to argue with the king and set him right."

Unspoken was the concept that American officers were incapable of commanding men in European warfare. Who, after all, had they ever fought? Indians in the early days and later? Mexican half-breeds in

1846–48? Then one another in the Civil War, a matter that the past century's soldier perhaps the greatest in German history, Helmuth von Moltke, said was an affair of two armed mobs chasing one another about the countryside? Then the Spaniards in Cuba, relics of a decaying, played-out empire? *Moros?* The bandit Pancho Villa? An unpleasant tone came into British and French voices and an implication less pleasant still. "I tell you one thing," Pershing said, "I'm going to jump right down the throat of the next man who asks me if I think the Americans will really fight. *Fight?* Americans?"

He banged his fist down on the table. He was at breakfast with someone from the long ago. She had written upon his arrival in France. "Dear General Pershing, My father was Chancellor Canfield of the University of Nebraska, and when I was a little girl I was in your class in geometry and you gave me some fencing lessons." Little Dorothy Canfield had grown up to be the eminent author Dorothy Canfield Fisher. Her husband was driving ambulances for the French wounded and she was working with their war-blinded. They had lived abroad for many years. Her former teacher had come to France just in time, she wrote him. There was a limit to what flesh and endurance could stand. "Thank God you are here!"

They sat together and she saw that what long ago when he was the lieut had been "an irresistible, friendly smile" was veiled, and that "none of the charm of his humorous comradely familiarity was to be seen." He seemed to her hard, intent, stern, like a doctor called to a sickroom. He made no claims of what he would accomplish, and said that until he got more firsthand information he could by no means be sure that he or anyone else could beat the Germans. When she said the sight of him made her again the little girl of great faith and that now she felt the war was over, he replied, "Child, it's just begun!" She was reminded that morning at breakfast of her dead father and the home people she had not seen for long years. "He was all my country come to France, purposeful, not overconfident, fully aware, and *determined.*"

He did not mean to let others fool him, or fool himself, he said as he walked in the Mills mansion garden with the former war correspondent Frederick Palmer, in whose company he had tramped Manchurian hills a decade and more before, to whose tent he had come one rainy day when the Japanese fought the Russians. Palmer was now in U.S. Army uniform, a major of the tiny nucleus of the AEF—the pioneers, they called themselves. He would not scatter the men starting to come over in droves now, feed them into the winds bit by bit for foreign armies, Pershing said to Major Palmer. He would not fight until his troops were ready. When he had a massive and cohesive force trained to smash through the Germans and send them running and destroy them as they ran—then he would strike. The British and French, he said, were too wedded to trench warfare. That spoke of defensive warfare. It was foreign to American nature, tradition, inheritance. Who believed in that weren't going to get their hands on his soldiers. They might appeal to Washington, they might eventually secure his relief from command. It was not unlikely. Indeed, not a single commander in chief of any of the great European armies had held that position when the war began. So it might be that Pershing under Wilson, like McClellan under Lincoln, would form an army to be fought to victory by a successor, Grant in McClellan's case, someone else in Pershing's.

Meanwhile, he would do his work. He transferred General Headquarters, AEF, 150 miles to Chaumont, where the frontiers of Burgundy and Champagne touched those of Lorraine. The town was in the rolling country of the upper Marne and had known Caesar on campaign against the Franks. Domrémy was near, where Joan of Arc was born and where she first heard voices calling upon her to save France. Along the road from Paris, Napoleon had begun the campaign of 1814, and in Chaumont in what was called the House of the Three Kings the rulers of Austria, Russia, and Prussia had met after Waterloo. The Americans took over the barracks that had housed infantry and artillery regiments, long four-story red tile-roofed buildings enclosing a quadrangle. There was an ornamental gate, and through it staff cars came and went, and motorcycles, and an enormous olive-drab Locomobile limousine with double wheels in back for traction on the muddy French roads and a flag on the fender flying four stars indicative of the major general's temporary new rank. The commander in chief's second-floor office was bare of any decorations. His desk was very plain, the seats in the room severe. Nothing but maps were on the walls. He kept a window open even in poor weather, and the temperature seemed twenty degrees colder in his room than elsewhere, or so people said.

His living quarters were five miles away in an old castle, Château Val des Écoliers. The orderly Frank Lanckton was with him, and had a new duty: maintenance of the general's Sam Browne belt. It was a contrivance that served no function. Before arriving in Paris, Lanckton had never seen one. But the thing immediately seized Pershing when he saw European officers wearing it. The Sam Browne made a man stand up straight. It looked snappy, martial, it made one look alert, smart, keen, ready, at attention—a soldier. In the years to follow, Lanckton wrote, he put in days, weeks, months, whole terms of enlistment washing and scrubbing and scouring the leather so that it was softer and shinier than the finest women's gloves. Metal snaps and bolts glittered. Soon an order was issued that all AEF officers would wear the Sam Browne belt. Fewer than 5 percent of the AEF's eventual officer corps were regulars, with ninety-nine out of one hundred lieutenants and captains newly commissioned and entirely without military experience, but they were going to look and act like soldiers. So would the enlisted men. High choker collars would stay buttoned at all times. Leggings would be pipe-clayed and neatly wound. Everybody would be closely shaved, every day.

Pershing's desire for order and cleanliness appeared extreme to the streams of men soon coming to France after hasty training in America. In a small group such as the corps of cadets in Nebraska, or in the little encapsulated force in the Philippines or in Mexico, his rigid insistences were submerged in men's view of him as someone who had other, human, qualities. That was not so in France, where his army grew to number millions. He seemed to his legions cold, hard-bitten, unreasonable, petty, rigid. A great Locomobile would appear and the commander in chief emerged seeking the slightest sign of sloppy housekeeping in billets and to take harsh notice of muddy shoes or headgear not set right, to critically regard how men moved about and held themselves, to go up ladders and look at the barn-loft sleeping quarters, inspect weapons and note if a marching unit was strung out too thinly and if its horses and mules showed evidence of recent grooming. If an officer issued orders in his presence Pershing was alert to any sign of a poor command voice. He himself seemed immune to dirt or the slightest crease on his uniform, appearing to J. Lawton Collins, a recent West Point graduate and the younger brother of Capt. James L. Collins, to be a figure in his polished Peale boots "stunning, commanding," seemingly taller than when met with in the past, always straight-backed, square-shouldered, moving forcefully, immaculate, impressive. The men found him forbidding and menacing. Most soldiers were afraid of him and were sometimes too nervous to answer coherently when questioned about the quality of their meals. In kitchens he asked the cooks about putting onions in the food, how often each week the garbage dump was inspected. He had questions about the sewerage system. When upon infrequent occasion a man found the courage to complain about something, he listened attentively and then pressed the soldier with questions demanding absolutely concrete answers.

He went to training camps and the quickly set up schools for military specialties, to ports to see the facilities for incoming ships. He was never at pains to be jovial, the commander affectionately pinching the adolescent enlisted man's cheek. Anyone standing in ranks who turned to look at him was lashed out at and the man's sergeant was told to take him out in the company street and keep him standing at attention with eyes front for half an hour. He arrived at a hospital to find the doctors lined up at the entrance as if, thought the junior officer Laurence Stallings, they expected a visit from the chairman of the board on Founder's Day. "Go back to your posts and stand at attention," Pershing said. He had hard eyes and set thin lips, Stallings thought. The Iron Commander. Pershing's favorite in the Bible, a soldier told the reporter Heywood Broun, was likely Joshua for making the sun and the moon stand at attention. "They will never call him 'Papa' Pershing," Broun wrote. Some of the staff at Chaumont thought him out of line to say such a thing. Pershing did not. He knew a fact when he saw it in print.

His duty-hours manner was no different with those he had soldiered with for long years than with those he had never met. Once a man known since West Point days came up and put out his hand and said, "John, I am—"

"Address your commanding officer as 'General.' " It did not matter if you had shared his tent on campaign in the West or out in the Philippines, that your wife had been Frankie's dear friend, that your children had played with Helen and Anne and Mary Margaret. If he thought you not up to your task, you were relieved of your post. He sent an estimation of senior commanders to Secretary of War Baker: "All the officers referred to are friends of mine, but that should count for nothing. General Morrison is very well informed on military history, but has very little experience in recent years in handling troops. He is quite inactive and unaggressive. General Green is too inactive. General Plummer is neither active nor strong. General Bartlett belongs to this same class of men who are old for their years. We want only strong, active men, and cannot afford to take chances on weaklings or others who have stood still." His recommendation was that to spare embarrassment to soldiers taught by fighting Indians, the war in Cuba, the Philippines, and in some cases by the Punitive Expedition, but who were not equipped for European warfare, they be kept at home as administrators for the great army coming into being. "General Barry is, I fear, too far along in years to undertake the handling of a division or to stand the arduous work very long." On General Hodges: "He is fifty-eight years of age and it is too late for him to begin to learn to be a soldier. It will simply be a waste of time, with no result except failure."

It was very difficult for him to have to deny those in whose company he spent his career the chance to shine in the greatest war in history, but it had to be done. To pick high leaders was the most difficult task he faced, he wrote Secretary Baker. The most difficult case of all was that of former chief of staff J. Franklin Bell. After begging for a chance to serve even as Pershing departed Governor's Island on the SS *Baltic*, Bell came to Europe to renew his pleas for an active command while reminding his former subordinate of the many things he had done for him in the past. Pershing saw a diabetic explaining away a weak appearance by saying he had been seasick on the ship coming over. Once Bell had been the U.S. Army's *beau ideal* of a soldier, holder of the Congressional Medal of Honor for charging Philippine insurgents with a pistol to force their surrender, a cavalry daredevil adventurous, fearless, with a pleasant look on his face in the midst of the most testing firestorm, sleepless, unconventional. His leadership of volunteers known in the Philippines as The Suicide Club led to likening him to a hurricane or a Wild West desperado. But his day had passed. "No officer has inspired me with a more sincere opinion of personal character and worth than you," Pershing wrote him. But: "Frankly, General, I do not think you can stand the work and I beg of you to accept this as final. No one has a higher regard for you personally and for this reason no one has had a more difficult decision to make in such a case." Bell would be restricted to training troops in the United States. That was where he belonged. "My personal advice to you, if I were not in command, would be exactly to the same effect. I must hold to this opinion. I appreciate our friendship more than I can say in words. Please accept my warmest personal regards now and throughout our lives." When Bell died and Pershing sent his widow condolences, the letter was answered by the late general's aide-de-camp.

"He can read a man's soul through his boots or his buttons," wrote Heywood Broun. Pershing sought dust, rust, dirt, and round shoulders as he looked at men learning and practicing mapmaking, mining, quarrying, forestry, electrical and mechanical work, highway construction, searchlight use, camouflage, and bridge-building; as he inspected fresh water suppliers, the communications units and telephone and telegraphs and homing pigeons, military post office workers, butcher companies, bakery companies, motor maintenance, cooks' school, remount units, truck and horse transportation troops, field and evacuation and base hospitals, ambulance companies, veterinary units, mobile surgical teams, graves registration men, great infantry and artillery formations. To the British and French he appeared the most useless of individuals leading a growing crowd of equally useless personages doing nothing whatsoever to help win the war. There were fully formed Allied armies ready to absorb American troops, the French and British said, yet in incomprehensible fashion General Pershing insisted on setting up his own parallel organization. And not a shot fired at the Germans. The barrage of criticism and the appeals to Washington became couched in such terms, General Robert Lee

Bullard thought, as to justify a Pershing refusal to speak to any foreign officer or official.

Pershing was very much alone in France, no one over him in any way, his own secretary of war and of state there, thought the financier Otto H. Kahn, and his own finance and diplomatic agent also. No American soldier had ever held such power; no soldier of any country, perhaps, save Napoleon when emperor. He sharpened the blade he would wield when he was ready, seeking officers with grasp—it was a favorite word. It seemed to him that the commander of his only complete division—the French and British had hundreds—lacked grasp. Maj. Gen. William Sibert of the First U.S. Infantry was an engineers officer of substantial technical competence. But it was a question as to whether he was a leader. He did not appear to inspire his officers or soldiers with confidence, men sent from Chaumont to look into matters reported—Pershing's "periscopes" and "crocodiles." General Sibert was not physically imposing and did not have an imposing personality. At a divisional review where Sibert's troops marched raggedly over poorly selected, uneven ground, Pershing erupted. Besides the matter of the undistinguished marching, he rasped in his harshly cold manner, Sibert's officers offered insufficiently pertinent observations regarding a practice attack on an entrenched enemy. It was all very unpleasant. "He just scarified us," remembered one of the First's officers. The outfit showed little evidence of proper training, Pershing said. Poor use had been made of its time. He grilled officers, got faltering replies, turned to go. The officer who remembered being scarified was perhaps not so much so, for he began to say something. Pershing turned away. The officer reached out and put his hand on the commander in chief's arm. "General Pershing, there's something to be said here." "What have you got to say?" The officer, "mad all over," he remembered, poured out a torrent. The lookers-on were "horrified." But Pershing listened and in future visits always took him to one side to ask how things were going. The officer never held anything back. "You could talk to him as if you were discussing somebody in the next country. He never held it against you for an instant. I never saw another commander I could do that with. It was one of his great strengths that he could listen to things." Here was someone, Pershing decided, who had grasp. It was George C. Marshall, Jr.

Another who had the quality was a First Division sentry who one rainy day halted the general's limousine. Orderly Frank Lanckton got out into what every AEF veteran never forgot, the French mud that outmudded all others. It was up to his ankles on this occasion, Lanckton remembered. He was a sergeant at the time. He told the sentry who was in the car. The man, a private, said his orders were that all vehicles along the road must disgorge all occupants to be recognized and identified. Lanckton reported the situation to the passengers in the Locomobile. The general's aide Col. Carl Boyd got out, his boots sinking into mud that covered his spurs. Flushed, he returned. Lanckton tried again. "Here, sentry, you better pass this car before you get into trouble."

"Sergeant, my orders are to have the occupants of every car dismount before I let them pass."

"But do you realize who this is? General Pershing."

"I don't give a damn if it's Jesus Christ. Those are my orders."

Pershing heard. He slowly got out. Rain was pouring down. He walked forward, his boots and even the bottom of his overcoat picking up heavy streaks of soft clay. The sentry executed a smart Present Arms with his rifle. "I am sorry that I had to make you get out of the car in all this mud and rain, but those were my orders," the sentry said.

Pershing returned to the car and told Colonel Boyd to get the man's name, rank, serial number, and organization. The next day the buck private sentry was jumped to sergeant. He had acted exactly as the commander in chief would have, were their situations reversed. That was what was desired. "Pershing was his own model," wrote the reporter Frank H. Simonds. "When you stumbled on a lost American doughboy in a God-forsaken Lorraine hamlet, his bearing, the set of his tunic, his salute, all authentically recalled the general who sat in Chaumont." He was hard and relentless, his soldiers uniformly believed, ruthless, inexorable, inflexible, stifling. And the last remove from lovable. The game was going to be played under the Pershing rules, reflected Maj. Frederick Palmer, and as they were not pleasant rules, Pershing was not loved. He was unconcerned about that and equally so that unlike Foch he was not dramatic, that unlike von Hindenburg he was not avuncular and magisterial, and that unlike Joffre, as Heywood Broun had pointed out, he was not Papa-like. Asked for interviews by the American correspondents, he granted none, saying that it ill became him to make declarations when U.S. American troops were not fighting despite the many pressures to make them do so. His army, he let it be known, would speak for him when it was ready.

None of his subordinate commanders gripped popular imagination as leaders of the Great War, and none ever would. The Civil War had generals with names instantly recognized and always remembered. No one in later years gave a thought to any AEF general other than Pershing. He was his army. To the doughboys—the term possibly derived from the Punitive Expedition's adobe-covered sloggers become 'dobes and then in France that by which they were remembered—it was his fault, and his alone, if the meat portion issued with the watery soup was no more than the size of a man's thumb, if there was a scarcity of tobacco and chewing gum, if the military doctors were unsympathetic, if sunny France of legend was found just as appealing to the boys Over There as winsome Virginia had to their predecessors in the frozen lines before Richmond and Petersburg seven decades and more earlier. The Americans had rushed to the recruiting stations with the declaration of war, ready to go over the seas and assert their nation and save the world and make it safe for democracy. The United States was privileged to spend its blood and treasure, President Wilson had said. Now its representatives sat in frozen mud and sleet and squalor and nothing was happening. All around the troops in the little manure-pile villages—ownership of a substantial mound was a sign of well-being to the Lorraine peasantry—were the French, whose poilus as with America's doughboys had once rushed to the troop trains taking them to the slaughterhouse of their generation—of the generations. It had begun with soldiers in *rouge pantaloon* hearing from their plumed officers carrying canes, "My dear friends, I ask you to join me in singing 'La Marseillaise' as we go over the top." It ended with French girls destined to live out their lives as members of that million-woman group known as The Waiting Ones, doting on others' children never permitted tin soldier toys because such would bring reminder of Auntie's husband who never was, lying under a grave marked *MORT POUR LE FRANCE.*

Now France was all but finished in this war. Logical, chilly, a man foreign to glamorous illusions, the field commander Gen. Henri Philippe Pétain frankly told Pershing that at one point after a catastrophic attack that Pétain had violently opposed but upon which his predecessor insisted, the army of the Republic was almost completely in mutiny, with but two dependable divisions standing between the Germans and Paris. Now it was Pétain's task to hold a shattered force together. He was doing so brilliantly, not wantonly shooting deserters, but telling his men he would not ask them to go up against entrenchments, sited machine guns, registered artillery, their flesh offered to the enemy's steel. They would hold for him, and for France, would they not? he asked. And any attacks would be of the most limited type. "We must wait for the tanks and the Americans," he said. Pershing cared for Pétain above all others met in the war, understood his reasonable and reasoning, realistic, humane manner, knew what he was and what he had done. To those who studied the great leaders of the war he himself seemed most akin in personality and demeanor to Sir Douglas Haig, head of the British Expeditionary Forces. Once they stood on a lawn of the park at Haig's château-headquarters where the glittering British lived in high dress-uniform-for-dinner style, few officers of background other than the landed gentry and the rich. (Haig himself somewhat raised eyebrows because his money came from Haig & Haig whisky, his family "in trade.") A German plane flew over and dropped a bomb. Standing with Sir Douglas's batman, Pershing's orderly, Sgt. Frank Lanckton, turned and ran. The concussion done with and the fragments down, Lanckton looked at the two commanders. Field marshal and general were found completely unperturbed, their conversation uninterrupted. "How did you like the air raid?" Pershing asked later. "Lanckton, bullets have a way of chasing those who run." Lanckton never ran again.

In his calmness, disregard of emotional display, acceptance of what must be, Pershing did in fact resemble Haig, who like himself had married late in life—to a maid of honor of Queen Alexandra. As with Pershing, Haig was a lifelong cavalry officer, always immaculate, polite when politeness was in order, never anything other than perfectly turned out, gloves, burnished spurs, crop or swagger stick, sometimes a cane, majestic to be sure, but cold, remote, aloof, untouchable, distant. But Haig was also hopelessly inarticulate, almost bringing to mind a bumblingly upper-class nobleman as seen on the stage, and showing not the slightest need for friends, human contact, exchange, humor. He had no interests beyond military ones. Pétain was far more the American's type, droll, quietly amusing, feelingly able to talk to poilus as Haig could never to other ranks, and, finally, akin to Pershing in another matter. Nothing could more typify him than when called upon to take command at Verdun he was found by an aide in the Hôtel Terminus at the Gare du Nord in a room before which stood a pair of his boots waiting to be shined by the night porter, accompanied, the aide remembered, "by some charming little *molière* slippers, utterly feminine." Wearing "the scantiest of costumes," Pétain opened to the aide's knock, heard that he must go to Verdun, said they would leave at first light, and returned to his companion who, he said later, first wept and then displayed such performance as would make the night memorable in the recollection of one who had known many such nights. "I have two passions," General Pétain said, "sex and the infantry." Pershing understood, save that he was of the cavalry.

From far-off California Nita Patton wrote, "It is just at the hour of dark, when all the world seems to bow its head in prayer. If you were only here we would go out onto the porch and watch daylight fade, but because you are so far away I do not go alone. It would make me sad. The hurt of our parting would be too severe. It was a Sunday evening when we kissed good-bye. So many weeks have gone since then. All kinds of things have happened. For you many wonderful things, experiences that have marked epochs in the world's history. But in it all our love has lain warm in our hearts. Just think if you had gone away before you asked me if I loved you. Unspoken love is such a feeble thing, a prey to so many doubts and fears. I thank God that He let us have those unforgettable weeks, that we could see each other and kiss away each other's tears before we parted."

To her brother George the matter between his sister and "Nita's suitor" was "certainly the most intense case I have ever seen," so he wrote home; but he added to his wife, Beatrice, that Nita should not come to France, as she had thought of doing. "It will be absolutely wrong for her to make her proposed trip. Be sure not to encourage her in any way." Officers' wives were not permitted to join their husbands overseas, and it would not do for the commander in chief to have Nita come over. There was more that Georgie did not add. Nita might send the general a newspaper clipping speaking of how a beautiful Pasadena blonde—"Sounds a bit chorus lady, doesn't it?"—was about to marry the AEF head; she might write, "John, I feel near you. I wonder if away over there you are thinking just a wee speck of me, right now. Anyway I love you with my whole heart"; but soon Nita's letters said, "Darling John, you seem very far away tonight, and detached from me. It is such ages since I heard from you. I feel as if you were a part almost of another existence. I do not like to feel this way."

She wrote, "Darlingest John, I think I'll divorce you if you don't write soon. Just now I want you, right here, I want to hear you say, 'I love you.' I am a lovesick maiden, and I am lonesome." The game was up for her. "A little tin god on wheels," she would bitterly say of him shortly. He had found others—found another.

Louise Cromwell Brooks, lustrous brown eyes and vivacious manner, was a great heiress of whom it was said that even had she been working behind a counter at Macy's would have "simply radiated sexual excitement." Her father was rich, but her stepfather, Thomas Stotesbury of J. P. Morgan's, was more than that, possessing $150 million. She was wayward, spoiled, erratic, wild. She had a Paris residence. She came into the sphere encompassed by the commander in chief of the American Expeditionary Forces. "It was inevitable that once these two magnets came within range of their forcefields he and Louise would end up in bed together." In time she suggested that they marry. But he knew her ways. "Louise," he said, "marrying you would be like buying a book for somebody else to read." They remained friends. She went on to others and he became ever more close to someone than whom no one less likely could be imagined.

Micheline Resco was a promising Paris artist. She asked to do the general's portrait. She was in the estimation of Pershing's chief of staff, James G. Harbord, "a little Russian girl."

Although Mlle. Resco was of Romanian and not Russian birth, the description was otherwise accurate, for she was of slight build and of an age that would have more logically suited her to be the sweetheart of a French lieutenant or corporal rather than the commander in chief of the Americans. Blond and blue-eyed, she was twenty-three years old. Summaries of Pershing's day for his staff's official diary began regularly to indicate that the general spent the evening "studying French." The individual with whom he conducted his seminars was never indicated. Sometimes the diary depicted him as sitting for his portrait, her name appearing, and the eventual work became, he said, the finest representation of him ever made. Their affair, of course, was impossible to conduct outside the knowledge of his official family, and there was never any pretense about it. She would receive a note from one of the junior officers asking if the general might come at a certain hour. Driving to her home, he sat up front next to the sergeant-chauffeur so as to be inconspicuous. Sometimes she was brought to his quarters. None of his people shook their heads at a man nearing sixty with a girl almost too young to vote—had the United States allowed women's suffrage. He was human. And he was lonely. Great power—supreme power, actually—cut him off from the world. At mealtimes talk of military matters was not permitted, and he could be light in touch as he talked about past times, laughed at funny things others said, even occasionally made little jokes about himself. But no one mistook the situation. Place card seating was rigidly determined by army rank; his position at the head of the table signified all that had to be said.

There circulated around him men he had known ever since he was a youth—his West Point classmate Avery Andrews, for instance, who long ago had attended Colonel Huse's preparation school for the Academy with the appointed cadet from Missouri, Mr. Pershing. It was Andrews who had introduced him to Teddy Roosevelt. They had known each other's wives and children. Now Andrews was on the staff as a colonel working on the railroad transport stretching from French debarkation ports with quickly built yards, docks, warehouses, machine shops, motor

depots three thousand to six thousand miles from U.S. ports of embarkation. Yet despite thirty-five years of close friendship, there was not a touch
of what Andrews called "undue familiarities" between the two men. "I
never allowed myself to forget that he was the commander in chief of a
great army and that I was his subordinate." Once their mutual classmate
T. Bentley Mott walked with Pershing in the Mills mansion garden to
hear of a delicate personal-nature problem regarding relations with the
French, who as with the British, opposed everything Pershing did, or, perhaps more to the point, did not do. Mott was his classmate's liaison with
the French general headquarters. The French remarks directed at him
about AEF inaction seemed really out of bounds, offensive, Pershing remarked. He was wondering just how to reply. Mott asked if the matter was
being raised in the capacity of old friend or of commander in chief. Pershing said, "Let it be John and Bentley." As soon as the talk was over they
reverted to their position-assigned roles. Pershing in those days of the war
had but one person with whom, apart from Micheline Resco, he could
ever really relax. That was Charles G. Dawes. A banker and great power
in Chicago whose situation brought him to be mentioned in the same
breath with Morgan, Carnegie, Astor, Vanderbilt, Rockefeller, and Harriman, struggling-lawyer days in Nebraska when he ate at the lunch
counter with Lieutenant Pershing at a cost to each of no more than fifteen cents long in the past, Dawes joined the army and went off to training in a private railway car. He rose to direct and coordinate all army purchases in Europe, deploying vast sums to buy guns and planes and
ammunition from the Allies, food from Scandinavia, horses from Spain,
railroad ties from Portugal, forage, mules, coal, vegetables. No less military a soul existed in the American forces, or probably in any of the other
forces. Once Harbord walked up to General Purchasing Agent Dawes as
he stood with a group of officers visiting a French headquarters. Dawes
was then a colonel. "This is a hell of a job for the chief of staff," Harbord
said, "but the general told me to do it." He buttoned up Dawes's overcoat,
including the hook at the top. "Charlie," Pershing told him, "when I'm in
front of the men, don't come up with your cigar in your mouth and say,
'Good morning, Jack.' I don't give a damn what you call me when we're
alone." It was hopeless. Once Dawes saluted his old friend with a cigar in

his mouth, hit it with his hand, and spewed ashes and embers over both of them. "I am going to be a real soldier yet," Dawes deadpanned. "This morning I remembered to put on my pants before my shoes." Pershing sighed, "Charlie, I once thought I would follow you into law, but I never imagined you would follow me into the army." Dawes let it be known that he had heard a photograph was taken in England of Pershing with breast pocket unbuttoned. "For this picture I am going to search that country." He saw himself in his supply capacity as someone to whom the dough-boys stretched out their arms asking for what they needed and what their leader, "my dear commander," wanted them to have. He was brilliant at his work, making his purchases with great efficiency and dispatch. Harried by a congressional committee years later for an accounting in detail of the immense sums he had expended so that the AEF might live and function, Dawes exploded with the expression that gave him his ever-after nickname: "Hell 'n Maria, we were trying to win a war!"

"Dawes to me is a pearl without price," Pershing said of him for his work. He might have said the same thing in a personal vein. Sgt. Henry Cooper, majordomo of Chaumont and the Mills mansion in Paris, remembered mornings when Dawes had spent the night. Pershing would take a walk with him, both still in their pajamas. "The general would have his arm around Dawes or it would be the other way. They always seemed to be the chums of their Nebraska days."

There was something else beyond shared youth that spoke from Charlie Dawes to Jack Pershing. He had had one child. As a young man in 1912 Rufus Fearing Dawes drowned on a Wisconsin vacation trip. His father never really recovered. "I do not seem to get over the loss of my dear, dear boy," Dawes told his diary years later. He made his Chicago mansion a home away from home for all his son's friends so as at least for the moment not to be so lonely for Rufus, and now in France with Rufus five years gone, junior officers as he probably would have been, they sought him out. That helped, but there was a limit to the help anyone could give. Once as he rode with Pershing in the back of the Locomobile there came what Charlie called "an instance of telepathy" when he was thinking of "my lost boy" and across the seat it came to him that into his companion's mind had come thoughts of his own great losses. They turned to one another, both in tears. "Even this war can't keep it out of my mind," Pershing said. There was no need for him to explain who he was speaking about. Once he was in his car with his aide Col. John G. Quekemeyer. The war was on for America then, the real war, with mule carts hauling back from the front the bodies of thousands of American soldiers, some slipping off to be dropped into the mud and likely denied Known Dead status but to be remembered as missing in action. "Frankie, Frankie," Pershing cried, burying his face in his hands, "my God, sometimes I don't know how I can go on."

Frankie came to him in dreams in those years, and after. Of her, of course, nothing was left but a little boy far away.

My dear Warren,

I have just had a very pretty horseback ride along the Marne. It is a beautiful river and has a canal along its entire course. The banks of the canal are level and grassy and, usually, lined with trees. This morning I rode along the banks for about two miles and came to a point where the canal runs across the river and into a tunnel through a mountain. The bridge that carries the canal is very deep of course and is made of iron. I thought you would be interested to know about this.

I have a very good horse, a bay. He has a splendid trot, a nice canter and gallops well when you want him to. The only thing that was lacking this morning in making my ride a complete joy was that you were not here to go with me. I often wish you were with me when I see beautiful things as I travel about the country. I would also like to have you with me always under all circumstances. I especially miss you at night.

I am just dictating this short note while I am eating breakfast, so good-bye. Write me very often.

With much love,

Papa.

Dear Papa,

I hope you are well. I have a bed on the sleeping porch.

We made a cake today.

Aunt Bess gave me $1.5 for my fireworks. We got
3 boxes torpedos
8 roman candles
5 boxes sparklers
5 lady crackers
4 big
3 rockets
6 son of a guns

I love you papa

Warren Pershing

My dear Warren,

Don't you wish you had a stenographer to whom you could dictate your letters, so you would not have to write them? I guess you do. At least I would think so from the way the bad pen and bad pencil seem to work for you. Ink is not always good, is it? Funny how ink will spill and spoil letters. I remember when I was a little boy I used to be just the same way. It is not so easy to write, but then you know little boys must learn to do things well, even if it is a little hard to learn. And it is always better to learn when you are a little boy because it comes easier than when you grow up. There are lots of things I wish I had learned better when I was a little boy.

You know a boy ought to be very careful about riding his wheel and not take chances about running into streetcars, and when he sees a streetcar coming (and he ought to be on the lookout for them all the time) he should stop until the streetcar passes by. How do you suppose I know about your running so close to a streetcar? I won't tell you now. I will have to tell you some other time. Maybe you can guess, but you must be very careful, because I would like to think of you as being careful.

I know little boys have to have a lot of time to play, and I want my little boy to have lots of time to play. I think he would get about as much out of play as he would writing letters, as a rule, but you know when anybody wants a letter from his little boy as much as I do, then maybe the boy might take a little less time to play and a little more to write letters. I hope you got well over the measles. You won't have to have them again.

Good night, many kisses.

Papa

The personal situation of the American general was very well known in France, and the image of a lonely man whose son was long miles away over the Atlantic seized a nation whose own sons had been so spent along the Western Front. It was noticed how he could choke up and hastily leave a room where there were little children with their mothers. Marshal Joffre's wife ordered an exact miniature duplicate of her husband's uniform, blue coat, old-style *rouge pantaloon*, cap of blue and gold and scarlet, and seven stars on the sleeve. It went off to Nebraska, and Warren wore it to school. "All the little boys and girls now know what a real Marshal of France looks like," Warren's father wrote. "I expect they will remember that a long time, a uniform like that, a nice sword and cap and everything," and now Warren must with the greatest attention to neatness send a carefully written letter of thanks to Mme. Joffre. Warren did, and also told his father of a dream he had: "I went to Germany to raise the American flag and just as I was putting up the flag aunty called me and I did not get to dream any more. With love and many kisses, Warren Pershing." He sent word of his new gloves, pen, sled, roller skates, ice skates, brown suit, cap and mailed off to Chaumont returned tests in which he got 100—these without doubt selected in preference to those in which he got lesser grades.

And: "Dear Papa, I am in Cheyenne having a fine time. They brought my ponys in. I am riding them every day. I washed them yesterday. They do not buck at all. One of them shies at automobiles and the other one does not shy at all. With love and many kisses—" and a dozen X's. Back came, "I am mighty proud to see that you are doing so well with your hand-writing. It is a delight to read your letters now, which I can do without any difficulty." Sometimes his aides wrote to Warren, those who did not know him saying they hoped to meet him one day to tell of the interesting things they had seen, and spend time with him. Senator Warren wrote his son-in-law in France that the boy was a fine rider, going thirty-five miles on a horse to see some outlying sheep just purchased. He caught one who ran off very proficiently, accomplishing the work as well and as quickly as any of the senator's hands. Warren himself sent thanks for a gift, appending two lines of X's with the notation that they represented one million kisses: "I am very glad to see how well you write," his father answered. "I think it is very good indeed. I am very glad to know that you liked the neckties." As always the letters were typed by a clerk and with a passed-by-censor stamped and initialed imprint on embossed stationery reading American Expeditionary Forces, Office of the Commander-in-Chief.

Other letters went out on that stationery. Ill-equipped for all that General Purchasing Agent Charlie Dawes could do, the pay often late, the food desolate, inflicting no damage on the enemy, wet and cold, "beggars in uniform" casting about for arms from the Allies, the men of the AEF compared their winter of 1917–18 to the one suffered through by earlier soldiers, at Valley Forge. In a way that was an uplifting concept, for eventually General Washington had triumphed. But the comparison did not sit well with Pershing. It spoke of down-at-the-mouth discouragement. He wanted resolution, energy, aggressiveness, a heads-up attitude, the infusion into his troops of certainty that the day was coming when unlike the French and British dependent on artillery and hand grenade they would depart trenches and trench warfare to seek out the enemy with rifles, the proper use of which, he believed, was given to Americans above all other peoples for the weapon having conquered the frontier from which he sprang and the West he had known. Logistics and transport and equipment and armaments and ordnance were one thing, and spirit and character another; and like Napoleon he held the moral to be as three to one against the material. Increasingly he wondered if the commander of the First Infantry Division, the initial division formed in France, his premier unit, the Big Red One, understood.

> Confidential.
> From: The Commander-in-Chief, A.E.F.
> To: Major General W. L. Sibert
> Subject: Pessimism.
>
> 1. Americans recently visiting our training areas and coming into contact with officers of high command have received a note of deep pessimism, including apprehension of undue hardships to be undergone. General officers prompted by soldierly duty, leadership, patriotism, fortitude and ambition, should maintain quite an opposite attitude.
> 2. While realizing that optimism cannot be created by order, it should be unnecessary to point out that such a state of mind on the part of officers in responsible positions is at once reflected among their troops, and it is not an over statement to say no officer worthy of command would give expression to thoughts of depression. A conservative firmness and faith is not inconsistent with a serious estimate, but I need hardly add that a temperament which gives way to weak complaining and querulously protests at hardships such as all soldiers must expect to endure, marks an unfitness for command.
> 3. The officer who cannot read hope in the conditions that confront us; who is not inspired and uplifted by the knowledge that the heart of our nation is in this war; who shrinks from hardship; who does not exert his personal influence to encourage his men; and who fails in the lofty attitude which should characterize the General who expects to succeed, should yield his position to others with more of our national courage. The consciousness of such an attitude should in honor dictate an application for relief. Whenever the visible effects of it on the command of such an officer reach me in future, it will constitute grounds for his removal without application.

John J. Pershing, Charlie Dawes felt, was "a master of English" whose personal attention to any document sent out above or below his name Charlie could instantly recognize. That was so in the writing of such brutal a memorandum that General Sibert of the First had the unhappy experience of receiving. Sibert, however, did not understand what he was being told, or did not want to know. He did not have grasp. Pershing had seen that at the inspection where George C. Marshall, Jr., fearlessly opened his mouth, a man who had grasp. Sibert was relieved of his command, Robert Lee Bullard replacing him. It did not matter to Pershing that he and Sibert had been together at the Point in the days thirty and more years gone when they had been boys along the Plain and in drill hall and summer encampment along the Hudson, comrades in the little enclosed and encapsulated army of before-the-war. The time was coming when in a day the AEF chief would relieve of the command of their divisions two classmates who long ago went with him from graduation to New York dinner and drinking and sightseeing and dinner again and pledge of undying friendship. The job of every member of the American Expeditionary Forces, it was said, hung by a thread. To question an order from the commander in chief, to indicate the slightest doubt that it could be successfully carried out, was to court dismissal from one's post. It was true even for Charlie Dawes. "When a conference was called there would not be much of any discussion. The general, while he asked our opinions, was really looking to see if any of us showed cold feet, so that if we did he could kick us through the transom."

But, of course, he could not do that with the French and British, who had fought so long and given so much. By early 1918 the Americans had 250,000 men in France. The few regulars had been gathered from their remote posts, the ones from the Philippines greeting old pals of the Days of the Empire by rubbing three fingers together to mimic the manner in which the gu-gus put rice in their mouths. All of their slight number were submerged in the great mass of those who had flocked to the recruiting stations to do what posters everywhere urged: Join the Colors and Make the World Safe for Democracy. They were strangers to the Old Army's drinking in tough bars and brawls under tropical moons, and all were doughboys now. But what had they *done,* the strapping soldiers of the

New World? To the French and British it seemed very likely that the war could end without America's hardly having fired a shot. Their appeals over Pershing's head to President Wilson and Secretary Baker for immediate amalgamation of American troops into Allied formations brought coldly worded remarks from Pershing about problems being worked out in France by people on the scene. "May I not suggest to you the inexpediency of communicating such matters to Washington by cable?" he wrote the president of the Council of Ministers, Georges Clemenceau. The Tiger did not trust soldiers—war was too important a matter to be left to generals, he famously said—and he did not trust the British; but he united with London to deal with the parasitic Americans. Pershing *must* give over his men. British prime minister David Lloyd George used threats, charm, innuendo for his appeals. If the war were lost by France and Britain, he told Pershing, it would be lost honorably by those countries, for they would have expended their last in the struggle. But the United States? It would have put forth less effort than tiny Belgium. Lloyd George did not move Pershing. He held to his views. He would not feed his units into Allied armies. "It's no use," Lloyd George concluded. "You can't budge him."

On March 21, 1918, a massive German bombardment of steel and poison gas crashed down on British positions on a front of some fifty miles. Sixty-four specially trained German divisions came on, many of the men brought from comatose Russia, storm troops who suddenly returned mobility to what had been a stationary fight for more than three years. They did not push forward as a line but as arrows, bypassing and isolating any strongpoints that held, a series of little rivulets, not a flood, jets and not waves. Their artillery came through on portable ramps and heavy duckboards so that the guns would not sink in mud fought over for so long. They got to open ground. They were in among and behind His Majesty's forces in France. The riddled British broke, and the Germans went nearly forty miles in a rush toward the railway center of Amiens, the base for the entire British effort along the Western Front. If they took it, the hinge of the French and British would be ruptured and there would be a separation which would see one ally fall back to Paris while the other looked for retreat to, and likely across, the Channel.

A second German attack would soon sweep over what had been deemed quiet sectors in the South, and over the Chemin des Dames, the Ladies' Way, ridges said to be named for their use as a favorite spot for riding by the daughters of a French king, or perhaps because local women liked to promenade there. Past its shattered defenses the road to Paris seemed open. Civilization itself seemed in peril, what it had been suddenly put in danger of replacement by what was represented by the always-uniformed Kaiser Wilhelm II of great upturned flaring mustaches and rearing metal eagle- and plumage-topped soaring helmet. His world, it was said, consisted of officers of the Guards shouting orders. A German officer whose passage on the sidewalk was blocked by a civilian, His Imperial Majesty had declared even in the peacetime years of earlier times, was entirely justified in cutting that civilian down with his saber. Now Wilhelm's soldiers were coming on. "With our backs to the wall and believing in the justice of our cause each one must fight on to the end," Field Marshal Sir Douglas Haig told his men in a grim Order of the Day. "Soldiers, I call upon you," said Gen. Henri Philippe Pétain. "The fate of France hangs in the balance."

Again and yet again the French and British now had at America's general. The abandonment of Paris would soon be in the air, with government officials packing to fly to Bordeaux, and Pétain telling Clemenceau that the Germans were going to defeat the British in the open country. Pershing had to waver in his stand that the Americans would do little until they had formed a completely independent army fighting under its own flag. He went to Marshal Ferdinand Foch, the just-named generalissimo of all Allied and Associated Forces, and said he was offering his men. There followed discussions of how those men would be used, and it was seen that Pershing of the Associated Force had ideas far from parallel to those of the Allied Forces. Was he ready to risk the French being driven all the way to the Loire River? Foch demanded.

"Yes," Pershing answered, "I am willing to take that risk. The time may come when the American Army will have to stand the brunt of the war, and it is not wise to fritter away our resources." Paris would soon be under artillery bombardment from the German guns—the Big Berthas. Refugees were streaming away from the scene of the fighting, frightened women and crying children walking by farm carts loaded with furniture, chickens, mattresses. Yet the man held to his naive, grandiose schemes, said the French and British. Foch cried that a fearsome destiny could overtake them all as Pershing tried "in vain to organize on lost battlefields over the graves of Allied soldiers." This man possessed "invincible obstinacy," said Lloyd George. "It is maddening." Pershing banged his fist down on a table and said, "Gentlemen, I have thought this over very deliberately and will not be coerced."

But he had to do something. America had been at war for one year and had suffered fewer than two hundred battle deaths. (Twenty thousand had died for Great Britain on the day the Battle of the Somme began, July 1, 1916, and it was said that France had seen a man die for every minute that the war had gone on.) He ordered the First Division to take Cantigny, a little village on a ridge northwest of Montdidier. A regiment would be assigned the job, four thousand Americans undertaking their country's first real action in the Great War. The town itself was relatively unimportant—its main use to the Germans was to offer observation points for their artillery. Its symbolism was immense. "We will refer this to your president," Lloyd George had told Pershing, speaking of the eternal question of amalgamation in the Allied armies, and Pershing had replied, "Refer and be damned"; but if he failed at Cantigny the president might well feel himself forced to bow to European demands. And he must not only take Cantigny but also hold it. The French had twice taken the town only to lose it again. The Americans must do better.

He assembled nine hundred officers of the First on the grounds of the château serving as divisional headquarters. "I did not want you to enter into real participation in this war without my having said a word to you." They must be alive to situations changing minute by minute once they got into action. They must not try to recall exact examples taught in drill, or patterns of particular type. Determination would win through, aggressiveness, their stamina and that of their men, character and the will to win. "I am not given to speechmaking, so only a word more. Our people today are hanging expectant upon your deeds. Our future part in this conflict depends upon your action. You are going forward, and your conduct will be an example for succeeding units of our army. I hope the standard you set will be high. I know it will be high." He was like a football coach talking to his team before the big game, Col. John L. Hines thought. Robert Lee Bullard found him his usual terse, businesslike self, but when speaking privately with the new First Division commander he was different as he discussed allied officers. "Do they patronize you?" he asked Bullard. "Do they assume superior airs with you? By Christ! They have been trying it with me, and I don't intend to stand a bit of it."

Zero Hour at Cantigny was 4:45 A.M., May 28, 1918. The war, it was said, had made a funeral pyre of the Europe that had been, and by extension of the entire world. It had thrown in the discard a thousand years of civilization's onward march, murdered the past and released the caveman from the sanctuary where he had thought to be imprisoned to let him red of tooth and fang run amuck in worship of the devil-god Moloch, who lived on human bodies. The witches' sabbath had made slaughter in hideous mud and endless death a shrine at which the great nations prayed and to which they sent their sons. The survivors who lived on, many of them, were spiritually as walking dead men, victims of the red years of butchery, of suicidal death. That the first name of the boy who shot the Austrian Archduke Franz Ferdinand and so unleashed the hurricane was Gabriel was not by mere chance, people said. Now the Americans had come to the war. A colossal two hours of artillery fire rained down on the German positions and reduced Cantigny to smashed rubble. Officers' whistles blew, and three lines of soldiers of the Twenty-eighth Infantry Regiment rose from their trenches and headed for the town on the ridge through what the doughboys termed Death Valley, past clouds of cordite smoke mixed with lingering poison gas and dust, earth showers from the rolling barrage going before, pieces of metal jammed into the ground, incinerated Germans, mangled bodies, pieces of bodies. A few enemy machine gunners held out, a few enemy infantrymen rose out of cellars. They were dispatched. The Yanks were in Cantigny. Their losses had been acceptable.

Pershing stood with Bullard and watched German prisoners being marched by. He said in the most emphatic manner that the town must be held against the inevitable German counterattack, and left. Soon a note was delivered to Bullard. It repeated in writing what Pershing had said verbally. "I need not suggest that you give this your personal attention, which I know you will do, of course, but am writing to show that I am rather anxious about it."

"Smarting under French and British doubts," Bullard said to himself, and went forward to the regimental commander whose men made the attack, Col. Hanson Ely. "You must hold your position and not give any ground at all." Bullard said. "The whole world is watching the Twenty-eighth Infantry and we must continue to hold Cantigny at all costs." Hundreds of bodies lay about, soon to swell up and discolor. The Americans dug in among the cellars of smashed houses and in the wrecked town cemetery of bone fragments, bashed-in headstones, ripped floral offerings. The counterattack came, the first of half a dozen, each preceded by monstrous artillery barrages on a town whose exact position was precisely known to German gunners. The Americans turned haggard. Eaten alive by lice—even General Bullard was infested—dirty, frightened, hungry, thirsty, sleepless for the noise, "half crazy," almost, Colonel Ely thought, "temporarily insane," hollow-eyed and with sunken eyes, they held for the three days that the Germans sought Cantigny. They lost close to one of every three men. The German counterattacks gave out. The Americans had held Cantigny. Dining with his staff, Pershing banged his fist on the table and shouted with joy.

The Germans poured over the Chemin des Dames, and the Aisne and the Vesle, heading for the Marne and the high road to Paris. Four days after elements of the First U.S. Infantry Division made their assault on Cantigny, elements of the Third arrived at the town of Château-Thierry. They spread out ten miles along the Marne. Pershing must put away his hopes for a completely independent American force. He must shore up the disintegrating French lines, for the French seemed beaten, forty divisions shattered. All along their front civilians hurried away, James Harbord feeling it was the most pathetic sight he had ever seen: terrified peasantry fleeing from a barbarian invader. Mixed in with the people were French soldiers. "The Boche is coming," poilus said; and they were finished with opposing him. Many of the men were drunk with wine looted from the houses of those who fled, and not in military formations but in little groups of three or four, a routed army on the run going one way while the Americans went the other.

The Germans arrived at Château-Thierry. Paris was but forty-five miles away. For eighty-two hours the Americans combatted the thrust of the spearhead and the Germans turned away; and ever after there were those who said the Yanks had held the road to Paris. Even as the fight went on, the Second Division and more elements of the Third moved into the Marne salient. They held the Germans. Then on June 6, the Second and the Marines went on the attack. The Germans counterattacked. Artillery, gas, mortars, fire from flamethrowers, rifle bullets in sleets: Belleau Wood. The big shells thundered over like express trains rushing through an endless tunnel to land with explosions lighting up a landscape come to resemble the surface of the moon, and ration parties lumbered up Gob Gully past broken trees from which dangled horribly wet legs trailing undone puttees to the ground. Rifle grenades came down and lifted horses up and left them as great hulks of meat grinning in death with lips drawn back in the last act of life, a scream very like that of a woman in agony. "Come on, you sons of bitches," a marine sergeant yelled at his men. "Do you want to live forever?" The Americans took Belleau Wood.

June was almost out, and Pershing had one million soldiers in France. He wanted his own sector, but complied with the French request that he join their Moroccan troops for an attack at Soissons. It was successful, though his casualties were very bad. It was the turn of the tide. After that, remembered Imperial Chancellor George von Hertling, even the most optimistic in Berlin knew the war was lost. The Germans moved back. Pershing by then controlled his army without restraint, and when Secretary Baker asked if perhaps General George W. Goethals, builder of the Panama Canal, should go to France to run the supply system, Pershing refused the offer: "The whole must remain absolutely under one hand. The responsibility is then fixed."

Summer came. His force increased immensely, ships sometimes bringing ten thousand soldiers in one day. Pershing went about with his four temporary-rank stars in his special train of eight coaches with its own power plant, telephone and telegraph apparatus, office car, sleeping cars, dining car, and his private one with dressing room and library. There was a French chef instructed by officers considering themselves amateur cooks in how to make wheat cakes to accompany the boiled eggs, toast, and tea for breakfast. Each day despite rain or, as occurred, German shells falling nearby, the AEF commander walked up and down the train's length for an hour in such swift fashion that Georgie Patton thought his exercise could only be termed "violent." Then he went back to work, appearing to the train's people to be a man tireless both mentally and physically. He planned his army's fight against the enemy and himself fought its fight against the French and British never giving up their hopes for its use in the amalgamated, and subordinated, manner that they but not he thought best. He looked wonderful. "I never saw General Pershing looking or feeling better," Charlie Dawes told his diary. "He is sleeping well. He is tremendously active." At home in the United States he was no less the symbol of his army than George Washington had been of his, and people spoke of another job waiting for him once he licked the Germans, the same position Washington assumed once he had beaten the British. Senator Warren had a warning about that: "Don't let the presidential bug get to boring into your topknot, as it is worse than moths, caterpillars, and other things that make a bad mess," he wrote his son-in-law from Washington. "Let it make you feel and say, like the prudish girl when the question is popped, 'This is so sudden! I am terribly surprised!'" Pershing wrote back, "As for the presidential bug, it is perfectly ridiculous. I should consider myself very much of an ass if I gave it one moment's consideration." He was in France to fight a war, he told the senator, and "you can rest assured, absolutely, that if I fail it will not be because I have any bug in my head."

Yet it was impossible to make him less of a public figure than he was. As such he wanted to spare his son any undue attention, and wrote Chicago's Lillian Bell of the Children's Patriotic League, whose members sent presents to French war orphans and worked to grow vegetables and to hold down household waste, and stood for love of country and supporting the men overseas, that he could not let Warren be publicized as a league volunteer. "I want him to be a very democratic boy. He is growing up in the public schools, and he is treated just like any other boy and I want him to continue to lead the very simplest kind of life and enter manhood without being handicapped by his father. I have to decline to allow his picture published or allow him to be featured in any way." But he could not entirely have his desires met in such matters, and was thrown into a fury when a newspaper article appeared in papers all over America. "GENERAL" PERSHING JR. LEADS ARMY LIKE HIS FAMOUS DAD, the piece was headlined. EIGHT-YEAR-OLD HAS FOUR BOY PRIVATES IN LINCOLN, NEB., TO SALUTE HIM. Warren's force included a Red Cross auxiliary of three little girls. The "small commander" had a miniature doughboy uniform in addition to the dress outfit of a marshal of France, the one given him by Mme. Joffre, and the article's accompanying picture showed him in it, solemn in campaign hat and puttees. "I'm going to be a real soldier when I grow up, just like my dad is," Warren was quoted. "Dad says that if I was a few years older I could go with him now and help lick the Germans." The commandant of Fort Crook in Omaha had invited him to review troops of the Forty-first Infantry, which was expecting early sailing orders, the article went on. "And they can tell Dad all about it when they get to France." Aunt May heard about that from her brother, as she did when she permitted his picture to be used for an insurance company advertisement: "I am perfectly furious."

But he knew how indebted he was to May and their sister Elizabeth— Bess—and could never remain angry at either of them. May wrote that a pendant he sent her was the loveliest piece of jewelry she ever had. "To think that you with all the weight of responsibilities on your shoulders took time to select all these beautiful gifts for us." Warren was singing in the Holy Trinity Episcopal Church choir, she told him, had appeared in a University of Nebraska production of *The Pied Piper*, attended dancing school on Saturday—but he knew about that: he had earlier told her to look into the school program to see if ballroom manners were taught correctly. (His own ballroom prowess had helped him win Frankie, he knew; "perfectly elegant dancer," she had written in her diary.) The night May wrote, Warren was dining at a friend's house and would then go with the friend and the friend's mother to see the film *Huck and Tom Sawyer*. For summer wear May and Bess got him a sailor suit with long trousers, and white sports shoes of leather and canvas to go with it. "I thank you very much for all you tell me of Warren," he wrote, "and what he is doing. Please hug him about a thousand times for me." Wherever he was, at the Mills mansion in Paris, at the Val des Écoliers outside Chaumont, in his special train, the first thing Frank Lanckton unpacked to put out was a picture of Warren. With him in the photograph were Frankie and the girls. It sometimes seemed to Lanckton that when the general looked at it he forgot, if only for a moment, that four of the five were gone.

In July the Germans came at him from Château-Thierry eastward almost to the Argonne Forest. He stopped them and went on the attack, the fighting close-in at times with the opponents bayoneting one another or using their rifles as clubs. Tens of thousands went down. There was unremitting rain. The Germans went back to make a stand on the Vesle. Through the three months of constant fighting the AEF head as always maintained the closest of controls. If infantry was half an hour leaving trenches after an artillery barrage, or alternately reserves were sent forward too early and so crowded the front lines, someone was instantly relieved to join other officers waiting for reassignment in a gloomy and downcast group at camp in Blois—they went blooey, the expression was. Formal letters of instruction regularly went from Chaumont even to men of so high a rank as Robert Lee Bullard, moved up from division commander to corps commander to lieutenant general commanding the First Army. Bullard was to stay in close contact with and keep in mind the condition of every unit under him, General Pershing had no hesitation in letting him know, and was not to leave such duties to his staff alone; he was to keep active control over his supply depots, his corps commanders and their staffs, his divisions, his regiments, even his battalions. Joseph Dickman and Pershing had been dear friends back in the Philippines and later; but "Let me say that it is the corps commander himself who must be held responsible for the success or failure of his troops. His obligations cannot be delegated." The commander in chief's old friend knew what that meant. If things went wrong he would be on his way to Blois.

To Maj. Gen. William Haan, commanding the Thirty-second Division, with whom he had shared quarters in the long ago, he then addressed by Pershing as "Bunkie," came a letter signed by the aide Col. Carl Boyd: "General Pershing directs me to inform you that during the visit he recently made to your division he noted that some of your regimental commanders wore soiled clothing, were unshaved and presented generally an untidy appearance. The commander in chief directs that you give this matter prompt and energetic attention." Along with other divisional commanders Haan was reminded not to be too far away from leading elements of his attacking columns so that control might be maintained and forward troops kept aggressively active. He must not leave too much to his staff, himself making it clear to junior officers that they must assume responsibility. War was not a question of all being equal, he must make clear to those juniors. A divisional commander must keep involved in questions of food preparation. He must take care of his unit's animals. "Every horse is worth its weight in gold." Attention must therefore be paid to grooming, loading, feed, water. As with all other divisional commanders Haan must impress his personality upon soldiers, talk to assembled groups, be out among his men supervising and directing. He must get himself well forward to the front, not discuss losses, be interested in questions of equipment, discourage tendencies among his men to consider themselves abused or overworked, make frequent inspections, take nothing for granted. "May I not say that my sole purpose in writing the above is, by friendly suggestion, and perhaps, some criticism, to help you if possible to meet the great responsibility which rests upon you." Everyone knew what was unstated: Be as much like the commander in chief as possible or prepare to go blooey.

With wounded soldiers Pershing could be very tender. "It's I who should salute you, lad," he said to a boy unable to do so for having lost his right arm and apologizing to his commander for not rendering the honor. He ruffled the soldier's red hair. At Base Hospital No. 1 in Neuilly he said a word to each patient and bent over to look at a young doughboy being brought in with a bullet through the stomach. Such a wound could have only one result. The soldier was still conscious. "Aren't you General Pershing?" "Yes, I am." The soldier asked to shake hands. They did so and then the commander in chief backed away, never removing his eyes from the boy, waving. "I shook hands with General Pershing. Did you see him smile?" were the soldier's last words.

Those two, the boy who lost his arm and the one who lost his life, had done their duty and paid a price. Their general had a different response to certain other members of the AEF. "When men run away in front of the enemy," he wrote his division commanders, "officers should take summary action to stop it, even to the point of shooting men down who are caught in such disgraceful conduct. No orders need be published on the subject."

"See here, General Pershing, are we *really* going to beat them?" Dorothy Canfield Fisher asked on the night the Battle of Château-Thierry began. "Are you *sure?* Things look so bleak." The friendship begun when he was her math teacher and fencing instructor back at the University of Nebraska and resumed when he came to France had blossomed. He looked forward to getting letters from her, seeing her when he could. Now he laughed at what she had said. They were at dinner. He seemed to her to be again the young officer of long ago. "The old charm, the old light-hearted sunniness were there again," she wrote.

"Why, you're not asking me that question seriously, are you?" he asked. He was fresh from the front. The grimness seen when they first met in France was entirely vanished. "You don't mean me to understand that you are employing the English language to express *doubt* in the matter?" She did not join in his laughter and must have looked troubled. "Why, child," he said in what she thought sounded like an organ note of his deep voice, "*of course* we're going to beat them." Two days later she saw American troops go forward through a wheatfield with horses pulling artillery pieces, her strong and erect young countrymen, and it seemed to her she heard again the lieut of Nebraska days telling his cadets at the Omaha contest, "Boys—I think—you're going—to win!"

She had sensed what was in his mind. He would do it with as little reference as possible to the British and French, feeling as he did that they had nothing to teach him or his men, and that he was fed up with their demands that he play a supporting role to their leading parts. They had with great reluctance finally accepted that he would never permit them the use of small groupings of Americans, but kept to their idea that he apportion out larger units to serve under their command. He would not do so on any permanent basis. There was a fierce scene with Foch. "Do you wish to take part in the battle?" challenged the generalissimo.

"Most assuredly, but as an American army and in no other way."

"Your French and English comrades are going into battle; are you coming with them?"

"Marshal Foch, you have no authority to call upon me to yield up my command of the American Army and have it scattered among the Allied forces where it will not be an American army at all."

"I must insist upon the arrangement."

"You may insist all you please, but I decline absolutely to agree to your plan. While our army will fight, it will not fight except as an independent American army." Both rose from the table at which they had argued for more than two hours, Foch pale with rage, and Pershing so in a fury that for a moment he thought of hitting the Frenchman. They worked it out that Pershing should attack what was called the St.-Mihiel salient, attempt to reduce it, and then in conjunction with Allied attacks elsewhere go at the Germans in the area of the Argonne Forest west of the Meuse River, some sixty miles from St.-Mihiel.

With some half a million soldiers he moved upon the salient, a bulge in the line twenty-five miles across and sixteen miles deep. The Germans had been there since 1914. They had put in barbed-wire entanglements, concrete pillboxes for machine guns, trench systems, emplaced artillery. Twice in 1915 the French had attempted the salient and twice were beaten back. The American troops moved by night. There were terrific rains. At one in the morning on September 12, the artillery opened, flames pouring from muzzles with such constancy that it would have been possible steadily to read a newspaper by their light. The railroad guns sixteen inches across fired on German transportation routes and road junctions and occupied villages; the lighter guns crushed trenches and dugouts. The tanks were ready to go and with them Georgie Patton, transferred there from Pershing's staff. There were some fifteen hundred airplanes to strafe the enemy.

After four hours the barrage lifted and the infantry left their muddy trenches—over the top and into no-man's-land of the World War, the Great War. They took hills, towns, prisoners. There were American assaults from varied angles, the units merging together to press on. Gaps were quickly closed, and from the start it was obvious the operation was a great success, a triumph garnering sixteen thousand prisoners and two hundred square miles of territory. The next day, Pershing's fifty-eighth birthday, a telegram came from James Harbord, former chief of staff of the AEF commander raised to leader of the Second Division at Belleau Wood and then made head of the Services of Supply, a major when *Baltic* sailed for France but a major general now: NEARLY THREE HUNDRED YEARS AGO OLIVER CROMWELL ON THE 13th OF SEPTEMBER WENT INTO BATTLE QUOTING PSALM 68: "LET GOD ARISE AND LET HIS ENEMIES BE SCATTERED: LET THEM ALSO THAT HATE HIM. LIKE AS THE SMOKE VANISHES, SO SHALT THOU DRIVE THEM AWAY." As with Cromwell Pershing was a cavalryman, and like Cromwell he now appeared to the Americans a great soldier chosen to lead their sons in something of a holy war to make the world clean and right, to find the New World redeeming the Old, to fight for, as Wilson said when he asked for war, all the things America held closest to its heart and to which America could, as Wilson said, dedicate everything she was and all that she had, with the pride of those who knew that the day had come when she could spend her blood and her might for the principles that gave her birth and happiness and the peace she had treasured. "God helping her, she can do no other," the president had ended. From the senators and congressmen came a great roar in which were heard the rebel yells of Southerners who as boys had served under Lee and Jackson. Now from all over the country poured telegrams combining birthday salutations with congratulations for the St.-Mihiel victory, the Children of the American Loyalty League, the All-Polish Congress, the Citizens' Vigilance Committee of Miami County, Indiana, the People and Mayor of Kingsville, Texas, the National Council of Traveling Salesmen, the Shriners, the Shipbuilders at Hog Island, Philadelphia, who celebrated the birthday by driving 195,000 rivets, more than on any other day, the Women's Auxiliary of the 165th Infantry, the mayor and common council of Harrison, New Jersey, the Chamber of Commerce of Des Moines, Iowa, the Citizens of Syracus, Kansas, the Board of Aldermen of St. Louis, the Rotary Club of Everett, Washington, the Indianapolis Optimists' Club, all saying they were working with General Pershing to beat the Hun, all answered by himself or one of his aides; the Women's Club of Cheyenne, Frankie's hometown, who informed him that in their Thrift Club Campaign they had for his birthday sold thirteen thousand thrift stamps, the Young Men's Business League of Beaumont, Texas, the El Paso Kiwanis Club, the Junior Order of United American Mechanics of Brooklyn, New York, the San Antonio Blue Bonnet League for National Service, the University Club of San Francisco, the Parents' Association of the state of Washington, the Children of the Irving School, Bloomington, Illinois, the Community War Council of Swarthmore. They were with him to a man. The phrase was constantly repeated. They spoke of him by the nickname created by newspapermen who could hardly use his actual one deriving from service with black troops, Nigger Jack, and substituted Black Jack instead.

With General Pétain he walked through the liberated town of St.-Mihiel, the inhabitants weeping for joy at seeing the Germans driven away. "We gave 'em a damn good licking, didn't we?" Pershing said. Across the lines Germany's Erich Ludendorff was so overcome as almost to be unable to speak coherently.

The Battle of the Meuse River and the Argonne Forest impended. It must begin in fewer than two weeks. He had given Foch his word. He closed down operations in the St.-Mihiel salient and hurried his soldiers south. There they would meet with other American units, more than one million men coming on to try to cut the railroad lines over which moved 250 trains a day supplying the German forces in northern France. There the British would attempt to break free at last of those thin opposing lines the cutting edges of great swords, where for so long and at such cost they had contested for tiny, muddy gains. Pershing came to the Argonne. The host he led was ten times the size of the combined Union and Confederate armies at Gettysburg and spoke a language and lived a life those of the blue and gray never could have understood. Eons, a world, time unmeasured divided it from the days of the Spanish War, and of days in the Philippines; indeed everything was different from when the Punitive Expedition came home from Mexico. The old broad-brim campaign hat was gone for the overseas cap, the spiral woolen legging replaced the canvas puttee, there were metal helmets, new trench knives, gas masks. Pershing had come to this moment with nothing behind him but the Old Army tradition, discipline, and West Point's code. From here came, so swiftly, the end of the America where the street paving ended at the town line trolley turnaround. Nothing would be the same afterward.

He looked at the Meuse-Argonne. "I send you a million kisses and I embrace you tenderly," he found time on September 29 to write his mistress Micheline Resco back in Paris; but the great battle was waiting. Napoleon had his Berthier as indispensable right hand, Blücher his Gneisenau, Ney his Jomini, Grant his Rawlings, Hindenburg his Ludendorff, and Foch his Weygand, but there was nobody like that for Pershing. He and he alone determined that the Americans would go forward in the Meuse-Argonne. Neither President Wilson nor Secretary of War Baker had suggestions, and neither offered plans. It was up to the general they had selected to do the job.

In an area of thickly wooded hills the American attackers faced belts, chains, of German fortifications, interlocking bands of fire, concrete bunkers and pillboxes, concealed machine-gun nests. Amid forests and up the ridges were barbed-wire entanglements and emplaced mortars and artillery pieces, all registered in so defenders could know precisely where a shell would land. Oncoming troops would be swept by fire, raked from end to end—enfiladed from reinforced concrete positions defiladed so that neither direct nor plunging counterfire was likely to be effective. "The most ideal defensive terrain" he had ever seen or read about, thought First Army chief of staff Hugh Drum; a place that made the Wilderness of terrible memory to Lee's men and Grant's men look like a park by comparison, remembered corps commander Hunter Liggett. James Harbord felt that what the Americans faced might be "the most comprehensive system of leisurely prepared field defense known to history."

To assault this redoubt Pershing could attempt no Lee-like feints and no Napoleonic echeloned waves rendezvousing on the scene of battle.

Over thin and winding country roads and trifling feeder railway lines he must marshal his forces and supplies and head-down go forward. There would be no big sweeping moves, glamorous charges with waving flags, field music of fife and drum, bright swords. The soldiers were loaded almost like mules with gas masks, bandoliers of ammunition, canteens, packs, grenades, rations of preserved beef with carrots. They plodded forward as anonymous automatons. Never was war so inhuman, so removed from human elements, so machinelike, thought Gen. Robert Lee Bullard. The artillery opened on the twenty-four-mile front, shells crashing through the trees and in the gullies and up the ridges. "It is well that war is so terrible, else men would learn to love it too much," Robert E. Lee said at Fredericksburg. No such thought came to John J. Pershing along the Meuse and in the Argonne. Coming over on *Baltic* he had said war was ruin and waste. Now he would do the war in. Germany's machine guns chattered like typewriters. Shells crashed. Fires broke out in the trees. Behind the American infantrymen were lines of military police brutal in their treatment of anyone who hesitated, or thought to go back.

The troops went forward. Some on the way or once there became ill. They fell strangely silent. Or they talked too much. In the end they cried or screamed or clawed at their mouths. It was unpredictable who would become undone, tough old soldier for years snarling "Close it up!" at drilling rookie, or fuzzy-cheeked college boy enlisted off his campus. Shell shock. That was the new term. Sometimes victims of war's new modernized horror recovered. Sometimes they did not, going from dressing station to base hospital and eventually hospitals for veterans in the States, where decades later, Wilson gone, Baker, Bullard, Hunter Liggett, and John Pershing at Arlington, they lived yet with what the Meuse-Argonne had been. People came sometimes to make them an outing with hot dogs and such. Some of those of their fellows who came from the World War safe went in the 1920s and 1930s to riotous American Legion conventions of silver-plated helmets and balloons filled with water dropped with great hilarity from high hotel rooms, touched battery-powered electric canes to the rear ends of girls young enough to be their daughters, paraded to the accompaniment of blaring drum and bugle corps. They were the boys who cracked the Hindenburg Line. They

drank at smokers in the Veterans of Foreign Wars clubhouse who were
the legions that won the war. Then there were the ones forever young
whose names were commemorated on bronze plaques or on the pedestal
below the statue of The Doughboy in the squares of a thousand towns or
in the new Roaring Twenties suburbs of new commuter rail lines out
from the central areas where stood the memorials for those who did what
they did for Lee in the South and Grant in the North. The Americans
went into the Argonne Forest.

"Things are going badly," Pershing said to Maj. Gen. Henry Allen of
the Ninetieth Division. "We are not getting on as we should. But by God,
Allen, I was never so much in earnest in my life and we are going to get
through." In fewer than forty days American casualties exceeded one
hundred thousand men, not that far off from the total forces engaged on
both sides at Gettysburg. The Argonne became uprooted trees, battered
wheels, shreds of wire, great chunks of metal, helmets in the mud, dead
horses and mules, ruined weapons, bodies, bits of bone, a skull, bits of
uniform, the stench of putrefying flesh mixing with that of cordite fumes.
(Poison gas decades later made caves still dangerous, hunters around a
fire would be blown to bits by a long-ago dud shell heated to sudden explosion, children finding a grenade would have an arm torn off, a leg.)
Transport by animals or truck was so difficult to get forward that infantrymen going up the line were handed shells to carry to up-close guns. The
days of going through northern cities for embarkation from Hoboken
with girls offering candy, fruit, coffee, their addresses for correspondence
from Over There, then the ship, then training days in France, maybe a
brief leave to Gay Paree, all that gave way to death and cripples brought
to aid stations in the long mule-drawn wagons slogging past bodies fallen
off into the mud. "There is no course except to fight it out," General Pershing said on October 4, fewer than ten days into the fight. The next day
Pétain came for lunch. "He said this is something which might have happened to anyone," Pershing recorded, "and there is only one course left
and that is to keep on driving. That is what we will do." One evening his
limousine ran out of gas and as the chauffeur sought more the commander in chief sat alone in the backseat. An old woman came along, bent
over, with a black knitted shawl over her head and wooden sabots on her

feet. She saw the car's flag with four stars and put her hand over her eyes to peer in. "*Monsieur, monsieur,*" she said. General Pershing looked at her. "Thank you," she said.

She went on. He wrote Micheline Resco back in Paris on October 13, "I am very sad that I am not able to see you, kiss you, lovingly embrace you. But the battle progresses. All to you, J."

He was constantly among his soldiers, sometimes standing in the middle of a roadway to unravel traffic heading up the line or returning from it. Field telephone wires lying on the ground or strung to tree stumps got cut, carrier pigeons failed to arrive, runners with messages fell hit into trenches or shell holes, the roads and trails collapsed into pools of muddy water despite engineers trying to shore them up by piling on rocks to form a base. In awful rain and quagmire sixteen thousand men came down with flu in the week ending October 5. Some twenty-five thousand tons of supplies daily had to be moved up to no-man's-land, smoke swirling about. On October 15 Pershing relieved of their commands his classmates John McMahon from the Fifth Division and Beaumont Buck from the Third. Both were major generals. The artillery barrages rained down on enemy batteries, roads, headquarters, bridges, reserve encampments. Everything was fog, whistles, the rolling thunder of the guns, the dispatch forward of ammunition, oil and gas, food, forage, road-building and bridging materials, equipment for the signals and motor and tank units, medical supplies, with gas shells from the enemy falling and mortars hitting home, screams for the medic to hurry. Georgie Patton went down and his orderly dragged him into a shallow crater to stop up a wound pouring blood, German bullets singing over both their heads. Pershing had a snarl for the chief of staff of the Forty-second, the Rainbow Division for its composition of men from every state in the Union. The men appeared sloppy and lackadaisical. "I'm going to hold you personally responsible for getting discipline and order into this division," he rasped. "I'm going to hold you personally responsible for correcting measures with the officers at fault. I won't stand for this. It's a disgrace."

"Yes, sir," replied Col. Douglas MacArthur.

One million two hundred thousand Yanks went at the enemy; the headquarters map's red strings showing American unit positions went forward; and out in the rain back past the masses of men who made those strings move came tens of thousands, one hundred thousand, one hundred seventy thousand sick and wounded and dead, evacuated rearward. So jammed were the roads with traffic coming and going that it appeared the U.S. Army in the Argonne might come to resemble a great turtle immobilized on its back and unable to move; but the Push, so they called it, went on. The head of the army's medical services came to Pershing to beg that he break off, and divisional commanders, weeping, asked for that; but those around the commander in chief saw such appeals had no meaning to him. "Men," he told a group of soldiers in the mud, "if you can stick this a little longer I'll have you out of here in a few weeks." He knew it was vital that he personally, he the commander, the man two million American soldiers in France viewed as one whose replacement was inconceivable, look fresh, sharp, dynamic, optimistic, uniform as always immaculate, boots glittering, "up" at all times. He could never permit himself to lower his head on his desk, he told Col. George C. Marshall, who had proved to be a staff officer brilliant at working out orders, for such an act might be nosed about as signifying depression and discouragement immediately and dangerously spread by rumor, as occurred when once he been seen slumping back in his car.

Secretary of War Baker came over to France. A couple of months earlier he had been to London, where he was told that Prime Minister Lloyd George, ill at his country residence, desired a conference on a matter of the utmost importance. If Baker could not come down, the prime minister, against doctors' orders, would come up. Baker went down to the country to hear Lloyd George tell him Pershing was impossible with his insistence on a separate American military entity, and that he, Lloyd George, regretted that he must ask for his removal. His discussion of Pershing's faults required fifteen minutes of monologue. When he finished there was a brief silence, followed by Baker's reply: "Mr. Prime Minister, we are not in need of advice from any foreign nation as to who should lead our armies." Now as the Argonne fight went on Baker asked Pershing if there was anything he could do. Pray, Pershing replied. As they spoke, as the battle raged, the French suggested that Pershing cede control of some half a million or more of his men. They would be put under French generals. In Paris Clemenceau was still saying that American battalions should be in French regiments, that the logical reasons for this were being withheld from Wilson and Baker by their general, who should have been relieved long ago.

The American commander in chief met with Generalissimo Foch for a frosty exchange of views. More than frosty, perhaps; the words "waspish," "sharp," "brusque," "scorn," "slur," "angry," and "harshly" were in the account of the meeting given by Laurence Stallings, who lost a leg in the Great War and would go on to write the play most associated with it: *What Price Glory*. The complaints and arguments did the French and British no good. Americans and Americans only would command their country's soldiers. Pershing divided his force into two armies, Hunter Liggett in charge of one, Robert Lee Bullard of the other, himself as an army group commander on a level with Great Britain's Sir Douglas Haig and France's Henri Philippe Pétain. Pershing's troops fought on. The Allies took note. When Generalissimo Foch ran into Bentley Mott and was asked how things were going, the Frenchman reached out and grabbed his questioner by the belt with one hand and lightly punched him in the chin with the other, followed by a hook to the ribs and one to the ear. *That* was how things were going, and what was being done to the Boche. Without a single word Foch went on, shouldering the stick he carried, relic of the lost world that had been the gentlemen's war of plume and gesture and elaborate horsehair and ostrich-feather helmet. Now all that was in the mud along the Western Front. Old Europe of land in the family for three hundred years, butler with silver tray, dress-for-dinner and teeming servants on one hand, and on the other position assured in that it was what one's great-grandfather held, gamekeeper or *sommelier*, perhaps—it was all going. It might hang on for a few years until the Crash of 1929, but the days were numbered. To replace it in the scheme of things came the Americans, brash, loud, unmannered by the standards of Pall Mall and the Sixteenth Arrondissement—and now they took the Argonne. In the north the British were also coming on; and the enemy began negotiating. They had to. German schoolboys going up the line found themselves called strikebreakers by those coming down in the dribs and drabs of broken array. Germany's ally Turkey surrendered, and as unrest and revolution seized Vienna and Budapest, Austria-Hungary broke apart. Bulgaria quit. Notes from Berlin went out to President Wilson.

An end to the fighting was in sight, and for the British and French it could not come too soon. Never mind the exact terms given the German. Let the Great War find its conclusion. There was something else. America was reaching its peak, men pouring in as soldiers of a country vibrant, pledged to do great things, resounding with the songs of 1918, "Over There," the others, while Great Britain and France were at their last resources. If the war went on, America must take the lead. That meant American dominance at the eventual peacemaking whose treaties would determine the future. It was understandable, what the Allies felt. They had given so much. Let the matter have done. Be over. Perish the details. Peace.

General Pershing did not see it that way. Long ago he had ordered his fellows to attention as across the Hudson from West Point there passed the funeral train of Ulysses S. Grant, nicknamed Unconditional Surrender for the terms he offered Buckner at Fort Donelson. Pershing wanted what Grant's first two initials stood for, with a smashing victory parade in Berlin, his troops banging and rattling their way down Unter den Linden, flags whipping, the bands playing. That was what had been seen in Paris at the end of the Franco-Prussian War. As the heirs to German troops of that day now fled away from later battlefields with unburied dead left lying behind, with tens of thousands of his Yanks ready to do or die, Pershing perhaps saw in imagination Grant's men swinging along in the great victory parade of 1865, their ranks predecessor to what he would offer in Germany's capital.

It was to Wilson, and not the French and British, to whom the Germans appealed for terms. Cablegrams flew to him from the Wilhelmstrasse. He also heard from his commander in France. No terms, Pershing said. Let the Germans stack arms in ceremonious surrender display, lay down their battle flags, go off as definitively beaten as Lee had been at Appomattox. He went to Paris to make known his views, but was not asked to the discussions of the Supreme War Council of the Allied and Associated Powers. Field Marshal Haig was, and gave it as his opinion that the enemy should be granted mild terms. President Wilson's representative, Edward M. House, indicated he was inclined to agree. "Mild terms!" Pershing burst out to his liaison officer at the British War Office, Lloyd Griscom, the bridge-playing minister to Japan during Russo-Japanese War days. It was October 27, 1918. They sat before a fireplace in a bedroom of the Mills mansion in the Rue des Varennes. Pershing was in a dressing gown with a blanket over his knees. A form of influenza had taken him. He ought to be in bed, Griscom said, and Pershing admitted it was so, but he had work to do. They talked about the proposed armistice. Armistice—that was a word most Americans had never heard before. "Truce" was what was used during the Civil War, and Grant had wanted precious little of that for his opponents.

As they spoke, Griscom found that Pershing's "habitual imperturbality" was gone. "Mild terms!" he burst out. "That's what Haig wants." He showed what Griscom called such "emotional vehemency" as his old Japanese-days acquaintance and Great War subordinate did not know he possessed. Haig wanted an end to the fighting because he had no more reserves, Pershing said, and had insultingly voiced doubts about the ability of the Americans to fill that lack if the Germans kept up a fight. "What right has anyone to make such a statement?" Pershing demanded. "We have the upper hand, and there is no reason why the terms shouldn't be stiff enough to prevent a war such as this ever having to be fought again." Griscom had never seen him so upset.

Three days later, Supreme War Council discussions still going on without him, he came down with another physical problem. Calling on him at the Mills place, his Old '86 classmate Mott found him walking up and down in his dressing gown, fearful profanity coming in an underbreath sometimes augmented by what Mott termed "a furious ejaculation."

"Don't pay any attention to my language," Pershing said. "I have had a horrible toothache all day." For years he had suffered from such problems, and would do so for years into the future. "The dentist has been here three times and the only thing he can offer by way of relief is to propose an opiate. I have too much need of all my senses to accept that, so the best I can do is to swear. It seems to relieve me a little bit." He told

Mott he had a letter he wanted his classmate personally to hand to Generalissimo Foch. It detailed why unconditional surrender must be demanded from the enemy. Without such the Boche could with rifles shouldered and big guns rolling and flags flying go back to welcome arches in a Germany that had known no trenches, barbed wire, or shell holes, and whose people might well decide their army really hadn't been beaten at all. What that might store up for the future could be imagined. Mott did as he was told, but Foch told him with a sweep of his hand to inform Pershing there was nothing to worry about. Pershing returned to Chaumont, from where he wrote Micheline Resco of his regret at being unable to see her when in town because of his illnesses and the press of important matters. "Do you wish to pardon me—do you wish to give me a long kiss like always and permit me to send you a million thoughts of chagrin?"

The war was going to be suspended, the Allies decided. An armistice. The Germans would march home in formation with weapons and flags. On the night of November 10, Mott wired from Foch's headquarters that all firing would cease at eleven the next morning—the eleventh hour of the eleventh day of the eleventh month, November 11, 1918.

The officers of the commander in chief's staff stayed up all night in the Val des Écoliers living quarters outside Chaumont. At six in the morning they drove to headquarters to find Pershing alone in his office. Everyone sat around looking at watches, waiting for eleven o'clock. The commanding officer showed no exaltation by word or gesture. There was not a hint in his demeanor that anything extraordinary was about to occur. "I suppose our campaigns are ended," he remarked, looking at the wall map. "But what an enormous difference a few days more would have made." Off to the distance could be heard the sound of big guns going off as doughboy artillerymen sought to have the last word.

Nobody spoke as eleven o'clock approached. Time had never passed so slowly. Then there was a last final salvo of cannons, and the Great War was over. Silence settled over the Western Front, and from the trenches men lifted themselves up to stand exposed as no one could have done without certain death for four years. A German took off his helmet, put on a soft cap, threw the helmet in the mud in front of him, bowed, waved, turned, and went away. In Pershing's office the officers broke into explosive yelling, slapping of backs, laughter, all talking at once. They made for the center of town and there met the populace coming their way dancing, singing, shouting, weeping. That night the staff put records on a Victrola and danced, together and alone, the general joining in. Champagne bottles packed into an ice-filled German helmet were popped by stewards.

Pershing in that moment came to the end of his career as a fighting soldier. He had dealt in his beginnings on a charger with Indians in the West, then the Spanish in Cuba, with Moros in the Philippines, Mexicans in Chihuahua, then the Germans with tanks, airplanes, short-range howitzer and long-range piece and the mustering of soldiers in undreamed-of numbers. What he had done in the Great War was to be recorded as displaying great intelligence, perfect soundness, immense resolution, energy, rectitude in thought and action, great determination and command of detail. Thousands of miles from home, his the task of controlling all strategy and administration and of dictating major and minor tactics for his soldiers, his the guiding hand of the enormous supply and maintenance services, he emanated, radiated, authority, while never known, remembered his staff officer John McA. Palmer, to do a tactless thing. From his soldiers he received no love. Perhaps it was that the World War was too inhuman for men to feel adoration for those who led them. Pershing was not incapable of feeling for the men who served under him. In the days after the Great War, preparing speeches for dedication of cemeteries of dead boys, he could tell his aides that he wasn't sure he could offer his remarks without breaking down. He never did. He was a man who had gotten through the loss of the love of his life by discipline, form, hardiness, willpower, getting things done, a soldier with a soldier's dedication. So he was understood by his men: honorable, dependable, worthy, admirable. But no more than these. When political figures canvassed men of the AEF with the thought in mind that a victorious general might make a likely presidential candidate, they swiftly found that there were few votes to be garnered by Pershing's victory.

His staff people with him day and night to a man revered him and in later years as individually industrialist, pioneering radio magnate, swashbuckling history-making soldier, hopeful of likely important future sadly dying young, rich man-diplomat, hope of American fascism, foremost-placed figure of military aviation, soldier-statesman with world-renowned great name, U.S. Army chief of staff, none ever had the first bad word to say about him. Men of acclamation and renown often leave broken friendships behind them. That was never true of John J. Pershing. He remained as he had been, an adherent of what Robert E. Lee was reputed to have said but never actually did, although the words accurately defined his view: *"Duty" is the most sublime word in the language.* Pershing could be kind, would always do what he could. Achievement, however, was what mattered.

When his battles were finished Othello said, *Farewell the plumed troop, and the big wars, farewell the neighing steed, and the shrill trump, the spirit-stirring drum, the ear-piercing fife, and all quality, pride, pomp and circumstance of glorious war.* When his battles were finished Pershing said to Charlie Dawes in their first post-Armistice contact that as the American people had supported them so magnificently it was their obligation in return to cut down on military expenditures and thus cost the taxpayers as little as possible.

Mr. Pershing of Missouri, First Captain of the Corps of Cadets in 1886.

Second lieutenant of the Sixth United States Cavalry.

Captain Pershing.

Brigadier General and Mrs. Pershing in Zamboanga, P.I., with Helen, Anne, and Warren. A fourth child, Mary Margaret, will shortly arrive.

In the Philippines. "He is today the one great American to the Moro mind. They regard him as a supernatural being."

Miss Anne Wilson Patton—Nita. Her brother, George
S. Patton, thought her romance with the head of the
American Expeditionary Forces was "certainly the most
intense case I have ever seen."

Major general, raised to that rank while chasing Pancho Villa in Mexico. "All the promotion in the world would make no difference now," Pershing wrote a classmate.

The AEF leader as sketched by Mlle. Micheline Resco, who would be his hidden mistress for thirty years. No usable pictures of her are known to exist.

"He can read a man's soul through his boots or his buttons," wrote the reporter Heywood Broun. "They will never call him 'Papa Pershing.'"

With Secretary of War Newton D. Baker.

The general with his overseas staff and his son, Warren.

The highest ranking officer in United States history often went to sporting events with his growing son.

"Named by the Washington Post as the best dressed man in the capital."

With his closest European friend, Marshal Henri Philippe Pétain, thirteen years after the war—1931.

Charles Gates Dawes, with whom as a young man Pershing shared fifteen-cent lunches in Lincoln, Nebraska, and who remained a lifelong intimate.

Above: World War II's Free French leader General Charles de Gaulle calls upon an aged Washington invalid.

Left: Warren holds the flag from his father's coffin as Aunt May stands by. Arlington Cemetery, July of 1948.

Mumu with her sons Dick, left, and Jack.

Warren with his two adolescents at the Stork Club, Jack wearing glasses.

Dick as a member of the Yale University lacrosse team.

Jack as a colonel of the army reserves.

✦ IV ✦

GENERAL OF THE ARMIES OF THE UNITED STATES

→ 13 ←

"BY ORDER OF THE SECRETARY OF WAR you are directed—" began the holder of that position.

"Say it again, Chief," said Warren Pershing, age nine, with a laugh. They were standing on the deck of *Leviathan* about to sail for France. Pershing had always promised his son he would bring him over when the war ended.

"By order of the secretary of war, you are to pose for these photographers," Newton Baker intoned. Warren gave him a look interpretable by the newspapermen as, "How do you get that way, eh?" and folded his arms across his chest. Flashbulbs popped. "The ship may roll like a chip in a bathtub when she gets on the ocean, and you may not feel like eating any meals for a day or two," a reporter remarked.

"Huh! I should worry. I'm going to see Dad." Warren alternated flipping dimes in the air and reaching up to take Secretary Baker's hand. It had been a long time since he'd seen his father, the secretary said with a smile. They might not recognize each other.

"Betcher I'll know Dad all right," Warren said. His hair was so blond as almost to be white, as it had been since babyhood. He wore a military-style coat with officers' braid on the cuffs. "You needn't think I am going to be sick, because I'm not," he told the reporters. "The only rolls I'm going to notice are those I have for breakfast. This is the biggest ship on the ocean and has movies and everything."

"Shall we tell your father you are coming to visit him, or shall we surprise him?" Baker asked.

"I would like to surprise him," Warren said, "but you know he's a mighty hard man to fool." As he flipped up a dime, a crumpled fifty-dollar bill fell to the deck from his coat pocket. It was retrieved by a regulars sergeant who had been wounded in the Argonne and detailed to training duties at home before returning for Occupation duty in Europe and with shipboard assignment to look after the commander in chief's boy. The days of Warren dropping out of his pocket a week's salary for a good-provider family man, two and a half months' pay for an army private, would cease immediately when his father reasserted direct control over him. Warren must not be made aware of the money he was heir to through his mother, the only daughter of the richest man in Wyoming. The irreverent tone Warren assumed with Secretary of War Baker would also swiftly vanish. A boy largely brought up by his doting old-maid Aunt May was in grave danger of being spoiled, General Pershing believed. In later years the adult Warren Pershing remembered his father's discussions of such potentiality. Often they took place as the general and his son posted along on horses. His father offered ongoing lessons in advanced philosophy, Warren would remark. Then he explained the substance of the courses: "Ass-chewing."

Leviathan steamed out of harbor to the accompaniment of whistles and toots and plumes of water shot up in the air by welcomers awaiting the imminent return home of Adm. William S. Sims, Pershing's navy equivalent in Europe, and willing additionally to salute the outward-bound Baker, a fifteen-man congressional delegation going over for an inspection tour, the new American ambassador to France, and Warren. The general was on the pier when *Leviathan* made Brest. In the days immediately following the Armistice he had been kissed by Foch, greeted by a Clemenceau broken down in tears. He had decorated Haig, spent time with the king and queen of the Belgians, stood behind Pétain as the general was handed the baton making him a marshal of France. Pershing did not see his responsibilities concluding with the conclusion of the fighting. The men of his forces must be kept busy and the army functioning correctly. Even on the day when Warren's ship was due to arrive, his fa-

ther inspected six thousand soldiers about to embark for home. He went
to the mess hall, looked at the sleeping quarters. All over the American
Zone troops were kept at military drill interspersed with athletics, theatrical presentations, horse shows, vocational schools, and the fourteen-
thousand-student AEF university at Beaune teaching college-level
courses.

The commander kept to an exacting schedule. It was said that not a
single man of his two million did not at one time or another come under
Pershing's direct gaze. To those heading home he offered brief speeches,
seven to ten minutes. America was grateful to them, he said. Wasn't it
splendid to have served in this great army, to be chosen, privileged to do
so? The men should never boast about it, but always be proud. "I thank
you again and again. Now, men, tell your friends who are not here this
morning that you have just had a friendly talk with the general." He
would leave the soldiers with a good taste in their mouths, he said. But of
course discipline must be maintained. He kept after the venereal disease
rate, which sank to a low never seen before in any army of the world's history—as might be expected when by Pershing's order any man returning
intoxicated to base was assumed to have been exposed to infection and
given treatment, forcibly if necessary. Pershing knew about gonorrhea—
had had it twice in years gone by.

Even as he presented decorations, tied ribbons with battle names on
regimental flags, reviewed from a stand great marching columns, his eyes
caught muddy boots. "The men were not so well set up physically," he
wrote responsible officers of the Forty-second Division, "and their clothing showed lack of proper care." Presenting Medal of Honor or Distinguished Service Cross, he could focus on what a unit's musketry scores
indicated of its marksmanship, even though it could be expected that
none of the soldiers would ever have to fight again, for they had just participated in the winning of The War to End War. In all his time abroad he
took one vacation, a week in Monte Carlo six weeks after the Armistice,
where he walked along the beach, played golf, took Turkish baths,
worked out with gymnastic apparatus. Then it was back to work noticing
if men used sufficient dubbin on their shoes, if the length of the march
step in the review was of proper length and the fixed bayonets aligned, the

condition of the horses. On the afternoon of March 14, 1919, he boarded a small boat taking him out to *Leviathan* and reunion with the son not seen for more than two years. As they walked to the limousine, Warren joined in returning salutes. From then on he was always with his father, sometimes a small figure in blue Buster Brown suit and blue cap in a sea of khaki, but more usually part of it in his miniature lieutenant's uniform. After a time he decided he preferred to be a sergeant, so bars were removed from shoulders and stripes sewn on sleeves and he was called by his new rank. He was a likable child, sturdy, adaptable. Once at a social affair in the thin strip along the Rhine that was Occupied Territory, a phone call for the general came from his headquarters. An officer seeking him found he had departed the ballroom for the bedroom assigned to Warren. He was sitting there watching his son sleep. "I like to be with my boy," Pershing said. "I have seen so little of him in the last few years that it seems as if we hardly know each other. I want to see all of him I can. I wouldn't feel right if I let the evening pass without spending part of it with my son, even if he is asleep."

Together they went to plays and revues staged by soldiers' theatrical groups whose predictable jokes and jibes about the brass made Pershing laugh along with everyone else. They were at the finals of the AEF football league, and in the Cirque de Paris for the championships of the AEF boxing tournament. (The winners were duly noted in the general's official diary kept by one of his junior staff officers, "Eugene Tunney of the Services of Supply" winning in the light-heavyweight division. A few years later, as a professional, he was twice to beat Jack Dempsey for the heavyweight championship.)

They went to band concerts, both enjoying music, as did all Pershings. Even before the war ended, the general talked about creating a great army band. He asked the musically prominent Walter Damrosch to advise on the project, and Charlie Dawes, who kept a grand piano in the Paris hotel suite constituting his quarters. A marvelous group resulted. Even more notable was what was called the Composite Regiment, a crack drill squad of more than three thousand men and officers whose marching, appearance, trimness, snappiness, and brilliant dispatch exceeded even the standards of the Brigade of Guards or the Corps of Cadets. Both band and marchers were termed "Pershing's Own."

With Warren he went to dinners, balls, receptions, parades, no soldier in the world looking more the part he had been designated to play, that of the supremely trim and just-right representative of America's showing in the Great War. He was always surrounded by a flurry of smart aides and attending orderlies, with Warren, of course, the pet and mascot—"Your sergeant-son" to Elizabeth, queen of the Belgians. Orderly Frank Lanckton was in charge of such matters as dispatch to bed at the proper time: "Sergeant Pershing, go to your quarters." Mlle. Resco fell to Warren's charm, considerable then as afterward, and took him about for confectionery treats and museum visits. The general's relationship to her was as it would be to the day of his death. It was not of an entirely uninterrupted nature. (Where Pershing went, observed George Marshall, made an aide after the Armistice, it was like a wind blowing amid the ladies.) He remained true, however, to the young Frenchwoman while oftentimes skating on thin ice: he had perhaps been "so busy and impatient," but she must forgive him. "You know me well enough to know that I did not mean anything. It would be a poor kind of love that would not overlook that." "I have just talked to you over the phone and was surprised that you should break down and cry, you Dear, but I do understand, and shall never again be harsh even in manner—my *heart* isn't harsh anyway. But Chérie you must give me some excuses. Make some allowance for me. And, Chérie, I want you to get a *beautiful* Easter coat as my present."

Received at the Duchy of Luxembourg with speeches by inhabitants anxious to thank the Americans who liberated them from the Germans, he delighted in one delivered by an old lady who was under the impression that he and his troops were the British. Her remarks included Admiral Nelson's familiar admonition that England expected every man to do his duty. "It added a little touch to the situation which I should have hated to miss," Pershing mused. On the balcony of the grand duchess's palace he stood with her as the U.S. units passed in review. Spectators shouting "Hip, hip, hooray" filled the air with sound. "But I must say that I was not particularly impressed with the Eighteenth. They had a businesslike air, but were a little sloppy." He had an argument with Clemenceau about the dimensions of the area assigned to Americans in occupied Germany, telling The Tiger he had not discussed it with Foch because the marshal was so very stubborn. Clemenceau caught him by the arm and said, "Well now, General. Don't you think that possibly you are a little stubborn at times?" They both broke into laughter, and Clemenceau said he would see what he could do about the situation.

Warren was with him for a combined sitting with the sculptor Jo Davidson and artist Joseph Cummings on May 24, six weeks after the boy's arrival, to hear his father tell of his adventures in the artists' quarter of Paris twenty years before, when as a captain he first went out to the East—"I did my best to preserve throughout my military composure," he said of his dealings with the art students—and then went with his son on Memorial Day for the dedication of the great cemetery of Romagne in the center of the Meuse-Argonne sector where would repose the bodies of thirty thousand of his soldiers. He worked on his speech until the last minute, coming in from a morning ride with Warren on the day of its delivery to add finishing touches. It was difficult to make clear what he felt for these fallen, he told the listeners, and ended by addressing the dead: "And now, dear comrades, Farewell. Here, under the clear skies, on the green hillsides amid the flowering fields of peace, we leave you forever in God's keeping."

He played tennis, ordered that soldiers' uniforms sent for delousing be returned to their wearers freshly pressed, gave out medals for track meets, was interested in the AEF crew preparing to compete in the Henley Regatta, and on July 14, Bastille Day, rode in the great parade that was the last Paris showing of the men who won the World War. At the head of the Composite Regiment with his silk four-starred flag held aloft by a mounted lieutenant and followed by horsed generals and his aides, and the massed banners of the forty-five American regiments still in France, he went with representatives of all the other forces through jammed streets to the Arc de Triomphe and down the Champs-Élysées to the Place de la République. The statues of Alsace and Lorraine in the Place de la Concorde were free for the first time in fifty years of the mourning crepe hung upon them when the Germans took the provinces after the Franco-Prussian War.

Then he was off to England for the July 19 victory parade there, crossing the Channel on the British destroyer *Orpheus* and going to Victoria

Station, where awaited royal carriages of the King's Stable and Sec. of State for War Winston Churchill and a guard of honor from the Scots Guards. He went to Buckingham Palace to sign the King's Book, the Prince of Wales's Book, Queen Alexandra's Book. He lunched with King George and Queen Mary and three of their children, and His Majesty matter-of-factly remarked, "You, of course, will be the next American president." The visitor changed the subject. His reaction when he learned that his brother Jim was also giving that as his opinion in Chicago speeches was less restrained. "May the good Lord deliver us from fool friends and more foolish relatives," he wrote Jim. "Why in the name of common sense you should go around shooting off your mouth is more than I can understand. I am not a candidate for anything, but if I were, with you running round like a blatant ass, it would not be long before we should all go to the scrap heap as a family of fools. If you and a few other choice individuals whom I might name were yoked together and thrown into Lake Michigan, the rest of us might then get along without embarrassment every day of our lives on account of what you say or what you do."

He was not being very kind to a brother to whom the world itself had not been very kind, who had gone bankrupt running an orchard, unsuccessfully tried to sell stocks, went from thing to thing. "I have not made an ass of myself," Jim wrote back. "Is there anyone on earth that would go farther or do more for you? Is there anyone in the world as proud of you as I am? Now you know I am neither an ass nor the damn fool nor any of the vile names you have abused me with. It's true I went broke, but does this take all my brains away and condemn me as an eternal scapegoat? Now, John, I would rather cut my leg off than to do anything to hurt you." Pershing perhaps felt a little ashamed of himself. He had "never for a single moment attributed to you anything except the finest motives," he wrote Jim. If Jim wanted to come over to France for a visit, his brother would give him a chance to see everything he could.

As for the presidency—"I can say this to you, which I would not say to any other person in the world," he wrote Senator Warren, "that if there should be an unanimous demand all over the country for such a thing, I do not see how any man can decline." No such demand was ever made. The soldiers Caesar, Cromwell, Napoleon, Wellington and Grant had gone on to political power in times past; but of high officers directly after the Great War only Hindenburg occupied political office, and as a figurehead only, who when he utilized power did so with catastrophic results. John Pershing in later years said he was glad there had been no call to the White House.

On July 19 the victory parade in London was as a great flowing river, church bells ringing, distant artillery firing salutes, military bands blaring, the massed standards of the Household Cavalry and those of the Brigade of Guards gorgeous to see, the American Composite Regiment going on so magnificently behind the AEF commander in chief that even Guards officers said they never saw better marching although the horses provided for Pershing's staff at Rotten Row left something to be desired. Cavorting and prancing, eyes rolling, tails swishing, they were almost unmanageable, and when he saw the one Pershing was supposed to ride, Lloyd Griscom got angrier than at any time during his time of liaison with the British War Office. A substitute was found for the general, but the one supplied George Marshall threw him off and broke his hand. Marshall remounted and with the others sat four hours in the saddle as the parade went out of Hyde Park Gate across Knightsbridge and down Sloane Street to the Royal Pavilion facing the Mall, where there were obelisks, giant pylons adorned with chaplets of laurel encircling affixed regimental badges of the British Army. The occupants of the reviewing stand included Warren Pershing. King George slapped him on the back and Queen Mary told a photographer to get her picture with the boy. Marshal Foch shook his hand and touched his lips to it and Queen Mother Alexandra gave him a hug and a kiss. General Pershing dismounted after going past and came up into the box, Warren jumping forward with, "Oh, Dad!" His father lifted him in his arms and they kissed. The Associated Press reported Warren's reaction to his mixing with royalty and the great of the world: "That big Scotch drum major with the dress on and the high thing on his head was the one I liked best."

Pershing was granted the Freedom of the City of London and Sword of Honour, the Court of Common Council in mazarine gowns and white kid gloves for the occasion and a battalion of the Grenadier Guards drawn up in Guildhall Yard. The lord mayor and lady mayoress luncheon followed the presentation at Mansion House, with that night dinner in the House of Commons, the Right Honourable Winston Churchill presiding. There was a luncheon with Their Majesties in Buckingham Palace's State Dining Room ablaze with red carnations and roses, an afternoon party in the garden, great fireworks, presentation by Lt. Gen. the earl of Cavan of a sword gold-mounted and richly decorated with the hilt showing figure of Britannia and figure of Liberty, the monogram JJP in diamonds and rubies, and the Stars and Stripes and Union Jack, and on enameled ribbons designations of the American battles of the war, Château-Thierry, the Meuse-Argonne, the others. Cambridge gave him an honorary degree, students massing to carry him on their shoulders to luncheon at Christ's College, shouting, "Good old Pershing." Oxford gave him an honorary degree.

He did not forget Micheline Resco back in Paris. "Small dear, during the days since I arrived in London I have not had a moment to myself until this hour, but there isn't a minute that I do not think of you." He nightly dreamed of her, he wrote her, wanted to hold her in his arms. He regularly offered his thoughts in coded telegrams sent to her No. 4 rue Descombes apartment. *Mireille* meant "millions of kisses," *Antony* was "I am very anxious," *Cecile* "Why the silence?," *Ophelia* "I am very sorry," *André* "I am very anxious to see you," *Beatrice* "All is well." *To you To you To you*, his letters ended. But there was another woman in his life—or at least there had been. Told by her brother Georgie that there was a chance General Pershing still had feelings for her, Nita Patton came to Europe. "How long are you staying?" Pershing asked. "And what are you going to do over here?"

She wrote home that he was "a little tin god on wheels," and followed her letter back to California. There she asked a favor of her family regarding her relationship to John Pershing: "Let us *never never* speak of it again."

He went about to the old battlefields to have a soldier long dead disinterred so he could see the condition of the coffin. It was found in acceptable shape, although the cover was slightly bent. A very little dirt had gotten in. The body was in good condition. He noticed that the paint on the crosses in the cemetery at Fismes was of a poorer grade than that used elsewhere and was not standing the rain as well. With Warren and his aides he steamed down the Rhine, went to Italy. At Turin during a buffet lunch a band offered "The Star-Spangled Banner" over and over again, not realizing the obligation of the visitors to stand at attention. Finally the Americans disregarded the custom, odd as it felt to be eating while the national anthem was sounding. The king had him for luncheon at the Quirinal Palace, and he went to the Verona opera for Ponchielli's *The Prodigal Son,* performed in an old Roman arena with, he thought, unequaled effect for the setting and the light. He toured Milan and Venice.

Almost the last of the American troops were gone, and it was time for him to follow. "My work is finished," he wrote Micheline. "One is not able to stay in a strange country always. You know how I love France and the French, especially my dear one. You also know how I regret that I am no longer young, but if I were still young I would not have been able to participate in the great war at the head of our army. I am at the end of my life. You are a great artist. You have all your life in the future with a commencement already brilliant." But perhaps, he went on, they might yet be together now and then—she could visit him in America.

If his letter was an attempt to let her down easy, it did not accomplish its intention. His words shattered her. "Very dear," he wrote a few days later, "the end of the world is not here." His love, he wrote, went to her. He loved her. "I am not able to stay happy when you are sad. I send you all my kisses and all my love. Always to you."

By July 31, 1919, the strength of the office of the commander in chief at Chaumont consisted of seven officers, two field clerks, and two enlisted men. The tiny force arriving on *Baltic* two years and two months earlier had swollen to two million and then dwindled to almost nothing. His Old '86 classmate Avery Andrews prepared to return to the civilian life he had departed for Great War service under his onetime fellow cadet. Andrews had been in France one and a half years. During that time he had never heard Pershing mention Frankie's name. Now as they dined together just before Andrews left, the general spoke of a dinner party he and she had given Andrews and Mrs. Andrews in the St. Francis Hotel, San Francisco, in March 1914, just after the Pershings came back from the Philippines.

Frankie by then, the spring of 1919, had been gone nearly four years. The wife of Senator Warren's son Fred, Frankie's brother, Pershing's brother-in-law, put flowers on her grave and those of the lost girls, the cost of which at the general's request she billed to him. Fred attended to the grass surrounding the markers, she wrote. He had had it spaded up and replanted. It looked fine. Andrews invited his classmate at their last dinner in France to make use of his home whenever he came to New York City, and Pershing said, "Give me a key so that I can come on short notice." They had a long talk, "all difference in rank," Andrews remembered, "now forgotten. Again we were cadets living together in the old First Division of cadet barracks at West Point. Never up to that hour had I allowed myself to forget that he was the commander in chief of a great army and that I was his subordinate." In the years that were coming, they would draw as close as they had been in the long ago. *Dear General Pershing* and *Dear Andrews* in their letters would change to *Dear Pershing* and *Dear Andrews*; and at the end it became *Dear John* and *Dear Avery*.

For the last time a tiny group stood at attention before the Chaumont buildings from which the American forces of the World War had been directed, and "Over There" was played. From Paris a special train took the men from the St.-Denis station to where *Leviathan* waited in the roadstead at Brest. Generalissimo the marshal of France Ferdinand Foch came to see off the American with whom he had so stormily argued so many times. Pershing had never cared for him, thinking him rigid and self-righteous, almost like a dogmatic priest of the Catholic religion Foch fervently espoused. On a personal level he had from the beginning infinitely preferred the marshal of France Henri Phillipe Pétain, finding him more human, more humorous, kinder, of greater scope. But now in the last moments Pershing almost broke down. Foch was deeply touched, he told Bentley Mott, who was staying on in Paris at his prewar job as American military attaché. Mott told the marshal that there was nothing cold in Pershing's nature and never had been, but that he always kept himself well in hand, as was necessary when dealing with things of importance and for comprehending things as they were, not as one desires them. As *Leviathan* departed Brest, French destroyers with sailors on the yardarms and bands playing on the deck escorted her out. Gun salutes sounded from the harbor forts. Foch was on a little cutter, waving a final good-bye.

The returning conquerer was shown to the palatial cabin designated for Kaiser Wilhelm's occupancy in the days when *Leviathan* was the *Vaterland,* and was asleep there when, a few days at sea, Warren came jumping up onto the bed to announce that the ship's radio had transmitted the news that his father had just been named to the rank of general of the armies of the United States. His four-star predecessors Grant, Sherman, and Sheridan had held the less-inclusive rank of general of the army. Pershing was granted the right to replace four stars with six on each of his shoulders—which he never did. When they made Hoboken on the morning of September 8, 1919, they found all the harbor's boats trimmed with flags, and sirens and whistles sounding everywhere as *Leviathan's* massive hull came through the fog, her horn screaming to acknowledge the tributes. The destroyer *Blakely* appeared with a welcome party led by Secretary of War Baker. From all sides came the shouting of sailors in every kind of craft along with bells, trumpets, drums, the firing of Fort Wadsworth's salute guns. Pershing came down the gangplank and to a space at the pier brilliantly flag-bedecked and with fixed-bayonet soldiers standing at attention. Baker handed over a commission as general of the armies, and Pershing gave it to his son for safekeeping. Warren tucked it into his breast pocket.

They were ferried over to Manhattan and a cavalcade of autos to City Hall and presentation of honors by Mayor John F. Hylan, confetti flying from every window of the route and covering the floors of the open cars. Fifty thousand schoolchildren given the day off were at the Sheep Meadow in Central Park, and Madison Square Garden was jammed with members of the American Legion greeting their former commander in chief. That evening Warren was taken behind the scenes to see the circus animals close up. When he joined his father in their box, the audience broke into great cheers. Warren stood and waved his cap. The next day they left on a special train for Washington to pass through hundreds of thousands of cheering people along the way. At Philadelphia a legal holiday had been declared, and at Independence Hall the general of the armies delivered a brief talk and was given a gold replica of the Liberty Bell. His father-in-law's second wife, the former Clara Morgan, was there to greet him along with the wife of his aide, Fox Conner. In the press of people the women had trouble getting to the Broad Street station where they would board his train for the trip to Washington, and Mrs. Conner's velvet hat was pushed over to one side of her head. "The next time," Pershing said when they finally showed up, "don't be late, and have your hats on straight." His eyes danced, Mrs. Conner saw. He was very fond of Clara Morgan Warren, who was some thirty years younger than her husband, hardly older than Frankie would have been, and more than a decade younger than the general. She was a cheery, irreverent soul who termed herself, using the familiar term for women's underwear, his "step-in-mother-in-law." She professed to be dedicated to finding him a wife. "I have a new widow for you," she could write, "millions, unqualified social position, wonderful home, and only slightly damaged character. I spoke to General Dawes about a matrimonial arrangement, and sometime I will tell you what he said, showing that he judged you, even if not kindly." "Of course character would not have to be subjected to too close scrutiny," Pershing wrote back, "as the millions, the social position, and the wonderful house would quite obscure any little taint. As to anything Dawes told you, I enter a general denial." (The *Chicago Tribune* News Service a month after his return to American soil remarked that he was at one time or another reported engaged to a total of twenty-three women.)

At Washington's Union Station, Baker and Vice President Thomas R. Marshall were waiting to greet him—President Wilson was away on his doomed coast-to-coast tour aimed at getting the United States to join the League of Nations. Pershing rode in an open car behind a clattering cavalry escort taking him to a suite at the Shoreham Hotel, where he would prepare for a parade five miles long and a short address to a joint session of Congress. The school year of 1919–20 was about to begin, so Warren departed to the home of his Aunt May and Aunt Bess Butler. He had been away six months. The children of his class broke into applause when he appeared, and he told them that New York, London, and Paris were all right, but that old Lincoln, Nebraska, was best. When another child who had been away came in, the teacher clapped her hands and had the class join in. She did not wish Warren featured in any different manner from others, she explained later, in accordance with his father's desires. She need not have been concerned. Pershing was deathly afraid that his son would get a swelled head for the attention showered on him, but no one who knew the boy ever said anything of the sort. The only person who ever thought Warren showed signs of being spoiled was his father.

The general of the armies was himself inundated with attention. President Wilson was entirely out of the public eye, stricken with a thrombosis producing symptoms similar to a stroke as he campaigned in the West for the League of Nations, and confined to his White House bed; and Pershing was by far the country's most prominent and visible citizen. He was mobbed wherever he went, and from everywhere came requests that he join or accept honorary membership in American Legion posts, the Curus Fishermen's College with degree of Doctor Piscator, Delta Delta Delta sorority, the Humane Society of Missouri, the International Medico-Legal Association, the Isaak Walton League, the Junior Polo Club of Narragansett Pier, Rotaries, Chambers of Commerce, Kiwanis, eating clubs, Masonic organizations, the Mark Twain Society, National Inland Waterways Association, Phi Alpha Delta law fraternity, country clubs and golf clubs by the dozens, the Third Division Officers' Mess of New York, the Washington, D.C., Wellesley Club—"We confess that we cannot accurately define the duties of an honorary member, particularly a masculine one. But there will certainly be opportunities: Wellesley expects every man to do his duty"—dentists' associations, air progress clubs, the Anti-Swearing League, whose members promised "before God to do my best to refrain from all manner of language that I would not use before my wife, my mother, my sister, or my sweetheart"—anticrime clubs, the American Friends of Lafayette, the American Christian Fund for Jewish Relief, the Big Brother and Big Sister Foundation, groups for modification of the Prohibition laws, groups opposed to antiliquor legislation altogether, anticruelty societies, animal shelters, libraries, the Adventurers Club of Los Angeles, "composed of Explorers, big game hunters, soldiers, and others who have left the beaten path in search of Adventure," the Missouri Negro Soldiers Memorial Society, Religious Films Incorporated, the National Society of Colonial Daughters, the U.S. Volunteer Intelligence Corps of white men over sixty who strove to "combat all alien predatory designs of the communistic, Bolshevistic, atheistic, or other un-American activities of destructive groups that are like rats gnawing at the very foundation and pillars of our American way of life."

A large portion of each day was devoted to deciding which invitations for appearances by the general would be accepted. Such comprised a tiny proportion of the thousands of requests, but each letter was replied to by aides, usually Colonel Marshall or Colonel Quekemeyer or Capt. George E. Adamson, a big, strong, silent civilian taken on as field clerk in Punitive Expedition days, then given a commission and taken to France and back, and destined to dedicate his life to John J. Pershing no less than did Micheline Resco hers, although, of course, in a far different manner. Each letter leaving the office was checked by the general, an excellent line editor. If it appeared to him that one word too many had been employed, the letter was done over.

There was also an enormous personal correspondence demanding attention, most letters signed by an aide, but some requiring Pershing's own signature. One such replied to a writer saying Pershing was leaving a "proud inheritance" for "your small son," and identifying herself as having been, and being, somewhat in Warren's position. "I hope you won't mind my saying rather personally that I am very glad to think my grandfather has had such a great successor." It was the granddaughter of Ulysses S. Grant.

People from the long ago wrote. In the Philippines Captain Pershing had served under Gen. Samuel S. Sumner, and later briefly in Oklahoma. It was on a leave from his duties there that he went to Wyoming to ask Sen. Francis Warren for his daughter's hand. Sumner was the son of the Union Army's eminent Gen. Edwin V. Sumner and had been commissioned as a lieutenant in his father's army at the beginning of the Civil War. By the end of the Great War he was of course long retired and a very aged old soldier. But for former rank distinctions to hold did not seem out of place to Pershing the six-star general; and so his old chief wrote to him as "Dear Pershing," and he replied, "Dear General Sumner." That this was so—well, the general of the armies was like that, George Marshall remembered in later years. "I found him as informal and as unpretentious almost as a boy and as youthful in his reactions." Once the two were on a train sharing some Scotch, Prohibition or no Prohibition, and Pershing thought they ought to go offer a glass to Sen. George Moses of New Hampshire in the next car, reclining in his Pullman. "Senator Moses," Pershing said, touching the closed curtain of a berth. There was no reply, so he raised it.

"What do you want?" snapped a woman's voice. They had the wrong berth. The general of the armies ran. He shot down the train aisle, spilling the Scotch. "He was running up my back," Marshall remembered. They got to their stateroom and slammed the door shut. Pershing laughed until he cried. Finally, wiping his eyes, he suggested Marshall go back and try again. "Get another aide," Marshall said. When the trip was over the general was the usual Pershing, all business, stern, focused, intent, aloof. For years he maintained a lighthearted correspondence with an old friend of his and Frankie's, Emma Mahoney. When she mailed him cigars on the Mexican border in 1917 he wrote that while he appreciated the Coronas sent, she had noted, with a letter also written on a Corona, he had given up tobacco. "As to having guessed wrong on your present," she replied, "just what dissolute habits have you retained? Tell me and I will remember." She told him of the latest from Manila having to do with a divorce and "the infatuation of the Mrs. and her intention to wed a good-looking army man. Not thou, by chance?" When he went to France Mrs. Mahoney had not entirely resisted the temptation to write him as before, but to the extent that she had, "certainly it has been my most important war work. I feel sure you have appreciated it, for their name must have been legion who remembered you affectionately, but too often." Yet he wanted still to hear from her, it wasn't true that he didn't, his replies from Chaumont showed. "They have all spelled to me," she wrote, "besides the very great pleasure they brought, that more wonderful thing: that despite the importance you have attained, despite the plaudits, the glory and the brilliant success you have not only earned, but received, you have still kept old friends, old standards, and the great simplicity which has ever been your charm. It does spell how great true Democracy can be. To you and Warren. I wonder just how it feels to be the son of you!"

Dinners, the address to Congress, the great Washington parade, he on a horse presented to him in New York by the American Legion, "Jeff," for Lt. Jefferson Feigl of the Seventh Field Artillery, the first gunner to die in France; congressmen and senators and cabinet members coming, presentation of a magnificently upholstered Cadillac sedan by the automobile's manufacturer, constant hubbub about him, and no lengthy vacation in years, not since returning with Frankie from the Philippines; and he slipped out of the servants' entrance of the Shoreham in civilian clothing with his inevitable entourage of aides and orderlies for some relaxation on the New England preserve of former governor of the Philippines Cameron Forbes. Naushon Island was some seven miles in length by three across, and ran parallel with Martha's Vineyard. He swam, sailed, slept, played what was called "High Seas" with a house party of young people and college students. It was done on horseback and involved Merchantmen and Cruisers being chased by Pirates from one island hill to another. It seemed to him that most of the time he was a prisoner captured by Pirates singling him out for predatory attention.

He fished for perch and bass, landing one day a dozen of the latter, sang with the other guests, asserted his position in the world to put them through a spirited cavalry drill. He left Naushon for a visit to the Adirondack Mountains summer place owned by the family of the wife of his aide, Fox Conner, in Brandreth, New York. It consisted of twenty-seven thousand acres purchased by Mrs. Conner's grandfather for fifteen cents an acre in 1851. It was closed for the season when Fox Conner suggested it as a spot where the privacy of the general of the armies could be maintained as securely as on Naushon Island. Virginia Conner was told simply to inform her family that a hunting party would be paying a visit, not to mention any names. She quickly collected a cook, two extra guides, maids of her mother and her sisters, and hurried up with her daughter and a gallon of the finest whisky furnished by her father.

The railroad stop nearest the camp had no station and no stationmaster. One halted a train by waving a flag. She and a sister met Pershing's party of six men in two horse-drawn buckboards for the seven-mile trip to the camp. The horses drew them along through trails in the deep forests. "They can't get me here," Pershing said.

"Who?"

"The gentlemen of the press. They have nearly driven me crazy."

Evening was coming on when they arrived at the lake where the camp was, rippleless and reflecting the sunset. Pershing entered a log house, threw his hat and coat on a chair. "I'm never going back!" They held a fancy-dress party for which he wore a headdress given Mrs. Conner's aunt years earlier in North Dakota by Sitting Bull's son Louis. (The aunt in return offered a stuffed bird from her hat. He stuck it on his head.) In his Indian guise the general called the figures for a square dance. Ten days passed. George Marshall got a deer. Pershing never saw one. On a chill evening Mrs. Conner's sister Paulina said, "General, if when you wake up there is snow or heavy frost, meet me in the kitchen at six. I know of a beech knoll where an old snorter hangs out and I think I can get you a shot." They departed with a guide at the hour named. They were back at three in the afternoon. He knocked on Virginia Conner's door. "I got him. Your sister took me to him. She was like a dog on a trail and I dropped him with one shot."

"And now you're after a drink of whisky."

At the evening meal he came to the table in a dinner jacket. He had made up his mind, he explained, that if he got a fine buck he would dress in honor of the occasion. A while later Virginia Conner told him two nuns associated with a high-country sanitarium were around to collect money for their place. She had known them for years and said he must come and greet them. "He looked terrified and said that he did not have any idea what to say to nuns; that he felt like Warren who, when in England, upon being taken to see a duchess, asked if she spoke English."

One stormy day, she remembered, Colonel Marshall appeared and asked for a rag. The silence from the room he had just left fairly shouted. "I know that you two have done something frightful," she called out. Pershing's voice was heard, speaking in what she remembered as a lugubrious tone. "Come in and look." She found a pond of ink on the rug. "I have ruined your mother's carpet," Pershing said. "She is kind enough to let me use her room and then I spill ink all over it." Virginia Conner got milk and teaspoons and the three sat on the floor pouring and scooping up until the stain was more or less gone. After nearly three weeks in the

Adirondack fastness, Marshall told her the general really must be on his way. Congress wanted him to offer information regarding the late war, and the king and queen of the Belgians were paying an American visit. The incapacitated President Wilson would be able to do little to offer honors beyond receiving the couple for a brief call to his sickroom; Pershing's presence in Washington was really a necessity. "And you have to send my general home," Marshall said.

"Go home!" she commanded, and Pershing said, "I know I have to, and I don't want to a bit, for I have never had such a good time. No one has given me a compliment the whole time I've been here. You don't even ask me if I want a second helping of cake." He went with his party down the mountain roads and to the Washington train. "Is your little boy too big to kiss?" was the last thing that the queen of the Belgians asked when parting from him, he wrote Aunt May in Lincoln. "If not, please send him a kiss for me." His letter of November 13, 1919, a year and two days after the Armistice, added that he wanted to see for approval a reading list Aunt May had gotten up for Warren, and also that his son should "please look out for colds and remember not to take too much exercise after eating." He told May he wished Warren to be aware of matters not taught in school. "I want him to know something about the relation of capital and labor, the cause of strikes, and so on. Then he might also become interested in some little business. Possibly during the summer he might want to work in some store and as a messenger boy, or he might want to go into some shop and study mechanics."

All that seemed a little too much for the plate of a child not yet eleven years of age, May hinted in her replies. She did not believe Warren should take a newspaper-delivery route. Let him concentrate on his schoolwork and music and plays. But that her brother would be seeing him for the coming Christmas vacation—"Needless to say Warren is quite excited and gives expression to his joy by yelling." The reunion would be sandwiched in between appearances the general of the armies had to make before and after, and for years to come. He became the most-traveled and most-viewed American of his time, perhaps all time. He went off for endless tours of military installations with a staff in private cars attached to regularly scheduled passenger trains, civilians of the areas visited falling over themselves to offer invitations but a tiny fraction of which could be accepted. He moved through a world of welcoming band and glee club, parades, banquets, the Rotary, the local American Legion post, Fort Jackson in South Carolina, artillery salutes, reviews of troops, Camp Lee in Virginia, Fort Bragg in North Carolina, state governors delivering speeches, schoolchildren assembled, receiving lines, the corps of cadets at The Citadel in South Carolina, aviation school, Chamber of Commerce, college Reserve Officers Training Corps, high school drill team, Gold Star Mothers, businessmen's lunch club, War Mothers Society, Camp Gordon and Fort Benning in Georgia, the Confederate Veterans, and then off to sections other than the South, hospital and barracks inspection, stables, Kiwanis Club, women of the Red Cross Motor Corps acting as chauffeurs and presentation of bouquets of flowers in silver baskets, saddles, bridles, spurs, alligator traveling bag, saber, medals, silver pitcher and tray. He went to the Rock Island Arsenal and Fort Riley's Cooks and Bakers School, saw horse shoers and veterinary hospital, state commanders of the Veterans of Foreign Wars boarding the train to escort him to the capital, the Civic and Commercial Association reception, the Catholic Women's Club, the Women's City Club, a women's group the names of whose members caused Maj. Gen. James Harbord to whisper, "I have a new position for you. King of the Jews."

He always had a brief tribute for soldiers of the places visited—no one had surpassed Iowa's boys; Ohio men perhaps had equals but no superiors—shook hands with aged Grand Army of the Republic members identifying themselves as The Boys of 1861–65, was given roses by a little Portland, Oregon, girl whose father died in France, was introduced for a talk by the Exalted Ruler of the Elks, saw fortifications and battery drill, army post boxing tournament, heard singing, witnessed tree-chopping contests, met with groups of former overseas nurses, heard talks on the meaning of true Americanism and warnings about Bolshevism and radicalism. He spoke to some ten thousand at the Greek Theater of the University of California at Berkeley, saw the university cadet regiment, was delivering a talk to American Legion men in Los Angeles's Exposition Park when an airplane flew over and dropped by parachute a gold key to the Goldwyn Studios, which he and his staff then visited to see scenes being filmed. In

San Diego he addressed what the papers estimated to be between twelve thousand and fifteen thousand listeners in Balboa Park, saw polo at El Paso between the Eighth Cavalry and the Eighty-second Field Artillery, saw motor transport repair depot and air service supply depot, got silver-mounted cane and gold-tipped horns, was in Dallas, Fort Worth, Fort Sill, got keys to cities, was presented a gold watch in Camp Pike, addressed an African-American Legion post in Memphis, went through the army supply base in New Orleans, broke earth for planting trees, opened roads, dedicated fountains honoring the war's local dead, was at the Mardi Gras Rex Parade, where the king of the carnival named him duke of victory and presented a jeweled badge.

He attended receptions in his honor by the Daughters of the American Revolution and the Sons of the American Revolution, saw the Waterveliet Arsenal, inspected seacoast cannons and field cannons, unveiled church tablets for the men who served, dedicated flagpoles erected to those who fell, attended in Philadelphia the launching of the U.S. Army transport *Chaumont* as the shipyard workers crowded around him in such fashion to get his uniform all greasy, laid wreaths, was presented with silver loving cups and gold-headed swagger sticks, got honorary degrees from Yale, Williams, and Harvard. When one city wired to ask recommendations for entertainment, his aide George Van Horne Moseley, brilliant during the war and a decade away from the future finding him the hope of American fascism praising Hitler and saying the Jews and other undesirables should be deported to some desert island, Madagascar perhaps, to stew in their own vile juices—Moseley must have gone crazy, Pershing told friends then—wired back that there should be pretty girls instead of aldermen's wives at the speakers' table, and no chicken or Thousand Island dressing. Pershing and his staff had eaten so many chickens at the endless dinners, Moseley remembered, that they felt they simply could not look another one in the face. And the Thousand Island dressing. It was "served everywhere, often three times in a single day."

Seattle, Tacoma, Oklahoma City, Wheeling, Bridgeport, one ancient saying, "A Civil War man wants to shake hands with you, sir," and another, an ex-Confederate, informing him he fought better than he gave speeches, and crowds always gathering around at between-trains stopovers. "Where are you going, little curly-head girl?" he asked a seven-year-old, stepping through the circle of people pressing in. "She certainly is pretty," he told the child's mother.

"She's from down in the corn-fed country," the mother said.

"She looks it." He went to Chicago to meet Warren just prior to a visit to his old Missouri hometown of Laclede. "My father is A.W.O.L.," Warren said to his Uncle Jim. "He said he would meet me at the Union Station at seven o'clock and he isn't here. We better take his pass away, don't you think so, Uncle?" The general's train finally arrived and they went to a Laclede whose entire population turned out. Former pupils of his schoolteacher days surrounded him. He remembered all their names. "I hope to see you in the White House," said one; "Mollie, don't get such foolish notions in your head," he replied. "I'll never forget you, Sallie," he told another, "for your accomplishments in mental arithmetic. There never was a time in school when I could count myself more than one lap ahead of you."

"I used to think I knew as much about mental arithmetic as you did, John."

A black man who had worked for him in farming days came up. "Al, where did you get that flour in your hair?" Pershing demanded, his own head now white. An old woman said, "Look in my face and see if you know me." "Sure, I know Mollie Glover. You married a Roland—Lew Roland." A one-legged man approached. "I'm R. M. Brewer," he said.

"Lord bless you, you rented my father's farm."

"You bet I did."

"And I took it over the next year and farmed it."

"You did."

"And made more corn than you did, Brewer."

"I won't admit that, General."

A woman wearing the insignia of the Gold Star Mothers and with a black mourning band on her sleeve came up, Mrs. Willis Hamilton. "My boy—" she said, and began to cry. Her son Joseph had died in the Argonne. The general of the armies bent and kissed her. "Be brave, little mother, be brave." He saw an old black woman who had cooked for his mother and seized her shoulders. "Maria, it's good to see you." "Johnny,

I'm glad to see you. You-all ain't changed a bit—just took a little age on, Johnny boy." He went to the white cottage of the aged Susan Hewitt, who used to give him treats from her boardinghouse dining room. She was sitting with her best shawl around her shoulders. She held out her arms. "I knew you'd come," she whispered. "I've looked for you all day, Johnny, you dear boy."

He saw a man wearing a high silk topper. It was one of the board members who had examined him for entrance to West Point, when he got the appointment for correctly parsing the sentence "I love to study." He cried, "Can it be possible? Can that be Professor Smith? And look at that hat!"

At a Muhlenbach Hotel dinner in Kansas City the Missouri commander of the American Legion told the men, "I've been sitting beside him all night. When I told him I was a corporal it didn't faze him a bit." The ex-servicemen erupted into cheers. "Chairman, Corporal, and comrade," Pershing responded. "I was once a corporal myself"—that had been at West Point—"and worked hard to get it. So I was able to appreciate the dignity and honor accorded to me at the dinner tonight when I was placed alongside his majesty, your commander, the corporal." In New Orleans he remarked to a dinner that he'd been waiting outside for a while, and someone shouted that would pay him back a little for the times in France soldiers stood waiting in formation for the commander in chief's arrival and inspection. Everybody whooped. A laughing Pershing said that maybe they'd all agree to call it even now.

In Washington he lived in a rented Chevy Chase place with his aides and orderlies. The study became a replica of his Chaumont office, furnished with the rug that had been there, the old government-issue desk, the map that had been on the wall, and the clock with its hands at eleven o'clock for the hour the war ended. He wanted a familylike situation, he told one of his orderlies, Sgt. Steve Cato, a gifted singer often asked to perform for everybody, and such prevailed, with Warren spending all his school vacations with his father and his father's people. Pershing took his son riding along the Potomac, and sometimes father and son boxed together. Once Warren landed a punch that knocked the general down. The next day Pershing had severe pains in his side, and fearing a broken rib, had X rays taken. They proved negative. The bouts continued. When Warren was back in Lincoln for school sessions, Sergeant Cato remembered, any letter he sent was placed on top of the great pile of mail daily presented to his father. "The center of all his interests was Warren." (Of course he had other interests, though; and Micheline Resco was brought to the United States for prolonged visits and installed in a discreet rented apartment or quiet residential hotel.) "Many times I have wished you were along," Warren heard from San Antonio, "especially when I have met the schoolchildren, but of course I could not take you without your missing school, and I think that is more important." The boy's answering letters never failed to tell his father to come to Lincoln. He was going to be Hop-O'-My Thumb in a play. "I wish you could be here to see the show." He had a drum to beat in time to music from the Victrola. He was submitting a bill for polishing his father's shoes when they were together, fifty cents. Aunt May had bought him some new football pants. "We did not play football when I was a boy," Pershing wrote, "and I have always been sorry because I think I would have made a good center or possibly a fullback. Anyway I always wanted to get into the game but never had an opportunity." But he was looking forward to pitching some baseballs to Warren when they got together. As for Warren's interest in golf, at which he swiftly became very good, capable of holding his own against Aunt May, a devotee of the sport, the general upon consideration did not think it was a good idea for Warren to attach a rubber string to a ball he could practice hitting in the yard. Suppose it flew back and hit him!

Dec 4, 1920
Gen John J Pershing
Gen of Armies of United States,
Dear Sir:
I received your letter of the 29 instant and also received your check of ($1.00) one dolor. This is the way we start a business letter in school.

When school was out, he took Warren with him on inspection trips. They went south by ship, and the father had trouble making clear exactly what parallels of longitude and latitude were. "Papa told me to ask Colonel Marshall about it." Marshall gave confused information, checked the matter, and in the evening explained everything correctly. In the Canal Zone a special train took them about. They took trips on sub chasers and the submarine *R-21*. A squadron of the Twelfth Cavalry was detailed to escort them, and on the plain north of Corozal the entire regiment passed in review at the trot, then the gallop, then the charge. "As the last movement was not executed satisfactorily I had them do it over again."

A swimming instructor was retained to give Warren lessons; the travelers fished with the general commanding the area, Pershing landing a 140-pound tarpon. They witnessed sixteen-inch guns firing at targets at a range of twelve thousand yards, rode through the jungle for a trailside lunch of coconut milk and hot tamales and iced pineapple, saw eggs that when cracked found baby alligators crawling out. Four little grandsons of the post commander were invited to a swimming party hosted by Warren, with ice cream and lemonade. They went to St. Thomas and were met by a company of marines with a band. There were teas, receptions, reviews, luncheons, dances. They made San Juan, and the general and his son won a rowing race against the orderly sergeants Lanckton and Sheetz, who seemed to experience difficulty synchronizing their efforts.

He wanted Warren to know about the outdoors and nature, and in Washington one school vacation hired a naturalist for discussions of plant and bird and animal life. With his instructor Warren studied flowers and went to Washington's Red Cross building to see a large collection of purple martins. At the Naushon Island retreat of former governor of the Philippines Cameron Forbes, Mrs. Forbes offered the boy sailing lessons. "He is most enthusiastic and apparently picks up the details very quickly," the general reported to May. "I am taking this opportunity to coach him a little on his mathematics and physics." They played cards together. Going out to Colorado to stay at the home of Senator Phipps and do some riding and fishing, the general tested Warren's spelling and read aloud to him. His son's health was constantly on his mind. It seemed to him that along with bowed legs—a legacy, he decided, from the intense early horse lessons in the Philippines—Warren had a tendency toward flat feet. He

took the boy to Walter Reed Army Hospital, where the officer commanding the facility assembled specialists. A major went with Warren and his
father to a shoe store to select remedial footwear.

No father could have been more involved with a son, and Warren's
letters never failed to end with lines and lines or filled boxes of X's representing kisses. And yet. In 1905, about to be married to Miss Frances Warren in Washington's Church of the Epiphany, Captain Pershing had
asked his friends the Harvey Middletons of Baltimore to reserve for the
wedding night a hotel suite in their city—"not too expensive." The following day the newlyweds would be heading west for a Japan-bound
steamer, but they would be pleased if before they left the Middletons
came for luncheon. Fifteen years and more had gone by when in July
1920 Cornelia Middleton wrote regarding the remaining issue of that
marriage, Warren. She hoped Warren's father would not think, after he
read what she had to say, that she had overstepped. "I am claiming the
privilege of being your old friend. I am writing you a great-grandmotherly
letter.

"General Pershing, this dear boy of yours has seen very little of you in
his little-boy life and he has been brought up almost entirely by women
who adored him and his father and who tried to fill every place in the
child's life for his happiness. As Warren is a splendid, beautiful, lovable
boy, it has probably been impossible for these dear women to discipline
him. It would be a miracle if he has escaped being a little self-willed, determined, and something of an autocrat, God bless him!

"You must appreciate all this in your dealing with him and you must
be very, very careful not to treat Warren as though he was the United
States Army. Disobedience and hesitation to obey without question is
something of a crime in your eyes—your education has been toward strict
discipline. When your boy does wrong, please do not put on your steel armor for a court-martial but show him your glorious self—gentle, tender,
and loving. Always make him feel your great undying love.

"Warren is going to do a great many wrong things. He is going to argue and object to your suggestions and decisions and you must be very,
very patient and keep remembering that he is just a boy. Of course he
may have to be disciplined but make him feel your great *love* in it. A great

love like yours cannot help but to glorify and bless. Love is the greatest thing in the world. There can be no substitute—money, beauty, title, position, nothing can mean happiness without absolute love. Love glorifies the one that loves and is the halo to the one that is loved. If Warren can be made to feel and appreciate your great love for him he cannot go wrong for long. In the end he must be what you would have him.

"Are you still smiling and understanding this, nice man?"

Whether he smiled or not, certainly he understood. Pershing hovered over his preteenaged son, his last act at night before retiring to go into the room Warren occupied when in Washington to make sure the blankets were tucked in. Despite his great fear that Warren would be spoiled—the boy must promptly write thank-you letters to all who entertained him, he must be kept on a very tight financial rein, he must not idle his time away but always be busy at worthwhile pursuits—Pershing himself was perhaps too indulgent. Over and over a pattern was repeated. It showed itself for years. He would lay down the law, then immediately rescind it. The shotgun he had sent to Lincoln for Warren's birthday must not be taken apart. It could only be looked at. Then came a postscript to the order: "After reading this over, I must say that it does not sound very rational to give a fine boy a fine gun and then tell him only to look at it. What I mean to say is that he can learn all about the mechanism, and practice aiming, etc., and then later on actually shoot with it. Papa."

Luckily for him—luckily for Warren—the boy was sweet and compliant. Ordered to keep a summer vacation diary, he did so, dictating it each day as directed to one of the general's clerks, who typed it up.

May 27th. After lunch got ready for the tea this afternoon. I put on my soldier suit and I was to be at the door to give out the automobile checks. We cleared the big room for dancing. The Marine Orchestra came and then the guests. About 120 people. The cars drove to the front door and I handed the guest a check and the car drove around to another street and parked. When the guests left each presented a check and the number would be called out through a big megaphone and the driver would come up to the door. This system seemed to work very good.

May 31st. We aired the bunks and then were going to Arlington for Memorial Day Exercises. Papa made a very good speech. He asked if I wanted to get in front of his car and be his orderly. I got up front and Colonel Quekemeyer was with him. He saw some lady and took her in the car and made Colonel Quekemeyer get out. We rode around and took this lady home and finally Papa came out and we went home. Papa had to go some place that night. I had a shower bath and then went to bed.

June 4th. This afternoon I went swimming with Jimmie. He bet he could swim ten times the length I could. I swam the pool three times so if he could have won the bet he would have to swim thirty times. He didn't win. The bet was an ice cream soda.

June 7th. Put on my good clothes because Papa was coming home from Maine today. He arrived and there were about five orderlies standing out in front of the door. I took his bags and took them up-stairs. Sunny was feeling pretty good and when I started to saddle him he would buck. Finally I got him saddled up and started him on a trot and Sunny gave about three bucks and when he found I was still on his back he didn't buck any more. I found a row of cherry trees and I'd stop and take a few. I rode in a circle, grabbing a few as I passed by. I put on my civilian clothes and went down to the YMCA to have a swimming lesson. They told me to swim the length of the pool you get a button. I wanted a button so I decided I would swim the length. I swam the length of the pool to be sure I would get my button.

June 8th. I decided I would be a mechanic. Lanckton told me it would be all right and I asked Papa and he also said it would be all right. So now I am special mechanic for Papa's car. I got a pair of overalls from Sergeant Hayes but they are a little too large for me. I rolled up my sleeves and Corporal Beckman who drives Papa's Cadil-lac gave me permission to clean the car. Then he told me what to do and I oiled it. Then I asked Sergeant White who drives one of the Locomobiles if he would let me clean and he said he would. I came in and it took about an hour to get my hands clean. I looked just like a negro. I put on my civilian clothes and had dinner. Then we went to the barber. Then we got some overalls.

June 9th. Had breakfast, after which I went on horse exercise. Then I acted as mechanic until noon. I cleaned the Cadillac and all the rest of the cars. I am special mechanic for the Cadillac. Papa told me to go downtown with him and I went to the YMCA to take my swimming lesson. I came home and got a bat and played ball.

June 12th. I heard some banging and found out it was Papa and Jimmie playing with the medicine ball. I went out and we all three played. Miss Lefevre came. She and I went around the circle in front of the house a few times in her car. Then Papa came down and he went out for a ride with her and after he came back it was time for bed.

July 4th. I got up early and Lanckton told me to shine Papa's belt while he shined Papa's boots and pressed his clothes. Then we woke Papa up and he told me that he tried to get some firecrackers last night but he could not get any. I told Papa I knew a store where there were some and so he told me to get some. I told one of the sergeants to get me some, so he went over and nearly bought the store out. Lanckton then told me to shine my belt because there was going to be a tea in the afternoon. After lunch Papa and I wrestled on the bed. I threw Papa on his back quite a few times but he threw me on my back most of the time. Then I had a bath and got ready for the tea. Miss Lefevre liked to hear the firecrackers but she was afraid when I fired them near her and would rush to get away from them.

July 5th. Papa and I played ball. Then we had a bath for supper and while we had supper Donald was outside singing "I'm Forever Blowing Bubbles." Papa said, "I guess your friend is getting a little anxious, isn't he?" I said, "I guess he is." So finally I went out and I had my firecrackers and we shot off a lot of small ones and some big three inch and two inch firecrackers and some torpedos. Then we lit a chinese chaser. It goes all around, curves and everything else. Then I got my sky rockets and candles and I lit a red light and then Donald and I lit an electric buster. After we had shot all our things off I went to bed and Donald went home.

July 6th. I came down to Papa's office and we went down to the Riding and Hunting Club and Papa told me to make Sunny gallop. I could not hold him at first. Lieutenant Cunningham and myself rode the horses out to the house and Lanckton had my bath ready. After I had my bath I had supper. It was nearly nine o'clock so I went to bed.

July 11th. After lunch everybody began to smoke, so I smoked too — only my cigarette was a chocolate one. Then we went to the train, where Colonel Marshall was waiting for us. We got on the train and played a game that you would choose a sign and see whose sign would come next, and if the one that came next was like yours you would win. Then we had supper. When we arrived in New York we went to the Waldorf-Astoria, and as I was tired I went to bed right away.

V

WARREN

→ 14 ←

THE GENERAL OF THE ARMIES of the United States went to London to award to the Unknown Warrior in Westminster Abbey the U.S. Congressional Medal of Honor, and across the channel did the same for one whose place was beneath an eternal flame under the Arc de Triomphe. For the funeral of his own country's Unknown he wore as he marched side by side with President Harding down Pennsylvania Avenue only the Victory Medal to which any American soldier of the war was entitled. A silent wall of spectators watched, dirges sounding, muffled drums. When the White House was reached, the president stepped out of the line of marchers, but Pershing went on, chief mourner, up to Georgetown and across the Potomac there and along the unpaved Rosslyn roads to Arlington.

He was in San Francisco when Harding died; he had spoken with Mrs. Harding the previous night. Named as an honorary pallbearer and asked by the new widow to accompany her back to Washington, he boarded the train with George Marshall. Pershing accompanied President Coolidge to Marion, Ohio, for Harding's interment, joined former food administrator Herbert Hoover in appeals for the starving children of half-destroyed Europe, went to France to discuss plans of the American Battle Monuments Commission to honor the fallen, was mentioned for the post of baseball commissioner, senator from Missouri, movie czar, head of the American Legion, secretary of war, received each day an immense number of letters the majority of which were answered in necessarily negative fashion: "The general is very much interested in the welfare of all ex-servicemen, of course, but . . ."

His financial situation was very comfortable, his salary and allowances amounting to $21,000 a year, second in the government only to that given the president. (The Chief Justice of the United States got $15,000, a cabinet member $12,500, Senate and House members $7,500.) So it was not from a desire to make money that he wrote his memoirs. The job took him more than ten years, of which he enjoyed not a minute. "I am hidden away in Paris trying to do some writing," he told a Pineville, Pennsylvania, cousin, "but it is an up-hill job under any circumstances." (He did not feel it needful to mention that the circumstances included the presence of Micheline Resco in her Paris apartment.) "I sometimes feel like chucking the whole thing and making no attempt to record my war experiences which will probably not interest anyone." He would rather fight four wars than write the history of one, he told George Marshall, holding the fort at the Washington offices. "I have done considerable work, but like all that previously done, it seems quite banal and stupid and I am not at all satisfied with any of it," he wrote his sister Bess in Lincoln. "Maybe I should drop it or file it away and leave for posterity to handle as I am sick, sore and tired of the whole thing from beginning to end." "This—book!" he wrote his sister May. His estimate of his work was correct. What finally emerged for publication in two volumes in 1931 was, while of value to historians of the Great War, almost unreadable for the public, even AEF veterans. Pershing was a student of economy in writing, he was conscientious, fair, evenhanded—but these capabilities combined to produce what read like an after-situation battle report, official and dull. He knew it. For another ten years he labored on a second book. It would be of personal reminiscences. Marshall helped him, his longtime clerk-secretary Capt. George Adamson, aides and assigned officers and friends—but the proposed book, done and redone in endless drafts, was hopelessly flat, turgid, impersonal, dry, dreary. Perhaps it was foreordained that this would be so for the restraint and self-restriction he displayed, the gentlemanly holding-

back standing against those writing him awkwardly deferential memo-
randums in the third person: "The general in the general's descriptions
of negotiations with the Moros appears too restrained in detailing . . ."
That a sketch of him by Micheline Resco faced the title page of the second volume of his published *My Experiences in The World War* with no
explanation of exactly who Micheline Resco was—that was understandable. That Frankie and the girls were barely mentioned in his proposed
second book was another matter. The work was sincere and open as its
putative author understood those terms, but it was also infinitely too formal and dry and ultimately unpublishable. He never ceased regretting
that.

"With reference to Warren," the general wrote Aunt May in Lincoln after
telling her to purchase a car at his expense ("don't haggle over the price
too much"), "all of his papers show carelessness, which ought not to be allowed in a boy. He writes in a very hasty and casual way. So please see if
you cannot get him to think of the word he is going to write before he
starts to write it and make him rewrite all his letters whenever they are not
well written. I wish you would pay particular attention to this. Second,
please have him make a study of the meaning of words. I consider this
one of the most important things in a boy's education. The exact meaning of words is more important to a man than anything I can think of.
The power of clear expression is very necessary to succeed in whatever
profession or business one may undertake, and I wish to emphasize this
very strongly. I do not mean to crowd him or anything of this sort, but I
am anxious that he should make a very careful study of words, their
meaning and their synonyms. Third, Warren likes to read, so I wish you
would go to the teacher or possibly some professor at the university and
lay out a course of reading for him which he can do outside of school.
Please do this and let me know about it at your earliest convenience because I wish to have something to say about it myself and will get whatever books are necessary. I do not want him to grow up as I did without
knowing a lot about history and literature. Please do these things and let

me know what progress you are making." Only a little time was left when the boy could be a boy.

Papa and I wrestled. We had two rooms that were connected with each other and I got into Papa's bed while he was undressing and I said I was going to sleep there and he told me I couldn't, so we had a wrestle and he picked me up and carried me in my room and then we wrestled quite a while and finally I went to bed.

Had breakfast and played until about 11 o'clock. Then went to the beach for a swim. After supper we played pounce. My foot hurt so I put it in hot water. Then two ladies came in and we played pounce all afternoon. Then I had supper and after supper played pounce again.

My foot is well. Played and then went swimming. Rode horseback for about two and a half hours. Had supper, played, and then went to bed.

Lanckton said they were waiting for me downstairs so I got dressed quickly, but when I got downstairs I found out they hadn't been waiting for me at all—Lanckton just said that to make me hurry. We went down to the wharf. Papa carried me way out where it was over my head. After lunch I went sailing. Colonel Quekemeyer gave me some lessons in riding.

I made two bulls eyes. Before I went to bed I took some castor oil.

After supper I blacked myself up like a negro and had a whole lot of ferns around my waist so that I looked like a cannibal. Then we went to a party. Papa was dressed like an Indian Chief. We had a lot of fun. At the party we danced the Virginia Reel.

After lunch we got in the car and went to Coney Island and we rode on every thing in Luna Park.

Papa and I are very lazy nowadays so we slept until a quarter to nine. I went to where the soldiers sleep. They have a rifle, a "22" which they shoot rats with, and I went out and shot sparrows. I went to the

YMCA and had a swim. I forgot to take some money with me so I could not buy a towel, so I had to stand around until I dried. Then I went home and had lunch.

As the summer of 1921 approached, Pershing told people that although he hated to be parted from him, he had decided that Warren must begin to be out on his own, distant from an existence of glitteringly booted and Sam Browne–belted officer aides and deferential enlisted personnel united in third-person address to Warren's father and never-ending usage of "sir." He selected for his son's summer vacation Camp Red Cloud near Brackney, Pennsylvania, in Susquehanna County on Silver Lake. Camp experience would develop character in his son, self-reliance. "For the spoiled boy there is no better place."

The camp director, Louis Lamborn, had served in the American Expeditionary Forces. (Pershing meticulously addressed him as "Major.") He was proud to serve through Warren his former commander in chief, he wrote the general. When partway through the summer Pershing indicated he would like to visit, Lamborn assured him that Warren had been cautioned not to speak of the matter—for the general no doubt did not wish to mix with "grown-ups," meaning parents of other campers who might show up. "Warren is looking forward eagerly to your arrival. He has made all arrangements for your sleeping in his tent. I happened in the tent the other night after the boys were in bed just before 'Taps.' The boy was lying there with a picture in his hand. I asked him what he had. He said, with all the pride in the world, 'That's my dad.' "

Pershing went to Camp Red Cloud, slept in Warren's tent, got up for early morning walks with the nature instructor. In the fall Warren went back to Aunts May and Bess in Nebraska. "I would like you to assure him that it was very difficult for me to decide that he should go back to school at Lincoln and that I wanted him very much to stay here, but I did not believe it was the best thing for him, which is the only issue in question." Mandatory retirement from army service was coming, the day he turned sixty-four, and for his time remaining he accepted the post of chief of staff, which meant frequent absences from Washington as, ever the teacher he had always been, he worked to build up army schools across the country. He did not relax his intense involvement with his son's education, health, and demeanor. "I should caution you that Warren must be watched very carefully to see that he does not read by a dim light, nor read in bed, and that he should take care of his eyes as he would any other precious thing. I was very sorry to have Warren leave because he was so much company and so delightful to have around the house although, as you may tell him, a good deal of a barbarian. I hope that you will smooth off a few of the rough edges which he has acquired in the summer camp. He thinks he is playing with a lot of boys and diving in the lake, or something of the sort, all of the time."

In the early spring of 1922 Pershing asked his son if he wanted to return to camp. They also had to think about his going away to boarding school. "I liked Camp Red Cloud very well," Warren replied, "and if you do not have any other plan for me I would be glad to go. You said something about going to Alaska, if you go I would rather go with you. As to a school I do not know what I would like to do. You know more about schools than I do so you have better decide that matter. It has been quite warm here this past week. It makes me think of the fun we used to have last summer riding, walking and boxing." He was getting in a lot of golf with Aunt May. In a recent match he played two holes in par. "With Much LOVE. Warren."

He went back to Red Cloud, coming in at 5-foot-1 and 98 pounds, Director Lamborn reported, and left weighing 102$\frac{1}{2}$. He returned for a third summer, leaving at 109 and standing 5-foot-2. "Warren has ability. The moment he realizes he must work and work hard to succeed he will progress very rapidly. He is taking a position of leadership among the boys." He was second in the voting for Gold Medal Camper, Red Cloud's highest honor. His chance to be first evaporated when another tent of campers asked for the loan of some equipment for water sports. Warren had replied that his tent's slogan was: "We lend them nothing." So the aggrieved members of the rejected tent voted against him in a body, costing him the election.

It was time for him to go away to school. *Papa* became *Pops* in his letters, and the X's indicating kisses began to disappear. Looking at his photograph in his long pants, Pershing wrote, made him feel Warren wasn't going to be a little boy any longer. "I was just a little bit sad to see you not in short trousers. However, we all have to grow up, and now that you have long trousers perhaps you will take a more serious view of things." But that was going, in the general's estimation, to take a while longer, for the school to which he had sent his son, Phillips Exeter, did not look like it was working out for him. "Warren's nature is a very cheerful one and he is rather given to an optimism that takes life easy," Pershing wrote from France to his aide Lt. John T. Schneider in Washington. "In other words, I fear that he is not given to continuous devotion to his studies—moreover he likes athletics better." Would Schneider run up to Exeter and see how things were going?

Schneider journied to New Hampsire and reported that while he carefully avoided quizzing the boy he had gained the impression that Warren had begun by frittering his time away during the day and not cracking a book until night. Then he stayed up late and as a result was sleepy all day. But of late his work seemed to be improving, although he had failed the monthly English test. Schneider spoke with the English teacher, who said Warren was doing better although the teacher was not offering him much encouragement for fear of giving him grounds for letting up. The general had to bear in mind, Schneider pointed out, that it was not easy to make the change from a public school to a private one of the highest standards. On a happier note, Warren was very popular with the other boys. "I noticed this by the fact that a good number of them were dropping in and out of his room during the time I was there and they all appeared to be good friends." Warren and his pals demonstrated hockey, skiing, and snowshoeing to the southern-born Schneider, whose ignorance of such activities "seemed to delight them all."

His father's interpretation, as reported to Aunt May, was: "He has just been trifling his time away. He has been deficient in some study each month. He has evidently gotten in with a crowd of triflers, loafers, very much to the detriment of his studies." He was getting his son out of Exeter, he decided. Perhaps it would be best to get him out of the United States itself. He entered Warren in the Institut Carnall in the Château de Rosey, Rolle, Switzerland. "It is quite an undertaking for a kiddie of fifteen years to go 3,000 miles from home to a strange land to school, but it may be the making of him," he wrote Bentley Mott in Paris. Warren would sail on *Leviathan* in the late summer of 1924, the general taking it for granted that there would be someone on the ship staff who would take him in hand—"Otherwise, we shall have to put him in a crate and chain him by ankle to an iron bar, like they do the monkey in a cage." (*Leviathan*'s captain sent word Warren would be put at a table with the juvenile movie star Jackie Coogan, and that the captain would additionally work to make sure he had a pleasant journey.)

Before leaving, the general wrote May, Warren had better spend the early part of the summer in Nebraska boning up on his French. She must ride herd on him: "Warren is long on promises but short on execution, so do not be carried away with any promises he may make about studying this summer." Then in the end, as he always did, he backed away from fire-breathing orders about his son. "I think upon receipt of this note you may as well drop his French and let him have the vacation entirely free from study." The general of the armies stood on the pier waving as Warren left.

In Paris he was taken around by Micheline Resco before reporting to his new school in Switzerland where he received reminders from his father that he must not overdo his heart when rowing on the lake, remember promptly to answer all letters received, send full details on what courses he was taking, and do the very best he could in his studies so as to take advantage of the splendid opportunities offered him. "With all good wishes in the world and a solicitude for your welfare that you cannot imagine, please consider me always your most confidential friend and your best chum."

His own life was also about to change. "Do you realize," he wrote James Harbord, who had gone to be president of the Radio Corporation of America so he could have enough money to buy his wife a house, "that I have just about one more year to serve before I become a wheedling, ossified, doddering old mendicant knocking on the doors of my friends here and there for a few kind words and crumbs?" The year passed. The day following his final day of army service, September 13, 1924, an interview conducted earlier by Samuel McCoy was published in many newspapers. The writer had talked with his subject in the offices of the general of the armies in the State, War, and Navy Building (now the Executive Office Building) across from the White House. There were fireplaces at each end of the general's room, highly ornamented ceilings, parquetry floor, a mahogany door with locks and hinges of brass, and busts and pictures of renowned American generals. There was a picture of American graves at the cemetery of Suresnes outside Paris. It faced Pershing's desk. The picture was captioned: The Doughboys Who Never Came Back. "Let's not talk high-sounding phrases," Pershing said. "Let's not use old words, shopworn words, words like 'glory' and 'peace' without thinking exactly what they mean."

"There's no 'glory' in killing. There's no 'glory' in maiming men. There are the glorious dead, but they would be more glorious living. The most glorious thing is life. And we who are alive must cling to it, each of us helping." He had given up the big Chevy Chase place by then for an apartment in the elegant Connecticut Avenue building where Senator and Mrs. Warren resided — he had remained close to his father-in-law and stepmother-in-law, the ineffable Clara. His apartment, reported Damon Runyon at the time of the general's retirement, was coldly formal. There was a large picture of Field Marshal Earl Haig on a table, pictures of Foch and Pétain. There was a large bronze depiction of American, French, and British soldiers joining in a bayonet charge, symbolically of import, perhaps, but precisely what the apartment's tenant had vociferously opposed in the days of 1917–18. The general received Runyon in a dinner jacket, smoking a cigarette. Runyon had known him since Punitive Expedition days when he left off reporting the spring training activities of the New York Giants baseball team in Texas to follow the chase after Pancho Villa; Runyon had been with the AEF in France. He had a somewhat gentler view of the AEF chief than did the equally renowned reporter Heywood Broun, with his lasting thought that nobody would call the chief "Papa Pershing." ("I guess he was right," Pershing used to say with a laugh in later days.) It seemed to Runyon the man wasn't quite as hardboiled as he was taken to be. "I wouldn't go so far as to call him effusive, but he is always friendly."

The offices in the State, War, and Navy Building were his for life, it was announced, so he worked on his memoirs there, went to Paris to see

Micheline and to Switzerland to see Warren. He and his adolescent son took a trip through the Alps, followed the Preuss River up to where the road branched off for the St.-Gotthard Pass, snowballed one another by a glacier. Warren spent two years at the Institut Carnall. In the summer of 1925 he asked to remain in Europe during vacation, saying he wanted to get a job, preferably one having to do with cars. Pershing asked Bentley Mott, still American military attaché in Paris, if he would look around. After checking the Citroën automobile plant Mott felt that the workmen of the assembly line did not appear perfect associates for a young boy. He got Warren a job in a repair shop where he could learn a good deal about cars and the men seemed a decent lot. The foreman soon reported to Mott, who passed the information on to Pershing, that Warren appeared promptly for work each morning at seven to perform his stint lasting until six in the evening, and was an entirely satisfactory employee. (His off-duty time was supervised by Aunt May, sent over by her brother to live with her nephew in a pension.) That the son of America's leader in the war was now found most of the day unrecognizably covered with grease and lying on his back with his legs sticking out from beneath a car at the Compagnie Maryland place on the Boulevard St.-Cyr surprised Paris. Such an existence would not likely have been the lot of a French idol's son. For a time, reported the New York World, Warren became "the most interviewed person in France." But the interviews were not very successful. "Won't you come out and talk to me?" coaxed a reporter. "I'm sorry, miss, really," was the answer from the depths of a sunken repair pit, "but my boss pays me to work and I'm here to work." He was still extremely blond, good-looking, tall—he had shot up in height from summer camp days.

Warren came back to America and to Phillips Exeter, where he did less than middling work, mostly C's and D's. Like many a bright boy, he was no scholastic star. As with many a father, that did not sit well with General Pershing. "I must say it is quite discouraging, and I am quite at a loss to know just what to do," he told Aunts May and Bess. "I wish you would write him just as strong a letter as you can and tell him what a dreadful thing it is to waste his time and disappoint you and me and his grandfather, and the school authorities. Try to impress upon him the necessity for effort. Do this at once, please."

It wasn't going to work. Warren Pershing from childhood on had said he wanted to be a banker—they knew about arithmetic and helped people, he wrote his father in the days when he still filled his letters with X's—and eventually he would get involved in something somewhat related, becoming a vastly successful and very rich stockbroker. But his grades were never much to write home about. (That his father's had not been so wonderful at West Point was not much discussed.) He was enormously likable, everyone said, and refreshingly free from the arrogance of youth, Bentley Mott told his father. In the summer of 1926 he took a long motor trip with three pals through Canada out to Lincoln with by the general's orders Sergeant Lanckton and a second orderly trailing along in Pershing's Cadillac to look out for the boys and tend to their car. After three days visiting Aunts May and Bess, Warren went off to the Citizens' Military Training Camp at Fort Snelling, Minnesota. "He was not keen about it at the start but eventually went with the idea of making good," Pershing wrote George Marshall, who had gone off to serve with the Fifteenth U.S. Infantry permanently stationed by treaty arrangement in Tientsin, China, and with whom long and gossipy letters were exchanged. ("I played golf for the first time in a year," Marshall reported, "and the spectacle was one for the gods, with flow of gutteral profanity as an accompaniment.") Warren did splendidly at Fort Snelling, winning out of two thousand summer trainees the Best First Year Soldier award marked with presentation of a gold watch from the St. Paul Kiwanis Club. "I wondered whether this had given him a taste for a military career," Pershing wrote Marshall, "but it did not seem to have made much of an impression on him so far as that was concerned." West Point, where, of course, he had always hoped Warren would go, was out. "It looks as though he might go to Yale, although I am inclined to favor a smaller college. However, I shall let him make the decision."

The decision was that he would make for New Haven, where he did reasonably well academically and very well socially, a fixture at dances and balls and participation in other activities which caused him, according to his father's lights, to spend too much money. Capt. George Adamson was given the not very desirable task of keeping Warren abreast of the value of a dollar. "Now, Warren, one other thing," Adamson wrote after saying that the senator and Clara wanted him to visit during Easter, "we have not yet received your expense account. As you know, the general is holding me responsible for your expenses, and there is no reason in the world to ignore my several requests. Please sit right down and bring it up to date and let me have it." Eventually Adamson received word that the Yale sophomore's outlays for May 1928 included telegrams, a trip to New Britain, breakfast, lunch, supper, soda, the repair of his Victrola, new golf shoes, toothpaste, Listerine, the repair of shoes, stamps, a show, a magazine, haircut, shoelaces and shine, for a total of $29.75, to which were added monthly golf expenses which came to $32.95 including taxi, caddy, and greens fee. He cabled his grades to his father in Paris's Hôtel Crillon: MARKS FOR TERM MATHEMATICS NINETY CHEMISTRY EIGHTY FIVE HISTORY EIGHTY FRENCH AND ENGLISH SEVENTY FIVE HEALTHY FINE LOVE WARREN. But Adamson had to write to New Haven that he was shocked to learn that Warren never sent a word of thanks to Senator Warren and Clara for his Easter stay with them, that they were quite hurt, and that the general if he found out was not going to be pleased. When Pershing got back from Paris he did in fact find out. "Now, Warren, that sort of thing just will not do. After all that I have said to you about the necessity of keeping yourself in good standing with your family and friends, you absolutely neglect writing a letter of thanks and appreciation after spending a week with your grandfather and grandmother. It seems they did many nice things for you, and yet you have no word of thanks for them. It is really a shame and I am very much chagrined that you should still continue to act as a little boy would act." Warren had also gone to Old Point Comfort in Virginia for the opening of a new hotel, been entertained there, and had not written his host a line of thanks. "What kind of a position do you think this leaves me in for you to go about accepting things in such an off-hand, matter of fact way, without sending a polite word? I receive criticism for bringing up such a boor and people say that of course he has not been properly reared. Nobody has ever had such obligations as these hammered into him as you have, all apparently to no effect. All this talk about cars and trips abroad and everything may very well vanish into thin air in the face of this sort of thing." The student managed to make things up with Senator and Mrs. Warren, spending most of each summer for three years with them on the Cheyenne ranches. He wanted his son not to be seen as a guest out there, the general decreed, but put to work; and so it was done, with riding herd Warren's daily work, checking water holes, grass, and fences; and becoming with his charm the light of the lives of his hosts-*de facto* employers. As for his father's thunder and lightning about cars and proposed trips abroad, when Warren did in fact go to Europe for a summer he took with him a new LaSalle, a General Motors junior Cadillac purchased for $2,870, black, with chromium-plated wire wheels, and spare tires mounted in the fenders, with which, it was said, he set speed records from New Haven to Poughkeepsie and Vassar College. "Daddy always had an eye for a pretty girl," his son said years later.

The grades improved. Warren made the Dean's List. His expenses did not decrease. For a September 1928 jaunt to New York City he listed dinner and show at $8.20, matinee for two $5.00, dance and supper $8.00, dinner for two $4.50 plus taxis, books, notebooks, ink., etc., for a total of $53.15. "I am trying to see if I can't evolve some scheme so that you will owe me some money," he wrote his father. The general was against his joining a social organization, but he did so anyway, Phi Theta Psi, and was voted its Number One man. His father had once been Papa, then Pops. Finally he became Père, to remain so until with the years he became Grandpère. The general of the armies of the United States never ceased to worry about his son's health, nor to rescind an order as soon as he gave it. "Do not neglect a cold, but take right hold of it at the beginning and knock it out. You know enough without instructions from me or the necessity of going to a doctor. Do not hesitate to go to a doctor, however, if you feel you need one."

As he was away from Washington so much, it seemed to the general an extravagance to maintain a grand apartment there, and so he departed the Connecticut Avenue building where the senator and Clara lived in favor of a suite in the majestic Carleton Hotel. His closeness to Frankie's father and stepmother did not decrease. When in 1928 a United Press article speaking of his sixty-eighth birthday remarked that he had three major interests—his work with the American Battle Monuments Commission, his efforts for ex-servicemen, and his memoirs—Clara sent a clip of the piece and wrote, "Delighted to know the object of your life as herein stated. This is far better than the earlier three. It is nice to know that you have at least given up *song*." She dearly loved Warren. She had made him play up to a girl with whom he was in bad standing for not replying to an invitation for a dance at the girl's smart finishing school, she wrote the general in August 1929 from Cheyenne, signing herself to her older-than-herself correspondent as "Mother Clara." She had told Warren "that he would walk right up and tell her that he was sorry that he had been so rude, or that he would be disowned the next day. He sent word he had seen his duty and done it nobly." When Clara read the general had suffered a minor illness she wrote, "The papers state that you are in bed with a trained nurse at Walter Reed Hospital, but as news items are often inaccurate, I am hoping this may be greatly exaggerated." When he went for a visit to the Arizona Inn in Tucson she wrote, "I am hoping that you are dancing on the lawn with Mrs. Winston when I trust you removed your hat, if not other things."

In 1929 Senator Warren died. He was eighty-five. He had served in the Senate for thirty-seven years, more than anyone before him, and his funeral was held there, President and Mrs. Hoover attending, both houses of Congress, the Supreme Court, and the cabinet. He was the last of the hundreds of veterans of the Union Army who had served in the Congress. The only government notables left from the Civil War were Representative Stedman of North Carolina, late of the Confederate Army, and Justice Holmes, late captain of Federal infantry. For the services the general of the armies got into uniform with black mourning band and then with his son rode the special train west to Wyoming, the lying in state at the capitol there, and interment in Cheyenne's Lakeview Cemetery next to Frankie and the girls gone the fourteen years. Others from a later war than fought in by Senator Warren were also passing on: I JOIN MILLIONS OF AMERICAN VETERANS WHO MOURN WITH YOU went out to Lady Haig. General Pershing was in attendance at the funeral of Marshal Foch. "Marshal Sarrail died a few days ago," he wrote Charles Dawes from France shortly afterward, "and was buried today. Bishop Brent, who was over here with us and whom you will remember, passed away at Lausanne day before yesterday. And so, Charlie, we are all going on, getting a little older every day, and the ranks are becoming thinner and thinner." Dawes had gone on from the war's chief purchasing agent in Europe to originator of the Dawes Plan to rehabilitate Germany's shattered finances, to vice president under Coolidge to ambassador to the Court of St. James's. His relationship with the former University of Nebraska commander of cadets did not change. Charlie did not change. As ambassador to Great Britain he hired the American comedian Leon Errol to serve at an embassy party that found Errol snatching away plates from diners before they finished eating, dropping a lobster into a duchess's lap, and finally with a candle lighting his way crawling about under the table, Dawes hysterical with laughter at his antics and at the stiff-upper-lip Britishers looking the other way. "We are both growing older," he wrote Pershing, "but as with Mrs. Wiggs of the Cabbage Patch our vicissitudes have not made us sour." He and Pershing and James Harbord were, the papers said, the Three Musketeers.

In the France where he spent a part of each year Pershing oversaw the creation of chapels, statues, peristyles, and sundials on the grounds where the AEF had fought and where lay those of its number who had died, a towering 175-foot Doric shaft in granite at Montfaucon, a great circular colonnade at Montsec, twin rows of majestic columns on Hill 204, and marble headstones to replace the original wooden ones. He was often with Marshal Pétain, finding him droll, ironic, forthright, companionable. His first call abroad on his yearly visit—after seeing Micheline—was always upon Pétain. They didn't talk much of the war, just about daily life, noted Bentley Mott. The marshal had stories to tell of the chicken farm he had bought in the Midi. " 'I don't know whether you have yet passed through the poultry-raising period,' " he had been warned by an expert in such endeavors, he told Pershing. " 'If not, be prepared for its hallucinations, for they will surely beset you.' " Pershing spoke of how he was unable to shake clear of the entirely believed-in conviction, often alluded to in speeches of introduction, that as Grant had said "I propose to fight it out on this line if it takes all summer," and Sherman "War is hell"—which was not precisely what Sherman said—so would resound in history what the AEF commander never said, nor claimed to have said: "Lafayette, we are here!"

Ah, well. Life had its moments. Once Pétain had a sore throat and went to a doctor who did not inquire his name but complimented him on his fine constitution. "You didn't have very much to fatigue you during the war, did you?" the physician asked. Then there was the time the marshal stopped at a town where long ago he had been a lieutenant. He called upon his former landlady, now toothless, and asked if she remembered him. She did. " 'And now I suppose you must have risen to be at least a major?' " "There are doubtless other lessons in humility stored up for me," the marshal told Pershing, witty in his manner and very fortunate indeed not to know what those terrible lessons would be, "but at least they cannot take me by surprise." They planned a dinner offered to Paris friends. It must be at La Cigogne in the rue Duphot, proclaimed the marshal, and there must be escargot and pigs' feet à la Ste.-Menehould, boiled in bouillon for two days, then breaded and baked. Sauerkraut would accompany the dish. The wine must be Alsatian Riesling, special reserve. Together they went over the guest list, Pétain demurring at Pershing's mention of a prominent French statesman. "I don't see that he would add anything to the gaiety of the occasion."

The general was the marshal's host when in 1931 the United States celebrated the 150th anniversary of Cornwallis's surrender at Yorktown, and Pétain headed the French delegation to the ceremonies. They were together constantly. "He is a master of the art of war," Pershing told a dinner of New York's France-America Society, "a leader who can inspire whole armies with his patriotism, determination, valor. My dear Marshal, I am proud to call you my friend." By then the Depression had taken hold and Pershing's mail was filled with desperate letters from ex-doughboys asking for assistance in obtaining jobs. Those of their former comrades who in the days of prosperity had betaken themselves on vacation jaunts to eat in the wartime restaurants they had frequented, visit their old billets, and crowd Paris's boulevards, came no more. Their financial plight was of a different order than that of their former commander, for he could still afford to go each year to Micheline and Pétain and Room No. 10 of the Hôtel de France in Chaumont, where now stood at his former headquarters a statue of a female figure taking the arm of a Yank, her other arm around a poilu. Yet the stock market collapse and cutting of dividends forced Captain Adamson to write Aunt May, "It is embarrassing for me to disclose that the general's income has been rather seriously reduced. Will you let me know the very lowest amount you can get along with." Despite his situation different from the past, there were some obligations he would not avoid. One was to Frank Helm, who held him in his arms as weeping he went to San Francisco when Frankie and the girls died, and took Warren on his lap when the father had shivered so violently he could not hold his son. The years had not been kind to Helm. A series of appeals went out to Pershing for loans, business backing, recommendations. They were always met. Once a telegram begging help got misplaced. Helm was facing the shutoff of his gas and water as he sent it, with eviction in the offing. He sent a second message, saying apparently friendship had no meaning. Pershing could well have ended the friendship right there, but instead sent money and: "I am always ready to help you, Frank, so don't run off on a tangent. I do not forget my friends so easily." Within two weeks Helm was asking for money again—"Now, John J., please don't think I am working a willing horse to death, but I have no one to turn to." More money was sent.

He was not so soft a touch for his nephew Richard Paddock Jr., the son of the former Grace Pershing and his old The Three Green P's friend of second lieutenant days in the West. Dick Paddock stayed with Uncle John and Aunt Frankie and the children in the Philippines when his parents died, went to West Point and an army career that ended when he became improperly involved with the wife of another officer. With the years he would marry three women, none of whom he supported for very long. He ran out on bills which ended up being submitted to his uncle, borrowed money never repaid. "These matters are piling up rapidly," Pershing wrote him. "My only fear is that I know only a part of it all as I am firmly convinced that you are entirely negligent and careless of your financial obligations, and more especially of your reputation, to say nothing of mine."

It did not help. "A short while ago Captain Adamson informed me that some months or perhaps years ago you borrowed of him $75, which has never been returned. This is very embarrassing to me and should cause you to blush, if it is still possible for you to do so." Paddock was not the blushing kind. Ex-wives got injunctions to prevent his selling mutually owned furniture. In time they ended up needing help—their children by the odious nephew needed food. They got checks from the general. The same was true for Pershing's nephews by his brother Jim. After Jim died he helped out his widow, eventually taking care of the medical expenses incidental to her last illness, and paying for the funeral. Everything at one point was done at least partially with money borrowed from the prominent financier Bernard Baruch. He and Pershing became great friends, going hunting at Baruch's South Carolina estate and writing one another letters arguing about who was the better shot, with dark innuendos that the other's guide had actually shot down birds accounted as part of the bag. At one time Pershing ran up obligations to Baruch of as much as $40,000, two years of his salary and allowances.

Meanwhile, Warren was finishing up at Yale, doing pretty well scholastically despite such stunts as riding two horses standing up to win a bet, a foot on the back of each, and despite jaunts to New York. At the renowned speakeasy run by Texas Guinan he sat down in a trick chair that gave electric shocks, then stuck the chair under a friend. "When we went to pay the bill, I felt the name of the place should have been changed to Ali Baba and his forty so-and-so's," Warren wrote. But he was working away so that when his father came to New Haven for the graduation ceremonies he wouldn't be handed a blank piece of paper. He was thinking about going to law school but actually didn't feel much like doing so. Meanwhile, he said, he was not only in danger of being thrown out of his living quarters but also out of college itself. "Do you suppose you might be able to engineer massive change in the disposition of the nation's resources and credit me with $350 good legal tender at the Riggs National Bank?" The general complied. As always he was filled with concern about Warren's health, which was excellent, and the frequent purveyor of dubious medical advice, including counsel about how Warren should utilize some tonic he sent to ward off the alarming loss of hair that would despite all make him quite bald at an early age. He came to understand that his son wasn't a kid anymore. Warren in later years felt able to pinpoint the moment. He was driving his father and May from Lincoln out to Cheyenne, and they ran into a heavy downpour. Usually Pershing sat in the back giving orders even though he himself had never learned to drive, but this time he was next to Warren, doing, Warren recalled, "a lot of backseat driving from the front seat." Warren got madder and madder, as is not unknown when fathers offer sons suggestions about automotive operations.

It was the only time, Warren remembered, that he was ever angry with his father. "Why in hell don't you stop telling me what to do?" he demanded. "After all, I'm driving the car."

"Yes, but it happens to be *my* car."

"But I happen to be the one who can drive *your* car."

The trip continued in silence. They came to North Platte, Nebraska, and Warren brought the luggage into a hotel. Aunt May had her room; father and son had adjoining ones with a bathroom between. From an old Gladstone bag Pershing took out a flask of brandy and waved it from the bathroom and said, "I think it's about time you and I had our first drink together." It was his way of apologizing for the unrequested driving instructions, Warren realized, and at the same time an acknowledgment that the boy was now a man. Warren was graduated from Yale in June 1931. He was named as Most Likely to Succeed, took third place in the voting for Best Looking, third for Best Dressed, fourth for Wittiest. In that year the book was published whose writing had poisoned the days and nights of the general of the armies for ten years, no friend or associate having failed to be informed that he had a hundred times longed to throw the manuscript into the fire. Its greatest success was in severely (and justifiably) condensed newspaper serialization.

Papers seeking local angles ran contests in which readers were asked to compete in telling of encounters with the memoir's author, $5 generally being offered as a prize for the letter judged best, with $3 for second place and $2 for third. A Frenchwoman who came to America as a war bride wrote of how when serving in a hospital she slipped and fell flat in front of the head of the AEF. As she scrambled to her feet he picked up and handed over her nurse's cap with a smile and a bow. "'Twas my big moment." A onetime stables sergeant told how the general complimented him on how nice the horse accommodations looked. A former military policeman wrote that as German shells poured down, the general's Locomobile came along and his driver asked if the road was clear and the writer replied, "Get to hell out of here if you don't want your head shot off." Ex-soldiers reading the newspaper condensations and related stories were moved to write the general telling of long-ago incidents when he had said a word to them, and women of the AEF telephone system of the time he asked for a dance. All letters were answered with an assertion—not given under oath, to be sure—that the general "vividly" recalled the incident alluded to. The most discussed passage of the memoirs had to do with Pershing's offhand detailing of how when he was walking in the ravaged town of Sampigny with the French president and his wife two doughboy artillerymen came along and, learning who the visitors were, seemed to regard the information "as an introduction." As Pershing had it, the soldiers "warmly shook hands with the President and Mme. Poincaré, and then quietly went about with us. The President and his wife were very gracious, though much amused by the cordial and rather unconventional manner of their guests." Newspapers and book reviewers and indeed the public found enchanting such a story in the two-volume work of 836 pages otherwise with little human interest or crescendo and largely composed of official letters, report extracts, and analyses of order-of-battle alignments. The general in his description of the Sampigny occurrence, it was said, had in marvelously succinct fashion identified the two greatest heroes of the war. Apparently America had been privileged to produce men whose courage was such that they would barge in on the fearsome and ferocious Black Jack Pershing as he escorted about the president of France and his lady.

One of the stalwart pair surfaced, Mahlon Monte, a carpenter of Locustville, New Jersey, five miles outside of Camden. He and a buddy were near a blown-up bridge, he told a representative of the North American Newspaper Alliance, which sent the story all over the country. So the general and the others came along. Private Monte and his buddy snapped to attention. So the general said, "As you were." The privates stood easy. Then the lady talked to them in English. She asked how old they were. They were both eighteen. Originally with the 112th Field Artillery, New Jersey National Guard, Monte had been transferred to the Seventh Field Artillery of the First Army Corps. Mme. Poincaré kept up the conversation, so he had no choice but to walk with her. His buddy didn't know what else to do, so he trailed along. The buddy was to die in action. Private Monte was shrapneled and gassed, and got four citations for gallantry.

If Monte had been eighteen in September 1918, when the incident occurred, he would have been thirty-one or thirty-two when the general's memoirs came out. To him and others the war was of the distant past submerged by present overriding economic worries, and there were plenty of Americans who said the country should never have entered a war for Europeans to whom Uncle Sam, pressing for the payment of war debts, was now Uncle Shylock—and to some in America Uncle Sap for having fought at all. But with the years the popular image of the army's leader in France softened. He had been, papers said, speaking of his memoirs and the letter contests and the memories coming back, the stiffest and hardest soldier America ever knew, yes, but also the most considerate one. He was a strained personality, columnists wrote, severe, reticent, cold, ruling with an iron hand in AEF days, a very harsh personage—but one whose first concern was to maintain the discipline needed to get his work done at the least possible cost to the men entrusted to his care. Of that there had never been any doubt; and in a world gone awry as the war's exploding time bomb of the Great Depression took effect, the earnest and honest and honorable John Pershing still presented the unchanging meaning and appearance and picture of what he had always been. "I often see you in the newspapers looking younger, more erect, more vigorous all the time, while I get whiter-haired and more elderly by the minute!" Dorothy Canfield Fisher wrote him in 1936. He had retained, she felt, a simple attitude toward life, and seemed unaltered from the past, still to her the lieut of Nebraska days.

The papers she mentioned reported that he had been named by the *Washington Post* as the best-dressed man in the capital for the manner in which he wore clothing, his demeanor and dignity in never-fussy but always clean-cut and trim attire set off perfectly by his upright stride as he walked along or entered a room. His yearly winter trips West were noted by the press also, with mention of rides in the desert outside Tucson, visits to ghost towns, archaeological ruins, Indian mounds, Spanish missions, often with Charlie Dawes or James Harbord along. He was photographed laying wreaths on the tomb of the Unknown Soldier on

Armistice Day, and dedicating monuments to the American dead in France, often with Marshal Pétain along. There were occasional stories to accompany the frequent photos—not many, for little that he did was really newsworthy in the sense of needing much written explanation: a picture with its caption usually did the job. Once he granted a brief interview remarking that he regretted that his men had thought him an unemotional martinet. "That is not the General Pershing as I have known him all my life. He is quite a different fellow with many a soft spot in his makeup. That has made some of the things he had to do painful at times. Military responsibility leaves little chance to show those kindly, human impulses we all so like in men we have to do with. I wish they could have known the real John Pershing over there as he knew himself."

In 1937, adorned in formal uniform suitable for court activities, he served as President Roosevelt's representative to the coronation of King George VI, braided and ostrich-feathered hat, gold belt with embossed oak leaves, ceremonial sword, knee-length coat with gold collar and cuffs, epaulettes and sash. Invitations poured down in London, the Executive Committee of the New Commonwealth Society lunch at the Dorchester Hotel to hear the Right Honourable Winston Churchill speak, the earl of Derby at the Guildhall, the duke of Kent, the American Women's Club ball, the Lord Steward in thickest gold-bordered great oversized hand-delivered envelope saying that having been so commanded by the king and queen he offered request to Gen. John Joseph Pershing for attendance at a state banquet at Buckingham Palace, the Lord Chamberlain telling that he was commanded by Their Majesties to tender invitation to a Palace ball, Secretary of State for Foreign Affairs and Mrs. Eden asking appearance at the Foreign Office, baronets, marquesses, earls, colossal Fleet review, and, of course, the coronation ceremonies themselves at Westminster Abbey.

He turned down as many of the invitations as he decently could. For his health was not good. Colds constantly took him—they were the reason he spent winters in Arizona. In summer he found muggy, warm weather difficult to sustain. The general of the armies was, after all, in his seventies. Years afflicted him. Even a decade earlier he felt himself to be growing old. "I suspect that my teeth (my beautiful teeth) must come out," he had written Micheline, ensconced for a time in New York's St. Huburt Hotel on West Fifty-seventh Street. "This is the harrowing conclusion—and a most depressing one—that the dreadful processes of time are hastening old age." Increasingly he thought of the past, as old men will. There was much all about him to encourage that he do so. When in 1935 Malin Craig was named as the army chief of staff and he sent congratulations, Craig replied, "I remember as clearly as though it were yesterday when you first joined the Sixth Cavalry and your tolerance for me even in those days when I must have been more or less of a pest." It was hardly calculated to make Pershing feel young that already monuments to him were being erected—there was one of him on horseback where the road from Paris descended into Versailles. Marshal Pétain headed the group that raised the funds, and every time Bentley Mott passed, he said to it, "Well, John, how are you feeling up there this morning?" When he had to turn down a cold-weather New York meeting of the Philippines Club composed of old hands from the Philippines for being in Arizona, he put his regrets into poetry, or perhaps doggerel, which nevertheless told something of his feelings:

When you grow old, asthmatic and rheumatic
When cold and snow and sleet have got your goat
When winters seventy three your hair has whitened
And summer heat has withered up your form
Then you'll be far more sympathetic
And understand more fully aged ills.
You'll give a veteran more consideration
Who hesitates to dare December chills.

His Yale graduate son went off to Wall Street despite a market-stricken father's reservations—"I am not especially pleased that Warren is going into a brokerage house," he wrote Aunt May. "This is a despiriting, unsettling sort of thing and I should like to see him get into some business which is not connected with gambling." As always there was quick withdrawal of any criticism of his son. "He should know, of course, how interested I am in the new work he is doing, but he doesn't see fit to write anything about it." Within a short time Warren's inheritances and very considerable abilities enabled him to create his own firm destined to become a substantial presence on the Street. "Very striking," George Marshall wrote Warren's father upon receiving an announcement card, "in the name, number, street and city—Pershing, No. 1 Wall Street, New York."

Something else about Warren occupied his father's attention. "You know there are a lot of girls waiting for someone to play with them and oftentimes it is hard to keep your mind on your work," the general had written his cheery de facto mother-in-law, Clara, in 1933, who after the death of Frankie's father had married again, her de facto grandson Warren giving her away at the wedding. The same work distractions afflicted that grandson, to Clara and the general in their letters become Young Hopeful, sometimes simply Hopeful. "Well," Pershing wrote from Paris in July of 1935, "what do you think of Young Hopeful's getting himself into the newspapers with this Miss Muriel Richards her name is, a very charming girl, so I am told. It is all very well to be attentive and go places but why get your name in the papers? I wish you would send for Hopeful and find out what all this means and whether there is anything serious in it or not. I sincerely hope not." When the general returned to the United States: "Please advise Young Hopeful, if you happen to see him, that his father is in Washington and would like to have some word from him whenever the spirit moves him." Any news of Warren, he complained to Aunt May, was increasingly transmitted through deplorable newspaper attention. Clara, he wrote May, had been stricken with blood pressure going up to 220— down to 148 when she was put to bed—and the cause was that she had read that Warren was engaged to Muriel Richards. "I told her I thought it was only a recrudescence of an old rumor and that I did not think there was a thing in it as I felt sure Warren would tell me or you, or both of us, before he let anything like that get into the press. I do not believe he has an intention in that direction at all, at all, at all."

He maintained for riding exercise at Fort Myer outside Washington the two horses he had ridden in the great parades of just after the war, Kidron in Paris, Jeff in New York and Washington, but increasingly it was not easy for him to sit them. So they spent much of their time for pasture and turning-out at the Army Remount Depot in Front Royal, Virginia, where often he stopped by to see how they were coming along. The two were, said the colonel commanding the depot, also a subject of interest to other visitors, in fact "the two most photographed horses of the country." Their owner, his riding days drawing to an end, kept alive interests in other things. One day a young lady at Washington's radio station WRC answered a phone to hear someone indicate a desire to learn how programs were put out over the air. "I'd like to come down and see a broadcast," the caller said. "Is that permitted?"

The young lady inquired who was calling and was told it was General Pershing. "Really. Now isn't that nice," she said, and referring to the widow of the late King George V and mother of George VI, added, "you come right down, General Pershing, and when you get here, ask for Queen Mary—that's who I am." Half an hour later the office receptionist announced a gentleman asking for Queen Mary. The young lady directed that the gentleman be told to take a seat—"Queen Mary will be right out." She left her office for the waiting room expecting a prankster friend to find herself greeting an astonishing visitor. John J. Pershing being spoofed seemed as implausible as that the two privates accompanied him on his walk with President and Mme. Poincaré, and when the story got around Washington, Captain Adamson was applied to for verification as to its authenticity. "It certainly is true," Adamson told the *Washington Herald*, "and General Pershing got a great kick out of it."

→ 15 ←

MISS MURIEL B. RICHARDS was a young woman whose name found frequent mentions in the Society sections of the New York papers showing pictures of such as she seen strolling Fifth Avenue or passing the season in Bermuda, the debutante daughters of luminaries, the prominent girls of Society. She was "eye-compelling, one of the more attractive members of our fashionable younger set," related the gossip-column chronicler Cholly Knickerbocker. She was an heiress, the "B" of her middle name standing for Bache. Her grandfather, the banker and financier Jules S. Bache, possessed one of the premier art collections of the world. It included works by Rembrandt, Titian, Raphael, Dürer, Holbein, Gainsborough, Fragonard, Velazquez, Fra Filippo Lippi and Filippino Lippi, Goya, Van Dyck, Frans Hals, Vermeer, Watteau, Romney, and Sir Joseph Reynolds. She sometimes acted as hostess in the Fifth Avenue mansion housing his accumulations, a residence more like a palace than a town house, with ten fireplaces, two elevators, and accommodations for a dozen servants.

Muriel Richards' parents were divorced. She had made her 1932 debut at the Turf and Field Club and from then on took, as Cholly Knickerbocker put it, "an active part in the social whirl in town, down at Palm Beach (where she spends a part of her winters with her grandfather) and over in London and Paris." Her education consisted of Manhattan's

Brearly School, Oldfields in Maryland, and Mlle. Boissier's in Paris. She was addressed as "Mu," "Mumu," "Momo."

She was one of three young women of similar interests, taste, background, all dark-haired and dark-eyed, who termed themselves the Black Bitches. "Heartbreakers," remembered the sister of one of the others, Jane Holland, they "drove every man to distraction." Jane and Mumu and their third friend, Ellie Reed, came of age just as Prohibition was ending—"sirens at seventeen," said Jane's sister. The existence in which they found their being was the Stork Club and Twenty-One, chic places in Greenwich Village, slumming in Harlem, hotel dances, frolicking on the beach at Narragansett, après-ski lifting of a glass in Québec, "rich and spoiled, fashionable, in-the-world," remembered Jane Holland's sister, "beaus and lovers and goings-on and nightclubs. There were weekends in Greenwich and all-night parties on the roof of the St. Regis and matchbooks from the Stork Club," a camp in the Adirondacks—the Bache one covered thousands of acres—tennis, golf, bright bathing suits and striped beach towels, boathouses, treasure hunts, liners to Europe, Caribbean cruises, costume parties. Their escorts were monied and Wall Street–connected, clubmen good at bass trolling and grouse shooting, graduates of Groton, Andover, Phillips Exeter, Deerfield, St. Paul's, a "gentleman's C" at Princeton or Yale to follow.

In September 1937 the engagement of Muriel Richards and Warren Pershing was announced. Rumors of its coming, said the Society pages, had kept abuzz the social sectors of Fifth and Park for months. The future bridegroom's father found his prospective daughter-in-law sensible and seemingly capable of growth. He remained distressed that photographs of the couple too regularly appeared in the papers, at the racetrack, in nightspots, at the fights at Madison Square Garden in formal attire. "They manage somehow to keep pretty much in the limelight a great deal too much, in my opinion," he wrote Aunt May. Perhaps he did not entirely understand what interest they commanded because she was Society and he was the son of the general of the armies of the United States. The wedding was set for April 22, 1938, at St. Thomas's in New York.

That winter the general as had become usual was in Arizona, Aunt May along, and there he fell ill. It was heart and kidney problems, uremic poisoning. Seventy-seven years old, he lay in a coma. Warren rushed West. On February 24 the Associated Press reported the patient "dangerously near death as anxious physicians worked desperately to preserve his waning strength." DEATH IS NEAR, said the *Chicago Tribune*. SINKS RAPIDLY said the *New York Herald Tribune*. The reports were not exaggerated. Captain Adamson cabled Micheline Resco in Paris. The end was believed near. From his post at Vancouver Barracks in Washington State, Brig. Gen. George Marshall was ordered to the sick man's bedside—Adamson told Chief of Staff Malin Craig that Pershing had always wanted his former aide to be involved in the settlement of his affairs when he died. He was extremely glad Marshall was coming, Warren cabled, and would meet him at the Tucson airport. That his father was not going to live seemed certain, and so Warren arranged for production by the printers Copenhaver of Washington of cards acknowledging with appreciation the condolences he and May soon expected to receive. A three-car funeral train was readied to bear the body back to the capital, and an army plane flew West with a uniform to clothe it.

In his oxygen tent the general stirred, seemed to gain some strength. Adamson cabled Micheline that a little improvement was seen. By then Adamson had been in communication with masses of Pershing's old friends and colleagues about attendance at the forthcoming state funeral. But the tide was turning. Shortly the papers reported that he had come out of a coma and was asking for a newspaper, a barber, and some lamb stew. At once a gigantic flow of letters and telegrams came to Tucson. Some were from people he knew, but there were hundreds and hundreds from organizations whose members the recovering patient had never met, get-well cards mixing with expressions of sympathy, and thousands from former soldiers saying the old buddies were with him in this fight as they had been in France, that they were praying for the man under whom they had been proud to serve.

The outpouring of affection from strangers was astounding and entirely unprecedented in his life—those who had written when Frankie and the girls died were, after all, personal acquaintances. Yet perhaps it was not so wondrous. Twenty years earlier the doughboys joined the colors to make, as Wilson said, the world safe for democracy, to fight the war to end war. What followed was communism, fascism, Nazism, military dictatorships, and brutal totalitarianism in half the world's countries—so much for democracy—and a growing fear that the threat of another war was very much in the air; so much for the lasting peace the Great War was supposed to bring. It came to the ex-doughboys, America's sons, Wilson's heroes, Pershing's men, that with the years the coin in which they had traded had become debased. The gold had turned to tinsel. All too soon, just twenty years, it had become apparent that to have been of the force that held the road to Paris and cracked the Hindenburg Line wouldn't mean much, soon enough. It wouldn't command what it had, not when Adolf Hitler—"a mad man," in Pershing's letters to such as Dawes and Harbord—looked to be the arbitrator of the world's destiny bent on another fight more terrible than the last. So perhaps the writers of letters and dispatchers of telegrams to the recovering chief of the old days found in those writings and dispatchings validation of what he and they had once done together, a reminder of days when all were younger and the world brighter. On April 17, 1938, fewer than two months after every expectation had been that death was imminent, the general of the armies boarded a private railroad car at the Tucson station for the trip East and Warren's wedding on the twenty-second. A crowd of five hundred gathered to see him off. There was a band to play the old songs. When it finished with "Mademoiselle from Armentières"—how once they sang it, his soldiers, hasn't been kissed for forty years, hinky-dinky, parley-voo—he said from the car's rear platform, "Thank you very much. Glad to see you all. Good-bye." With him were a doctor, the doctor's wife, a nurse, several orderlies, and Captain Adamson come from Washington to send replies to every message received during the recent illness.

He went across the country to New York and a special siding of the railroad tracks under the Waldorf-Astoria, where a wheelchair ordered up by Warren awaited. His father disdained its use and walked to the elevator taking him up to his suite, a flag of four white stars on a red field broken out on the flagpoles over the hotel's Park and Lexington Avenue entrances. For the wedding Muriel Bache Richards was in an ivory satin princess gown with rose point lace and long court train, her bridesmaids, including the other two Black Bitches, in icy blue satin with short train, veils, and long, ice blue opera gloves. Warren was in batwing collar and spats. Dudley Thayer, his Yale roommate, was best man. (It had been announced that the groom's father would so serve, but that was beyond his strength.) The maid of honor was the bride's sister Dorothy. Having broken an ankle skiing at Sun Valley, she walked with the aid of a white staff at the top of which was a bouquet of flowers.

General Pershing stepped out of his limousine thin and pale, but when the onlookers jamming the sidewalks to see guests arrive for what was called Society's outstanding wedding of the season broke into applause, he took off his silk hat, and standing straight with his old-time military form, waved for the photographers. He entered St. Thomas's from a side door. As he came in, the two thousand persons present stood and remained standing until he reached his seat in the front pew. Mumu came down the aisle, her shimmering train reaching the length of six pews. She was twenty-three to Warren's twenty-nine. The cream of New York looked on as vows were exchanged.

The reception was at the 814 Fifth Avenue mansion of her grandfather, the great art collection eventually destined for the Metropolitan Museum of Art hanging on the walls. A detail of policemen and detectives checked guests coming to the door. At the church there had been masses of rambler roses at the base of the chancel, apple and dogwood blossoms in the form of trees, vases of Easter lilies on both sides of the altar, white birch and cedar trees and banks and cornucopias of spring flowers at the pillars, blue delphinium and bridal wreath marking the pew ends; at the reception the bridal party received in a bower of pink and white dogwood. The guests dined on small tables. Emil Coleman's orchestra played for dancing. "Brilliant reception," said the *New York World-Telegram*. Several columns were required to print the names of those attending, including such names as Vanderbilt, Dawes, Harriman, Foy, Straus, Whalen, Taylor, Woodward, Weicker, Dodge, Lowndes, Ewing, Frelinghuysen, Froelich, Baruch, Gary, Gruntal, Warburg, de Cordoba, Gimbel, Guggenheim, Oblensky, Thaw, Thayer, Chrysler, and a few hundred more. Among their number was listed Miss May Pershing, but not the general. His slight reserves of strength had been used up to smile at the church in his cutaway and dark gray-striped trousers, stiffly to sit erect in his pew while grasping the rail for support, to incline his head as the bride went past. When he arose to depart, a doctor assisted him from one side while an orderly did the same from the other. Coming down the church steps, they asked if he wanted to rest a minute. "No, thank you," he said. "We'll go right along." He smiled as people broke into applause on the sidewalk and then went to the Waldorf-Astoria, where earlier Dr. Roland Davison told reporters he hoped the ceremonies would not be too wearing on a man but weeks removed from a near-fatal illness, that "the emotional strain of his son's wedding will not tax the general's strength or nervous system to too great an extent." He was in fact affected in such fashion as immediately to be put to bed in the hotel and, when in a few days he was able to travel, to go directly to Washington's Walter Reed Army Hospital for three months of quiet rest followed by a trip to France to take the waters. Mr. and Mrs. F. Warren Pershing the day after their wedding made for Newark Airport and a United Air Lines plane for a three-stop flight to San Francisco and from there by boat on to a honeymoon trip that would see them visit Honolulu, then on to Hong Kong by Pan American Clipper, boat passage to Singapore to follow. Java, Bali, the Malay Peninsula, India, Bangkok—many "places of interest" would be viewed, the papers said. They would go on to Egypt and into Europe, Budapest, Rome, Paris, London—four months, around the world. They were very good about writing home.

To my new Father-in-law and Aunt—

First of all I want you to know how proud I am to be able to call you the above. I only hope that I will be able to make you proud of me.

General Pershing, it made me so happy to see you at the end of the aisle. It made my wedding day the happiest of my life. To you, Aunt May, I owe all my gratitude for being so sweet to me.

At last, I know what it means to be divinely happily married. Warren has been the perfect husband—always sweet and thoughtful. We are having a grand trip, and as I know that he has written details I won't repeat them. You will hear from us again in the very near future.

Devotedly,
Muriel.

In Manila they called upon Douglas MacArthur, commanding the armed forces of the Philippines—"he couldn't have been nicer," Warren wrote. MacArthur had married Pershing's long-ago Paris fling the rich and wild Louise Cromwell Brooks. (It wouldn't last long.) In Manila the travelers also called upon President Quezon, who showed them around his residence, which Warren's father had known as the Malacaña Palace of the governor general in the old days. Quezon, Warren thought, was very pleasant but almost childlike as he discussed improvements he was putting in, a dressing room with blue glass mirrors on all the walls, a fifty-foot mahogany bar and nightclub downstairs, two high towers on the place's wings. Egypt's pyramids Mumu found larger than expected; she described the trip by air out of Vienna as *"ghastly"* for the plane being hit by lightning: "I thought we were on our way to heaven." In London they saw the musical *Me and My Gal*, which featured the new Lambeth Walk dance, which they learned. They returned home to an apartment at 320 Park Avenue. "We have our fingers crossed," Warren soon reported, "as the cook has produced nothing but very excellent food and has complained not at all which is, I am told, a very unusual status for cooks to assume." They were at the Jules Bache place in Palm Beach, visited friends on Long Island whose house had two swimming pools, squash courts, bowling alleys, and shooting galleries, went skiing in Canada, were seen in newspaper photos describing them as prominent and popular members of the younger married set. The servant situation deteriorated, Warren wrote his father. There was "a very serious domestic problem which we are attempting to solve. It seems the cook and the maid are unable to agree on the general facts of life and both are threatening to quit unless we fire the other one. The unfortunate part is that both of them are excellent and we have been attempting to point out why they should learn to overlook the other one's faults. I might add I don't look for any tremendous success. We are trying to hang on to the cook long enough for you to come and sample her wares as she is truly excellent." A month later, April 1939, he likened matters to events occurring in Europe. "Our life has been complicated by a series of domestic crises similar in intensity to those abroad. We have now gotten somewhat shock-proof and are contemplating a revolving door as the last couple stayed so short a time it would have been a great deal easier if they had kept right on going out on their entrance." The young Pershings were off to Bermuda.

Two months later, the general made for Paris. But the weather was cold, gloomy, cloudy—not the best prescription for rheumatism. The waters in the South seemed less able to rejuvenate him than in former years. It seemed to him, that summer, that French fears about German intentions were misplaced. It did not appear that way to Warren in New York. "I would appreciate very much hearing from you," he wrote his father, "as the newspapers here scare us to death about every other day with screaming headlines of troop movements with ultimatums." He was a summer bachelor, Mumu at her grandfather's Adirondacks place most of the summer, Camp Wenon'ah in Tupper Lake. He would be up there every weekend and for a week or two in August.

Europe in that summer was coming to the last weeks and days of the period between the wars. It appeared to Washington that General Pershing ought to get out of there and back to America. He arrived on *Manhattan*, docking in New York on August 17. He had cut it pretty close. Two weeks later the Germans went into Poland. In Walter Reed Hospital for rest and observation, it seemed to the commander of America's overseas forces in what was no longer the Great War or the World War, but now so suddenly the First World War, almost too painful to accept that all the sacrifices of the earlier and terrible fight appeared to have gone for nothing. He was almost dazed by the concept that now another war was underway. He had felt that "such a thing was not within the range of reasonable possibilities," he wrote Charlie Dawes. But then, Adolf Hitler was a "mad man, not feeling the ordinary reactions of a sane person. So the world is thrown into another sad catastrophe, the end of which no one can foretell. It is a tragic thought for all of us who fought in the last World

War and who believed that such a calamity could not come again upon the people. I cannot help being greatly depressed."

Even as he wrote Charlie, the Germans were almost leveling Warsaw. Days later, cameramen came to Walter Reed asking the general to pose for photographs marking his seventy-ninth birthday. He did so on the lawn, natty in blue striped shirt and wearing a gray felt hat, carrying a cane, but soberly making reference to tragic events abroad.

After the Polish surrender what came to be called the Phony War, *la guerre de drôle,* ensued. Nothing happened along 1914–18's old front lines of haunted memory where the curtain came down for the youth of a generation, a civilization, and a way of life. Roses bloomed in the graveyards, 150 of them for the British dead in the Ypres sector alone. The final American one of great marble statuary and monument had been dedicated at Montsec by General Pershing in 1937, two years before the guns began to sound again in Europe and the troops to move, he then speaking of how futile war was, of the weight history would lay upon false leaders who might bring again such horror. Now it had come. Armistice Day of 1939 arrived, and with it for the general of the armies telegrams commemorating the day twenty-one years gone, as telegrams always did to mark the day of his debarking at France off *Baltic,* and the days his great battles began. It all seemed hollow now. With the warm weather of 1940 the Germans moved in the West, their advance more like a conquerer's march-past than a battle campaign. For the French ran away or surrendered. It took the Germans fifteen minutes to traverse the Verdun fields of glory for the holding of which the French gave up hundreds of thousands of dead in the earlier war. In the end General Pershing's dear friend came forward and asked the Germans for peace. Pétain was eighty-four. Sometimes his mind drifted. When its in-and-out focus cleared, it was upon one great principle: that he, old, must protect the young. He could not bear it that the sons of his soldiers of the First World War, so many of whom had died, should go to die in the Second. Let it end, and soon, the fighting. Nothing else mattered. ("You think too much of the French, and not enough of France," an aide said to the marshal. Perhaps Pétain loved not wisely but too well.) In time he would be judged by some as having tossed away his country's honor. He shook hands with Adolf Hitler.

To his friend at Walter Reed it was unthinkable that Pétain could forswear his obligations. "My thoughts are constantly with you in these tragic days," Pershing wrote him two days after he became what was called Head of the State ruling a portion of France left unoccupied, his headquarters in the watering resort of Vichy. He could not believe, Pershing wrote Micheline Resco, that Germany's "ruthless ruffians" were meant to rule the world. (Armed with thousands of dollars he sent her in addition to Captain Adamson's monthly-dispatched remittance, and copies of a signed appeal asking aid of all U.S. diplomatic and consular officials, she had escaped France for New York, Warren meeting her on the pier at his father's request, to go from there to be ensconced in Washington's Shoreham Hotel.) Six weeks after the fall of France the British were off the Continent, most of the Empire's military equipment left behind on the beach at Dunkirk. Pershing asked for radio time from America's major broadcasting systems and from the suite he still maintained at the Carlton Hotel despite spending far more time at Walter Reed Hospital, offered some views to his country's people. It was unprecedented, the papers said, for although he had often delivered ceremonial addresses since the Armistice, never before had he undertaken to speak out on national policy. "Fellow citizens," he said, "I am speaking tonight because I consider it my duty. It is my duty to tell you that in my opinion we face problems of the utmost seriousness."

He was in a black suit, Black Jack sitting erect at a table on which was a phalanx of microphones reaching millions of people and saying America must face the truth. That America must rise up, arm, justify its independence, democracy, constitutional liberty, its resistance to fanaticism, tyranny, brutism. "Warren was so proud of you," Mumu wrote. Others were most strongly moved that an old warrior had girded on his armor of long service, long taken off, to tell a people deeply opposed to war and intervention in Europe's problems that alas, those problems were America's, too. "We must be ready to meet force with a stronger force. We must build up our army and navy. We must have the strength of character to face the truths. A new kind of war is loose in the world. It is a war against civilization, it is a revolution against the values which we have cherished. It must be faced with daring and devotion. We must lift up our hearts. We must reaffirm our noble traditions. We must make ourselves so strong that the tradition we live by shall not perish. I thank you."

He had written the speech with the inevitable assistance of the aides upon whom he had always settled responsibility, but without the influence of anyone in the U.S. government. Speaking solely for himself and as a "hard duty" he had, said the *Louisville Courier-Journal*, told the "cold and solemn truth." Another, entirely by coincidence, had on Sunday, August 4, 1940, also addressed the nation. It was Charles Lindbergh. He was a great aviator, conquerer of the Atlantic, attractive and with an attractive wife, recipient of the world's sympathy for the fatal kidnapping of his little son eight years earlier, but also famously pro-Nazi. His speech said that Germany should rule Europe and that such rule should find American compliance, and "friendly agreement." Here stood, papers said, someone who knew nothing of human nature, a mechanic, really, ignorant of history, fatuous and "without capacity," said the *Courier-Journal*; and here in epochal contrast stood someone who offered a "noble call to truth-telling and to courage." It was John Joseph Pershing's last great contribution.

He was rising eighty—would reach it in five weeks—and, like Pétain, he drifted in and out, like Pétain able sometimes to discuss the most demanding subjects before falling into vagueness and forgetful noncomprehension. The public did not know it, nor many of his friends, but he was never the same after the siege of illness at Tucson. With his condition came pronounced physical weakness. Those not with him steadily could not realize the situation; and so in December 1940, four months after his radio address, President Roosevelt asked him to become U.S. ambassador to Vichy France, rump France, that portion of the country where the Germans permitted Pétain to be Head of the State. In such capacity, the president reasoned, he could shore up his old friend in opposing German demands for French aid in the fight against Britain. One very old man might help another very old man to do, go on, be. But it was impossible, and Pershing knew it. "My condition is such as to make my successful accomplishment of the mission very improbable." He did not wish to fool himself nor fool others, he had told the correspondent Frederick Palmer long before as they walked in the garden of the Mills mansion in Paris, and that had not changed, that desire, although he himself had. When Georgie Patton, brigadier general of tankers now, wrote from Georgia asking his old chief to come to Fort Benning so they could do some riding together as cavalry officers together they had in France and, before that, Mexico, the general of the armies replied that he would love to but that he was afraid it would be a little too much for him. Days in the saddle were over. Kidron and Jeff lived on at Front Royal unridden, word of their health regularly sent on to their owner.

Raised to army chief of staff, George Marshall was a frequent caller to Walter Reed. He often found rising in his mind, as he performed his duties, that which he termed a "perfect picture" of the way General Pershing had appeared in 1917–18 and afterward, and of the manner in which he had gone about his work. From that picture, Marshall said to his wife, he had learned the importance of refusal to lose one's temper. It wasted energy better used in the performance of duty. He had learned also from the Pershing-who-was, not the old man up in Walter Reed, a coldly dispassionate judgment of men, no matter their personal relationship to the judge. Every job in the American Expeditionary Forces hung by a thread, even his, Charlie Dawes had said in the old days, and as America vastly increased her army for what was coming, George Marshall put to test in war games and maneuvers, and ruthlessly found wanting, officers he had soldiered with for years and who had once been the rising heroes of the AEF. Of the twenty-one U.S. Army major generals of the line on the day Marshall became chief of staff in 1939, nineteen were given nothing of matter to do in the war so soon to come. Their wives wrote begging important assignments for them, referred to old friendships with Marshall and his wife, dinners at his home—it did not matter. Pershing had taught him adherence to efficiency. Who had done great things in high position in 1918 was by 1939 almost certainly too old, rigid, set in his ways. Pershing had seen that in 1917–18 in great leaders for the Spanish War and the Philippines. So it was to those who had been young captains and majors in the First World War that Marshall looked to for leadership in the Second. Loyal, however, not only to the concepts of the Pershing that had been, but to the Pershing who was, Marshall personally went around Washington in the spring of 1941 looking for a replacement for the general of the armies' little-used Carlton Hotel suite. Getting to his rooms there even with the assistance of orderlies and the nurse always assigned to him by the Walter Reed authorities was proving too much for the general's strength. Marshall studied apartments available for sublease, paying particular attention to those whose garages had no steps and whose lobbies would not require a long walk to reach the street. None was satisfactory for the fragile state of Walter Reed's semipermanent resident, and after luncheon with their mutual old chief on May 22, 1941, Marshall wrote Charlie Dawes an unhappy truth: "I fear you will have a great shock when you see General Pershing. Confidentially, it is very, very sad to see the change in him in the last few weeks."

He took slow walks about the Walter Reed grounds and went for automobile rides, kept up a limited correspondence with old friends. It was, of course, a great thrill for him when Mumu gave birth to little John Warren Pershing in New York in January 1941. "Dearest Père—now Grandpère," the new mother wrote. Her father-in-law's picture was right next to the one of Warren on her Doctors' Hospital bed table, her letter said. "Now to try and tell you about your grandson. I would say that he looks exactly like Warren. He has blond hair, blue eyes, the same shaped head & face as his father. The doctor tells me he is perfect. People have been so kind—Mr. Baruch telephoned and sent flowers, Miss Resco sent an adorable hat and coat for John Warren, General Marshall wrote Warren a perfectly charming letter. As for your son—he is so happy and proud. It makes me so thrilled. Both of us wanted a boy so much and neither one of us dared to admit it—until now. Do write to me and give me the news of yourself and Aunt May. Fondest love, your devoted daughter-in-law."

To recover from her confinement she went with Warren to Jamaica, then to Cuba and then up to her grandfather's Palm Beach place, little John Warren—immediately "Jackie"—at the Park Avenue residence with his nurse. In Cuba, Warren wrote, they saw where in the Spanish-American War the Rough Riders and Captain Pershing of the black Tenth Cavalry had been: "San Juan Hill et al., and with our guide refought the battle very successfully." One of the people at F. Warren Pershing & Co. mailed the general a portrait of his grandson: "That was a fine photograph that Mr. Froelich kindly sent me, and a very striking one inasmuch as John Warren is eyeing someone very directly and also has his right fist ready to give whoever it is he is looking at a good punch in the nose." A June christening had been planned for New York, but the trip would have been a great strain for the infant's grandfather in what was likely to be warm weather, so the ceremony was transferred to Washington's National Cathedral. Then the young Pershings went off to the Adirondacks camp, where a nursery and playroom had been added to the bungalow reserved for them there. "It was grand to see you and the family down here," the general of the armies wrote his son. "The young man certainly is a winner. He is not only a fine looking little fellow, but he behaved himself as a real boy should. John Warren behaved as one would expect a big husky, as he is, to do, and stood up for what he considered his rights. I am mighty proud of him."

But being on his feet for a long period during the cathedral ceremonies took a great deal out of Jackie's grandfather. He found himself unable to attend the fifty-fifth reunion of his West Point class. A loudspeaker telephone hookup would have to substitute, and over it he talked with those present, addressing them as "old duffers" and then saying a personal word to each. "I have studied the photograph taken at the class dinner again and again," he soon wrote Avery Andrews. Of the seventy-six with whom he had graduated, all but a dozen and a half had gone on. Two months later his eighty-first birthday came, and among the congratulatory telegrams was one from Jules Bache: "The Little Corporal joins me in fondest greetings and heartfelt wishes for perfect health." Pershing in his reply promoted the grandson to the Little Colonel. "Warren and Muriel flew down to spend a few hours with me and I was gratified to hear from them how well you and the little fellow are getting along. I wish that we could all have been together at the lake." He envied Bache for being able to see Jackie every day in New York, he remarked. Muriel was very fond of her grandfather, referred to by her as "Mr. B." In newspaper articles it was always mentioned that the great financier, in addition to having one of the world's preeminent art collections, was also what was termed a *bon vivant*. Once after dining at the Fourteenth Street German restaurant Lüchow's, Warren and Cliff Michel, who was married to one of Mumu's two sisters—the other was the wife of the theatrical figure Gilbert Miller—decided to step into a nearby burlesque house to see the strippers and hear the jokes. As they approached the box office a limousine glided up to have the chauffeur hold open the door for their wives' grandfather. Mr. B. walked in without buying a ticket. Perhaps the bon vivant had a permanent box, Warren and Cliff Michel decided. Perhaps he was a friend of one of the young ladies. They could not doubt that it would be best for them to seek entertainment elsewhere.

With crafted speedboats and limber wooden fishing rods in the Adirondacks camp, and pool parties at Palm Beach in the winter, and Persian carpets and crystal sconce and chandelier and silver candelabra, and ice bucket and silver cocktail shaker and strainer for the drinking no less a part of their life than eating, beautifully dressed and always well turned out, the young Pershings lived their Society life as Warren went ahead on the Street. He was very good at his work. Things occurred in the stock market that would not bear well the light of scrutiny—but never when the principal of Pershing & Company was involved. Warren was, people said, almost painfully honest. He was also very well liked, very charming, and loyal to his people, even those who really drank a little too much. With dining out in the homes or clubs of persons very much like themselves, well bred, polite, mannered, monied, there were routine litanies of jokes about FDR and Eleanor, and remarks about the Jews. Warren was rarely called by his first name. Even Mumu addressed him as "Persh."

The general's closeness to his sister never decreased. He told May to get herself a new car, and she bought a blue Buick whose picture she mailed him. "Isn't it beautiful? I'm delighted!" She was almost as thrilled as he about little John Warren, and sent a tray, bowl, knife, fork, and spoon, the infant's name engraved on the porringer of sterling of good weight. "Our new Baby," she termed him in letters replying to those of her brother detailing the boy's progress as seen in Washington visits: "John seems to be getting along very well, just as vigorous as ever. He is certainly a fine youngster. I think he has about six teeth now and is able to crawl all over the place. He tries often to stand up and it is amusing to see his efforts to do so, but they are trying to keep him from doing that so as

he will not acquire legs like his father and his great-grandfather Warren."
He had always thought his son's bow legs came from the early riding
lessons back in the Philippines, but apparently the trait was genetic—
John Warren was going to have legs unable, as the saying went, to stop a
runaway hog. The grandfather was always appreciative in the highest degree when the child was brought to Washington. "It would be next to impossible to describe the great pleasure I had when you visited," he wrote
Warren and Mumu. "To see the progress that has been made by my
grandson was very gratifying, and I thank you both most sincerely for
bringing him down."

His friends of the old days of the Old Army and Mexico and the war were
gone or going, their letters speaking, as his did, of grandchildren and of
age's infirmities. "He is cheerful and philosophical in spite of having to
move about in a wheelchair," wrote Mrs. Malvern Hill Barnum of her
husband, the "P.T." of West Point days and of those of the Tenth Cavalry
in Cuba, and divisional command in the war. "The years do have a way of
catching up with all of us." Soon there came from her what brought a re-
sponding telegram from Walter Reed: DEEPLY GRIEVED BY THE
SAD NEWS OF THE PASSING OF YOUR DISTINGUISHED HUS-
BAND, MY CLASSMATE AND DEAR FRIEND. PLEASE ACCEPT
MY PROFOUND SYMPATHY.

    At the news of what had occurred at Pearl Harbor, the general of the
armies wrote to President Roosevelt that as with all Americans he wished
to partake in the defense of the country. "As one among those millions, I
offer my services, in any way in which my experience and strength, to the
last ounce, will be of help in the fight." Back came, "Dear General, You
are magnificent. You always have been—and you always will be. Your services will be of great value." Yet what really could he contribute? "I think
his desire was to hear the president say he would utilize the general's services as a military adviser," Chief of Staff Marshall told Secretary of War
Henry L. Stimson. But such a work was far beyond his strength. "This war
does not seem the real thing without you at the head of it," Avery Andrews

wrote his old classmate. "But I guess it is a youngsters' job." Andrews turned to discussion of what was more appropriate for correspondence between two warriors whose fighting days were long gone: "I do hope you are as well as we oldsters can reasonably expect, even if we do have a few creaks and cracks in our joints."

Such description did not apply to Warren. Yet he was equally not definable as the youngsters of whom Andrews had spoken, thirty-two years old, father of a child and with a second soon on the way, head of a Wall Street firm. General Marshall offered a civilian job in the War Department from which Warren could work up to be commissioned a captain in the army's finance department. It was a perfectly legitimate opportunity for service and one that a great many other men of Warren's age and position would have scooped up in an instant. Warren did not. He wished his father's position not to play a role in his participation in the Second World War; and shortly papers throughout the country reported that on February 4, 1942, fewer than two months after Pearl Harbor, he had enlisted in the army as a buck private. Marshall had him assigned to basic training near Washington and wrote the new soldier that his father was going to be very pleased and proud. There followed a widely reprinted photograph of Pvt. Francis Warren Pershing of Company B, Fifth Battalion, U.S. Engineers at Fort Belvoir, Virginia, seated on his bunk polishing his shoes. He wore strap-under leggings. He had lost eight pounds from his six-foot frame since joining the service two months earlier, he soon told newspapermen, and was down to 187 pounds. (To speak to reporters was not something Warren sought, but for him to do so was considered a good move by the army's public relations people.) When interviewed he was doing some landscape work. "I've been shoveling dirt and planting grass seed today," he remarked. "You'll have to ask my captain what I'll be doing tomorrow." He had visited his father at Walter Reed, he said, to be told that his uniform fitted him mighty well. His marksmanship had gained a sharpshooters' designation. His company commander told the newspapermen that he was one of the battalion's top soldiers. "We made him right guard of his platoon, not because he is Private Pershing, but because he was the best soldier we had for the job." Warren did not speak of the commander in chief of the AEF to the men around him. Once a fellow soldier asked if he was related to General Pershing. "You look something like him," the man said. "I'm a distant relative," Warren replied. A listener pooh-poohed the idea. "He's no kin to General Pershing. If he were, he'd have one of those easy political jobs." But the truth of the matter, of course, got around Fort Belvoir, and once when Warren on a night exercise was using a sledgehammer to drive spikes into timber serving as part of a bridge, a sergeant of regulars in the time-approved manner of putting the rookies in their place came by and offered out of the side of his mouth, "You'll never be the man your father was."

Warren broke into laughter. "Don't I know it!"

After basic training he was appointed to the cadre retained at Fort Belvoir for instructing new recruits, with attendant promotion. Corporal Pershing's application to and acceptance for the base officer candidate school followed. Marshall forwarded to Walter Reed the results of his first four weeks there; grades of 97 in Maps and Aerial Photos, 95 in Command and Leadership, 94 in Explosives and Demolition, 85 in Engineer Tools, 100 in Rifle Marksmanship, 100 in Rigging, 91 in Floating Bridges, and similar high marks close to the top of the class in camouflage, obstacles, scouting and patrol, fixed bridges, use of the machine gun, sanitation, and hygiene. Marshall came to graduation to hand him his commission—the health of the general of the armies prohibited his attendance. In August 1942 Lieutenant Pershing was assigned to the 275th Engineer Battalion of the Seventy-fifth Infantry Division at Fort Leonard Wood, Missouri. (Decades earlier his father had his problems with General Wood, but all that was ancient history now.) Warren did not care for his new assignment. He wanted to get overseas, he told his father. There was a war on, and he didn't want to fight it in the backwaters. Warren certainly was an enthusiastic soldier, the general wrote Aunt May. He never talked about the market or business at all, and military service details consumed him. Back in New York Mumu was doing her bit. Cholly Knickerbocker's Society in the War Effort column related that the "tall, dark, and beautiful" former Muriel Bache Richards was "one of our most active war workers." She acted as nurse's aide in the army dispensary at Whitehall Street and was a visiting nurse for the Henry Street Settlement House. On

Monday nights from eight to midnight she ran the "multiplication dances and conga lines at the Open House for Officers at Delmonico's, and every Friday for four hours pours beer for officers at the gala dance." The days weren't long enough for this "very busy and popular lady." Sons of the odious nephew Richard Paddock by various wives wrote from army bases to tell Uncle John they had joined the colors. He sent letters to them and their mothers expressing his pride and pleasure.

For himself, he sometimes departed Walter Reed dressed in a dark suit for a slow automobile ride through wartime Washington, his car as it passed through the hospital grounds going by young men on crutches or in wheelchairs. More and more he used a rolling chair as he moved about his third-floor three-room suite dressed in pajamas, an orderly always with him. George Adamson, raised from captain to colonel just before his retirement from military service, held down in civilian capacity the elaborate offices in the former State, War, and Navy Building where was engraved in gold above the door The General of the Armies. (Now, of course, there were new buildings, the Pentagon dwarfing everything else in the Washington area.) Adamson came to Walter Reed every other day to report on what business required discussion. There wasn't much. May Pershing was at the hospital in constant attendance, the Nebraska home closed and the Buick in storage. She lived in a guest house on the Walter Reed grounds, read from the papers to her brother when he was up to it, helped him with his food, received the infrequent callers. One arrival found himself unrecognized despite an acquaintance dating back a quarter of a century and more. When he spoke, his old chief came to himself and his mind became clear. "He looks very old," George Patton wrote in his diary. The affair with Nita was so long ago. She had never married.

They talked about chasing Pancho Villa and how the then Lieutenant Patton shot two Mexicans. He was taking the pistol he used to his new duty assignment, Georgie said, and Pershing said he hoped Patton would kill some Germans with it. "He said that at the start of the war he was hurt because no one consulted him, but he was now resigned to sit on the sidelines with his feet hanging over. He almost cried. It is pathetic how little he knows of the war." At the end Patton knelt and took his old commander's hand in his own and kissed it and asked for a blessing. "Good-bye,

Georgie," Pershing said. "God bless you and keep you, and give you victory." "I put on my hat and saluted, and he returned it like he used to, and twenty-five years seemed to drop from him." Patton left for Bolling Field and a plane to Norfolk and the ship taking him to the Allied landings on the Moroccan coast of North Africa. He wrote from there one month later on the stationery of the Headquarters Western Task Force, Office of the Commanding General, speaking of how during the hospital visit he had wanted to talk of his assignment—"I wanted desperately to tell you"—but that adherence to enforcements of silence about impending ship movements had forbidden it. Now the task force had successfully accomplished its mission. "I think of you and try to conduct my operations as I think you would have done. I realize that when I make such an attempt I am entering the field of impossible competition." The night before the landings, Patton wrote, he kept in mind his old chief's ability to put aside worry even in the face of the most testing situation, and in the tense nighttime hours lay down in full pack on the ship and slept for two hours "in order to prove to myself I could emulate you." His letters continued regularly to come to Walter Reed. "I can assure you that whatever ability I have shown or shall show as a soldier is the result of a studious endeavor to copy the greatest American soldier, yourself." General Patton of great reputation and glory and indeed legend would in time as he rampaged through France and into Germany send snapshots of the old AEF Chaumont headquarters taken by his Third Army's forward thrust from the Germans. Some of the barracks which had contained offices were roofless from artillery fire. At the Val des Écoliers the housekeeper told Patton that at the desk where once Pershing worked another soldier had also: Field Marshal Erwin Rommel.

Upon rare occasions other visitors were shown into the hospital suite where an old man's days droned their hours away. One was very tall and hawk-nosed and physically awkward. General Pershing registered upon the uniform of a French officer and inquired after Marshal Pétain. So far as he was aware, replied Charles de Gaulle, the marshal's health was excellent. He did not allude to the death sentence in absentia he had passed upon Pétain, nor the same that the marshal in Vichy had passed upon him. With his visitor Pershing talked of his desire in 1918 that no armistice be extended to the Germans, that they should have been forced into an unconditional surrender. If that had been done, he told de Gaulle, there probably would not be a second war going on. That was an abiding theme among those who had to deal with the Second World War knowing that alone of all the chieftains of the First it was Pershing and Pershing only who wanted total victory and had warned of the consequences if there were no total victory. In his 1943 congratulatory telegram for the Walter Reed patient's eighty-third birthday, President Roosevelt said the occasion "forcibly" brought "to mind that you wanted to go through to Berlin in 1918." In the following year the president's greetings included: "None of us will forget that in 1918 you wanted to go through to Berlin. How right you were!"

The demands upon Chief of Staff George Marshall were such that he could not easily break away from work and go up to Walter Reed, but Mrs. Marshall sometimes came, or sent a cake she had baked. In return the general of the armies had Adamson send plants for her garden or terrarium. Once a month Charlie Dawes came, stopping in Washington for lunch while traveling from Chicago to New York for a meeting of the board of directors of James Harbord's Radio Corporation of America. But the years were telling on Charlie also, and sometimes he was confined to his house. "Last Sunday was a lonely day for me," Pershing wrote him in April 1943. "It was a day when you should have been here for luncheon, and I hope you will not be compelled to miss another one. I shall look forward to seeing you at the regular time next month." The years were also telling on Harbord, the other of what the papers used to call the Three Musketeers. He had more friends in Arlington Cemetery than elsewhere, he said. The living graduates of Old '86 were down to fewer than a dozen. Yet the past still had its grip, and when officials of the University of Wyoming asked if General Pershing would accept an honorary degree, he replied he would do so in Frankie's memory. There must be no publicity. On the university's June graduation day the Wyoming alumnus Adm. Emory S. Land came to Walter Reed with diploma and academic hood to make the presentation before an audience consisting of an army doctor and nurse and a couple of hospital people, the general's orderlies, and May. The grass had been growing over Frankie's Cheyenne grave by then for nearly thirty years, and on those of Helen and Anne and Mary Margaret. To Frankie's son, the girls' brother, and his two little boys—the second one, Richard, born in October 1942—was given all the focus General Pershing could muster up. Mumu was very good about bringing the grandsons for visits and sending word of their doings. "Dickie is so darling I'm sure you'd be proud of him. He has a little blond fuzz on top of his head, a bit darker than Jackie. They look exactly alike and Jackie seems to be very happy about the new brother. Dickie is coming along beautifully and laughs and coos all the time—he is the exact image of Jackie and is really sweet. Warren I suppose has told you that I'm bringing them to see you at the end of March."

The visit came off as scheduled when Mumu stopped on the way north from Palm Beach en route to the Park Avenue apartment, and the general wrote his son in Fort Leonard Wood, "It was perfectly fine to see the two kiddies as they came through here with their dear mother. Both were looking well—extremely healthy and active. Little Jackie is about the most active thing I have ever seen. He never walks any place at all, but must run. I think little Dickie is the handsomest baby I ever saw. I hope he holds on to some of his good looks when he reaches manhood." By then Warren had been promoted. "I was fifteen years reaching the grade of captain," his father wrote, " and you have been fifteen months. If you keep up the same relative speed you will reach some of the higher ranks some day, but it is all more or less a matter of chance, so my advice is to be content with what you have." Still the most enthusiastic of soldiers although disappointed to be a staff officer and not a company commander, which was what he wanted, Warren was looking forward to a visit from Mumu commemorating the fifth anniversary of their marriage. "It certainly doesn't seem to have been that long ago." Perhaps his next anniversary would find everyone in a more peaceful world. Of the boys: "I really miss those two rascals who I understand are becoming very tough citizens. Wish I could see them again." Soon Mumu wrote details of her Missouri trip and the latest on the grandsons: "The babies are both very well—Jackie grows more grown up every minute—he really is beginning to be a little man—never stops talking and makes very good sense. Dickie now has four teeth and spends his placid little life cooing contentedly. He really is so sweet."

In the summer of 1943 she visited Warren again in Fort Leonard Wood and then went with the children to her grandfather's Camp Wenon'ah in the Adirondacks. "Dickie is enormous now and looks so much like you," she wrote her father-in-law in Walter Reed. "I took Jackie out in a canoe this morning and he was so good. He really makes very good sense now. If it is convenient for you I will bring the children to see you in the beginning of October as I think you'd enjoy them. Do let me know." Of course the answer was affirmative, and Warren wrote from Leonard Wood, "I envy you your chance to see those kids—Muriel tells me Dickie is really coming along and is now old enough to totter around." Warren had gotten his company and was learning what a commanding officer should know, or at least a portion of it. "Not much but some." But he wanted to get overseas, he told his father. General MacArthur had once indicated he'd like him as an aide, and General Marshall let him know he'd take him along if assigned to command the coming invasion of Europe. Meanwhile he languished in Missouri. Couldn't his father get him to someplace more interesting? "I have rarely asked for a favor, but this is one I am really asking for, so think it over and see if there isn't some way of working it out. I've been in the army almost two years now, and would certainly like to get a little closer to some action."

Marshall was applied to. Warren got orders for the European Theater of Operations preceded by a January 1944 furlough with Mumu and the boys in Palm Beach. She wrote, "Dearest Père, Just a short line to say hello and tell you that your babies are very well—Jackie is learning how to swim and is a real little water rat. Dickie as yet is not too sure he likes it, but is walking all over the place and trying desperately to talk—so far it sounds like Chinese. Warren left here Tuesday night and I spoke to him on the telephone Wednesday night and Thursday night—but no call last night so I gather he has left these shores. It was awfully hard to say goodbye to him but my pride in him makes up for the heartache a little bit. He is the most wonderful and lovable person that I've ever known. I only pray this war will soon be over so we can all be together again." Soon she was writing that Dickie had fifteen teeth and each day looked more like his father and grandfather. "Jackie is a source of delight to everyone. He is very much the little man and is interested in everything and everybody. He plays host for me whenever I have friends over. He is full of conversation that actually makes quite a bit of sense. Jackie now swims all over the pool by himself with a pair of water-wings and my greatest worry at the moment is to try to get him out. He loves the water so much he hates to get out. Dickie is a bit timid still. I am feeling very well altho' I miss *our boy* terribly—however as I said before I'm really proud of him." Warren by then was with the Engineering Section of the Headquarters of the U.S. First Army in England, living, he wrote, in a former boys' school with Gothic architecture reminiscent of Yale's. His fellow junior officers he found a nice bunch of fellows. His mattress felt as if stuffed with rocks. All of Britain was amazingly blacked out to protect against German bombers, with not a light to be seen anywhere. Making his way to an Officers' Club dance on his first night on the post, Warren wrote, he fell flat on his face in the darkness. He was hoping to learn to find his way around a little better or he would really be in trouble.

For Easter of 1944 Mumu took the boys down to Washington. "The kiddies are certainly prospective commandos," the general told his son, "and I think Jackie could qualify right now. Dickie demonstrated that he has the lung power, and needs only to develop a little more physically." He had gathered up all his strength to take everybody to lunch at the Carlton Hotel, hoping to follow up with Easter services at the National Cathedral or in Arlington, but it had proved too much to attempt, so he stayed indoors. "No need to tell you that you are constantly in our thoughts, and that our greatest pleasure is hearing from you." Warren replied he only wished he could have been along for the family get-together. He had recently been to Oxford for a visit, where his thoughts went back to the day in 1919 when as a child he had seen his father receive an honorary degree there. On April 20, 1944, the Associated Press filed a story datelined a U.S. Army Unit Headquarters in Britain: "Captain Warren Pershing, by his own estimation a 'small potato' in this war, has come over to help finish off Hitler's armies as his father did the Kaiser's.

"The strapping son of General John J. Pershing is in the Engineer Corps and up to his ears in pre-invasion paper work.

" 'Write about those fellows who are flying the bombers and fighters,' he said. 'They're the ones who are doing the fighting now.

" 'Anything I would have to say would be pre-season talk. Wait until we get over there and do something. And if I have something to do with it, come around then.' "

By then, mid-1944, the general had almost ceased the writing of letters to anyone but Warren and Muriel, Aunt May when she left Washington for brief trips. "General Pershing is not quite up to making personal acknowledgment of his correspondence these days," Adamson wrote in response to mail coming in. The old friend who had held him in his arms as he wept for Frankie's death could write saying it really rankled that the Japanese, "those yellow devils," were in places remembered from long-ago days in the Philippines and using the port facilities and buildings and roads put in in the Days of the Empire, but Frank Helm got nothing back beyond Adamson's reply that the general was glad to hear from him. Even James Harbord must understand there could be no answers to his letters, although the general took great pleasure in them. "In view of what you state about his interest, I will continue to send them once in a while," Harbord told Adamson, "but if at any time it seems to you I am overworking him, please call me off." Other old friends confined themselves to birthday telegrams with mention that they were thinking of Ould Lang Syne in the Philippines, or days in Mexico or France, or of Frankie in the long ago. When Avery Andrews' son telegraphed his mother was dead, Pershing managed to telegraph condolences to the classmate of days long gone by, a last communication to someone known more than sixty years.

For the summer of 1944 Mumu went to Narragansett Pier—Jules Bache was dead, and the days in the Adirondacks were over. A Swedish couple came along to take care of the house and the children. Aunt May went north to be with them and enjoy the seashore, and from there wrote Adamson that she was concerned about how her brother was taking the news that Warren landed in France directly after the D-Day invasion. "While it is difficult to guess the general's innermost feelings regarding Warren," Adamson replied, "I may say he gives no indication of undue concern. Of course Warren is very much in his thoughts these days, undoubtedly, but he has voiced no alarm regarding his situation."

Warren's letters all through his time in England were cheery, breezy, cleverly done, easy, filled with details and touches of the type that evaded his father in the published memoirs and long-worked-on but unpublished attempt at a more personalized autobiography. He had been to London for a few days, he wrote, thinking he would like to be stationed there instead of at the former boys' school out in the country. "After my visit I was very glad to come home to roost. There is a good deal too much brass floating around there for a lowly captain. I am much better off right here." As an officer courier he stumbled into a blacked-out train compartment at three in the morning, stretched out, and when light came awoke to find a woman sleeping on the opposite seat. "First time I ever slept with a strange woman and didn't know it." Warren's letters could also turn serious, thoughtful. General Eisenhower had visited his post. "He is a fine looking gent and impressed everyone very much. He spoke briefly to the officers. The meeting was held in the delightful old chapel of the school. I couldn't help thinking, as he spoke, of what a topsy-turvey world this is where a church is used for a meeting place for a group who are devoting their every effort toward war. Even the churches who formally are against it are enlisted in this struggle. It is a very sobering thought." His letters from France as the Allied forces pushed forward rarely alluded to combat experiences but spoke of the nature of field service: "I may learn to like living in the great outdoors, but I am afraid the army started on me too young." He was involved with staff work, doing up orders and consolidating operations reports. He was extremely sorry not to have met with General Marshal, who had made an effort to see him while visiting the area of operations, but unfortunately he'd been off on a mission.

> Excuse the paper, but it is the best the Government is providing in this war so it will have to do. It seems there is something of a shortage, and confidentially, if you think this is bad as a substitute for writing paper, you should see the stuff that is provided for that other daily necessity. It would make a better file. But I can't say we suffer too much. Of course, a real egg is hailed as a rarity, and please notice that I used the singular, because that is exactly what we get about

once a month. We are quite well provided with the powdered variety, which seems to produce sufficient energy and no doubt are the equal of the shelled egg in vitamins. But I am sure the last war would have lasted longer if you had to face powdered eggs every morning, instead of having a nice cosy three-minute boiled pair as you did. You are really lucky that science had not made the strides it has in the last few years, and it is now one of the horrors of modern warfare.

Back came: "I have enjoyed your learned treatise on Scientific Advances and their Relation to the Life of the Modern Soldier." However, the patient at Walter Reed could not agree with his son's belief that the invention of the powdered egg had notably increased the difficulties of army life, for a soldier always griped about food and everything else. Science was extraneous to "that old and universal army pastime." For himself, he had little news. "I am getting along about as usual. I continue to lead a rather cloistered existence. However, now that the weather is nice I hope to get out for a drive occasionally."

The war went on and Warren with the others of the American armies went forward into France. "The food, which I believe I discussed at some length previously in somewhat unfavorable terms, is excellent, including upon occasion a bottle of captured wine, so for the moment at least war is somewhat less than hell." He was with a small flying headquarters and at the time of writing in a lovely valley whose settlements had been obliterated by artillery fire. "The towns are in such ruins that we just put a shovel to work scooping it into trucks and spread it out. Haven't run into anyone I knew before lately, but everyone here that I talk to always inquires very kindly about you, and the older ones who served under you are most interested. At the moment am keeping house in a one-ton cargo trailer, which has all the disadvantages of a lower berth but few if any of its advantages, but at that is an improvement over the lowly pup tent. When this is over, I doubt that you will find me going on any camping trips for quite a spell."

General Marshall came over again and this time Warren got to see him and to receive a gift package sent by his father and aunt. The four days' speed of delivery from Walter Reed seemed to him wondrous — "But

considering the caliber of the mailman, it is not too amazing." Warren
gave Marshall handkerchiefs to take home to his father, and a tablecloth
for Mumu. "I wish I could smuggle myself into the tail of that plane, but
I guess that will have to wait a little longer. I certainly would like to see
you and May again. I miss you both very much, and send you all my
love." The cigarette ration was one pack a week, so he was really happy
about the carton delivered by the "courier," with whom he spoke for ten
or fifteen minutes.

In Walter Reed there were almost no visitors. Fred Ferguson of the
United Press two years earlier had been granted a brief interview. He
found the general with sunken cheeks and thin face. The day was chilly,
wasn't it, he had told Ferguson, who found the temperature perfectly
comfortable. The general took out a folded shawl but had trouble getting
it undone, and Ferguson did the job and then draped it across his host's
fragile back. As he did so his mind went back a quarter century to the days
when he could never have even dreamed of putting a shawl around the
broad shoulders of the commander in chief of the American Expeditionary Forces. It seemed to Ferguson that perhaps the same thought as to
the change the years had brought came into the general's mind, for as he
sat back in his chair he smiled and asked, "Do you remember when you
were a boy how the old folks always wore shawls around their shoulders?"

"I said that I did," Ferguson wrote, "and that I remembered very distinctly a little shawl with white checks that my mother wore around her
shoulders, and he smiled again and said, 'Yes, mine too.'" After that there
were no more interviews.

Fall of 1944 came, and Warren wrote of enjoying a beautiful Indian
summer's day. He didn't look forward to field living when the weather got
colder and hoped things were the same for the enemy, only more so. "I
could use an end to this whole business without any trouble at all. There
is considerable talk about the Germans folding up, which I hope will turn
out to be true, but as you know, you can't count on the so-and-so's. Con-
sequently, we spend all our time trying to kill them off and don't have too
much time to speculate on what will happen if they decide they have had
enough." It was one of his very few references to what earned him five
battle stars. Instead he talked about his fellow soldiers, chow, and his one-

ton trailer residence. "I have gotten so attached to it, I am thinking of parking it in the street next to our apartment after the war. The food is at the moment being supplemented by captured German delicacies such as *paté de fois gras*, pickles, preserves, to say nothing of a spot of wine here and there, so we don't do badly at all, especially since we captured some Worchestershire sauce to flavor the Spam." He was involved in forcing river crossing, doing the work usually assigned a major as he supervised four other Engineers captains who addressed him as First Vice President. "They are all a nice bunch of boys, so it is pleasant all around. We are occupying the shooting lodge of some successful German, which is built in the typical heavy style and furnished with heavily carved, solidly built, and thoroughly unattractive furniture. But of course its principal attraction is that it keeps out the snow, rain, and sleet. I thought of you, Père, the other day, or rather evening, when I was having dinner in one of the local bistros. The owner of the place announced he had some oysters. They were not half as good as those we used to have at the Carlton, but after a year without them, they tasted mighty fine, the only flaw the fact that we had to use a sort of lemon extract because they haven't seen a lemon over here in more than four years." He was going to miss the fun of using his French now that he was in Germany. "I was coming along a little and beginning to get a little confidence, and now I shall probably forget it all again."

I like to think that you are with me as we traverse this area, in spirit anyway, as you certainly tried to convince people that we should have made this march in 1918. What a shame it is that we didn't. We might have been spared this war. I think you would have enjoyed going through this part of the country. The other day as I rode down the Rhine I was reminded of our trip in the boat, as you will remember. A funny thing happened some months ago, it was back last August when we were still on the other side of Paris. The colonel asked me if I had ever been on the Rhine and I said I had. He then asked a lot of technical questions about the width and speed of the current. I could only guess, but told him it was around eleven hundred feet across and had a current of about seven or eight miles an hour.

Lately we have had a good chance to check out these measurements as we have built a number of bridges across it. They vary from just under a thousand feet to thirteen hundred, and the current has been measured at about seven miles an hour. So, little did you think, or I either, that as we cruised down the Rhine and I asked all the questions that a boy of ten always asks, that the information would turn out to be of any practical use!

He wrote to Mumu of how he thought of her when having dinner with one of the most beautiful things in the world—an omelette soufflé. "But what a soufflé. I certainly must bring back the recipe. Sounds like a tough war, doesn't it? I ask everyone I know who is going back to look you up. The latest is a correspondent for a Chicago paper. He said he would give you a call. My God, how I envy these gents that get to go home. It seems so far away I don't think I will know how to act when I do get back." Warren grew to hate the Germans. He found it a thing of beauty to see the smashed German towns. It would teach them a lesson. In the Battle of the Bulge he sat drinking a martini by the light of a flashlight as overhead the ack-ack searched for a "bastardly Jerry" plane. He'd taken up quarters in a bottling works where he slept between cases of soda water and orange pop stacked up to the ceiling. "It would have been exceedingly handy if we only had a little Scotch and a little ice." He had received the packages she sent her wandering boy, had been to Paris, where he found the Crillon of former visits closed and his father's statue demolished by the Germans. He ran into a fellow he'd known back at school in Switzerland and went with him to his home to meet his five children, the youngest aged two and four, the same as Jackie and Dickie. "They make me realize what I am missing at home." The war couldn't last much longer, he told Mumu. "Let's hope that maybe Jackie and Dickie can avoid what tripped up both their father and grandfather, and I might add even their great-grandfather. It looks to me as though the law of averages ought to begin to operate in their favor and maybe skip their generation. If so, the last years will not have been in vain."

President Roosevelt died; and in the month he became president, April 1945, Harry Truman came to Walter Reed to attend church services with the patients, shake hands with boys in wheelchairs, and spend a little time in the suite of the general of the armies. The war in Europe finished up and it was suggested to Maj. F. Warren Pershing that if he stayed on a while for Occupation duty he could have a lieutenant colonelcy. "The hell with that," he said. He wanted to get home to Mumu and the boys and see his father, who, the papers said, had been too ill to pose for pictures or issue a statement on the day the Germans surrendered. For September 13 Truman sent him: "This should be one of the happiest of your birthdays as you remember that this time we went all the way thru to Berlin as you counseled in 1918." He was eighty-five. An army band came to be on the lawn beneath his rooms and to play the old songs of the First World War. He stood in the shade of an awning protecting him from Washington's sun and gazed down. In conquered Japan, MacArthur cabled: "From Tokyo, the entire command joins me in affectionate greetings on this your birthday."

Warren saw released concentration camp prisoners swarming over Germany's wrecked roads, "Frenchmen, Czechs, Russians, Belgians, and I don't know how many other nationalities," many carrying crudely fashioned flags of their countries, all smiling and bowing to the Americans, singing—"A thrilling sight to see these people once more free men and women"; saw the defeated German soldiery truckload after truckload tucked in so tightly they had to stand perfectly still and rigid, "their faces reflecting just glum indifference," and felt no sympathy and indeed felt contempt for the German civilians insisting they had never been in agreement with Hitler. "Amazing, all the people were just waiting until we came along to liberate them from the Nazis." He collected a box of things for shipment to Jackie and Dickie, "caps, goggles, canteens, etc. I remember enjoying similar equipment, model 1918, and I don't think they will be much different." The day came when little Jackie looked at a tall stranger in uniform, not so much at the stranger but at his belt at a level with Jackie's eyes. In later years he remembered nothing above or below the belt but also that he knew this wasn't a family friend or passing-through visitor, that it was his father home from the war. The family went down to Washington, the boys on an airplane for the first time in their lives. Jackie took with him his cigar box filled with toy soldiers.

They went to an old man in a very elaborate red brocade bathrobe, old-fashioned and with tassels. His mustache tickled when he kissed you. He had a deep voice. Years later, decades later, a friend got hold of an old record of General of the Armies of the United States John J. Pershing speaking and had it worked on by audio people to clear up the sound, and gave it to Jackie; and at once he recognized that voice from when he was five years old. In Walter Reed he got out his cigar box and he and the man in the red brocade bathrobe—in later years Warren used to wear it— played soldiers. "I whipped him. I made the rules." The little boy swept the soldiers of the general of the armies to the floor when he felt like it.

By a year later it seemed to Warren, he wrote his father, that the war had never been, that as he and Mumu passed bathing-suit Bermuda vacation days it was almost beyond remembrance that twelve months earlier he had been in his one-ton trailer and heard the bombs and saw the dead. In his Wall Street offices of Pershing & Company he worked to raise his annual income to reach what came to Mumu by inheritance. That was Warren's great desire. It took him years and years to do it. Meanwhile the boys lived the life into which they had been born, maids, nannies in white, the Buckley School of ties and knee socks with shorts worn in warm weather, brown oxfords, dark blue cap with a silver "B," dancing school of waltz and fox-trot and the social graces, doors at home with glass knobs, Persian rugs, polished mahogany, Japanese screens, leatherbound books, the oils in frames. One's father had been at New Haven, as was said for Yale attendance, one's mother at Farmington, as was said for Miss Porter's—although that was not so for Mumu; and indeed Jackie and Dickie debated in later years whether in fact she was a graduate of any high or prep school, and together decided she probably wasn't.

Sons of what the papers' still-extant Society sections and shiny-page rotogravures of the late 1940s described as the Fifth and Park Avenue sectors of New York, they were directed, as detailed by the son of Warren's employee Archibald Douglas, to pass the hors d'oeuvres and told to cover up your ears, young man, when jokes about breasts or bedrooms or Polish bridegrooms on wedding nights were told to screaming-laughter listeners. (Sometimes fractured French was used in front of children.) Jew jokes and Jew songs were a specialty of Archibald Douglas. You could always identify a particularly loud barrage of hilarity coming from a group around Archie as signifying that he had done his basketball song accompanied by grotesque leapings around representative, he said, of the way Jews at Columbia University played the game. (He had briefly attended the school but found it impossible to be in class or on campus with such people.) Archibald Douglas's wife, Ellie, was one of the three Black Bitches. Her son, hers and Archie's, contemporary of Jackie and Dickie Pershing, remembered that it was unthinkable to see his mother and father's set absent a bottle. Impossible to consider. Drinking was a necessity, Geoffrey Douglas remembered, at parties, after golf or tennis at the club, at the beach, while building snowmen on the slopes, around picnic tables—there must always be a glass in hand, and smiles and grand laughter. Children were given sips of gin or whisky concoctions or champagne—vodka was unknown in the America of those years just after the war. That Upper East Side life, Geoffrey Douglas remembered, was in fact a drenched life of drinking. Of the women it often came to be said that they were nervous—a nervous condition, a nervous breakdown, with stay in a sanitarium to dry out. They went in for decorating, being a Gray Lady at the hospital, went to hairdressers, for sales, then long and wet lunches in what Geoffrey Douglas saw as the parched little world in which he and Jackie and Dickie found their being. In maturity Geoffrey kept the photographs of Archie and Ellie Douglas seen on the slopes of St. Agathe or at the Dunes Club, Narragansett, Warren and Mumu Pershing with them, smiling, drinking, in the background at Adirondacks places boathouses with gable roofs and wide French doors on the second floor opening onto balconies from which merrymakers on windless nights called to one another across the lake, and there were bright bathing suits and the women with broad straw hats on gaity-filled weekends, treasure hunts, birch canoe races, ghost stories around campfires stoked by Canadian guides, two-pound rainbow trout, Nanny with hair in a tight bun, outboards with brass fittings and mahogany trim, blond girls in torn sneakers; and in the end the alcoholic Archie Douglas a source of embarrassment and sadness but kept on nevertheless at Pershing & Company. He was loyal, Warren. Ellie Douglas had constant migraine headaches, as was not uncommon in women of her set, and spent days her son remembered as "vacant and useless, followed by nights that stretched endlessly, pointlessly, toward a sleep that rarely came before dawn." One rang for the maid to bring in the tray when one awoke. The sister of another of the Black Bitches looked at Jane Holland's four marriages, several breakdowns, a suicide attempt, a life of alcoholism, the wealth and good looks and being well born and socially prominent perhaps not so very much when put in the balance against the morning blackouts after a night out, so typical of Jane Holland's women friends. "They wanted so badly, and so desperately, to *be* somebody. It was such a waste. It's so sad, so tragic. Such an awful waste."

There was for Jackie and Dickie the Narragansett Pier summer house now that with the death of Jules Bache the Adirondacks place was gone — and for Jackie a savage, deadly, cold, brutal, terrifying beating by his father with the slipper used for going to the beach when Warren came in from golf to find his older son playing with matches. Jackie never forgot, and as a soldier years later was a bit of a fanatic, he knew, when he hectored his junior officers about being goddamned careful when using butane lamps turned up for pup tent warmth in cold-weather field exercises. He had, he understood, a fire hangup. Kids today don't understand what a naked flame is, Jackie decided, decades after the beating he took as a little boy, decades and decades after his grandmother Frankie and little aunts Helen and Anne and Mary Margaret had turned to dust in their Cheyenne graves.

Sometimes the family journeyed down to Washington for a visit to Walter Reed and the general and Aunt May and Micheline Resco coming over from the Shoreham Hotel, as she did every day to read to the patient and play cards with him for trivial stakes when he was up to it. She was never enthusiastically received by Aunt May. Pershing sat up in entirely straight fashion when nurses changed his bed linen; he had had a lot of practice at that sort of posture maintenance, he told them. Often he was confused, sometimes for as long as ten days in succession, but they saw that he *knew* he was confused. In lucid moments he spoke with wonderment at what had befallen Henri Philippe Pétain. Put on trial for collaboration with the Germans, the former head of the Vichy regime offered no defense. A marshal of France, he said, did not offer explanations.

Condemned to die, his sentence had been reduced to life imprisonment by Charles de Gaulle. It was inconceivable, the Walter Reed patient said, that his old friend was now held to be a traitor to France.

To the extent that they came to thought in the public mind, the two old soldiers were linked. But of course they did not come to mind much. A 1947 article by the *Chicago Tribune* Press Service reporter Henry Wales defined them as "two heroes of World War I, today forgotten men." When Wales had attempted to call on Pershing, he found May barring his passage. She was sorry, she said, but the doctors did not wish the general excited in any way, and so only those of his immediate entourage were permitted in. Wales had had to ask several people in Walter Reed where the general's rooms were before finding someone who knew, and when he had called the War Department the switchboard took quite a time to find the correct number for his offices. They would soon be removed from the old State, War, and Navy Building to two small cubbyholes in the Pentagon. "We must make way for progress, it seems," George Adamson observed. "There has been another war, other idols now." Most of the mementos of the old offices, presentation swords, medals, awards, pictures, busts, the great cherrywood desk far too large for the new accommodations, were crated up and stored away. Pershing never knew. "We have kept the fact from him," Adamson said, "because he has never given up hope of returning to his office someday."

Her brother had a surprisingly good appetite, May Pershing told the reporter Wales. The previous day, she said, he had bean soup for luncheon and asked for a second helping. He was able to eat meat, and had his coffee. He did not smoke. He seldom left his bed and his sight was not good, but for occasions he was placed in a wheelchair, such as when his son and daughter-in-law came down for a birthday party, bringing a cake. For a moment May let Wales come into the general's room to see him propped up with four pillows on his bed, a sergeant-orderly sitting by. It seemed to the reporter that the eyes flickered with recognition for someone known in past days, but May tugged at the visitor's arm. "I'm sorry I can't let you talk to him." Wales left to do his story on the two forgotten heroes and of how May Pershing said, "Yes, my brother frequently mentions Marshal Pétain." Sometimes Mme. Pétain wrote of her husband from the hotel where she lived on the little windswept island off La Rochelle where he was imprisoned.

> The very strict rules which are applied to him in the painful detention forbid him from responding to you himself. Even today during the hour which is accorded me to spend with him (between two guards) we spoke about the past and all the reasons the marshal had to like and admire General Pershing. Never have I heard him say anything other than "my friend Pershing" when he spoke of the general. These are his emotional thanks which I address to you. Never has he doubted the sentiments of friendship the general holds for him. I express my friendly and affectionate sentiments to you, my dear general, the same as I hold for your dear family.

Annie Pétain's letter was sent in July of 1948. She could not know that even as she wrote, its intended recipient was dead.

✦ VI ✦

DICK

✦ 16 ✦

IT WAS NOT DIFFICULT for the newspapers to find almost unimaginable differences in the world to which he was born and in which he lived, and the world of his death. He had known rebel bullets of the Civil War killing men when the raider Holtzclaw came to Laclede in Missouri, had in cavalry blue chased Indians out on the Plains, gone up against the Spanish in Cuba, dealt with Moros from the dawn of civilization in the Philippines, gone after Pancho Villa, cracked the Kaiser's lines. Who in Washington's crowds watching as his funeral went its way to Arlington on July 19, 1948, had recently given much thought to all of that? The Russian land blockade of Berlin was in its third week of being circumvented by the great airlift mounted by the Western Allies; the State of Israel, formed two months earlier, was battling Arab enemies. A world thought in terms of atom bomb and jet plane; and the dead man came from horse and saber. Behind his casket, American generals of the Second World War were out in mass, Kenney, Spaatz, Vandenberg, McAuliffe, Lemnitzer, Norstad, Devers, Clark, Hodges, Gerow, Walker. (Georgie Patton was dead and buried in Europe.) Rain came, and the two generals leading the others conferred about getting into trailing automobiles.

"Brad, what do you think?" Dwight Eisenhower asked the army chief of staff.

"For Black Jack Pershing," Omar Bradley said, "I think it would be proper if we walked in the rain."

Behind the horse Black Diamond of empty saddle and reversed boots in the stirrups came automobiles carrying honorary pallbearers from out of the past, officers of the First World War grown old. (Avery Andrews of Old '86 was among them, survivor of a West Point class whose number could literally be counted on one hand.) After their war it had been decided that as an aid for record-keeping officers should be given serial numbers. The man being buried was given the first: 0-1.

After services at the amphitheatre the coffin was taken on its horse-drawn caisson to the gravesite, where Warren stood with May leaning heavily on his arm, she in heavy veil. The honorary pallbearer Charlie Dawes was with them, traveling to Washington for the last time in his life. (The other of the Three Musketeers, James Harbord, had been in Arlington for a year.) George Marshall stood by. As President Truman's secretary of state he had officially circulated a notification to foreign governments of the passing of the late general of the armies. On the day after his father's death, the day before his funeral, Warren had delivered to Micheline Resco a large check and a letter his father had written her in 1929 for delivery upon this occasion. It said that God had sent her to him, that she had made him happy, that he did not wish her to weep at his death. In 1946 a priest had in effect joined them in a symbolic secret marriage.

"Taps" sounded, echoed by an unseen bugler. By the time the succession of lone sentries mounting guard for three days concluded their duties, Warren and Mumu had rejoined their sons at their summer place. (Mumu had not thought them old enough to be present at the funeral.) The general's estate, some $250,000, was left in trust to May, reversion to Warren upon her death.

The end of the summer of 1948 came, and Warren's family removed to their Park Avenue apartment, departing it at vacation times for Palm Beach or a Canadian fishing camp or Narragansett or their place at Round Hill in Jamaica. Warren was a part owner of a hotel there, and all the owners had villas sprinkled about the property. May often came to be with them, impressing her little great-nephews as a tall, severe, somewhat frightening figure. She brought to Jackie's mind the image of Ray Bolger in women's clothing in the play *Charley's Aunt*. (She was in fact a Victorian-era disciplinarian figure about whom even Mumu trod carefully.) Jackie was reaching a time when he disdained the diminutive of his name. "I'm Jack!" he told his mother, who kept forgetting and addressed him as she had in earlier years. Not that he or Dick saw a great deal of her, for in families of their set it was the domestic staff who really raised the children. They rarely were with their mother, Jackie and Dickie. They smelled her perfume; that told them she was around. The boys found Warren remote. It seemed to them that he was like an onion in that no matter how many layers you peeled off, you never got to the core. That was what they called him to one another: Onion.

Warren was, as he had been from childhood on—although his school grades sometimes didn't show it—a good mathematician. He could figure bond yields down to the fourth decimal in an instant, could extrapolate to the fourth number in his head. He often carried a slide rule. He was interested in architecture and loved to look at blueprints. He had a trombone he liked to play. When Jack got to about the age that Warren had been when the general sent him off to Switzerland, Warren dispatched his son to his old school. Jack was unhappy there, not infrequently on detention for passing notes in class and feeling he was getting nowhere, although in later life he retained the French he learned. His letters home were far from cheerful. On Sunday nights the boys had to sit in a particular hall at a long desk and write their parents, and a fellow student, equally unhappy at the Institut de Carnall, suggested to Jack that they go into the washroom and sprinkle their letters with water so that their parents would draw a logical conclusion. It worked with Mumu. "My God, he was weeping!" she cried to Warren, who wasn't fooled. He'd learned the trick in his days in Switzerland.

After Jack had been there a year, Dick was sent over to join him. There was a crowd that was hazing a Jewish boy, and Dick joined in until a fellow said to him that his own ancestry wasn't so pure—the fellow's mother had told him so. To their bewilderment Jack and Dick soon heard anti-Semitic remarks coming their way. They put in a transatlantic call to Warren—far from a matter of routine in the mid-1950s—and for the first time learned that Jules Bache had been a Jew. (Theirs was not the first Social Register family of background considered questionable and best undiscussed.) They must not apologize for their great-grandfather, Warren told them, but show respect for him and be proud of his achievements. In the summer of 1955 Warren and Mumu came over to Europe, bringing along a majestic Chrysler convertible for travel with their sons. At tourist sites Warren would retain the services of a guide and say, "You've got one hour." The guide inevitably replied that the wonders on display could not be shown and discussed in such a short time. "One hour," Warren would repeat. He had teenagers, he understood what was possible. The boys termed the period the Cultures Hour, and when getting up in the morning discussed what they would do when it was over. (Warren's strategy worked. In later years Jack never stopped in Paris without visiting the Louvre.) In the settings where just after the First World War he had been with kings and queens and presidents and field marshals, Warren was of course quite at home in *première classe* hotels and restaurants; and there returned to him also his more recent memories of the Second World War ten years in the past. For half an hour he stood silently staring at where he and the other Americans had crossed the Rhine at Remagen and where he had worked to put up Bailey bridges, at some cost to many of his fellows. "Don't bug him, leave him alone," Mumu told her sons.

Jack came home after two years, Dick remaining behind, to begin at Phillips Exeter, where Warren had gone before and after Switzerland. It didn't work out—at Exeter you could smoke, go off-campus; it was more than Jack could handle. As unhappy with Jack's performance as the general had been with his own, when Warren's showing brought critical letters and investigatory visits from military aides, Warren transferred Jack to the Gunnery School, where things went no better. Warren learned from the situation, and when Dick came back from Switzerland, he was enrolled at Fessenden, where a tighter rein was applied. It worked. Dick was good at turning in top grades. Then he went to Exeter, where he again did well. He still wasn't ready for his father's Yale, his father felt, so he was sent for a postgraduate year at Lawrenceville. Jack by then had transferred to Collegiate, where he came to himself—more or less, for Jack was no great student, although he got very active on the yearbook.

He wasn't getting along with his father. They ceased speaking for a time. Jack took himself down to Florida and went to college there—more or less—and then asked himself who he was hurting by all this, and entered Boston University, where he became a big wheel in the Pershing Rifles, the nationwide military honor society and social fraternity whose beginnings were in the group commanded seven decades earlier by the lieut of the University of Nebraska. The Pershing Rifles were hard to get through, with only a percentage of pledges ever making it to full membership and with the greater number of men harassed out by push-ups, running in place, hazing orders to go out and obtain the addresses of twenty-five girls, and their measurements, or suffer a demerit. Pledges got yelled at, got marched around, were liable on their way to classes to be ordered to brace up against a wall. On the plus side, there were parties and dances in addition to the drills held at the Boston Army Base. Everyone knew who Jack was, and saw him as a blond, good-looking, fun guy who was a hell of a dancer doing the UT, a wild and frenetic jump-around college dance of the day. It was the heyday of the Rifles, its last great moment before Vietnam and the protests. Jack led a panty raid at B.U., screaming guys racing into girls' rooms to grab their undergarments out of the chest of drawers, and was severely punished for it even as the college official ordering the penalty secretly thought that at least what he and the others had done was *American* and in collegiate hijinks tradition, as the growing demonstrations against involvement in Vietnam were not, in the official's opinion, he being a naval reservist who grew to dread crossing the campus in uniform for what students would say at seeing him. Jack in later years remembered the Pershing Rifles as the best part of Boston University days. Years later, when he met Gen. Colin Powell, he instantly established a good rapport when they discussed their former membership in the organization.

Dick in his postgraduate year really blossomed at Lawrenceville. In fact, his performance there was remarkable. He simply *exploded* on the scene, remembered his classmate David Schlossberg of Trenton, New Jersey. That wasn't at all an easy thing to do for a new kid coming into a situation where 95 percent of the others knew each other from freshman year. But no one at Lawrenceville had ever seen anyone like Dick, so-

phisticated and seemingly bursting with any number of abilities that
came to him with maddening ease. He could listen to someone playing a
harmonica, ask to borrow it a minute, and produce tunes. One time he
watched a fellow working with charcoal and paper, asked if he could give
it a try, and turned out a very good sketch. He was a splendid singer. He
was terrific at soccer, and as a lacrosse player was of such quality that
those who knew the sport said that with application he could rise to proficiency on the national level. His highest calling was in being funny—hilarious, even. Then and later, people said he could make a living per-
forming, or as a comedy writer. Dick had great presence. "You know,"
David Schlossberg's mother told her son, "he has a way of taking over a
room, dominating it." As a newcomer to a school where the long-standing
students had paired off as roommates, Dick was assigned to live with another recent arrival, Donald Parsons of Dundee, Illinois. Parsons took a
couple of looks at his new roommate and said to himself what everyone
else at Lawrenceville similarly concluded: This is one hot-shit type of guy.
Everybody liked being around Dick. The faculty members regularly had
him over to their homes, where his Germanic-sounding doubletalk gibberish recitations reminiscent of those done by the comedian Sid Caesar
left people screaming with laughter. Parsons' girlfriend Arlene, coming in
from her Denver school for the senior prom, was struck by what a good-
looking guy Dick was, how much fun it was to be with him. "I would say,
very, very attractive. Heck of a nice guy, good athlete, he was the type of
guy who appealed to me—but I had my guy, Don."

Graduation Day for the Class of 1962 at Lawrenceville came. A
bunch had been accepted at Yale, including Dick and Parsons and
Schlossberg, and they decided to room together up there at New Haven.
Schlossberg had been a day student commuting each day from Trenton,
and as such not as close to Dick as he later became; but for all four Yale
years they were together as the staples of a rooming situation where others
came and went. At first glance David Schlossberg would not have seemed
the likeliest candidate to become Richard Pershing's dearest friend. He
was a Jew. David had good manners and was smart, destined to be a
prominent doctor with a string of books on medical matters to his name.
One of the varied roommates was the engineering major Ronald Singer

of Roslyn, New York, a terrific student garnering top grades and awards. Singer was one-quarter Jewish by virtue of a Czech grandfather, and Schlossberg proclaimed that if you added everything up with Dick and Ron and himself, their room was on average at least half Jewish. (When Ron and Dick were tapped for Skull and Bones, however, and David was not, it was made perfectly apparent how certain aspects of things operated in the Yale of the mid-1960s.)

If Ron Singer was a super student, and David Schlossberg a very good one, they were not in that regard joined together at the hip with Dick Pershing. Dick was tied up with debutante parties, girls, excursions, stunts, the expenditure of what seemed to the others colossal sums of money. He loved to call up the Rotisserie Normand, a stylish New Haven restaurant, and in his Institut de Carnal French announce, *"Ici parle M. Pershing, je voudrais . . ."* and order a meal in advance for himself and a date, stipulating the white he desired, and the red, and the *dégustif* to follow. The money he spent was hair-raising, and sometimes he got erupting letters from his father to be read aloud to his friends. Mike Dalby of Skull and Bones thought it was like a parlor game to figure out how Dick would get away with his latest escapade. How on earth could anybody *ever* weather blowing tuition for the entire school year, lodging, allowance, everything, before Christmas? If I did that, people exclaimed! "Got to run down to New York, see the old man," Dick said. When he got back to Yale he reported everything was okay. Precisely in the fashion of his own father raving and ranting about obligations and almost immediately following up with gift of elegant new LaSalle to be taken for a European jaunt, Warren capitulated and let Dick's doings go and so, everybody saw, let him back in the chips again. But of course Dick made that a likely outcome, David Schlossberg reasoned, for Dick was the king bullshit artist of all time. He could talk anybody into anything, and likewise pull off anything.

To his Yale friends, Dick's parents were a mystery no one even tried to solve. Their apartment to Ron Singer was like the abode of royalty, this elegantly done-up multifloored place on the corner of Seventy-second and Park with the Social Register in telephone tables along with the New York phone book; and then there was that wonderful big house at Southampton replacing the Narragansett one, and the Jamaica place they called a "cottage"—which it wasn't. To Dick's lacrosse team friend Jimmy Howard, the Pershings lived in a different world than anyone Jimmy or any of the other boys knew, with someone named Robert going around offering drinks from a tray. Mr. Pershing the Yalies found handsome, impressive, cool, distant. Aloof, stiff, thought Singer—austere. Reserved, hard to get in focus, thought Mike Dalby.

Mumu simply buffaloed the Yale boys. She stalked around this magnificent duplex of an apartment with dens, studies, libraries, interior staircases, wide hallways, grand drawing rooms, great formal dining room, massive doors in the fashion, the students thought, of a reigning queen. She was of a time and place when a name and old money meant something, Dalby decided. That had to do with her imperious, regal, mince-no-words way. To Singer she was almost a joke, she was so stuffy. Don Parsons just threw up his hands. She was too chi chi for a guy from Dundee, Illinois, he concluded. Behind her back she was referred to as the Grand Dragon, a designation of unknown origin but frequent employment. Maybe Schlossberg made it up—he couldn't remember. Dick used to imitate the Grand Dragon's sweeping manner of going about, his friends reduced to helpless laughter at the performance. Mumu liked Schlossberg the most of all the fellows. "Make me a mart, dear," she would say, and Schlossberg took gin and vermouth and ice, vodka sometimes—it didn't matter to her—and turned one out. (He had never seen anything like the way the Pershings drank before, during, and after lunch, and the same for dinner.) Mumu could be kind, generous. At the Round Hill place in Jamaica Schlossberg spoke of the beauty of the spot, the home of William Paley of the Columbia Broadcasting System adjoining that of the Pershings, and Mumu said, "You'll have your honeymoon here," for Schlossberg was engaged all through college and so not a participant in the others' pursuit of girls which Jack, not noted for the purity of his language, defined with another phrase. Mumu was good to her word, insisting that David and his bride go down right after their marriage, which was celebrated the day before the graduation of the Yale Class of 1966, Dick acting as usher in formal attire and dancing the *hora* in exuberant fashion. The James Coburn movie *Our Man Flint* was being shot at the hotel of which Warren was part owner, so it was barred to the newlyweds, but they stayed at the Pershing cottage with two servants in attendance. David was extremely fond of the Pershings—as friends. To have them as parents? "Well . . ."

Sometimes at Park Avenue late at night the Grand Dragon materialized as the Gray Ghost, coming down to the first floor drawing room to order that collegiate jollity be made less noisome. A particular divan there was under a great oil painting of the general of the armies of the United States. It was the only point in the room that his eyes could not reach, and upon it occurred activities not so remarkable for college boys and their young lady friends. "I've had that recovered twice, and I don't want to do it again," Mumu eventually declaimed. The Illinoisan Don Parsons was a big Chicago Blackhawks hockey fan, and often he and Dick came down from New Haven to watch the team battle the Rangers; and from this Mumu in her high-handed way deduced that Parsons was a bad influence on Dick and responsible for his mediocre grades. (General Pershing in Warren's student days also railed against what he termed "loafers" standing in the way of his son's scholastic progress.) Mumu's charge against poor Don was, as all the Yalies knew, complete bosh, for Dick was quite capable of getting so-so grades without Don's help. The end of each semester produced a completely predictable scene: Dick sitting up all night with a couple of bottles of Rosé d'Anjou and a carton of Pall Malls and drinking and chain-smoking as he prepared for the next day's final. The day before the end-of-term exam in Russian history he said to David Schlossberg: "I better get the book." He bought one, sat up all night, and passed. He was so goddamned smart, David thought, he could pull off this kind of crap—even at Yale. An English major, as was brother Jack at Boston University—against their father's wishes, Warren holding that such a field of study was useful only if you wanted to teach, which seemed an unlikely destiny for either young man—Dick hardly killed himself working on his supposed specialty. David remembered his asking for a look at his roommate's paper on Henry James.

"I worked hard on that paper," David said suspiciously. "Just need a few ideas," Dick replied. Soon the paper surfaced for Dick in a lit course. "Yeah. Just ideas," David said. Once Dick purchased a paper off a guy and became righteously indignant when he discovered he wasn't the paper's sole proprietor; the guy had sold it to someone else also. From his one-night immersion in the history of Russia, Dick derived the concept that "David Schlossberg" was an insufficiently impressive name, and ruled that his roommate required the middle name of "Kuropatkin-Bazill" while almost certainly knowing no details of Capt. John J. Pershing's involvement with those who routed the Czarist general Aleksyey Kuropatkin during his military attaché days of the Russo-Japanese War. He successfully schemed to slip the addition in Yale records in the form of the initials "K-B," where they remain inserted into David's name to this day and presumably forever. Dick was, thought Don Parsons, a throwback to the Ivy League playgrounds of former eras with a "gentleman's C." It characterized Dick for Jimmy Howard that while his lacrosse teammate, articulate, bright, quick, someone who got concepts quickly, was a terrific player who had a good shot and was encouraged by the coach to shoot while being reasonably generous about passing to others, he did not give the maximum to do what was necessary to turn himself into the nationally ranked player he might have become. Ron Singer was not a person who made friends easily, and in later years he saw Dick as one of the best friends he ever had in his life, an outgoing and light-hearted individual of great spirit and style and elegance making a major impact on people; yet also an irresponsible screw-off. Singer had a brother, Gerald, who tried college for a few months and, unlike Ron, found it not to his liking. Gerry used to go up from Long Island to see Ron at Yale, where he found Dick the most similar to himself of all the fellows met at New Haven: a harum-scarum, wild, hell-raiser type. Mike Dalby found his Skull and Bones pal Dick almost certainly the most charming guy he ever knew, gifted in extreme measure, funny, verbally clever, someone people felt at ease with and liked to be around. An intellectual—no. And lacking the obsessions or passions of some of the other Yalies, but someone who had luck, blarney, and could get away with anything. Don Parsons thought: Engaging, charming, a tremendous guy, the kind that everybody wishes they were in his shoes. He would be enormously successful when he got things figured out and decided what to do, Don figured. Dick wasn't perfect, but Don was certain it was in the cards that one day he'd have the world by the ass.

To his parents' discomfiture, Dick began a romance with a Smith College girl the activities of whose socially prominent family were, Warren and Mumu felt, too much chronicled in newspapers and magazines. (They had forgotten, or chose to forget, the manner in which General Pershing had complained to Aunt May about what he felt were too-frequent press mentions of his son and daughter-in-law.) The Smith girl's family were products of late 1950s and early 1960s airplane technology—charter members of the jet set seen in Paris or the Med or the Indies or in New York clubs. The girl was funny, irreverent, on the ball, wild—a feminine version of Dick. He himself was, of course, also a jet-setter. He went off to Hawaii to become the subject of reports filtering home that he there spent his time hustling suckers for bets in Honolulu pool halls, using to advantage his skill in the game plus the special take-apart and screw-together cue Jack had given him. His father and mother ordered him out of Hawaii to the Wyoming sheep ranches of his late great-grandfather Senator Warren, still in the family and run by a son of Frankie's brother. A hard-bitten old foreman who years earlier at the general's orders had supervised in cold-eyed fashion the range work of Dick's father was given the task of putting Dick in order. Perhaps thinking to put the fear of God into the eastern playboy, the foreman set Dick to eviscerating dead sheep. He had mistaken his man. Dick instantly turned into a crazed professor of Biology 101, spewing scientific-sounding gibberish while flinging and draping entrails about. Everyone howled.

The romance with the Smith girl eventually ran its course and concluded, to Warren and Mumu's relief. At least it hadn't garnered the horrendous national attention given a matter in which Dick and Jack had figured, the former more prominently. The New York City and Southampton debutante Fernanda Weatherill gave a summertime affair that saw the celebrants retire to an unoccupied shoreside mansion. All was reasonably in order when Jack departed for a private rendezvous elsewhere with a young lady. Back at the mansion, things got pretty wild, as the New York tabloids headlined the following day. Sons and daughters of the social-set rich, the papers reported, had simply ripped the place apart. A shambles, chaos, wild destruction—the mansion was completely trashed, as a later generation would put it.

In the morning hours Jack returned from his rendezvous to the site of the party to find his brother lying outside in evening clothes, sleeping in the sun. Jack asked what the hell happened. "It seemed like a good idea at the time," Dick offered. The papers spoke of arrogance, decadence, loss of values, mindless irresponsibility; and it transpired that a photographer had snapped pictures, one of which showed Richard Pershing about to do something to which hypothetical reference is often made while being in fact seen by few and done by even fewer. Standing on a fireplace mantle, he was holding in his hand the ceiling lighting device. The picture portrayed Dick about to swing from the chandelier.

Someone fortunately knew someone who happily knew someone, and the negative was obtained and destroyed. Graduation Day for Yale's Class of 1966 approached.

By that time Jack was in the army, a first lieutenant of Special Forces. Besides his Pershing Rifles doings, he had been designated a Distinguished Military Graduate of the Reserve Officers Training Corps at Boston University, and at a Fort Devens ceremony commanded a two-thousand-man formation. Warren and Mumu came. She was unable to pick her son out in the mass of uniforms on the drill field. "Where's Jack?" she asked. Just look through the legs of the fellow out front, you could see the whole detachment, Warren replied. That identified the fellow as Jack. The origin of his bowleggedness traced back, perhaps, to the days in the Philippines when General Pershing had his orderly Frank Lanckton teach the tiny Warren to sit a pony almost before he could toddle. That had resulted, so the general believed, in Warren's growing up with knees distant from one another. He walked on the outside of his feet, and as a kid Jack imitated him and so, perhaps, ended up with similar legs. Or perhaps it was heredity. Jack loved the army. He went to jump school and got his parachute insignia, obligatorily referred to as Flying Ice Cream Cones, even as his Special Forces—Science Fiction—beret was termed the Green Beanie. West Point had always been out for both Jack and Dick—they had terrible eyes, Jack's worse. He was blind as a bat without his glasses, and when making training drops never went out of the plane without several pairs of extra specs fastened to or stashed in his equipment, for if when he hit the ground he lost the ones on his nose he'd be in a hell of a fix without an immediate replacement. The brothers spent as much time with one another as they could, as they always had, they having really raised one another with the aid of servants, their friends knew, in a family where the parents weren't much around. Once in New Haven they started sparring around when totally smashed, and Dick unleashed a punch that splattered Jack's nose. God, said the staggering-around David Schlossberg, equally loaded, you'd really think Jack's schnozz was broken. That *crack* when Dick's fist landed, it was so realistic! And the way Jack's nose was practically wound around his ear. It was really a great imitation of a broken nose.

Eventually the three managed to figure out that indeed the nose required medical attention. "Goddamn—gee, I'm sorry," Dick kept saying in the hospital emergency room. David lost track of things and kept mumbling that it was really a great fake, the way Dick pretended to break Jack's nose—no small achievement, that, he said. He noticed the apologizing Dick kept looking admiringly at the fist that had done the job. When the brothers were apart they sent each other long and elaborate letters using elegant similes and metaphors and written on little portable Olivettis. Assigned by the army to Germany, Jack tried his hand there at poetry: *Ode to a Night Drop.* "It was terrible. I loved it."

By the time of graduation, Dick was keeping steady company with a young woman. She was Miss Shirley Gay Hildreth of Southampton, the site of the Pershings' summer house, a "townie." (She preferred the term a "local.") Shirley was called Shirl the Pearl by some of her friends, sometimes simply Pearl, and was good-looking enough to remind people of the movie star Ali MacGraw. Shirley was lively, funny, fun-loving, smart. Her family was an old Long Island one and had owned Hildreth's in Southampton for going on to 150 years, one of the longest-held family department stores in the country, perhaps the longest. She had gone to prep school at Northfields and then to Bennett Junior College on scholarships. Her family could not begin to dream of competing financially with that of Dick Pershing's, but she was of social background, her situation bringing to David Schlossberg's mind the image of a fine old family place where several rooms are closed off for lack of money to heat them. Jack liked his brother's girl very well. "Any more at home like her, any dupes on her?" he asked. There weren't. Her sister was of a different type. After junior college Shirley got a job with *Vogue* magazine in New York. It was great. You were paid a pittance but had terrific perks, ins with Seventh Avenue dress houses. She went on lots of fashion shoots for the magazine. Her boss hated writing up the blurbs for the pictures, so she did it. It was lots of fun, great Diana Vreeland days, a roller coaster, all kinds of dynamic things going on. She lived with other young women in an East Nineties apartment.

Shirley found Mr. and Mrs. Pershing stern, demanding, by-the-book, cold. Warren, she thought, could be warm and loving, but essentially he was very stiff-upper-lip. Mumu she found very grand, someone who cowed others, was busy hostessing, doing events by the rules, a person who ruled the roost and had no warmth. They expected, Shirley saw, their sons to be strong leaders and contributors. They were in her eyes alcoholics without doubt. Gen. John J. Pershing to their thinking, she felt, was a great historical figure of impeccable form and performance. By then, when Shirley came on the scene, Micheline Resco was an old lady with raddled teeth living in Paris on the money left her by the general and added to by remittances from Warren, and, it seemed to Shirley, somewhat of an embarrassment in her apartment decorated with mementos of the general, a shrine to him, and with her existence proving that he was not just this stern and perfect gentleman, but someone who was passionate and loving, who didn't just keep everything inside the way Mr. and Mrs. Pershing did. So, Shirley concluded, the money sent to Paris was keeping-away money. That was not the impression garnered by Jack and Dick, who saw how protective their father was when talking of old times with the old lady they were told to address as Aunt Micheline and who had long ago taken around Paris the little son of the commander in chief of the American Expeditionary Forces in his miniature sergeant's uniform and who had devoted her life to being Warren's father's hidden mistress — although, of course, they could not know that as children. Aunt May had never liked her, or rather never liked the situation, and in the long Walter

Reed years had been less than forthcoming about offering a welcome when Micheline came each day to play cards with the general or read to him. Sometimes she declined to send a car to the Shoreham Hotel for Micheline, saying it and the driver were needed elsewhere. But then, the boys were not crazy about the fearsome Aunt May, while Micheline in Paris was exotic and dramatic and unthreatening as she held a handkerchief to her mouth to conceal the bad teeth.

Commencement day at Yale came. You were supposed to offer for the records and yearbook an indication of your future plans, and for most of the new grads that presented no problem, Jimmy Howard to the University of Pennsylvania Law School, David Schlossberg to Tufts Medical School, Mike Dalby to Harvard for Chinese studies and an eventual Ph.D. in management consulting there, Ron Singer to England on a Mellon Fellowship, Don Parsons to Northwestern's Business School.

Dick put down for his future plans: law. He just pulled the concept out of the air, had no intention of following through on it. You had to put down something. But what was he going to do with himself? In faraway Indochina a war was going on into which American troops were being committed in numbers so small and remote from the involvements and plans of Yale graduates as to make little impression in New Haven. It wasn't like the Great War finding half the Americans charging Belleau Wood fresh from their campuses, nor the Second World War which found such as the rising young brokerage firm head Warren Pershing joining up as a buck private, nor the Korean War which saw men getting draft calls the moment they had their college diplomas in hand. At one time Jack had told Dick he ought to do something in Yale's ROTC unit, and received a dismissive reply from his brother: "It's not cool."

But one is only young once, and being a soldier is certainly an experience, and Dick's name after all was Pershing, and maybe it was expected of him, and perhaps he felt a need to validate and legitimize himself, and find out how he shaped up with Gen. John J. Pershing and Maj. F. Warren Pershing, and there was such a thing as not shirking a perceived duty, and there did exist, after all, some privileged young men who felt the Indochina matter was the only war in town and so ought to be checked out; it was more or less the Our War of their generation demanding the fulfillment of a patriotic obligation to join up after the fashion of their fathers and grandfathers, or perhaps John Wayne movies. It made a lot of sense for Dick to volunteer for the draft bringing into the service people mostly from the South Bronx or Harlem or southern mill towns or Pennsylvania mining places or West Virginia hollows, figured Dick's friends bound for other destinies; for Dick, charming, rich, with no compulsion to take up anything else, Dick who had always skated along being Dick and having a good time, he had to do *something*.

He took basic, put in for Officers' Candidate School, was accepted, began the course at Georgia's Fort Benning. First Lieutenant of Special Forces John W. Pershing called from his post in Germany and alluding to his brother's past dismissal of ROTC inquired the officer-aspirant's appraisal of OCS. "Is it cool?"

"Yes, Jack."

"THAT'S 'SIR' TO YOU, ASSHOLE!"

Back in New York Shirley was having roommate problems and so Warren and Mumu asked her to move into Dick's room, a good deal for her. By then the war in Indochina was no longer so remote a matter for Americans. Jack got orders for Vietnam; they were canceled. He wondered if there was a conspiracy to keep him out of harm's way because his name was Pershing. Jack didn't like that.

Dick did great at OCS and was on his way to graduating as first-ranking man of his class, or second at the worst, when he got caught in an off-limits and restricted-time pizza run the demerits for which queered his chances for a super-high finish while not putting in danger his commissioning as a second lieutenant of the 101st Airborne. The U.S. Army has never possessed elite outfits in the European fashion which for centuries found certain units ranked above others—in Great Britain each regiment held a precisely determined and understood place—but the 101st, one of America's two jump divisions, had a particular place in military thinking. As did the Special Forces. Why did both Pershing boys, neither ever any part of an outstanding student in college, shoot for top places in the army? Well, hell, if you're going to do something, do it right. And let's face it, there's a certain mystique about the Special Forces and the Airborne. In the spring of 1967 Jack managed a port call to get from

Germany to Benning so he could swear Dick in, a right available to any-one holding a commission. The night before the ceremony they got bombed in a Columbus bottle club outside the post. As always they fin-ished one another's sentences, got caught up in talking about things that demanded that one interrupt the other. In the morning they raised their right hands and Dick became a second lieutenant. That was in August 1967. Eighty-one years and two months had passed since John J. Pershing achieved that rank.

In December two brigades of the 101st got orders for Vietnam. At that moment Jack in Germany also had received orders for the same destina-tion. They were canceled under the army's rule prohibiting all sons of a family from being sent to a combat zone. Dick was in-country in Vietnam on December 13, 1967, at a base camp some twenty miles north of Saigon. At a barracks there he looked up Ron Singer's brother Gerry, a pri-vate first class who like Dick was breaking in and going through training missions. It was murderously hot. Dick had received a tape from Shirley, to whom he was now formally engaged, he told Gerry, and was looking for a player so he could hear it. The couple had thought of getting married be-fore he shipped out. Warren was against it. He had seen quick wartime marriages end up with the boy not coming back and the girl a young widow with a child to bring up on her own — not a good scene.

Dick seemed eager to get out of the steamy training base, Gerry saw, ready to go. He said he couldn't wait. There was no officer-enlisted man business as he talked with his roommate Ron's brother, there was no "sir" required. He was still Dick to Gerry, who found him the same friendly, jazzy guy he had been at Yale. Off in England, Ron was violently against the war, a view that did not change with time. In years to come he was un-able to discuss Vietnam rationally with Gerry, so the brothers in unspo-ken manner agreed not to refer to it. Ron's viewpoint was not a unique one in the America of early 1968. At a Palm Beach dinner party someone remarked that possibly America was on the wrong track in Vietnam. "I have two sons serving, and one is over there," Mumu declared, and rose from the table. "Come, Persh." She swept out, Warren in her wake.

The training at the camp north of Saigon ended suddenly and with a bang; for in February what was called the Tet Offensive erupted all over

Vietnam. Both Dick and Gerry along with others were flown north to Danang, then convoyed out in trucks to firebases just south of Hue, the focus of American television and newspaper reports inevitably identifying it as the old imperial capital now suddenly and unexpectedly and terrifyingly infiltrated by the enemy. Gerry was in the 326th Combat Engineers and involved with demolition and communications work and keeping roads clear, based at Camp Evans surrounded by Landing Zone Jane and Landing Zone Sharon, when he was sent to a camp some eight miles north of his own to pick up something. There he came across Dick Pershing. He was just standing there. He had just come from a mission, he told Gerry. He had lost half a platoon, maybe two-thirds. Now he had to arrange the tagging and the bagging of the dead, and the securing of their personal property for sending home. And then the letters to the next of kin.

He had, Gerry saw, a look of great resolution on his face, an air of being very involved. He looked fatigued but very, very disciplined. The area was up to here in mud, for the Tet Offensive came during the monsoon season. It wasn't anything like as stifling as it had been in the south, when they were in the camp near Saigon. You had to wear a field jacket at night. Dick with that resolved look on his face indicated to Gerry without saying it directly that he was being offered a chance to get out of the field but that he was not going to go. He was not going to leave his men. It was of course, Gerry said in later years, an entirely subjective impression on his part, but that was what he believed. Acted as if he had a mission, very disciplined, so extremely focused. He didn't seem bitter about the losses of his men, but he had that look of absolute determination and was so steely-eyed; he was going to get this thing done, he had a clear and strong sense of duty, was going to play the cards he'd been dealt. Dick was not the same individual Gerry had seen at the north-of-Saigon base camp just weeks earlier. Later he heard that Dick had definitely refused rotation but didn't know for certain that it was true. Gerry's letter to his father on February 9, 1968, reported that he had spoken with Ron's friend Lieutenant Pershing who was going through some bad times, had lost a lot of his platoon, lots of casualties. "It is undoubtedly having a strong effect upon him." The letter still existed thirty years later when Gerry was no longer the wild kid but the head of the trophies and medallion business his father founded, bearing still the scars incurred when an American truck drove over a mine which went off and lacerated his leg. Some days later Dick was on a search-and-destroy mission when his platoon ran into a North Vietnamese Army unit present in strong force. His people were badly cut up. They attempted to block off the North Vietnamese. An American went down in open space. Dick went to drag him to safety. The air was filled with rocket and small-arms fire.

After his graduation from West Point in 1936, when Gen. John J. Pershing came to celebrate the fiftieth anniversary of his own graduation there, the visitor's half-century-later successor as first captain of the Corps of Cadets went off to a field artillery unit at Fort Sill, Oklahoma, where he broke remounts destined to pull Model 1887 French 75s with wooden wheels. Then World War II came, and the postwar world, and William C. Westmoreland attained high rank. As four-star general commanding U.S. Army units in Vietnam, it was his habit each morning to read over a list of men killed the previous day. He did not know that had also been the practice of General Pershing in France in 1918. On a particular February morning in 1968 a particular name caught General Westmoreland's attention. As superintendent at West Point in 1960, he had presided over a commemoration of what would have been General Pershing's one-hundredth birthday. The general's son, Warren, and Warren's wife attended, along with their two sons. Two cadets had been told off to show the teenage sons around, and later they and their parents had been received by General and Mrs. Westmoreland in the superintendent's quarters. Could the 2d Lt. Richard W. Pershing named in the list be one of those boys? Westmoreland wondered. He had not known whether or not a grandson of General Pershing was in Vietnam serving under him. He told someone to check the matter out. He soon had an answer.

On that day in New York, a Sunday, Jack Pershing was awakened quite early in his room on the upper floor of his family's duplex. Jack was back from service in Germany. It was a maid who woke him up to say a uniformed army colonel wished to see him downstairs. Jack had recently received a one-upping letter from Dick, telling his captain of Special Forces brother that he had the Combat Infantryman's Badge for which Jack, who had never seen fighting, was of course ineligible. "Up your green beret," Dick wrote. Jack had recently sent his brother a CARE package, two items of which were a multipurpose knife and a box of condoms. The reason that a colonel would call upon a captain before nine o'clock on a Sunday morning immediately suggested itself to Jack. He was slow about shaving and dressing. He went downstairs, and any faint hopes he had about being mistaken regarding the colonel's visit vanished when he saw the colonel's face. "Good morning, sir," Jack said.

The colonel was the commander at Fort Hamilton. "I'm afraid I've got bad news," he said. The 101st had been in contact with the enemy, and Lieutenant Pershing was dead. Later Dick was posthumously awarded a Silver Star and a Bronze Star for trying to rescue the wounded man of his unit.

Jack asked if the colonel would mind waiting while he told his parents. First he placed a call to the family doctor, who lived nearby, up the street. Warren had recently undergone open-heart surgery, had a valve put in, and Jack thought it best to have the doctor ready if some sort of sedative was called for. He went into Warren's room and awakened him. Then they went to tell Mumu. She emitted the same sound Jack was later to hear from a Harlem mother, and one in Greenwich Village, to whose apartments he went on the same mission as the colonel: a wail. That was the only way to describe it. He asked the colonel if he could be appointed survivors' assistance officer, and the colonel said he could. Jack called Shirley, who was out at Southampton for her father's birthday, and told her parents; she was still asleep. She heard her parents whispering outside her door, awakened, immediately knew what had happened, and began to scream and scream.

That the grandson of Gen. John J. Pershing had been killed in action was a reported in a great number of America's newspapers, although it is a question of what proportion of readers immediately identified the name in the headline. In Vietnam Gerry Singer heard about it, and read the brief article in *Stars and Stripes*, and wrote his father, "I don't know what to say about Lt. Pershing being killed. I'm terribly outraged at the entire world. Why in almighty hell and for what?" When Gerry recovered from his leg wound resulting from the blown mine, his tour of duty was nearing an end. He was offered a sergeancy if he stayed on, reupped. "Thanks, I think I've had enough," he said.

A few days later David Schlossberg sat down in a Tufts Medical School class in histology, tissue study, next to a fellow student who was glancing through *Time* magazine before the professor started talking. The "Milestones" column listed as the dead of the previous week Joe W. Brown, the judge of the Jack Ruby trial for the shooting of Lee Harvey Oswald; the cartoonist Peter Arno; former senator Scott Lucas of Illinois; Thomas Byrd, last of the eminent Virginia brothers *Time* identified as Tom, Dick, and Harry; the novelist Fannie Hurst; and William G. Mennen, head of the toiletries company bearing his name. The first name on the list was that of Lt. Richard Pershing, Yale '66, killed leading a patrol near Quang Tri as he searched for a wounded member of his platoon.

The fellow sitting by David knew he was Yale '66. "Know him?" he asked, pointing to the item.

"My best friend."

"No, I'm serious."

Following the church services in New York when after a time the remains were returned from Vietnam, mourners gathered in the Pershing apartment before going down to Washington for the interment at Arlington. Warren and Mumu went to a second-floor sitting room, and people walked upstairs in small groups to be with them. Schlossberg had very little to say when he came in. Jewish teaching, he knew, says you should say nothing because nothing is appropriate, nothing appropriate can be said, that you should let the others speak. That was, he knew, sitting *shiva* methodology.

"You know, to lose him for this," Warren said. "I'm not even sure we should be there." *Let's hope that maybe Jackie and Dickie can avoid what tripped up both their father and grandfather, and I might add even their great-grandfather,* Warren had written from Germany as a combat officer of Engineers. *It looks to me as though the law of averages ought to begin to operate in their favor and maybe skip their generation.* "These military funerals are pretty rugged," he said to David. "Are you sure you want to go?" To many of the Yalies his attitude, and that of Mumu, seemed difficult to fathom. They seemed so restrained, so cold. But they knew the rules, Jack thought. This was a military family. The great portrait of the general of the armies looked down on the people gathered in the main drawing room, below it the divan upon which had taken place those college boy-girl friend activities that called for the two recoverings Mumu had ordered. Something very unpleasant took place there in the drawing room as the people gathered. Right after the newspaper articles and *Time* item, certain phone calls were received in the apartment. One was from someone saying he was a sergeant to whom Dick had lost money at cards. He wanted payment from Dick's parents. Others were from antiwar protest callers saying this militaristic pig got precisely what he deserved. A reporter came to be served a cup of coffee and to ask Jack if his brother's death turned him against the Vietnam War. It wasn't just the question, Jack felt, it was the sneer that went with it. He asked the reporter if he would please immediately leave—he didn't want to have to hit him and spill coffee all over the rug. Once a soldier's money was no good in a bar, Jack knew—guys bought a fellow in uniform his drinks—but now in West Coast airports army men had red paint signifying blood tossed at them, heard themselves called baby-killers. In the lower floor of the apartment right after the church services a future high elected official of the government, active in the antiwar movement, worked the room for backing. Jack charged him, had to be physically restrained. Horrible, awful at such a time, Schlossberg thought. In the coming years Schlossberg was surrounded by people figuring angles to get out of military service. He couldn't join in their maneuverings. He had easy opportunities to avoid wearing a uniform but couldn't do so—couldn't do so because of Dick. He went into the navy as a doctor, a volunteer. "I'm a lieutenant commander!" he told Jack on the telephone.

"What! You don't even know what a goddamn lieutenant commander is!"

"Yeah! But I'm a lieutenant commander!" In later years Mike Dalby of Skull and Bones put in time doing *pro bono* work in connection with making the Presidio in San Francisco a national park. Dalby did it because Dick's grandmother and little aunts died there. At the funeral Dalby helped the debutante Fernanda Weatherhill, at whose party Dick swung from the chandelier, into a car. His arm sank into her fur coat, he remembered.

As his friends aged while forever young he was in his grave next to that of the general of the armies, Dick became the subject of wistful memory to those who had known him. David Schlossberg, an ardent amateur photographer, often felt how sad it was that Dick wasn't around to look at David's best shots, to share them. Jimmy Howard found himself unable to see Dick's name on The Wall in Washington without bursting into tears. With Dick gone, Warren and Mumu told his fiancée that she could continue to occupy his room until she got her feet under her, and Jack, out of the army and working as a floor broker for his father, took her along on dates, or out for a movie and a bite. One night Jack was at a club talking to a couple of Warren's friends, and found himself telling the men that it was coming to him that he was in love with Shirley. "Why don't you go home and tell her?" one asked.

Shirley was asleep. Jack woke her up. "I've been feeling the same way," she said. As in the fashion of Leviticus's biblical injunction, Jack married his dead brother's girl. For a time Jack had nothing to do with the army, but then he got active in the Reserves. It became his major interest, and he devoted weeks and months to it each year, eventually rising to the rank of colonel while hoping that he could yet become a second General Pershing. To put in the time he did, you couldn't be involved with worry about paying a mortgage, but of course, that was not a problem for Jack. He was always ready to go off on a Reserves mission—at his own expense, if necessary. He moved in high army circles, called Westmoreland "Westie" and Chief of Staff General Gordon Sullivan "Sully." On the seventy-fifth anniversary of the landing of the doughboys in France, Jack went there as special representative of the secretary of war to dedicate a statue. His conversation was filled with army jargon. He was addressed as "Colonel," and identified himself as such on his homes' answering machines.

Mumu fell ill. In the hospital, Jack picked up the word "stat" on the communications system. She died in the hospital. "Nasty shock," Warren told Dr. David Schlossberg, reserved and Waspy, David thought, as always. Warren was lonely without Mumu, and asked Jack if he would mind if he married again. Jack felt odd about being asked, but had no objections. Warren married. When he became ill at the Southampton place, David examined him, found extensive internal bleeding, and told Jack he must be gotten to Mount Sinai Hospital in Manhattan at once. David knew two doctors there who could save him if anyone could. "We'll chopper him in," Jack said in his military fashion, and they got a helicopter. The immediately done operation was not a success. But of course Warren had been on borrowed time for all the years since the Presidio fire of 1915. Mumu had been cremated, and so was he.

The Fifth Avenue mansion that had seen their wedding reception was gone by then, replaced by an apartment building in which had resided at one time Richard M. Nixon and Nelson Rockefeller. The house was sold after Jules Bache's death to the colorful if notorious financial manipulator Serge Rubinstein, who was found murdered in one of the bedrooms, a highly publicized homicide that was never solved. Jack gave up the apartment in which he and Dick were raised. It was far too large for just himself and Shirley—for they had no children. Jack and Shirley were married for more than fifteen years, and then she left him. He came to feel her doing so saved his life, for in the wake of the breakup he consented to enter a Minnesota institution that specialized in helping people give up alcohol. For years Jack had been drinking. He did not touch anything for the period elapsing between the bell opening stock trading and the bell ending it, but he drank before and after. He had his first drink before seven in the morning, something-and-orange juice—vodka or gin. After Shirley left, a group of friends sat him down and told him he had to quit. David Schlossberg frankly told Jack that in his medical opinion he was going to die soon if he didn't give up the bottle.

He proved a model recovering alcoholic, offering guests access to liquor kept in his homes but never touched by himself. When Pershing & Company was absorbed by another firm, Jack got involved with manufacture of an automatic weapon rivaling the AK-47 and the Uzi. He traveled extensively, going off to Iceland for the fishing, going to South America on a Reserves mission or to England for grouse shooting. Shirley had in the divorce settlement gotten the Aspen house. She remarried and lived in it with her new husband. Jack also remarried, and with the second Mrs. Pershing, the former Sandra Sinclair, an exceptionally youthful-looking grandmother retired from the real estate business, lives very well in homes in Manhattan, Long Island, along the Rhode Island shoreline, and Florida. It has recently become a difficult matter to arrange interment at Arlington, for the cemetery is running out of space in the wake of America's wars and its servicemen killed in action or dying of natural causes. But Jack had put in more than thirty years of active and Reserves time, and in addition he was who he was. So it was intimated to him that when the time came he could go to be with his grandfather the general of the armies and his brother the second lieutenant. His burial, then, would mark the conclusion of a family that served in all the wars from before the Revolution to Vietnam, in all the ranks, places, theaters of operation, situations—or almost all—and then everything would be over.

SOURCE NOTES

A GREAT PROPORTION of the information utilized to write this book was obtained from the John J. Pershing Papers in the Manuscript Division of the Library of Congress. If not otherwise indicated in the Notes, Pershing Papers involvement for any attribution may be assumed.

As discussed in the text, General Pershing labored for some ten years on an informal autobiography. He never completed the job. The abbreviation JJP mem indicates allusion to these unfinished memoirs.

The text frequently mentions letters sent to General Pershing, or letters he wrote. If the text makes a sender or recipient's identity clear, and if no particular reason exists to give the exact date of a letter, the Notes will pass the matter by. For very important communications, or when dates appear pertinent, dates will be given.

vii–x. Washington newspapers extensively described the funeral.

    x. "Perfectly elegant dancer": Miss Warren, the future Mrs. Pershing, kept irregularly attended to diaries at various times in her life.

    4. Men arrived: A typed copy of an article from a paper identified as *The Union* for June 24, 1864, is in the Papers.

    5. "I recall distinctly": JJP mem.

    7. "The words would not come": Ibid.

    9. "The conclusion in the family": Ibid.

9. not the only sin of his youth: Samuel Carothers wrote his former playmate a reminiscing letter when both were mature men.

10. conquering Musquakie king: A Brookfield, Mo., newspaper clipping for Feb. 27, 1938.

10. "made a brave effort": JJP mem.

12. "Nigger!": An undated *Kansas City Star* clipping with byline of Burris A. Jenkins.

12. "that board down there": Undated clipping of the *Webb City* (Mo.) *Globe and News Herald.*

13. "here to run this school": JJP mem.

15. "But John, you are not": Ibid.

17. "simply incredible": Andrews, pp. 19-20.

17. In the pages: As with his wife, General Pershing attempted to maintain a diary every now and then.

18. indicated Moderate: The filled-in form is in the Archives of the U.S. Military Academy at West Point.

18. to find its approximate parallels: Mott, p. 29.

19. *long life be yours: Laclede News,* Dec. 29, 1881.

20ff. As a West Point student company commander, Pershing detailed infractions of his men.

20. "nearest approach thereto": Andrews, p. 25.

20. Walcutt remembered: Ibid., p. 25.

21. "Let's get where we're going": A song written by John Huston Finley for John McCormack, briefly popular, noted Pershing's use of the expression.

21. "a burnt match": JJP mem.

22. "His exercise of authority": Bullard, *Personalities and Reminiscences of the War,* p. 42.

22. "Land o' mercy": JJP mem.

22. "to stand first": Bullard, *Personalities and Reminiscences of the War,* p. 43.

23. Mark Twain came: JJP mem.

23. "He knew his way around": Harbord, *The American Army in France,* p. 39.

23ff. Pershing detailed his memories in a letter to the class reunion of 1911.

24ff. An irregularly kept diary details the New York City stay.

26. "A jollier crowd than ours": Andrews, p. 41, quotes an 1887 Pershing circular letter to classmates.

26. "land of the burro": Class of 1886 circular letter for 1887.

27. Sixth Cavalry services are described in JJP mem.

29. "permission to eat that snow?": Conner, pp. 92-93, gives a somewhat jumbled description of the incident as related to her by Pershing.

30. "Our chinaman": Penn to his mother and sister in Batavia, Ohio, Christmas Day 1887, Manuscripts Division, Library of Congress.

30. "only thing lacking is": Pershing to Penn, Oct. 10, 1887.

31. "We are going to take those men away": D. P. Dolsen to Pershing, Oct. 22, 1906.

31. "Everywhere the naked, hungry, dirty": Davis, p. 31.

32. out of his saddle: Smythe, *Guerrilla Warrior*, p. 20.

33. "I have been there so long": JJP to Penn, Sept. 30, 1890.

33. "Sure, and that I do!": Poe, pp. 280-81.

33ff. It was a two-hundred-mile trip: Stotsenberg's description of the journey can be found in *Arizona and the West*, Autumn 1961.

36. Half a century on: JJP wrote a circular letter to his Class of 1886 on Apr. 20, 1937.

36ff. Ghost Dance details are found throughout in James P. Boyd.

37. Troop B: names are noted in JJP mem.

38. "Three or four of the boys": JJP to Penn, Feb. 14, 1891.

38. "What General Miles has shown you": James P. Boyd, p. 287.

39. "disciplined, really trained": Dorothy Canfield Fisher to JJP, June 25, 1917.

39. "one thousand of whom": W. H. Morrill of Lincoln to JJP, Jan. 28, 1905, offering wedding congratulations.

41. "electrified" them: University of Nebraska's *The Pershing Rifleman*, May 1935.

41. "the remotest classroom on the campus": Dorothy Canfield Fisher in *The Red Cross Magazine*, Sept. 1919.

41. "or has made a deeper impression": Chancellor James H. Canfield statement, May 27, 1895.

41. "The boys all loved": Harry D. Estabrook in *The National Magazine*, Oct. 1915.

41. "Horace Greeley's advice": Timmons, p. 18.

42. With friends he celebrated: Harry Zehrung, later mayor of Lincoln, sent JJP a reminiscing letter on Jan. 21, 1919.

42. "pretty well from your scholars": Dawes to JJP, Dec. 18, 1939.

42. if you needed crutches: Dorothy Canfield Fisher in *The Red Cross Magazine*, Sept. 1919.

43. His appearance was a colossal absurdity: Ibid.

44. "Boys—I think": Ibid.

44. "I say without the slightest reserve": Quoted by Andrews, p. 46.

45. "Too much credit cannot be given": A copy of Major Fechet's report of Oct. 17, 1895, is in the Papers.

45. Campaign ribbons of a kind: *Boston Sunday Globe*, Aug. 5, 1917.

46. knock them into a river: JJP mem.

47. What fun it had been: JJP to his long-ago classmate and fellow lieutenant Malvern Hill Barnum, Apr. 11, 1940.

47. "What in hell are you doing here?": Guy Preston to JJP, May 13, 1924.

47. Could he hope to be there?: Guy Preston to JJP, Jan. 6, 1934.

48. the silencing is discussed in Smythe, *Guerrilla Warrior*, pp. 40ff., and in the unpublished memoirs of George Van Horne Moseley, Manuscripts Division, Library of Congress, pp. 35ff.

49. Farmer John, the Keg: Moseley, op. cit., p. 41.

50. "May I be relieved from here?": JJP mem.

54. "cool as a bowl of cracked ice": Smythe, *Guerrilla Warrior*, p. 52, quotes Capt. Charles Ayres.

54. bravest man under fire: Baldwin to JJP, Nov. 30, 1898.

54. "could have taken our black heroes in our arms": JJP speech to the Hyde Park (Ill.) Methodist Church, Nov. 28, 1898. His parents were parishioners there.

55. "did some tall rustling": Baldwin to JJP, Nov. 30, 1898.

55. "done valiant service": Quoted by Vandiver, Vol. I, p. 216.

56. He sailed for the East: JJP mem.

56. "How did you stand the ordeal, General?": Chase, p. 27.

59. actually found out things: Bullard, *Personalities and Reminiscences of the War*, p. 44.

59. "I'm going to send you to Iligan": JJP mem.

59ff. "gone and went and done it": *Minneapolis Journal*, Sept. 23, 1923, article bylined Top Sergeant Archer.

60. "Praised be God": Dozens of letters from Moro leaders are in the Papers.

61. "more important than his gun": Lanckton's memories were detailed by Robert Ginsburgh in *The American Legion Monthly*, Oct. 1928.

61. "I do not recall ever having seen": JJP mem.

62. "On one of those visits": Ibid.

63ff. "I am very glad to meet the commanding officer": Numerous typed copies of stenographic reports are in the Papers.

64. "let them die!": Quoted by Smythe, *Guerrilla Warrior*, p. 94.

65. "today the one great American": Lt. George Bowman of the Fifteenth Cavalry to Ass't. Sec. of War William Cary Sanger, May 15, 1903.

65. "some fool officer": Bullard, *Personalities and Reminiscences of the War*, p. 45.

65. "ideal administrator": *Philadelphia North American*, Apr. 1903.

65. "brilliant record": Ibid.

65. "privileges and beneficences": *New York Sun* clipping of May 1903.

66. "steady, Lord": JJP mem.

66. a military genius: McGovern, *By Bolo and Krag*, p. 233.

68. A lot of courage: Lieutenant Bowman to Assistant Secretary Sanger, letter cited above.

68ff. The Bacleod campaign is described in Landor, p. 285ff., Smythe, *Guerrilla Warrior*, p. 95ff., and JJP mem.

70. "If the Americans want to fight us": Quoted by Landor, p. 293.

75. "greatest shepherd since Abraham": *New York World*, Oct. 29, 1929, quotes Sen. Jonathan Prentiss Dolliver of Iowa as so describing Senator Warren.

75ff. Details on Senator Warren are found in a 1924 election pamphlet and in the *New York Morning Telegraph* of Aug. 18, 1918.

76. "maiden chatelaine": *Washington Mirror Magazine*, Jan. 28, 1905.

76. "Though but a Miss": *San Francisco Call*, Aug. 26, 1900.

76. "Felt an inspiration": As earlier mentioned, Miss Warren, later Mrs. Pershing, occasionally attempted to keep a diary.

78. "met the girl God made for me!": Quoted by Smythe, *Guerrilla Warrior*, p. 113.

78. "I see now": Senator Warren is quoted by Harold F. Wheeler, *Ladies' Home Journal*, Juiy 1919.

78. "My dear Captain": As late as Mar. 1904 that remained her greeting.

78. "Share your embraces": Gen. George B. Davis to JJP, June 16, 1903.

79. "Get in": Miss Warren's diary.

80. "That's right": Quoted by Smythe, *Guerrilla Warrior*, pp. 117–18.

81. "John L. Sullivan and Jake Kilrain": JJP to F. S. Wood of West Chester, Pa., May 15, 1926, in response to a letter asking impressions of Theodore Roosevelt for publication in a proposed book.

81. *I thought you would:* The Papers have dozens of congratulatory messages.

82. Wedding decorations and events are described in *Washington Mirror Magazine,* Jan. 28, 1905, the *Philadelphia Press,* Jan. 28, 1905, and *Life* magazine, Feb. 4, 1905.

83. "Love her more and more": JJP irregular diary.

83. "jolly and friendly": Griscom, p. 252.

85. "natives allowed to ride first class?": Dunn, p. 123, quotes the question.

86. "This is great!": Quoted in Palmer, *With Kuroki in Manchuria,* p. 270.

86. "harrowing": JJP mem.

87. "We are paying for this": Quoted by Palmer, *With My Own Eyes,* p. 248.

88. "most pleasingly human": Palmer, *John J. Pershing,* p. 59.

93. "you know": Guy Preston to JJP, Nov. 27, 1906.

95. "How are you, Colonel?": George MacAdam in *The World's Work,* May 1919.

95. nervous and ill at ease: Smythe, *Guerrilla Warrior,* p. 136, on the basis of an interview with a woman present at Fort McKinley at the time described.

96. "I never ask": Quoted by Andrews, p. 69.

97. The valet had forgotten to pack: JJP mem.

97. "everybody on the street": Warren to JJP, Jan. 25, 1908.

98. "It gave added charm": Nurse Lustig wrote of her experiences in 1941 for a projected magazine article; a copy was sent to JJP. The proposed article was never printed.

100. "cordial, kindly": Undated *The Army and Navy Journal* clipping.

101. "heavy as lead": JJP mem.

101. "the heathen rage": Mrs. Pershing diary.

101. "Jack, what shall we do?" JJP quotes his wife in JJP mem.

103. "swang a censer": Mrs. Pershing diary.

103. "Jack got into the game": Ibid.

105. "we have subjected you": JJP mem.

106. "fit for duty": Ibid.

108. "That's the way, General!": *American Legion Monthly,* Oct. 1928, op. cit.

109. the last baby of '86: JJP wrote thanking Duncan for the thought on Dec. 4, 1912.

109. quite alone just then: JJP to Joseph Dickman, Jan. 5, 1912.

109. "It is hardly worthwhile": JJP to his sister, Mary Elizabeth Butler, Sept. 13, 1910.

109. "I wish that I had gone": JJP to William Tracy Page, Oct. 11, 1910.

109. "I was both glad and sorry": Senator Warren to his daughter, Apr. 11, 1910.

110. Canned Mystery: McGovern, *When the Krag Is Laid Away*, p. 110.

110. hold up an entire troop movement: Smythe, *Guerrilla Warrior*, p. 137.

110. "I think you two": *American Legion Monthly*, October 1928, op. cit.

111. "Stay in China!": Ibid.

111. pacifist and not a warrior: Bullard, *Personalities and Reminiscences of the War*, pp. 91–92.

112. began with caviar and oyster cocktails: The June 12, 1911, menu card is in the Papers.

112. as if they were a boy and girl in love: Unidentified and undated Iowa newspaper clipping about Mrs. Bloedel.

114. "Don't sizzle your time away": His 1886 classmate Deshon to JJP, Nov. 18, 1913.

114. "Leave, Jack": John A. Ryan to JJP, May 5, 1912.

114ff. The Moro Province Fair: Extensively described in JJP mem, and in an article JJP sent at the time to *Travel Magazine*, which eventually published it in Nov. 1918.

116. "I am sorry to know": Dec. 6, 1911, letter to various Moro leaders.

118. "I romped and played with them": JJP mem.

118. "so rapid and remarkable": *San Francisco Examiner*, Jan. 13, 1914.

119. "There was a crash": Mrs. Pershing sent her father a long description of the Apr. 5, 1914, accident; JJP had it copied for dispatch to his sisters May Pershing and Mary Elizabeth Butler.

120. "It reminded me of old times": JJP mem.

122. favored the Elite Confectionery: Martinez shows Villa at the shop in a photo facing p. 97.

122. "Take off your hat": Turner, p. 203.

122. give an account of oneself: Bullard, *Fighting Generals*, p. 1, and *Personalities and Reminiscences of the War*, p. 20.

124. "I'm tired of living alone": George MacAdam quotes JJP in *The World's Work*, June 1919.

125. "I had a letter": Laura McClernand to JJP, Sept. 6, 1915.

125. given hats to wear: articles by Sophie C. Hart and Caroline Hazard in *Wellesley College News*, Autumn 1915.

126. "Miss Hart": Ibid.

127. Another guest: Major Henry H. Whitney to Senator Warren, Aug. 31, 1915; copy of letter is in the Papers.

129. "more news on the Presidio fire": Quoted by Smythe, *Guerrilla Warrior*, p. 210.

130. "Frank! Frank!": Undated letter from Lt. Walter O. Boswell to JJP directly after the fire, quoting his wife, Anne Orr Boswell; also Major Whitney's letter to Senator Warren, op. cit.; also newspaper articles describing the tragedy.

130. "nobody left in there": Smythe, *Guerilla Warrior*, p. 209, on the basis of an interview with a man who was present at the fire.

131. "not nearly all!": Frank Helm quoted JJP in a long letter to the Pershing aide George Adamson, Oct. 7, 1948.

132. "Mama takes us often": Ibid.

132. *Tell her, O gracious Lord*: General Pershing put a paper containing the words with consolatory telegrams from his nearest friends and relatives.

133. playing with matches: Col. John W. Pershing to author.

133. Our beloved friend: A folder in the Papers holds condolence messages in their great number.

136. "Last year": JJP to Senator Warren, June 19, 1916.

136. "O, he just jumped up": May Pershing to JJP, June 25, 1916, the day after Warren Pershing's seventh birthday.

139. nothing to do with so militaristic a body: George Van Horne Moseley unpublished memoirs, op. cit.

140. "I suppose": Ibid. Moseley was present in the room.

141. "stables": *Baltimore Sun* article by Worthington Hollyday, Jan. 27, 1929.

141. "Everyone wants to go": Blumenson, Vol. I, p. 320.

141. "Beaus galore": Patton, p. 147.

143. situation wasn't very good: Frank B. Elser, *American Legion Monthly*, July 1932.

144. "as good as mine": Quoted by Dunn, p. 230.

145. "favorite tune of Mrs. Pershing": Frank B. Elser, op. cit.

146. The Bandit: Patton to his wife, May 17, 1916, quoted in Semmes.

146. "All right, send it": Frank B. Elser, op. cit.

146. "All the promotion in the world": JJP to T. Bentley Mott, Oct. 2, 1916.

146. "Dear Major General Pershing": Anne Wilson Patton to JJP, Oct. 17, 1916.

148. "Nita may rank us yet": Patton to his wife, quoted in Blumenson, Vol. I, p. 350.

148. "I will say the wrong thing": Patton, p. 157.

149. I am ordered to Washington: JJP to May Pershing, May 5, 1917.

149. "diminuitive": John J. Pershing, Vol. I, p. 17.

150. could not have made a better choice: Andrews, p. 80.

150. undertaken by Jason and the Argonauts: Harbord, *Leaves from a War Diary*, p. 3.

152. King George telling America's general: From the time of arrival in France to some months after the end of the war, Pershing dictated a brief daily diary to a member of his staff.

153. *"Vive l'Amérique!"*: The *Hartford Daily Courant* for Sept. 21, 1918, reported on a talk by Floyd Gibbons describing JJP's arrival in France.

154. The war as it had been and would be: *Washington Post*, Dec. 15, 1941, article by Clementine Phelps.

154ff. great honor to greet an old soldier: *New York World*, June 15, 1917.

155. "What a magnificent gesture!": *Army-Navy Journal*, July 17, 1948.

155. he did not feel worthy: Mitchell, p. 141.

156. a dream of Paradise: Harbord, *The American Army in France*, p. 89.

156. "Don't it beat hell": Quoted by Dawes, p. 23.

156. "so unusual for an American": Quoted by Pitt, p. 68.

157. "formed an army worthy of the American people": Quoted by Bullard, *Personalities and Reminiscences of the War*, p. 94.

157. "I should have liked to argue": Staff diary.

158. "I tell you one thing": Dorothy Canfield Fisher, op. cit.

158. "Dear General Pershing": Mrs. Fisher to JJP, June 15, 1917.

158. "irresistible, friendly smile": Dorothy Canfield Fisher, op. cit.

158. *determined*: Ibid.

158. or fool himself: Palmer, *With My Own Eyes*, p. 345.

160. whole terms of enlistment: Lanckton as interviewed in the *American Legion Monthly*, Nov. 1928.

161. "stunning, commanding": Collins, p. 27.

161. "Go back to your posts": Quoted in Stallings, p. 41.

161. "never call him 'Papa' Pershing": Broun, p. 92. *The Detroit Free Press* of Feb. 5, 1922, reported JJP as saying of the remark, with a laugh: "I guess he was right."

161. "John, I am—": *Chicago News*, Jan. 14, 1931.

162. "All the officers referred to": JJP to Secretary of War Newton D. Baker, Oct. 4, 1917.

163. "No officer has inspired me": JJP to Bell, June 25, 1918.

163. "through his boots or his buttons": Broun, p. 93.

164. his own secretary of war and of state: The staff diary for Dec. 8, 1917, quotes a remark to JJP by the financier Otto Kahn.

164. "He just scarified us": Bland, p. 122.

164. "You could talk to him": Quoted by Pogue, p. 153.

165. "Here, sentry": *American Legion Monthly*, Nov. 1928.

165. "his own model": Simonds, p. 1.

165. going to be played under the Pershing rules: Palmer, *With My Own Eyes*, p. 356.

167. "How did you like the air raid?": *American Legion Monthly*, Nov. 1928.

167ff. Details on Haig are found throughout Smith, *The Ends of Greatness*.

168ff. Details on Pétain are found throughout Smith, *The Ends of Greatness*.

168. "just at the hour of dark": Anne Wilson Patton to JJP, Oct. 14, 1917.

168. "Nita's suitor": Patton to his wife, June 25, 1917, quoted in Blumenson, Vol. I, p. 402.

169. "a bit chorus lady": Anne Wilson Patton to JJP, Oct. 12, 1917.

169. "I do not like to feel this way": Anne Wilson Patton to JJP, Oct. 11, 1917.

169. "I am lonesome": Anne Wilson Patton to JJP, Oct. 13, 1917.

169. "little tin god on wheels": Patton, p. 189.

169. "radiated sexual excitement": Perret, *Old Soldiers Never Die*, p. 124.

169. "end up in bed together": Ibid., p. 125.

170. "little Russian girl": Harbord, *Leaves from a War Diary*, entry for Oct. 27, 1917.

171. "undue familiarities": Andrews, p. 264.

171. "Let it be John and Bentley": Mott, p. 294.

171. "hell of a job": Dawes, pp. 98-99.

171. "I don't give a damn": Quoted by Griscom, p. 411.

172. "Charlie, I once thought": Quoted by Timmons, pp. 165-66.

172. "of their Nebraska days": *Cleveland Plain Dealer* interview with former sergeant major Harry Cooper of JJP overseas staff, Jan. 8, 1931.

172. "my dear, dear boy": Dawes, p. 73.

173. "Even this war": Ibid., pp. 22-23.

173. "Frankie, Frankie": Quoted by O'Connor, p. 182.

175. could choke up: *Army and Navy News*, undated but apparently summer 1918.

177. Confidential: The letter was sent on Dec. 18, 1917.

178. "master of English": Quoted by Timmons, p. 185.

178. "When a conference was called": Dawes sent JJP a copy of a speech made in Chicago on Dec. 21, 1919.

178. rubbing three fingers together: Palmer, *With My Own Eyes*, p. 161.

179. "You can't budge him": Quoted by Simonds, p. 13.

180. "I am willing": Quoted by Smythe, *Pershing: General of the Armies*, p. 115.

181. "Refer and be damned": Ibid., p. 135.

182. like a football coach: Bullard, *Personalities and Reminiscences of the War*, p. 357.

182. "Do they patronize you?": Ibid., p. 198.

183. "You must hold your position": Ibid., p. 366.

183. "half crazy": Quoted by Smythe, *Pershing: General of the Armies*, p. 128.

185. "violent": Blumenson quotes Patton, Vol. I, p. 431.

185. "I never saw": Dawes, p. 153.

185. "Don't let the presidential bug": Senator Warren to JJP, July 11, 1917.

185. "it is perfectly ridiculous": JJP to Senator Warren, July 31, 1917.

186. "I want him": JJP to Lillian Bell, May 24, 1917.

187. "Let me say": JJP to corps commander Joseph Dickman, Oct. 28, 1918.

188. "General Pershing directs me": Colonel Boyd to Maj. Gen. William Haan, commanding the Thirty-second Division, June 2, 1918.

188. "I who should salute": *Cleveland Plain Dealer*, Feb. 14, 1931.

188. "Did you see him smile?" *American Legion Monthly*, November 1928.

189. "When men run away": A copy of the Oct. 24, 1918, letter was sent to all divisional commanders.

189. "See here": *Red Cross Magazine*, September 1919.

190. "Do you wish": JJP to Micheline Resco, Nov. 2, 1918, Archives of John Carroll University, University Heights, Ohio.

191. THREE HUNDRED YEARS: Harbord, *Leaves from a War Diary*, p. 353.

192. "a damn good licking": Quoted by Smythe, *Pershing: General of the Armies*, p. 186.

193. "most ideal defensive terrain": Quoted by Smythe, ibid., p. 186.

193. like a park by comparison: Quoted by Smythe, ibid., p. 191.

193. "most comprehensive system": Harbord, *The American Army in France*, p. 433.

194. Never was war so inhuman: Bullard, *Personalities and Reminiscences of the War*, p. 161.

195. "Things are going badly": Quoted by Simonds, pp. 18-19.

195. "He said this is something": Staff diary.

196. "*Monsieur, monsieur*": Thoms (sic) M. Johnson, a wartime correspondent, interviewed General Pershing in the late 1920s and produced a manuscript apparently intended for publication. The general slightly edited Johnson's effort. It apparently never found its way into print.

196. "I'm going to hold you personally responsible": Quoted by Perret, *Old Soldiers Never Die*, p. 91.

197. "if you can stick this a little longer": Former field artillery officer Clinton Bundy in the *Pittsburgh Sunday Telegraph*, July 8, 1931.

197. "we are not in need of advice": Quoted by Griscom, p. 435.

198. frosty exchange: Stallings, pp. 379-81.

198. the Frenchman reached out: Mott, p. 227.

200. "Mild terms!": Griscom, p. 440.

200. "Don't pay any attention": Quoted by Mott, p. 261.

201. "I suppose our campaigns are ended": Quoted by Griscom, p. 446.

217. "By order of the secretary of war": *New York World*, Apr. 8, 1919.

218. "Ass-chewing": Quoted by Col. John W. Pershing to author.

219. "I thank you again and again": Quoted by Harriman, p. 321.

219. had it twice in years gone by: Smythe, *Pershing: General of the Armies*, p. 250.

220. "I like to be with my boy": *Pittsburgh Sun*, Aug. 16, 1919.

220. "Eugene Tunney": Staff diary.

221. wind blowing amid the ladies: Pogue, p. 227.

221. "so busy and impatient": JJP to Micheline Resco, Mar. 23, 1925, archives of John Carroll University.

221. "It added a little touch": Staff diary.

222. "Well now, General": Staff diary.

222. "I did my best": Quoted by Chase, p. 27.

222. "And now, dear comrades": Staff diary, describing Memorial Day of 1919.

223. "You, of course": Staff diary, July 17, 1919.

223. "May the good Lord deliver us": JJP to James F. Pershing, Dec. 27, 1918.

223. "I have not": James F. Pershing to JJP, Jan. 28, 1919.

223. "I can say this to you": JJP to Senator Warren, Jan. 11, 1919.

224. got angrier than at any time: Griscom, pp. 456ff.

224. threw him off and broke his hand: Pogue, p. 200.

224. "Oh, Dad!": *Baltimore Sun*, July 20, 1919.

225. *Mireille*: A copy of the code is in Micheline Resco's Papers, John Carroll University.

225. "Let us *never*": Quoted by Patton, p. 190.

226. "One is not able": JJP to Micheline Resco, May 15, 1919.

226. never heard Pershing mention Frankie's name: Andrews, p. 264.

227. nothing cold: T. Bentley Mott to JJP, Nov. 8, 1919.

229. "The next time": Quoted by Conner, p. 87.

229. "I have a new widow": Clara Morgan Warren to JJP, Aug. 25, 1929.

230. did not wish Warren featured: *New York Sun*, Sept. 16, 1919.

231. "I hope you won't mind my saying": Princess Cantacuzene to JJP, Sept. 12, 1924.

232. "running up my back": Pogue, pp. 224-25.

232. "what dissolute habits": Emma Mahoney to JJP, Mar. 25, 1917.

232. "how it feels to be the son of you!": Emma Mahoney to JJP, undated but late 1919.

233. most of the time he was a prisoner: Staff diary, Sept 23, 1919.

233. "They can't get me here": Quoted by Conner, p. 90.

234. "asked if she spoke English": Quoted by Conner, p. 92.

235. "send him a kiss for me": JJP to May Pershing, Nov. 13, 1919, quoting Queen Elizabeth of the Belgians.

237. "three times in a single day": Moseley in what was meant to be Vol. II of his never-published autobiography, p. 15.

238–39. "where are you going . . . ?" *St. Louis Dispatch*, April 21, 1920.

238. "My father is A.W.O.L.": United News Service, Apr. 24, 1920.

238. "I hope to see you in the White House": *New York Sun*, Dec. 25, 1919.

238. "My boy—": *New York Tribune*, Dec. 27, 1919.

239. "Can it be possible?": *Missouri Magazine*, Aug. 1931.

239. knocked the general down: *American Legion Monthly*, in Robert Ginsburgh article about the Pershing orderly Sgt. Steve Cato.

241. "ask Colonel Marshall about it": Warren's dictated and then typed-up diary is in the Pershing Papers.

241. "I had them do it over again": Staff diary, Apr. 28, 1920.

243ff. May 27th: Warren's diary.

250. "I am hidden away": JJP to his cousin Bethed (sic) Pershing of Pineville, Pa.

253. "For the spoiled boy": JJP to Louis Lamborn, Dec. 12, 1921.

253. "Warren is looking forward": Louis Lamborn to JJP, July 29, 1921.

254. "Warren has ability": Louis Lamborn to JJP, Nov. 13, 1922.

255. "I noticed this": Lt. John T. Schneider to JJP, Feb. 11, 1924.

256. "Do you realize": JJP to James Harbord, Apr. 28, 1923.

259. "I played golf": Marshall to JJP, Sept. 29, 1924.

259. "Now, Warren": George Adamson to Warren, Mar. 2, 1928.

261. "an eye for a pretty girl": Col. John W. Pershing to author.

262. "Marshal Sarrail died": JJP to Dawes, Mar. 28, 1929.

263. "We are both growing older": Quoted by Timmons, p. 332.

263. "the poultry-raising period": Quoted by Mott, p. 317.

264. "You didn't have very much to fatigue you": Quoted by Mott, p. 317.

264. "I don't see that he would add anything": Quoted by Mott, p. 314.

265. "It is embarrassing to me": George Adamson to May Pershing, June 5, 1934.

265. "I am always ready to help you": JJP to Frank Helm, Dec. 11, 1929.

265. "These matters are piling up rapidly": JJP to Richard Paddock, Apr. 19, 1934.

265. "A short while ago": JJP to Richard Paddock, Aug. 1, 1938.

266. as much as $40,000: Schwarz, p. 337.

266ff. able to pinpoint the moment: O'Connor, pp. 374-375.

268. "as an introduction": John J. Pershing, Vol. II, pp. 274-75.

270. "as I have known him": *Pensacola Journal*, Apr. 6, 1935.

270–71. "I suspect that my teeth": JJP to Micheline Resco, Jan. 20, 1926.

271. "I remember as clearly as though it were yesterday": Craig to JJP, Oct. 31, 1935.

271. "Well, John, how are you feeling . . . ?" T. Bentley Mott to a Class of 1886 annual circular letter.

271. *When you grow old:* A copy of the poem is in the Philippines Club File, Pershing Papers.

273. "the two most photographed horses": *Washington Daily News* interview with depot commander at Front Royal, Col. Warren Whitside.

273. "I'd like to come down": *Washington Herald*, Sept. 13, 1936.

276. "Heartbreakers": Quoted by Douglas, pp. 119-26.

283. "You think too much of the French": Quoted by Smith, *The Ends of Greatness*, p. 176.

285. "My condition is such": JJP to Roosevelt, Nov. 16, 1940.

287. "I fear you will have a great shock": Marshall to Dawes, May 22, 1941.

289. best for them to seek entertainment elsewhere: Col. John W. Pershing to author.

290. "I think his desire": Bland, Vol. III, p. 13.

292. "You look something like him": *Washington Star*, Apr. 8, 1942.

293ff. General Patton's call is described in Patton, p. 251, and Smythe, *Guerrilla Warrior*, pp. 263-64, on the basis of an interview with General Patton's daughter.

294. "I wanted desperately to tell you": Patton to JJP, Nov. 24, 1942.

294ff. the uniform of a French officer: O'Connor, pp. 387-88.

295. more friends in Arlington: Harbord to JJP, Apr. 11, 1946.

302. a brief interview: Fred S. Ferguson of United Press International wrote on July 21, 1948, of the Jan. 23, 1942, visit.

304. "But what a soufflé": Upon occasion Mumu sent extracts from Warren's letters to her for General Pershing's enjoyment.

304. "will not have been in vain": Warren to Mumu, and copied by her for the general.

305. "The hell with that": Quoted by Col. John W. Pershing to author.

305. the day came: Col. John W. Pershing to author.

306. Warren's great desire: Ibid.

306ff. they were directed: Douglas, p. 155.

308. "vacant and useless": Quoted by Douglas, p. 160.

308. "They wanted so badly": Ibid., p. 121.

308. as long as ten days: Smythe, *Pershing: General of the Armies*, p. 306.

314. In 1946 a priest: Micheline Resco was an ardent Catholic. The priest in question, Jules A. Baisnée of the Society of St. Sulpice, wrote a statement, preserved in the Pershing Papers, that he "blessed the marriage" of Mlle. Resco and JJP. She later told people they had been married. No legal arrangements normal for a surviving widow appear to have been made, and the financial allotments Warren Pershing gave to Mlle. Resco for the rest of her life appear to have been entirely of a voluntary nature. Mlle. Resco's references to a marriage, therefore, seem to have had reference to a union in God's eyes.

317. Everyone knew who Jack was: Library of Congress employee Gerald W. Gewalt, a fellow member of the Pershing Rifles in Boston during John W. Pershing's time, to the author.

317. secretly thought: The college official years later related his feelings to Col. John W. Pershing, who described them to the author.

317. performance there was remarkable: Dr. David Schlossberg to author.

318. took a couple of looks: Donald Parsons to author.

318. what a good-looking guy: Arlene Parsons to author.

319. "*Ici parle M. Pershing*": Quoted by Dr. David Schlossberg to author.

319. a parlor game: Michael Dalby to author.

319. abode of royalty: Ronald Singer to author.

320. a different world: James Howard to author.

322. most similar to himself: Gerald Singer to author.

326. stern, demanding, by-the-book: Shirley (Hildreth) Cleveland to author.

327. it and the driver were needed elsewhere: Smythe, *Pershing: General of the Armies*, p. 307.

331. it was his habit: Gen. William C. Westmoreland to author. Hoyt, p. 145, relates that Damon Runyon was impressed with General Pershing's humane qualities when he found that the general each morning studied the names of those who had died under his command during 1917–18.

BIBLIOGRAPHY

Andrews, Avery DeLano. *My Friend and Classmate John J. Pershing.* Harrisburg, Pa.: Military Service Publishing, 1939.

Biddle, Ellen McGowan. *Reminiscences of a Soldier's Wife.* Philadelphia: J. B. Lippincott, 1907.

Bigelow, John Jr. *Reminiscences of the Santiago Campaign.* New York: Harper & Brothers, 1899.

Bland, Larry I., ed. *The Papers of George Catlett Marshall.* Baltimore: Johns Hopkins University Press, 1981.

Blumenson, Martin. *The Patton Papers.* 2 vols. Boston: Houghton Mifflin, 1972–74.

Boyd, James P. *Recent Indian Wars Under the Lead of Sitting Bull and Other Chiefs.* Philadelphia: Franklin News, 1891.

Boyd, Thomas A. *Simon Girty: The White Savage.* New York: Minton, Balch, 1928.

Braddy, Haldeen. *Pershing's Mission in Mexico.* El Paso, Tex.: Western Press, 1965.

Braim, Paul F. *The Test of Battle.* Newark: University of Delaware Press, 1987.

Broun, Heywood. *The A.E.F.* New York: D. Appleton, 1918.

Bullard, Robert Lee. *American Soldiers Also Fought.* New York: Maurice A. Lewis, 1939.

——. *Fighting Generals.* Ann Arbor, Mich.: J. W. Edwards, 1944.

——. *Personalities and Reminiscences of the War.* Garden City, N.Y.: Doubleday, Page, 1925.

Chase, Joseph Cummings. *Soldiers All.* New York: George H. Doran, 1920.

Cloman, Sydney A. *Myself and a Few Moros.* Garden City, N.Y.: Doubleday, 1923.

Coffman, Edward M. *The Hilt of the Sword: The Career of Peyton C. March.* Madison: University of Wisconsin Press, 1966.

Collins, J. Lawton. *Lightning Joe.* Baton Rouge: Louisiana State University Press, 1979.

Conner, Virginia. *What Father Forbad.* Philadelphia: Dorrance, 1951.

Davis, Britton. *The Truth About Geronimo.* New Haven, Conn.: Yale University Press, 1929.

Dawes, Charles G. *A Journal of The Great War.* Boston: Houghton Mifflin, 1929.

Douglas, Geoffrey. *Class: The Wreckage of an American Family.* New York: Henry Holt, 1992.

Dunn, Robert. *World Alive.* New York: Crown, 1956.

Eisenhower, John S. D. *Intervention: The United States and the Mexican Revolution.* New York: W. W. Norton, 1993.

Fredericks, Pierce G. *The Great Adventure.* New York: E. P. Dutton, 1960.

Freidel, Frank. *The Splendid Little War.* New York: Bramhall House, 1958.

Griscom, Lloyd. *Diplomatically Speaking.* Boston: Little, Brown, 1940.

Harbord, James G. *The American Army in France.* Boston: Little, Brown, 1936.

———. *Leaves from a War Diary.* New York: Dodd, Mead, 1925.

Harriman, J. Borden. *From Pinafores to Politics.* New York: Henry Holt, 1923.

Howland, Harry S. *America in Battle.* Paris: Herbert Clarke, 1920.

Hoyt, Edwin P. *A Gentleman of Broadway.* Boston: Little, Brown, 1964.

Landor, A. Henry Savage. *The Gems of the East.* New York: Harper & Brothers, 1904.

Liddell Hart, B. H. *The War in Outline.* New York: Random House, 1936.

Machado, Manuel A. Jr. *Centaur of the North.* Austin: Eakin Press, 1988.

Marshall, Katherine Tupper. *Together: Annals of an Army Wife.* New York: Tupper and Love, 1946.

Martinez, Oscar J. *Fragments of the Mexican Revolution.* Albuquerque: University of New Mexico Press, 1983.

McGovern, Chauncey. *By Bolo and Krag.* Manila: Escolta Press, 1910.

———. *When the Krag Is Laid Away.* Manila: Escolta Press, 1907.

Millett, Allan. *The General: Robert L. Bullard.* Westport, Conn.: Greenwood Press, 1975.

Mitchell, William. *Memoirs of World War I.* New York: Random House, 1960.

Moseley, George Van Horne. "One Soldier's Journey." 2 vols. Unpublished manuscript in Moseley Papers, Library of Congress.

Mott, T. Bentley. *Twenty Years as Military Attaché.* New York: Oxford University Press, 1937.

O'Connor, Richard. *Black Jack Pershing.* Garden City, N.Y.: Doubleday, 1961.

Palmer, Frederick. *John J. Pershing.* Harrisburg, Pa.: Military Service Publishing, 1948.

——. *With Kuroki in Manchuria.* New York: Charles Scribner's Sons, 1904.

——. *With My Own Eyes.* Indianapolis, Ind.: Bobbs-Merrill, 1932.

Parker, James. *The Old Army.* Philadelphia: Dorrance, 1929.

Patton, Robert H. *The Pattons.* New York: Crown, 1994.

Perret, Geoffrey. *A Country Made by War.* New York: Vintage Books, 1990.

——. *Old Soldiers Never Die: The Life of Douglas MacArthur.* New York: Random House, 1996.

Pershing, Edgar J. *The Pershing Family in America.* Philadelphia: George S. Ferguson, 1924.

Pershing, John J. *My Experiences in the World War.* 2 vols. New York: Frederick A. Stokes, 1931.

Pitt, Barrie. *1918: The Last Act.* New York: W. W. Norton, 1962.

Poe, Sophie A. *Buckboard Days.* Caldwell, Idaho: Caxton Printers, 1936, 1963.

Pogue, Forrest C. *George C. Marshall: Education of a General.* New York: Viking, 1964.

Schwarz, Jordan. *The Speculator.* Chapel Hill: University of North Carolina Press, 1981.

Scott, Hugh Lenox. *Some Memories of a Soldier.* New York: Century, 1928.

Semmes, Harry H. *Portrait of Patton.* New York: Appleton-Century-Crofts, 1955.

Simonds, Frank H. *They Won The War.* New York: Harper & Brothers, 1931.

Smith, Gene. *The Ends of Greatness.* New York: Crown, 1990.

———. *Still Quiet on The Western Front: Fifty Years Later.* New York: William Morrow, 1965.

Smythe, Donald. *Guerrilla Warrior: The Early Life of John J. Pershing.* New York: Charles Scribner's Sons, 1973.

———. *Pershing: General of the Armies.* Bloomington: Indiana University Press, 1986.

Stallings, Laurence. *The Doughboys.* New York: Harper & Row, 1963.

Timmons, Bascom N. *Portrait of an American: Charles G. Dawes.* New York: Henry Holt, 1953.

Tomkins, Frank. *Chasing Villa.* Harrisburg, Pa.: Military Service Publishing, 1934.

Toulmin, H. A. Jr. *With Pershing in Mexico.* Harrisburg, Pa.: Military Service Publishing, 1935.

Turner, Timothy G. *Bullets, Bottles, and Gardenias.* Dallas: South-West Press, 1935.

Utley, Robert M. *The Last Days of the Sioux Nation.* New Haven, Conn.: Yale University Press, 1963.

Vandiver, Frank E. *Black Jack.* 2 vols. College Station: Texas A & M University Press, 1977.

Vestal, Stanley. *Sitting Bull.* Boston: Houghton Mifflin, 1932.

Wooster, Robert. *Nelson A. Miles.* Lincoln: University of Nebraska Press, 1993.

INDEX

Page numbers in *italics* indicate illustrations.

Abe, Colonel, 91
Adamson, George E., 231, 273
   and Pershing's financial affairs, 265,
      284
   and Pershing's later years, 277, 293,
      295, 299, 309
   and Pershing's memoirs, 250
   and Pershing's son Warren, 259–60
AEF (American Expeditionary Forces).
      See World War I
Agga (Philippine maharaja), 112
Ah Chong, 108
Ahmai-Manibilang (Moro chief), 60–62
Ahmai Tampogao (Moro chief), 89
Alexandra, queen of England, 167, 224
Alfonso, prince of Spain, 108
Alger, Russell A., 55
Allen, Henry, 195
American Battle Monuments Commis-
      sion, 261
American Expeditionary Forces (AEF).
      See World War I
Andrews, Avery, 17, 49, 288, 290–91, 299
   at Pershing's funeral, 314
   at West Point, 20, 22
   World War I service, 170–71, 226–27
anti-Semitism, 315–16, 319

Apache Indians, 32
Argonne Forest, Battle of (1918), 193–98
Arlington National Cemetery, viii-xi, 333,
      337
Arno, Peter, 333
Arthur, Chester, 75
Arthur of Connaught (prince of
      England), 108
Astor, John Jacob, 53
Austria-Hungary, 199

Bache, Jules S., 275, 288–89, 299,
      315–16
Bacleod, sultan of, 67, 68, 69
Baker, Newton D., 209, 228, 229
   and Mexican crisis, 139, 140
   pacifism of, 139
   and Pershing's son Warren, 217–18
   World War I policies, 149, 162, 179,
      184, 193, 197, 198
Baldwin, Theodore, 54, 55
Balfour, Arthur James, 152
Barnum, Malvern Hill, 46–47, 112, 290
Barry, General, 162
Bartlett, General, 162
Baruch, Bernard, 266, 287
Bean, Wiley, 24–25, 26

Bear Nose (Oglala scout), 37
Beckman, Corporal, 244
Bell, J. Franklin, 104, 150, 162–63
Bell, Lillian, 185
Belleau Wood, Battle of (1918), 184
Berthier, Louis-Alexandre, 193
Big Charger (Oglala scout), 37
Big Foot (Sioux chief), 37
Black Fox (Oglala scout), 37
Bliss, Tasker H., 140
Bloedel, Bonnie, 112
Bloedel, Robert, 112
Blücher, Gebhard von, 193
Bolger, Ray, 314–15
Bond, Mrs., 113
Boston University, 317, 321
Boswell, Anne Decker Orr, 82–83, 97,
    125, 136
  and Pershing home fire, 127, 128, 130,
    132
Boswell, James, 127, 130–31
Boswell, Philip, 127, 130–31
Boswell, Walter O., 97
Bowman, George, 65, 67–68
Boyd, Carl, 165, 188
Bradley, Omar, viii, 313–14
Branch, Lieutenant, 77
Brent, Bishop, 262
Brewer, R. M., 238
British Expeditionary Force, 167
Broken Leg (Oglala scout), 37
Brooks, Louise Cromwell, 169–70, 281
Broun, Heywood, 161, 163, 165, 209, 257
Brown, Joe W., 333
Bryan, William Jennings, 42
Buck, Beaumont, 196
Buckner, Simon Bolivar, 199
Buffalo Bill. See Cody, William F.
Bulgaria, 199
Bullard, Robert Lee, 111, 122
  Philippines tour of duty, 59, 65, 68
  at West Point, 22, 23
  World War I service, 163–64, 178,
    182–83, 187, 194, 198
Butler, Elizabeth Pershing (Bess; sister),
    14, 109, 250
  and Warren Pershing, 135, 186, 187,
    229, 253, 258, 259

Byrd, Thomas, 333

Caesar, Julius, 159, 223
Caesar, Sid, 318
Campbell, William Pitcairn, 151
Canfield, James H., 40, 41, 42, 43,
    44–45, 49
Cantigny, Battle of (1918), 181–83
Cárdenas, Julio, 145
Carothers, Samuel, 9–10
Cather, Willa, 42
Cato, Steve, 239, 240
Cavan, earl of, 225
Church, Margaretta Gray, 127–28, 130
Churchill, Winston, 152, 223, 225, 270
Churchill School, 124
Civil War, U.S.
  Grant's generalship style, 159, 195,
    199, 200
  Pershing family experiences, 3–6, 8
Clark, General, 313
Clark, Senator, 78
Clemenceau, Georges, 179, 180, 198,
    218, 221–22
Cody, William F. (Buffalo Bill), 120
Coleman, Emil, 279
Collegiate School, 316
Collins, James L., 117, 129, 131, 135,
    145, 149, 150
Collins, J. Lawton, 161
Colonel Huse's School (Highland Falls,
    N.Y.), 17–18
Columbus (New Mexico), 139–40
Conner, Fox, 229, 233
Conner, Virginia, 229, 233, 234–35
Coogan, Jackie, 256
Coolidge, Calvin, 249
Coolidge, Grace, viii
Cooper, Henry, 172
Craig, Malin, 48, 271, 277
Cree Indians, 46
Cromwell, Oliver, 191, 223
Crow-on-Head (Oglala scout), 37
Cummings, Joseph, 222
Cunningham, Lieutenant, 246
Curzon, Lord, 152
Custer, George Armstrong, 18–19, 37
Custer, Libby, 150

Dalby, Mike, 319, 320, 322, 327, 334–35
Damrosch, Walter, 220
Datto Acoti (Moro chief), 64
Datto Gundar (Moro chief), 63
Davidson, Jo, 56, 222
Davis, Britton, 31
Davis, George W., 59, 60, 78
Davis, Jefferson, 47
Davison, Roland, 280
Dawes, Charles G., 56, 211, 229, 278, 287
  friendship with Pershing, 41–42, 46, 156, 171, 203, 262–63, 282
  later years, 269, 295
  at Pershing's funeral, 314
  political appointments, 263
  respect for Pershing's abilities, 178, 185
  and U.S. Army band, 220
  wealth and influence of, 171–72, 263
  and World War I, 156, 171–73, 176, 263, 286
Dawes Plan, 263
Dawes, Rufus Fearing, 172
de Gaulle, Charles, 212, 294–95, 309
Dempsey, Jack, 220
Derby, Lord, 152
Deshon, George, 105, 106, 114
Devers, General, 313
Dewey, George, 51, 54
Diaz, Porfirio, 121
Dickman, Joseph, 109, 187
Douglas, Archibald, 306–7
Douglas, Ellie Reed, 276, 307–8
Douglas, Geoffrey, 307
Drake, Francis, 51
Drum, Hugh, 193
Duncan, George, 25, 109

Eagle Chief (Oglala scout), 37
Eden, Anthony, 270
Eisenhower, Dwight, viii, 300, 313–14
Elizabeth, queen of the Belgians, 221
Elser, Frank, 143, 146
Ely, Hanson, 183
England. See Great Britain
Equal Franchise League of El Paso, 125
Errol, Leon, 263
Estabrook, Harry D., 41

Fairbanks, Senator, 78
Fechet, E. G., 45
Feigel, Jefferson, 233
Ferguson, Fred, 302
Ferrar, Geraldine, 104
Fessenden School, 316
First Volunteer Cavalry. See Rough Riders
Fisher, Dorothy Canfield, 39, 41, 42, 43, 44, 158, 189, 269
Foch, Ferdinand, 257, 262
  and World War I, 157, 165, 180, 181, 190, 192, 193, 198, 201
  and years after World War I, 218, 221–22, 224, 227–28
Forbes, Cameron, 112, 233
Forbes, Mrs., 241
Fort Apache, 32
Fort Huachuca, 32
Fort Stanton, 32, 33
Fort William McKinley (Manila), 95, 96–97
Fort Wingate, 32, 33
France
  diplomacy after World War I, 221–22
  Pershing's departure from, 227–28
  and World War I, 153–57, 163–68, 171, 179–84, 189–93, 195, 197–99, 201
  and World War II, 283–84
  See also Foch, Ferdinand; Pétain, Henri Philippe
Francis Ferdinand, archduke of Austria, 123, 182
Franco-Prussian War (1870–71), 10, 199, 222
Frederick the Great, king of Prussia, 18
French, Lord, 152
Froelich, Mr., 288

Ganassi, sultan of, 69, 89
George V, king of Great Britain, 152, 157, 223, 224
George VI, king of Great Britain, 270
Germany
  and World War I, 156, 179–80, 182–84, 187, 199, 201
  and World War II, 282–83, 305

Geronimo, 28
Gerow, General, 313
Ghost Bull (Oglala scout), 37
Ghost Dance, 36–38
Gibbons, Floyd, 153
Gladstone, William, 132
Glover, Mollie, 238
Glover, Roland (Lew), 238
Gneisenau (German officer), 193
Goethals, George W., 184
Grant, Ulysses S., 159, 195, 200, 223, 263
    funeral train, 23, 199
    leadership style, 40
    military rank, xi, 72, 228
    "Unconditional Surrender" nickname,
        199
Great Britain, 56, 263, 270, 328
    and Haig as military commander,
        167–68
    and Pershing's victory reception in,
        222–23, 224
    and World War I, 151–52, 157, 163,
        167–68, 179, 180–81, 189–90,
        197–99
    and World War II, 284
Green, General, 162
Griscom, Lloyd, 83–84, 200, 224
Guinan, Texas, 266
Gunnery School, 316

Haan, William, 187–88
Haig, Sir Douglas, 180, 198, 218, 257
    background and persona, 167–68
    impression of Pershing, 156, 157
    and World War I armistice terms,
        199–200
Haig, Lady, 262
Hamilton, Joseph, 238
Hamilton, Mrs. Willis, 238
Harbord, James G., 23, 236, 278, 314
    later years, 256, 263, 269, 295, 299
    on Micheline Resco, 170
    and World War I, 151, 156, 171, 183,
        191, 193
Harding, Florence, 249
Harding, Warren G., 249
Hargreave, Mr., 9
Harrison, Benjamin, 75

Hart, Sophie, 126
Has-White-Face-Horse (Oglala scout), 37
Hay, John, 54
Hayes, Sergeant, 244
Hazard, Caroline, 125, 134
Hearst, William Randolph, 52
Helm, Frank P., ix, 97, 127, 131, 132,
        265, 299
Helm, Laurie, 127
Herrera, Luis, 143
Hertling, George von, 184
Hewitt, Susan, 12, 239
Hildredth, Shirley Gay
    and Dick Pershing, 325–26, 328, 329,
        332
    and Jack Pershing, 335, 336–37
Hindenburg, Paul von, 165, 193, 224
Hines, John L., 182
Hitler, Adolf, 237, 278, 282, 283
Hoar, Senator, 78
Hodges, General (World War II), 313
Hoffman, Max von, 87
Holland, Jane, 276, 308
Holmes, Oliver Wendell, 262
Holtzclaw, Clifton, 4, 5, 313
Holtzclaw Raid (1864), 4–5
Hooker, Joseph, 53
Hoover, Herbert, ix, 249, 262
House, Edward M., 200
Howard, Jimmy, 320, 322, 327, 335
Howard, Oliver Otis, 18
Hurst, Fannie, 333
Hylan, John F., 228

Ignacio, Joaquina Bondoy, 92
Indians. See Native Americans; specific
        leaders and tribes
Institut Carnall, 255–56, 258–59, 315–16
Iron Cloud (Oglala scout), 37
Irving, Henry, 78
Islam, 57
Iwao Oyama, prince of Japan, 87

James, Frank and Jesse, 6
Japan, 83–84, 85–91, 85–93 (see also
        Russo-Japanese War)
Jellicoe, Admiral, 152
Joan of Arc, 159

Joffre, Madame, 175, 186
Joffre, Marshal, 154–55, 165–66
Johnson, Bill, 107–8, 110, 111, 135
Jomini, Henri de, 193

Kahn, Otto H., 164
Kenney, General, 313
Kills Alone (Oglala scout), 37
Kilrain, Jake, 81
Kingsbury, Henry, 95
Kipling, Rudyard, 63
Knickerbocker, Cholly, 275, 292
Knox, Philander C., 108, 109
Kuchiba, Colonel, 91
Kumamoto, General, 91
Kuroki, Tamemoto, 87
Kuropatkin, Aleksyey, 109, 322

Lamborn, Louis, 253, 254
Lanckton, Frank, 61, 108, 110–11, 241
    and Warren Pershing, 111, 135, 221,
        244, 245, 246, 252, 259, 324
    World War I service, 152, 160, 165,
        167, 187
Land, Emory S., 295
Landis, Kenesaw Mountain, 46
Landor, A. Henry Savage, 70
Lawrenceville academy, 316, 317–18
Lee, Robert E., 23, 194, 195, 199, 203
Lefevre, Miss, 245
Lemnitzer, General, 313
Lewis, Edson, 131
Liaoyang, Battle of, 85–86, 90
Liggett, Hunter, 193, 198
Lincoln, Abraham, 4, 159
Lindbergh, Charles, 285
Lisnet, Mrs. Frank, 33
Lloyd George, David, 152, 179, 181, 197
Lodge, Henry Cabot, 134
Louis (Sitting Bull's son), 234
Lucas, Scott, 333
Ludendorff, Erich, 192, 193
Lustig, Gertrude, 98–99, 100

MacArthur, Arthur, 83, 84, 86, 87
MacArthur, Mrs. Arthur, 83, 134
MacArthur, Douglas, 83, 196, 281, 297,
    305

Magoon, Charles, 78, 82
Magruder family, 77
Maguindanaw, princess of, 114
Mahoney, Emma, 232
Manchuria, 85, 86
Mangus (Apache chief), 28
March, Peyton C., 53, 86
Marshall, George C., Jr., 259, 277
    and Harding funeral, 249
    as Pershing's aide, 221, 224, 231–32,
        234–35, 250
    and Pershing's funeral, ix, 314
    and Warren Pershing, 241, 246,
        272, 287, 291, 292, 297, 300,
        301–2
    and World War I, 164, 178, 197
    and World War II, 286–87, 290, 295
Marshall, Mrs. George C., 295
Marshall, Thomas R., 229
Mary, queen of Great Britain, 223, 224
McAdoo, William Gibbs, 134
McAuliffe, General, 313
McClellan, George, 159
McClernand, Laura, 125
McCoy, Samuel, 256–57
McKinley, William, 50, 51, 56, 72
McMahon, John, 196
Meiklejohn, George D., 49–50, 55–56
Mennen, William G., 333
Merrit, Wesley, 18–19
Mexico, 121, 122, 139–48, 166
Michel, Cliff, 289
Middleton, Cornelia, 242–43
Miles, Cecilia, 47
Miles, Nelson A., 37, 47, 50
Military Academy, U.S. See West Point
Millard family, 77
Miller, Gilbert, 289
Miller, Luther D., ix
Mills, Darius Ogden, 156
Mills, Ogden, 155–56
Mindanao island, 57
Minus, 33, 34, 35
Mitchell, Billy, 155
Moltke, Helmuth von, 158
Monte, Mahlon, 268–69
Morgan, Clara. See Warren, Clara Mor-
    gan

Moro Province Fair (1911), 114–15
Moros
  as Islamic warriors, 57
  Pershing's disarming of, 115–18
  Pershing's relations with, 58–59,
    60–71, 89, 111
Morrill, C. H., 39
Morrison, General, 162
Moseley, George Van Horne, 237
Moses, George, 232
Mott, T. Bentley, 146, 256, 263, 271
  as military attaché in Paris, 35, 227
  and Warren Pershing, 258, 259
  at West Point, 18, 21
  and World War I, 171, 198, 200–201
Mukden, Battle of, 83, 86, 90
Mullins, Alexander, 11
Mutsuhito, emperor of Japan, 108–9
My Experiences in The World War
  (Pershing), 250–52

Napoleon Bonaparte, 102, 155, 159, 164,
  176, 193, 223
Native Americans, 30–33, 46
  Ghost Dance movement, 36–38
  See also specific leaders and tribes
Navajo Indians, 3
Nelson, Horatio, 221
Newscome, Fred, 131
Ney, Michel, 193
Nixon, Richard, 336
Nogi, Maresuke, 109
Norstad, General, 313

Oglala Indian scouts, 37
Orr, Anne Decker. *See* Boswell, Anne
  Decker Orr

Paddock, Richard (father), 29, 40, 97
Paddock, Richard (son), 97, 135, 265–66,
  293
Page, William Tracy, 109, 121
Painlevé, Paul, 154
Paley, William, 320
Palmer, Frederick, 87–88, 158–59, 165,
  286
Palmer, John McA., 155, 202
"Paloma, La" (song), 145

Panama-Pacific International Exposition
  of 1915, 119, 124
Panglima Diki-Diki, 115
Parker, James, 49
Parsons, Donald, 318, 320, 321, 322,
  327
Pasaim (Philippine iman), 112
Patton, Anne (Nita), 141, 146, 148, 149,
  168–69, 207, 225, 293
Patton, Beatrice, 148, 169
Patton, George S., Jr., 313
  and Punitive Expedition, 141, 142–43,
    145–46
  and sister's romance with Pershing,
    148, 168–69, 207, 225
  World War I service, 149–50, 152, 185,
    190, 196
  World War II service, 286, 293–94
Paulina (V. Conner's sister), 234
Pendleton, Miss, 126
Penn, Julius, 29–30, 33, 38
Pershing, Anna May (May; sister), 82, 97,
  149, 250, 265
  and great-nephews, 289–90, 314–15,
    327
  and Muriel Pershing, 280, 315
  and Warren Pershing, 135, 136, 146,
    186–87, 218, 229, 235, 240, 251–52,
    253, 255, 256, 258, 259, 266–67,
    271, 272, 276, 279
  and Pershing's death, 212, 314
  and Pershing's later years, 293, 295,
    299, 308, 309
  and Micheline Resco, 326–27
Pershing, Anne Elizabeth Thompson
  (mother), 3–8, 11, 12, 15
Pershing, Anne Orr (daughter)
  birth of, 99
  childhood years, 100, 103, 109, 118,
    122, 125, 128, 206
  correspondence with father, 123
  death and burial, 131, 132
  schooling, 112–13, 121, 124
Pershing, Daniel (great-grandfather), 18
Pershing, Elizabeth (sister). *See* Butler,
  Elizabeth
Pershing, Francis Warren (Warren; son),
  289, 331

and aunts May and Bess, 135–36, 146, 186–87, 218, 229–30, 235, 240, 251–52, 253–54, 255, 256, 258, 259, 266–67, 271, 272, 276, 279
at boarding school, 254–56, 258–59
childhood years with mother, 106, 107, 111, 118, 121, 206
college years, 259–62, 266–67
death of, 336
drinking problem of, 326
European trip, 210, 217–18, 220, 221, 222, 224, 226, 228
and father, 106, 111, 132, 135–36, 146, 173–76, 185–87, 217–18, 220–22, 224, 226, 228–30, 235, 238, 239–46, 251–56, 258–61, 266–67, 271–72, 276–77, 278–82, 297, 298, 299–304, 306
and father's death and burial, 212, 314
and father's near-fatal illness, 277
as fire survivor, 131, 132–33
first marriage of, 272, 276, 278–82
at military training camp, 259
remarriage, 336
and Micheline Resco, 221, 256, 284, 314, 326
son Dick's death, 332–35
and sons, 213, 287, 296, 315–17, 319–20, 321, 323, 324, 329
as stockbroker, 259, 271–72, 289, 306
summer camp experiences, 253, 254
summer job in France, 258
vacations with father, 239–46, 252–53
and wife's death, 335–36
World War I years, 173–76, 186–87
World War II service, 291–92, 296, 297, 298–304, 305
Pershing, Grace (later Paddock; sister), 40, 97, 265
Pershing, Helen (daughter)
birth of, 92
childhood years, 93, 97, 98, 99, 103, 109, 118, 122, 206
correspondence with father, 121, 123
death and burial, 131, 132
schooling, 112–13, 121, 124

Pershing, Helen Frances Warren (Frankie; wife)
births of children, 92, 98–99, 106, 109
carriage accident, 119–20
correspondence with husband, 121–23, 124, 125, 126–27
courtship and wedding, 77–80, 81–83, 242
death and burial, 130–32, 133
family background, 75–76
and Filipino woman's paternity allegations against husband, 92, 93
husband's remembrances of, 173, 186, 226–27
in Japan, 83–84, 88–89, 91–92
1908 return to United States, 100–104, 148–49
1913 return to United States, 118
in Philippines, 96, 97–100, 107, 108–9, 113, 118, 206
in San Francisco, 119–20, 124–28
social accomplishments as young woman, 76–77
Pershing, Jim (brother), 5, 9, 11–12, 119, 223, 238, 266
Pershing, John Fletcher (father), 3–6, 8, 11
Pershing, John Joseph
as army chief of staff, 253–54
as author, 250–51, 267–68
background and youth, 4–12
and births of children, 92, 99, 106, 109
career summation, 313
and controversy over promotion to general, 92–93
and daughter-in-law Muriel, 280–81, 284, 287, 297–98
death and burial of, vii–xi, 313–14
and deaths of wife and daughter, 129–35
financial help given by, 265–66
as general of the armies, 228–33, 235–39, 249–50
and grandsons, 287–88, 290, 296, 297, 298, 305–6, 331, 332
health concerns, 55, 72, 100, 105–6, 200, 219, 270–71, 276–78, 285–86, 287
ladies' man reputation, 23, 30, 62, 229
law studies and degree, 11, 12, 44

Pershing, John Joseph, (*continued*)
 marriage. *See* Pershing, Helen Frances
  Warren
 memoirs, 250–51
 and Mexican campaign, 121, 122, 124,
  135, 140–48, 207
 as Miles's aide-de-camp, 47
 military decorations and honors, x,
  224–25
 Native American relations, 30–32, 37,
  46
 nickname origin, 48–49, 192
 1908 return to United States, 100–104
 1913 return to United States, 118
 paternity scandal allegations, 92–93
 and posting to Japan, 83–84, 85–93
 and posting to the Philippines, 56–72,
  89, 92–93, 95–100, 106–18, 206
 and posting to U.S. West, 26, 27–38,
  205
 and posting to Washington, D.C., 55–56
 post-World War I operations, 218–28
 post-World War I vacation, 233–35
 as presidential aspirant, 185, 202,
  223–24
 as Presidio of San Francisco commander, 118–20, 124
 relationship with son Warren, 106,
  111, 132, 135–36, 146, 173–76,
  185–87, 217–18, 220, 221, 222, 224,
  226, 228, 229–30, 235, 238, 239–46,
  251–56, 258–61, 266–67, 271–72,
  276–77, 278–82, 297, 298, 299–304,
  306
 retirement and later years, 256–58,
  261–64, 269–70, 272–73, 293–306,
  308–10
 romance with Louise Brooks, 169
 romance with Micheline Resco. *See*
  Resco, Micheline
 romance with Nita Patton, 141, 146,
  148, 149, 168–69, 207, 225, 293
 as schoolteacher, 12–14
 as Southern Department commander,
  148
 Spanish-American War service, 49–55
 and Tenth Cavalry, 46–47, 50, 52, 54,
  55, 92
 and University of Nebraska, 38, 39–45
 as West Point cadet, 14–15, 17–26, 205
 as West Point instructor, 47–49
 as World War I Army Expeditionary
  Force commander, 148–68, 170–73,
  176–85, 187–203, 208-9
 and World War II, 282–86, 290–91,
  293–95, 305–6
Pershing, John Warren (Jack; grandson),
  326
 at boarding school, 315–16
 and brother's death, 331–32, 334
 childhood, 132–33, 213, 287–88,
  289–90, 296–98, 305, 308, 314–15
 college years, 317, 321, 323–24
 drinking problem of, 336
 and father's remarriage, 336
 marriages, 335, 336, 337
 military service, 214, 324–25, 328–29,
  335
Pershing, Joseph (grandfather), 18
Pershing, Mary Margaret (daughter), 109,
  118, 121, 131, 134–35
Pershing, Muriel B. Richards (Mumu;
  daughter-in-law), 299, 304, 331
 background, 275–76
 courtship and wedding, 272, 276,
  278–81
 death of, 335–36
 and death of son Dick, 332, 333–34,
  335
 drinking problem of, 326
 and father-in-law's funeral, 314
 relationship with father-in-law, 280–81,
  284, 287, 297–98
 and sons, 213, 287, 296, 315, 316, 320,
  321, 323, 324, 329
 World War II years, 292–93
Pershing, Richard (Dick; grandson), 325
 at boarding school, 315–16, 317–18
 childhood, 213, 296–98, 306, 308, 315
 college years, 214, 318–24, 327
 death in Vietnam and military funeral,
  xi, 331–35
 and fiancée Shirley Hildreth, 325–26,
  328, 329, 332
 military service, 327–31
Pershing Rifles, 43–44, 317

"Pershing's Own," 220
Pétain, Annie, 309–10
Pétain, Henri Philippe, 218, 257, 270, 271
    friendship with Pershing, *211*, 227, 263–64, 310
    imprisonment of, 308–10
    and World War I, 167, 168, 180, 192, 195, 198
    and World War II, 283–84, 285, 294
Phelps, Clementine, 154
Philippines, 55, 56–72, 89, 92–93, 95–100, 106–18
    Pershing's first impressions of, 56–59
Phillips Exeter Academy, 255, 316
Phipps, Senator, 241
Pine Ridge reservation (South Dakota), 37
Plummer, General, 162
Poincaré, President and Mme., 268
Poland, 282
Powell, Colin, 317
Presidio of San Francisco, 118–20, 124
Preston, Guy, 47, 93
Pulitzer, Joseph A., 52
Punitive Expedition (1916–17), 140–48, 166
    background, 139–40

Quekemeyer, John G., 173, 231, 244, 252
Quezon, President, 281

Raleigh, Walter, 152
Rawlings (Union officer), 193
Red Feather (Oglala scout), 37
Reed, Ellie. *See* Douglas, Ellie Reed
Resco, Micheline, *208*
    first meeting and wartime affair with Pershing, 170, 171, 193, 196, 201
    later trysts with Pershing, 240, 250, 258, 263
    and Pershing's death, 314
    and Pershing's family, 221, 225, 226, 256, 284, 287, 314, 326–27
    and Pershing's infidelity, 221
    and Pershing's later years, 271, 277, 308
    and Pershing's memoirs, 251
    as World War II exile, 284

Rhodes, Charles, 22
Richards, Dorothy, 279
Richards, Muriel B. *See* Pershing, Muriel B. Richards
Robertson (Imperial General Staff chief), 152
Rockefeller, Nelson, 336
Rommel, Erwin, 294
Roosevelt, Alice, 81, 89
Roosevelt, Franklin, 285, 290, 295, 304
Roosevelt, Theodore, 72, 88
    and Pershing, 80–81, 92, 134, 170
    as Rough Rider, 49, 51, 54, 92
Root, Elihu, 78
Rosecrans, William, 24
Rough Riders (First Volunteer Cavalry), 49, 51, 53, 92
Rubinstein, Serge, 336
Running Shield (Oglala scout), 37
Runyon, Damon, 257
Russo-Japanese War, 80, 83, 85–88, 96
Ryan, John A., 114

Sam (Navajo interpreter), 33, 34, 35
San Francisco, 118–20, 124–28
Sanger, William Cary, 65
Sarrail, Marshal, 262
Schlossberg, David, 327, 336
    close friendship with Dick Pershing, 318–22, 325
    and Dick Pershing's death, 333–34, 335
    on Dick Pershing's persona, 317
    Vietnam War service, 333
Schneider, John T., 255
Scott, David, 150
Scott, Hugh L., 149, 150
Shaho, Battle of, 90
Shaw, George C., 70
Sheetz, Sergeant, 241
Sheldon, George, 43
Sheridan, Philip, 19, 24, 228
Sherman, William Tecumseh, 23, 29, 228, 263
Sibert, William, 164, 177–78
Sidebottom, Preacher, 10
Simonds, Frank H., 165
Sims, William S., 218

Sinclair, Sandra (Mrs. Jack Pershing), 337
Singer, Gerald, 322, 329, 330–31, 332–33
Singer, Ronald, 318–19, 320, 322, 327, 329
Sioux Indians, 37–38
Sitting Bull, 36, 37
Skull and Bones, 319
Smith, Professor, 239
South Dakota, 37
Spaatz, Carl, 313
Spanish-American War, 49–55
Spurgeon, Charley, 22
Stallings, Laurence, 161, 198
Stanton, Charles F., 155
Stedman, Representative, 262
Stewart, Senator, 82
Stimson, Henry L., 290
Stotesbury, Thomas, 169
Stotsenberg, John, 33–35, 58
Strauss, Richard, 104
Sullivan, Gordon, 335
Sullivan, John L., 81
Sulu, sultan of, 114
Sumner, Edwin V., 231
Sumner, Samuel S., 71, 79, 231
Supreme War Council of the Allied and Associated Powers, 199–200
sword of Austerlitz, 155

Taft, William Howard, 58, 80, 89, 97, 105, 108, 127
Tenth Cavalry, U.S. Army, 46–47, 50, 52, 54, 55, 92
Thayer, Dudley, 279
Thompson, Anne Elizabeth. See Pershing, Anne Elizabeth Thompson
Thunder Bull (Oglala scout), 37
Truman, Harry, vii, 304–5
Tunney, Eugene (Gene), 220
Turkey, 199
Twain, Mark, 23

"Unconditional Surrender" policy, 199
U.S. Military Academy. See West Point
University of Nebraska, 38, 39–41, 42–45, 156
University of Wyoming, 295

Vandenberg, General, 313
Vietnam War, xi, 327–34
Villa, Francisco (Pancho), 313
    Columbus (New Mexico) raid, 139–40
    death of, 148
    as folk hero, 147
    Pershing's expedition against, 140–43
    persona, 122
    unknown fate of, 145, 146
Vreeland, Diana, 326

Waiting Ones, The, 166
Walcutt, Charles, 20–21
Wales, Henry, 309
Walker, General, 313
Walker, Norman, 129
Walthall, Polly Storm, 127
Warren, Bessie, 132, 227
Warren, Clara Morgan (Pershing's mother-in-law), 118, 121, 132, 229, 257, 260–62, 272
Warren, Francis Emroy (Pershing's father-in-law), 257
    background, 75–76
    and daughter Frankie, 77, 78, 83, 89, 97–98, 109, 119, 121, 231
    and daughter's death, 132
    death and burial of, 262
    and grandson Warren, 176, 260–61
    marriage to Clara Morgan, 118
    and Pershing's health, 105
    and Pershing's military career, 92, 93, 148–49
    and Pershing's presidential aspirations, 185, 223
Warren, Fred, 132, 227
Warren, Helen (mother), 76
Warren, Helen Frances (daughter). See Pershing, Helen Frances Warren
Washington, D.C., 55–56, 76–77, 257
Washington, George, xi, 176, 185
Watanabe, General, 91
Watta-Wa-Na, 10
Weatherill, Fernanda, 323, 335
Wellesley College, 75, 121, 124, 125–26, 230
Wellington, duke of, 72, 223
Westmoreland, William C., 331, 335

West Point (U.S. Military Academy), 14,
    17, 18–24, 47–49, 331
Weygand, Maxime, 193
What Price Glory (Stallings), 198
Wheeler, Joseph, 53, 54
White, Sergeant, 244
White Hawk (Oglala scout), 37
Whitney, Henry H., 128, 132
Wilde, Oscar, 104
Wilhelm II, German emperor, 152, 180
Wilson, Edith, viii
Wilson, Tug, 13
Wilson, Woodrow
    incapacitation of, 229, 230, 235
    and Mexican Punitive Expedition, 121,
        139, 140
    World War I policies, 148, 159, 166,
        179, 191, 193, 198, 199, 277
Wood, Leonard, 116
World War I, 148–68, 176–85, 187–203
    armistice negotiations, 199–201
    and calls for Pershing's removal, 197–98
    and Pershing's appointment as army
        commander, 148–49
    and Pershing's arrival in Europe, 151–54

U.S. military battle involvement,
    181–85, 187, 190–91, 192–97
U.S. military preparation for, 155, 156,
    159–66, 176–78
    *See also specific battles, military com-
        manders, and participating countries*
World War II, 282–87, 290–91, 293–95,
    300–305
Wounded Horse (Oglala scout), 37
Wounded Knee massacre, 37
Wovoka, 36
Wyoming, 75

Yale University, xi, 318–20, 321, 322, 327,
    334
Yamada, General, 91
Yellow Bear (Oglala scout), 37
Yoshida, H., 91
Yoshida, S., 91
Younger brothers' gang, 6
Yuhi, Colonel, 91

Zamboanga (Philippines), 57, 109, 118
Zamboanga Country Club (Philippines),
    113